GTO

GREAT TEACHER ONIZUKA

Vol. 6

By
Tohru Fujisawa

Los Angeles . Tokyo

Translator – Dan Papia
Retouch and Lettering – Tim Law
Cover Design – Gary Shum

Editor – Luis Reyes
Associate Editor - Tim Law
Production Manager – Mario M. Rodriguez
Art Director – Matthew Alford
Brand Manager – Joel Baral
VP Production – Ron Klamert
Publisher – Stuart Levy

Email: editor@TOKYOPOP.com
Come visit us online at www.TOKYOPOP.com

A **TOKYOPOP**® manga
TOKYOPOP® is an imprint of Mixx Entertainment, Inc.
5900 Wilshire Blvd. Ste 2000, Los Angeles, CA 90036

ISBN: 1-59182-030-8

First TOKYOPOP® printing: September 2002

10 9 8 7 6 5 4 3 2 1

Printed in the USA.

Kichijoji One-Day Dating Service
Give Us a Day, We'll Get You A Date

- Client Bio Form -

Name:
Eikichi Onizuka (a.k.a Great Teacher Onizuka, a.k.a Elephant Man)

Age:
22 (but, I look younger and love older)

Personal Statement:
First the dinosaurs roamed the Earth, eating nothing but cavemen and eucalyptus plants. Then a nuclear bomb went off and made them all extinct, which gave rise to the radioactive people who illuminated the eternal night that followed. Then it was boring for a long time until the late seventies (that's 1970's) when I was born, Eikichi Onizuka, 22 years old, destined to be a great teacher.

Greatest Achievements: (prepare to be amazed)
1. Passing my student teaching by tough loving the kids into respecting me (basically, hanging the three toughest up by their ankles and dunking them in a pond until they found it in their hearts to respect me).
2. Becoming a big rig driver and making it from Akita to Tokyo in 9 hours to attend a second job interview at Holy Forest Academy when I thought I had bombed out because I suplexed the vice-principal after the first one. I liked truck driving.
3. Making it as a temporary teacher at Holy Forest Academy, moving onto school grounds, and, on my first night, watching a couple make out, chasing off a space cult calling for an extra-terrestrial messiah, and saving one of my students, Noburo, who had flung himself from the roof hoping to escape the cruelty of an uncaring student body.
4. Winning over class four. Now, you have to understand, class four is a rough class, but that's because the school had pretty much bailed on them. They went through three different teachers last year and almost got rid of me, first by trying to shame me out of the job (little did they know, I have no shame), and then by physically trying to kill me. But I don't hold grudges.
5. Saving Noburo from killing himself again, same reason, same way. But this time we got revenge on the girls that beat him up. Which brings me to ...
6. One of those girls was the daughter of the president of the PTA, who was determined to get me fired for humiliating her daughter and blah, blah, blah. But really, all it took was Noburo getting naked to get me off... off the hook with the PTA.
7. Turning Tomoko into a star. She's one of my students who everyone thought was a stupid girl with big breasts. But I saw her for the talented, dynamic, caring, intuitive girl with big breasts that she is.
8. Maintaining my virginity until... tonight... maybe?

CONTENTS

GTO

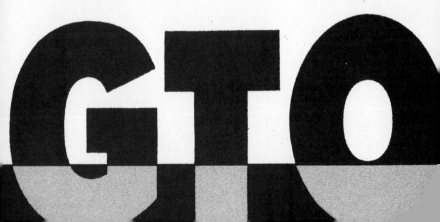

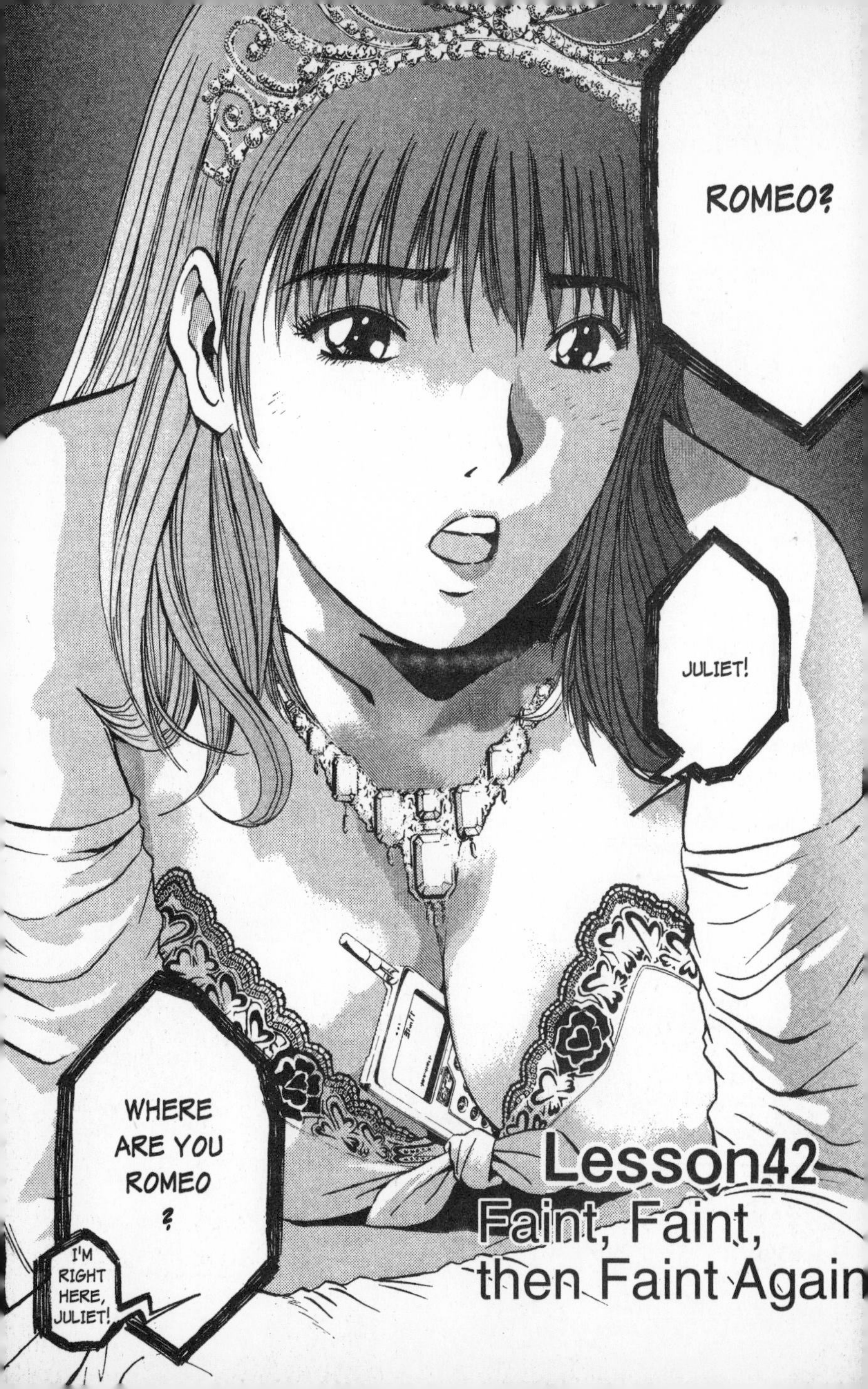
ROMEO?
JULIET!
WHERE ARE YOU ROMEO ?
I'M RIGHT HERE, JULIET!

Lesson42 Faint, Faint, then Faint Again

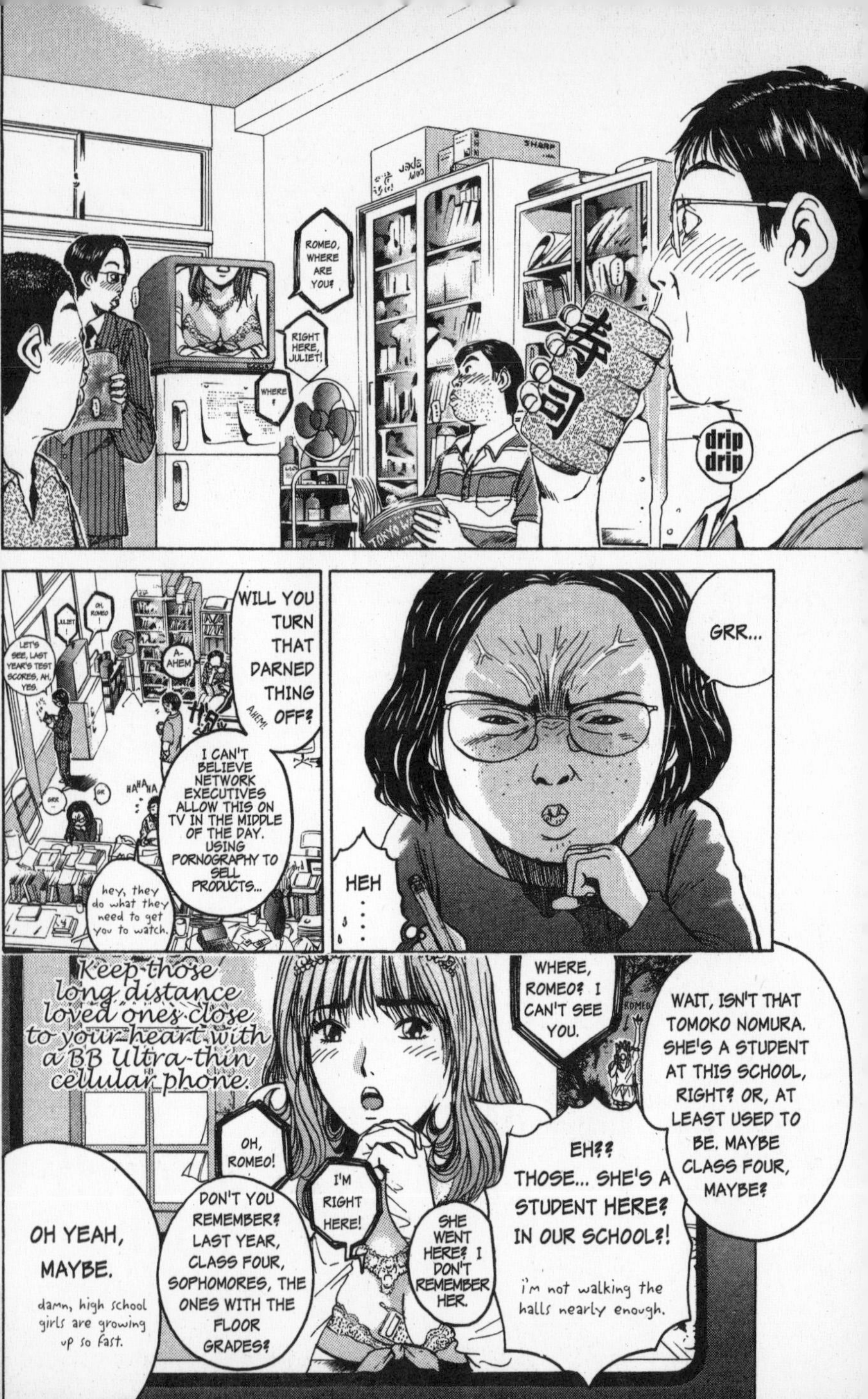
drip drip
ROMEO, WHERE ARE YOU?
RIGHT HERE, JULIET!
WHERE?
GRR...
HEH...
WILL YOU TURN THAT DARNED THING OFF?
OH, ROMEO
JULIET!
LET'S SEE, LAST YEAR'S TEST SCORES, AH, YES.
A-AHEM
AHEM!
I CAN'T BELIEVE NETWORK EXECUTIVES ALLOW THIS ON TV IN THE MIDDLE OF THE DAY. USING PORNOGRAPHY TO SELL PRODUCTS...
HAHAHA
GRR
hey, they do what they need to get you to watch.
WAIT, ISN'T THAT TOMOKO NOMURA. SHE'S A STUDENT AT THIS SCHOOL, RIGHT? OR, AT LEAST USED TO BE. MAYBE CLASS FOUR, MAYBE?
WHERE, ROMEO? I CAN'T SEE YOU.
ROMEO
Keep those long distance loved ones close to your heart with a BB Ultra-thin cellular phone.
EH?? THOSE... SHE'S A STUDENT HERE? IN OUR SCHOOL?!
i'm not walking the halls nearly enough.
OH, ROMEO!
I'M RIGHT HERE!
SHE WENT HERE? I DON'T REMEMBER HER.
DON'T YOU REMEMBER? LAST YEAR, CLASS FOUR, SOPHOMORES, THE ONES WITH THE FLOOR GRADES?
OH YEAH, MAYBE.
damn, high school girls are growing up so fast.

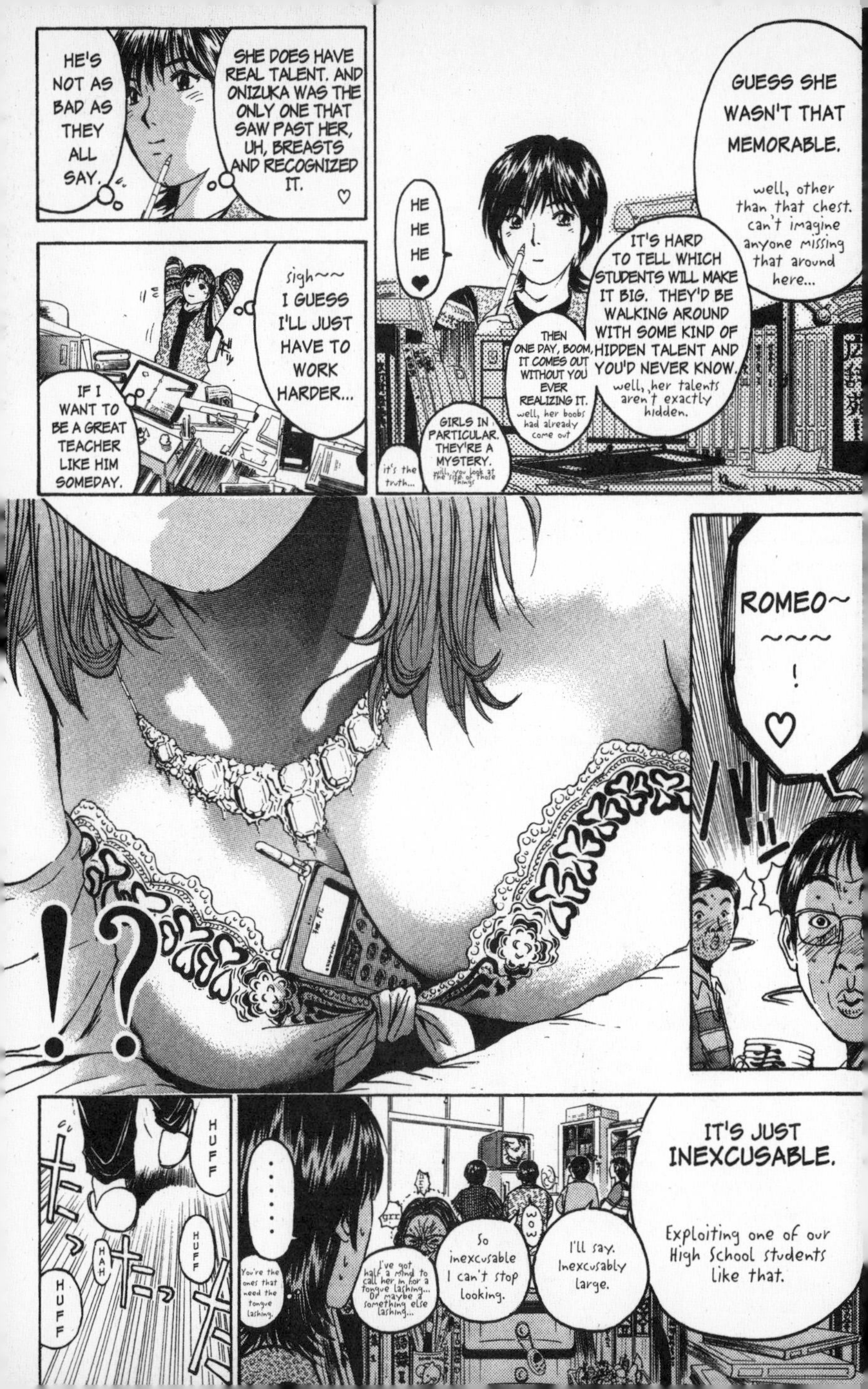
GUESS SHE WASN'T THAT MEMORABLE.
well, other than that chest. can't imagine anyone missing that around here...
HE HE HE ♥
IT'S HARD TO TELL WHICH STUDENTS WILL MAKE IT BIG. THEY'D BE WALKING AROUND WITH SOME KIND OF HIDDEN TALENT AND YOU'D NEVER KNOW.
well, her talents aren't exactly hidden.
THEN ONE DAY, BOOM, IT COMES OUT WITHOUT YOU EVER REALIZING IT.
well, her boobs had already come out
GIRLS IN PARTICULAR. THEY'RE A MYSTERY.
well, you look at the size of those things
it's the truth...
SHE DOES HAVE REAL TALENT. AND ONIZUKA WAS THE ONLY ONE THAT SAW PAST HER, UH, BREASTS AND RECOGNIZED IT. ♡
HE'S NOT AS BAD AS THEY ALL SAY.
sigh~~ I GUESS I'LL JUST HAVE TO WORK HARDER...
IF I WANT TO BE A GREAT TEACHER LIKE HIM SOMEDAY.
ROMEO~ ~~~ ! ♡
!?
IT'S JUST INEXCUSABLE.
Exploiting one of our High School students like that.
I'll say. Inexcusably large.
WOW
So inexcusable I can't stop looking.
I've got half a mind to call her in for a tongue lashing... Or maybe a something else lashing...
grr
You're the ones that need the tongue lashing.
......
HUFF
HUFF
HAH
HUFF

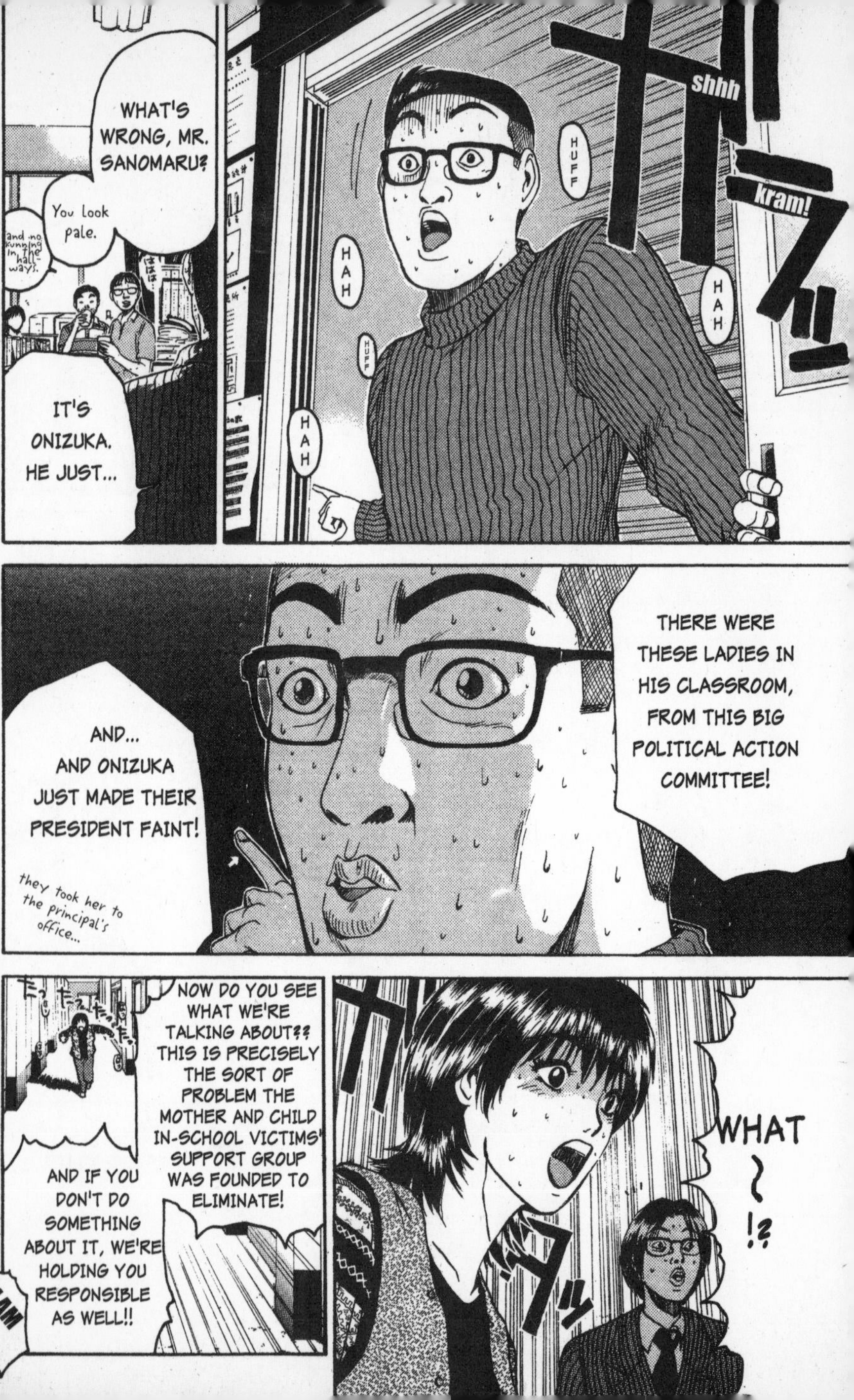
shhh
kram!
HUFF
HAH
HAH
HUFF
HAH
WHAT'S WRONG, MR. SANOMARU?
You look pale.
and no running in the hallways.
IT'S ONIZUKA. HE JUST...
THERE WERE THESE LADIES IN HIS CLASSROOM, FROM THIS BIG POLITICAL ACTION COMMITTEE!
AND... AND ONIZUKA JUST MADE THEIR PRESIDENT FAINT!
they took her to the principal's office...
WHAT~!?
NOW DO YOU SEE WHAT WE'RE TALKING ABOUT?? THIS IS PRECISELY THE SORT OF PROBLEM THE MOTHER AND CHILD IN-SCHOOL VICTIMS' SUPPORT GROUP WAS FOUNDED TO ELIMINATE!
AND IF YOU DON'T DO SOMETHING ABOUT IT, WE'RE HOLDING YOU RESPONSIBLE AS WELL!!
SLAM

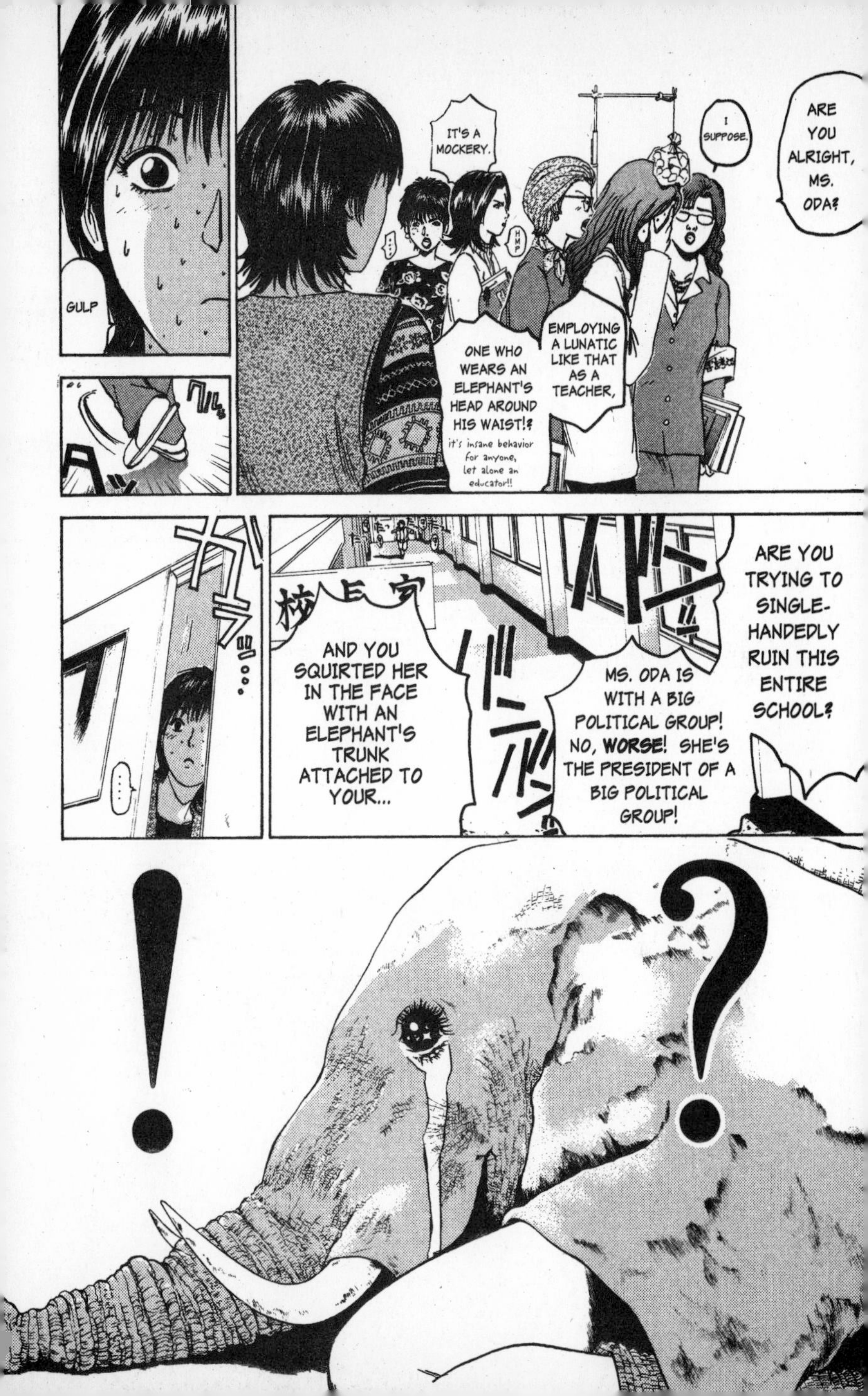
ARE YOU ALRIGHT, MS. ODA?
I SUPPOSE.
IT'S A MOCKERY.
HMP
EMPLOYING A LUNATIC LIKE THAT AS A TEACHER,
ONE WHO WEARS AN ELEPHANT'S HEAD AROUND HIS WAIST!?
it's insane behavior for anyone, let alone an educator!!
GULP
ARE YOU TRYING TO SINGLE-HANDEDLY RUIN THIS ENTIRE SCHOOL?
MS. ODA IS WITH A BIG POLITICAL GROUP! NO, **WORSE**! SHE'S THE PRESIDENT OF A BIG POLITICAL GROUP!
AND YOU SQUIRTED HER IN THE FACE WITH AN ELEPHANT'S TRUNK ATTACHED TO YOUR...

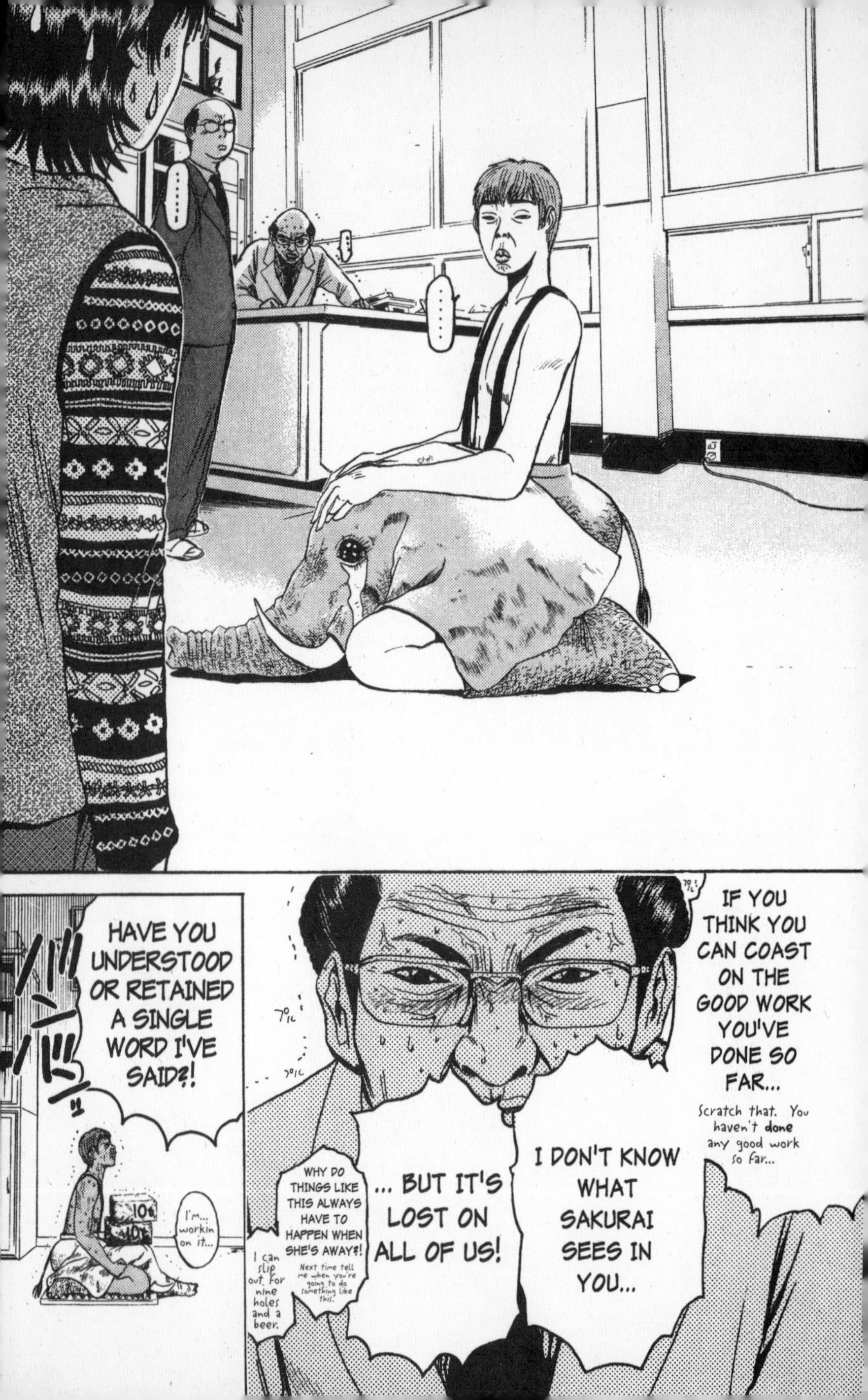
IF YOU THINK YOU CAN COAST ON THE GOOD WORK YOU'VE DONE SO FAR...
Scratch that. You haven't done any good work so far...
I DON'T KNOW WHAT SAKURAI SEES IN YOU...
... BUT IT'S LOST ON ALL OF US!
WHY DO THINGS LIKE THIS ALWAYS HAVE TO HAPPEN WHEN SHE'S AWAY?!
Next time tell me when you're going to do something like this.
I can slip out for nine holes and a beer.
HAVE YOU UNDERSTOOD OR RETAINED A SINGLE WORD I'VE SAID?!
I'm... workin on it...

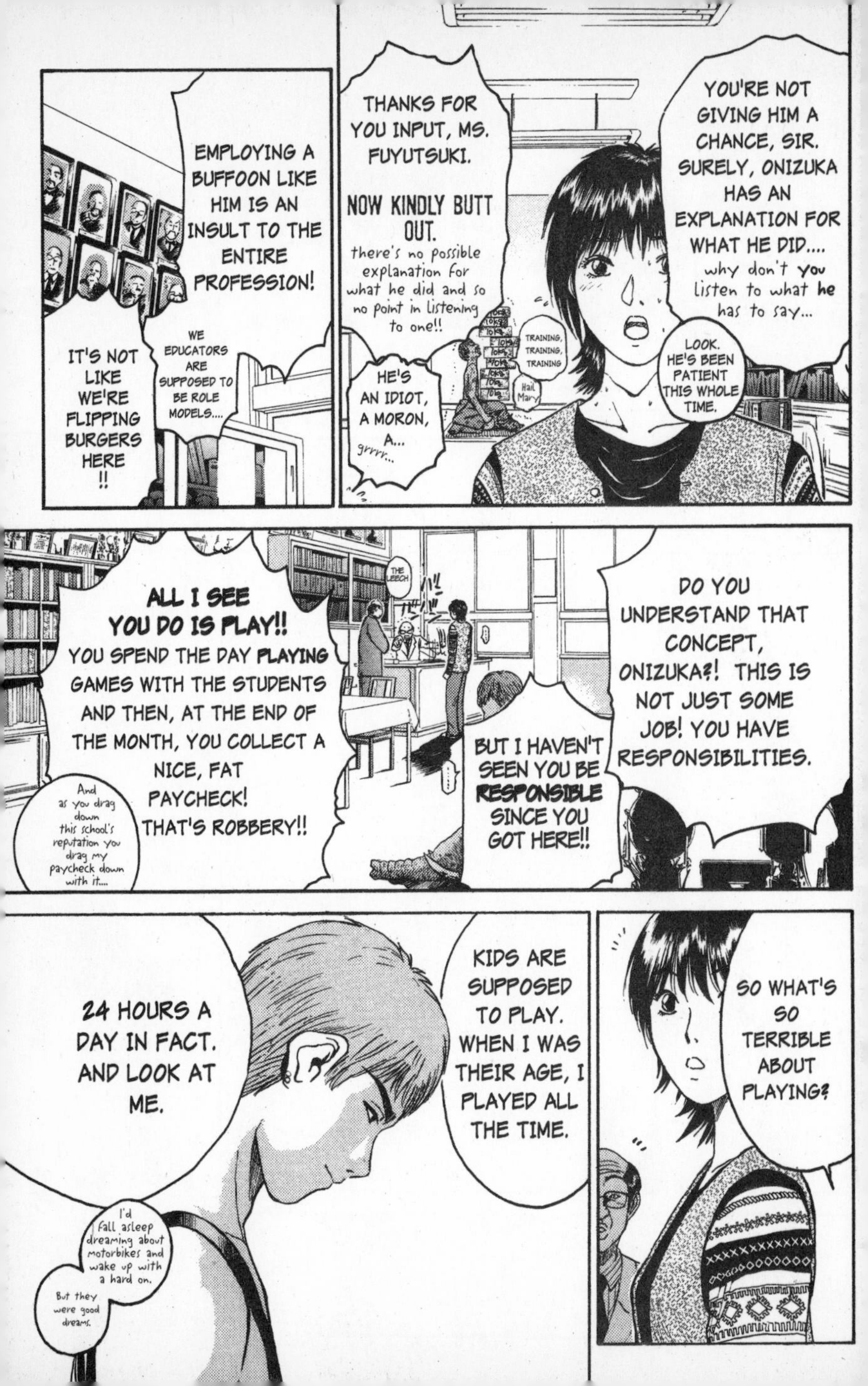

YOU'RE NOT GIVING HIM A CHANCE, SIR. SURELY, ONIZUKA HAS AN EXPLANATION FOR WHAT HE DID....
why don't you listen to what he has to say...
LOOK. HE'S BEEN PATIENT THIS WHOLE TIME.
THANKS FOR YOU INPUT, MS. FUYUTSUKI.
NOW KINDLY BUTT OUT.
there's no possible explanation for what he did and so no point in listening to one!!
TRAINING, TRAINING, TRAINING
Hail Mary
HE'S AN IDIOT, A MORON, A...
grrrr...
EMPLOYING A BUFFOON LIKE HIM IS AN INSULT TO THE ENTIRE PROFESSION!
WE EDUCATORS ARE SUPPOSED TO BE ROLE MODELS....
IT'S NOT LIKE WE'RE FLIPPING BURGERS HERE !!
DO YOU UNDERSTAND THAT CONCEPT, ONIZUKA?! THIS IS NOT JUST SOME JOB! YOU HAVE RESPONSIBILITIES.
BUT I HAVEN'T SEEN YOU BE RESPONSIBLE SINCE YOU GOT HERE!!
THE LEECH
ALL I SEE YOU DO IS PLAY!! YOU SPEND THE DAY PLAYING GAMES WITH THE STUDENTS AND THEN, AT THE END OF THE MONTH, YOU COLLECT A NICE, FAT PAYCHECK! THAT'S ROBBERY!!
And as you drag down this school's reputation you drag my paycheck down with it....
SO WHAT'S SO TERRIBLE ABOUT PLAYING?
KIDS ARE SUPPOSED TO PLAY. WHEN I WAS THEIR AGE, I PLAYED ALL THE TIME.
24 HOURS A DAY IN FACT. AND LOOK AT ME.
I'd fall asleep dreaming about motorbikes and wake up with a hard on.
But they were good dreams.

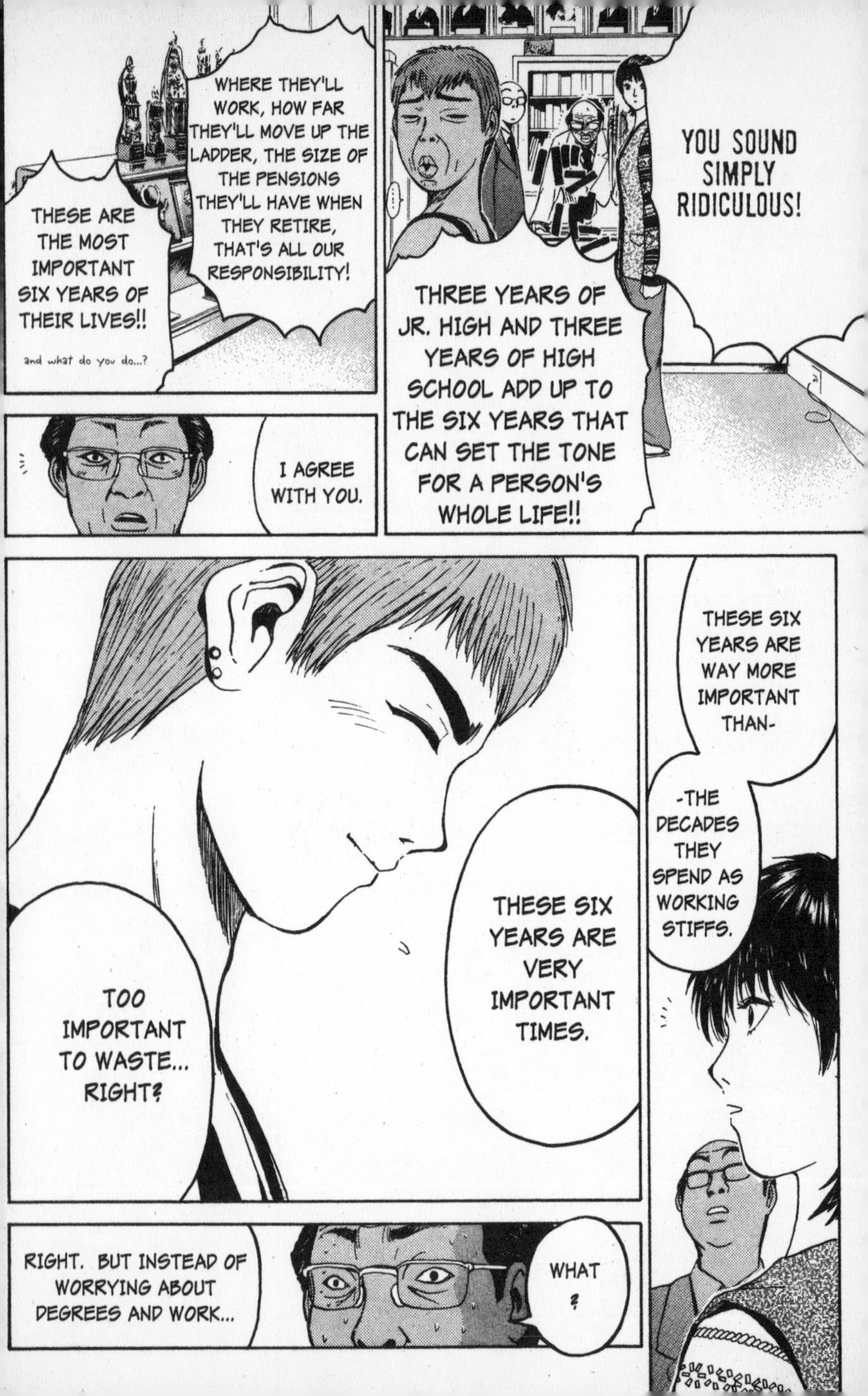
YOU SOUND SIMPLY RIDICULOUS!
THREE YEARS OF JR. HIGH AND THREE YEARS OF HIGH SCHOOL ADD UP TO THE SIX YEARS THAT CAN SET THE TONE FOR A PERSON'S WHOLE LIFE!!
WHERE THEY'LL WORK, HOW FAR THEY'LL MOVE UP THE LADDER, THE SIZE OF THE PENSIONS THEY'LL HAVE WHEN THEY RETIRE, THAT'S ALL OUR RESPONSIBILITY!
THESE ARE THE MOST IMPORTANT SIX YEARS OF THEIR LIVES!!
and what do you do...?
I AGREE WITH YOU.
THESE SIX YEARS ARE WAY MORE IMPORTANT THAN-
-THE DECADES THEY SPEND AS WORKING STIFFS.
THESE SIX YEARS ARE VERY IMPORTANT TIMES.
TOO IMPORTANT TO WASTE... RIGHT?
WHAT?
RIGHT. BUT INSTEAD OF WORRYING ABOUT DEGREES AND WORK...

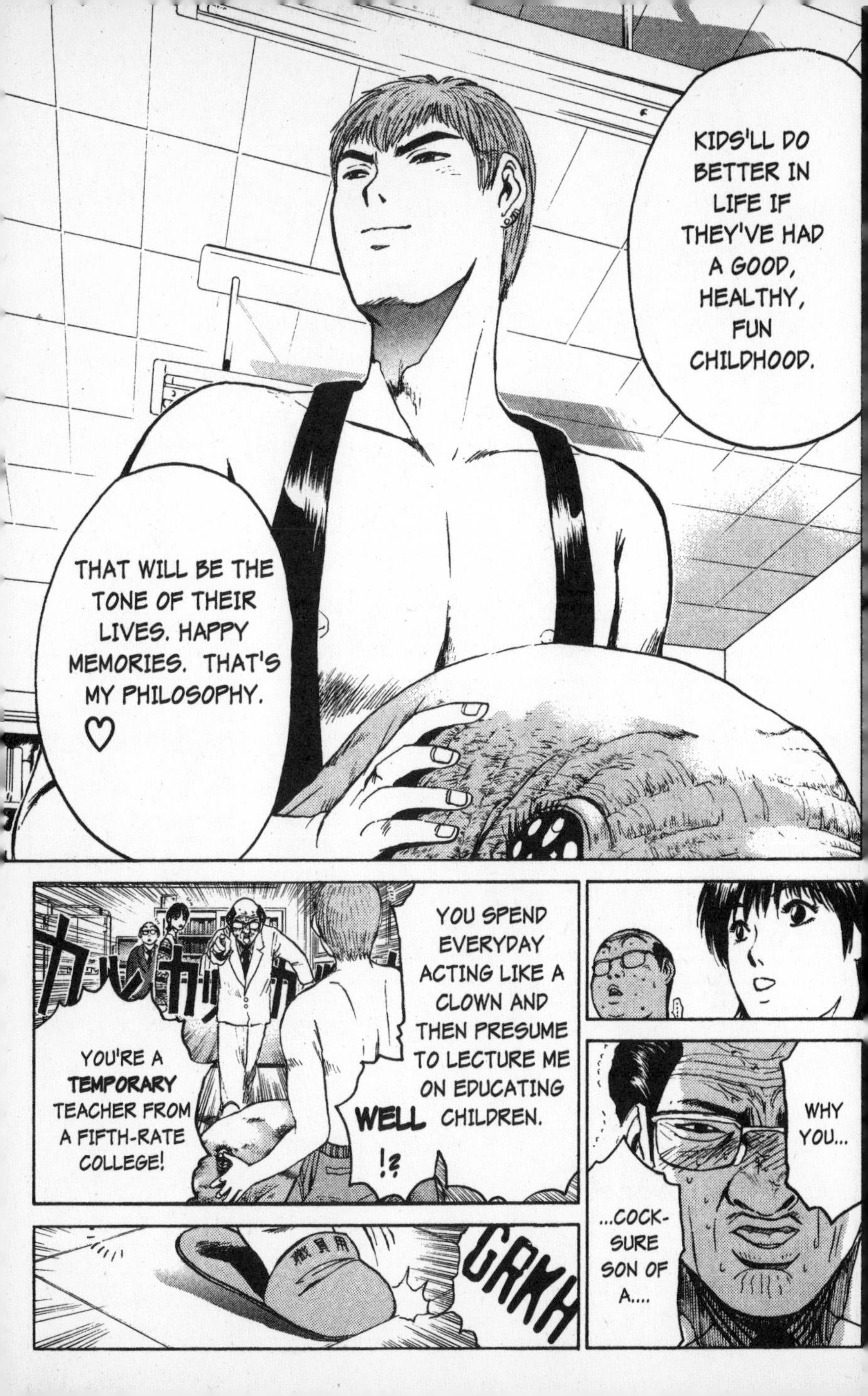
KIDS'LL DO BETTER IN LIFE IF THEY'VE HAD A GOOD, HEALTHY, FUN CHILDHOOD.
THAT WILL BE THE TONE OF THEIR LIVES. HAPPY MEMORIES. THAT'S MY PHILOSOPHY. ♡
YOU SPEND EVERYDAY ACTING LIKE A CLOWN AND THEN PRESUME TO LECTURE ME ON EDUCATING CHILDREN.
WELL
!?
YOU'RE A **TEMPORARY** TEACHER FROM A FIFTH-RATE COLLEGE!
GRKH
WHY YOU...
...COCK-SURE SON OF A....

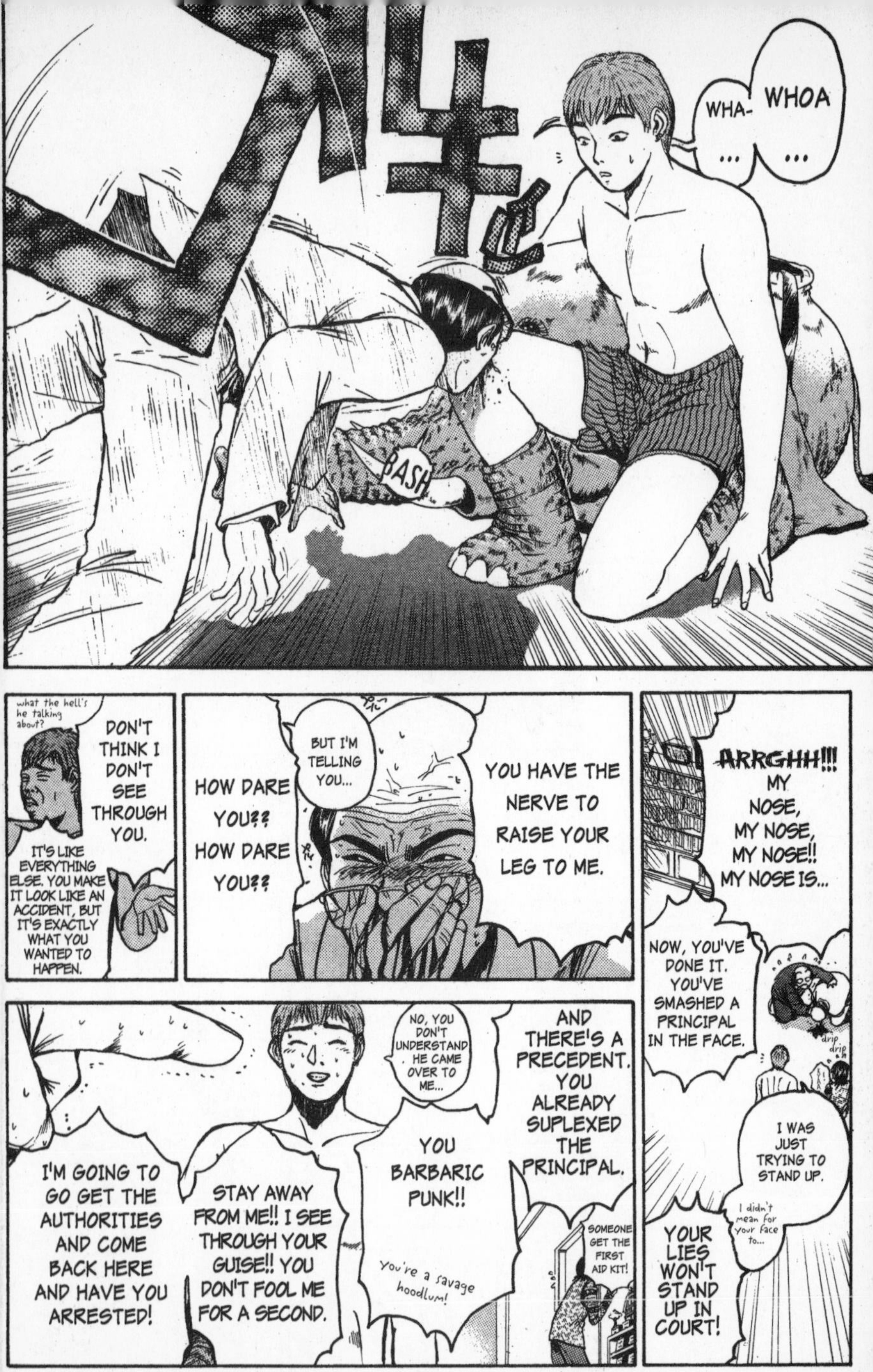
BASH
WHOA ...
WHA- ...
ARRGHH!!!
MY NOSE, MY NOSE, MY NOSE!! MY NOSE IS...
NOW, YOU'VE DONE IT. YOU'VE SMASHED A PRINCIPAL IN THE FACE.
drip drip
I WAS JUST TRYING TO STAND UP.
I didn't mean for your face to...
YOUR LIES WON'T STAND UP IN COURT!
YOU HAVE THE NERVE TO RAISE YOUR LEG TO ME.
BUT I'M TELLING YOU...
HOW DARE YOU?? HOW DARE YOU??
DON'T THINK I DON'T SEE THROUGH YOU.
what the hell's he talking about?
IT'S LIKE EVERYTHING ELSE. YOU MAKE IT LOOK LIKE AN ACCIDENT, BUT IT'S EXACTLY WHAT YOU WANTED TO HAPPEN.
AND THERE'S A PRECEDENT. YOU ALREADY SUPLEXED THE PRINCIPAL.
SOMEONE GET THE FIRST AID KIT!
NO, YOU DON'T UNDERSTAND. HE CAME OVER TO ME...
YOU BARBARIC PUNK!!
You're a savage hoodlum!
STAY AWAY FROM ME!! I SEE THROUGH YOUR GUISE!! YOU DON'T FOOL ME FOR A SECOND.
I'M GOING TO GO GET THE AUTHORITIES AND COME BACK HERE AND HAVE YOU ARRESTED!

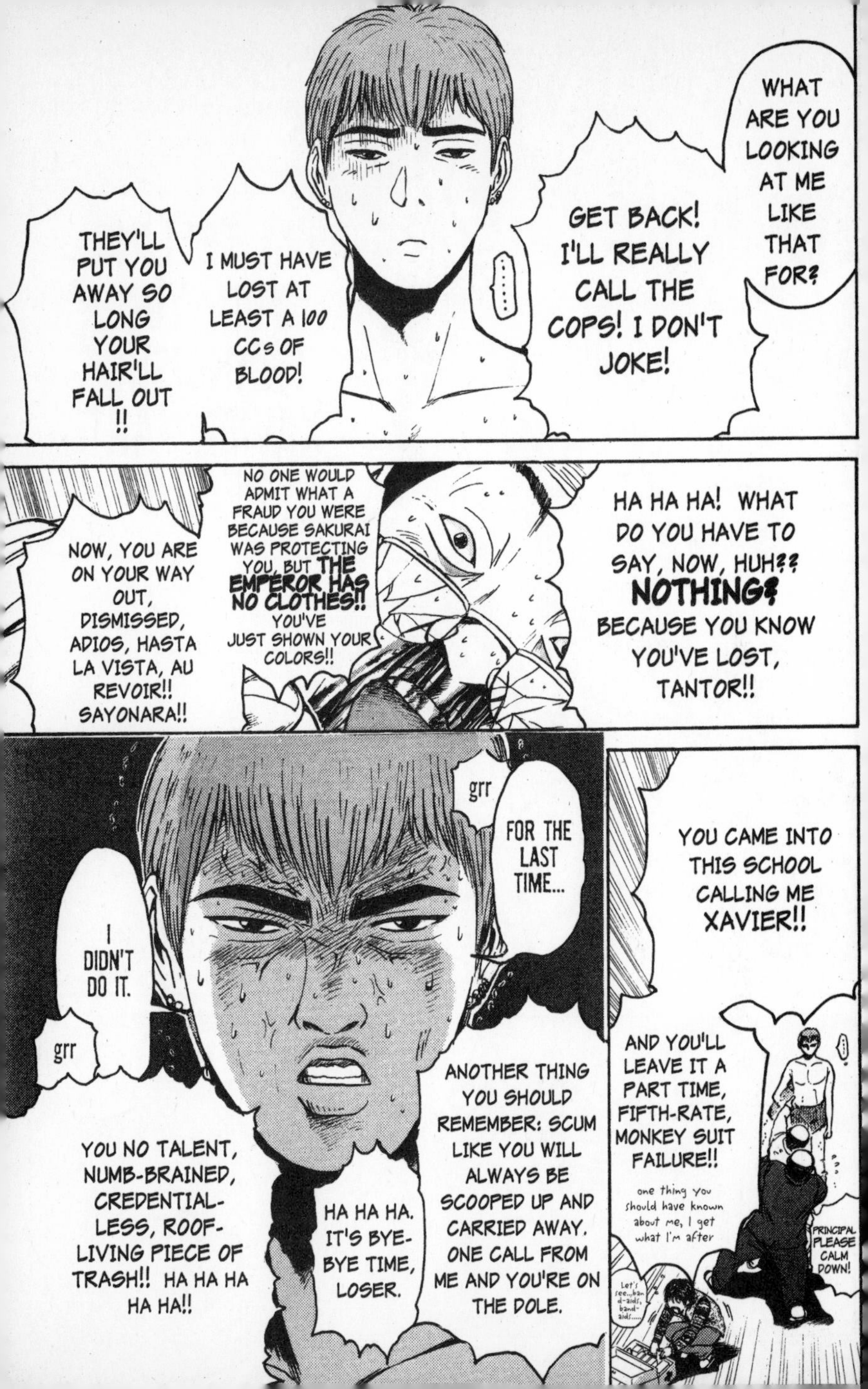
WHAT ARE YOU LOOKING AT ME LIKE THAT FOR?
GET BACK! I'LL REALLY CALL THE COPS! I DON'T JOKE!
......
I MUST HAVE LOST AT LEAST A 100 CCs OF BLOOD!
THEY'LL PUT YOU AWAY SO LONG YOUR HAIR'LL FALL OUT!!
HA HA HA! WHAT DO YOU HAVE TO SAY, NOW, HUH?? NOTHING? BECAUSE YOU KNOW YOU'VE LOST, TANTOR!!
NO ONE WOULD ADMIT WHAT A FRAUD YOU WERE BECAUSE SAKURAI WAS PROTECTING YOU, BUT THE EMPEROR HAS NO CLOTHES!! YOU'VE JUST SHOWN YOUR COLORS!!
NOW, YOU ARE ON YOUR WAY OUT, DISMISSED, ADIOS, HASTA LA VISTA, AU REVOIR!! SAYONARA!!
YOU CAME INTO THIS SCHOOL CALLING ME XAVIER!!
...
AND YOU'LL LEAVE IT A PART TIME, FIFTH-RATE, MONKEY SUIT FAILURE!!
one thing you should have known about me, I get what I'm after
PRINCIPAL PLEASE CALM DOWN!
Let's see...band-aids, band-aids......
grr
FOR THE LAST TIME...
I DIDN'T DO IT.
grr
ANOTHER THING YOU SHOULD REMEMBER: SCUM LIKE YOU WILL ALWAYS BE SCOOPED UP AND CARRIED AWAY. ONE CALL FROM ME AND YOU'RE ON THE DOLE.
HA HA HA. IT'S BYE-BYE TIME, LOSER.
YOU NO TALENT, NUMB-BRAINED, CREDENTIAL-LESS, ROOF-LIVING PIECE OF TRASH!! HA HA HA HA HA!!

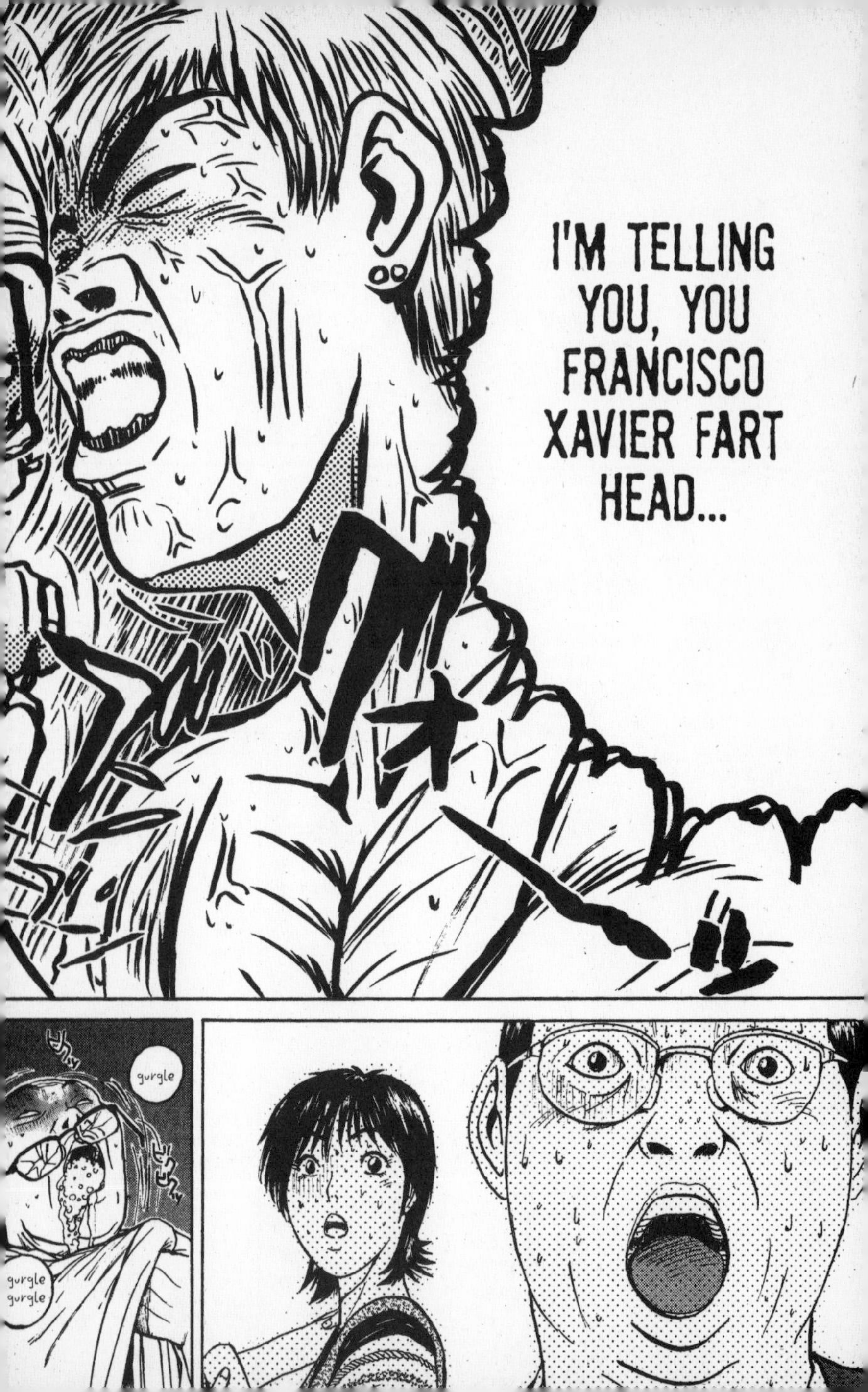
I'M TELLING YOU, YOU FRANCISCO XAVIER FART HEAD...
gurgle
gurgle gurgle

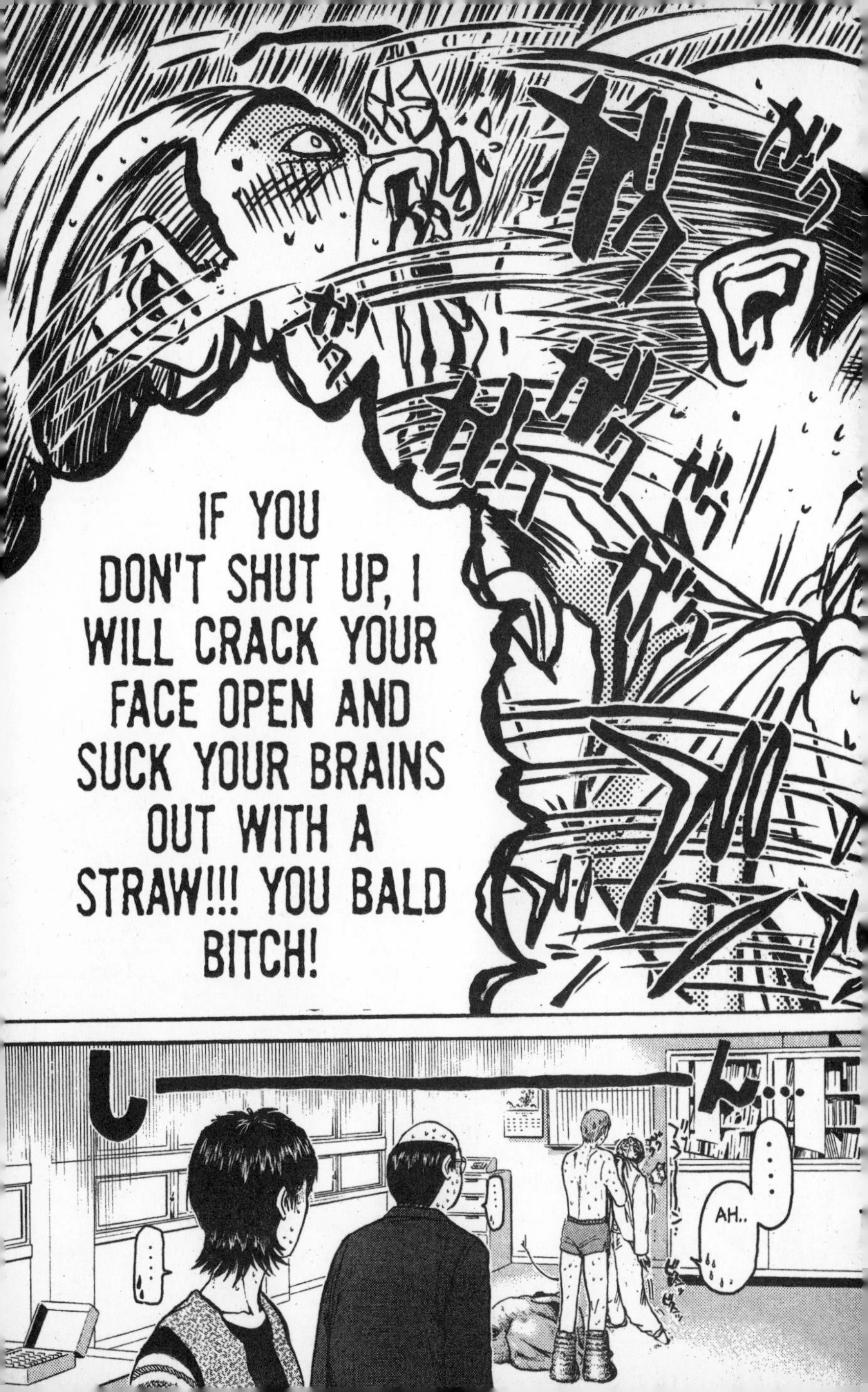
IF YOU DON'T SHUT UP, I WILL CRACK YOUR FACE OPEN AND SUCK YOUR BRAINS OUT WITH A STRAW!!! YOU BALD BITCH!
AH..

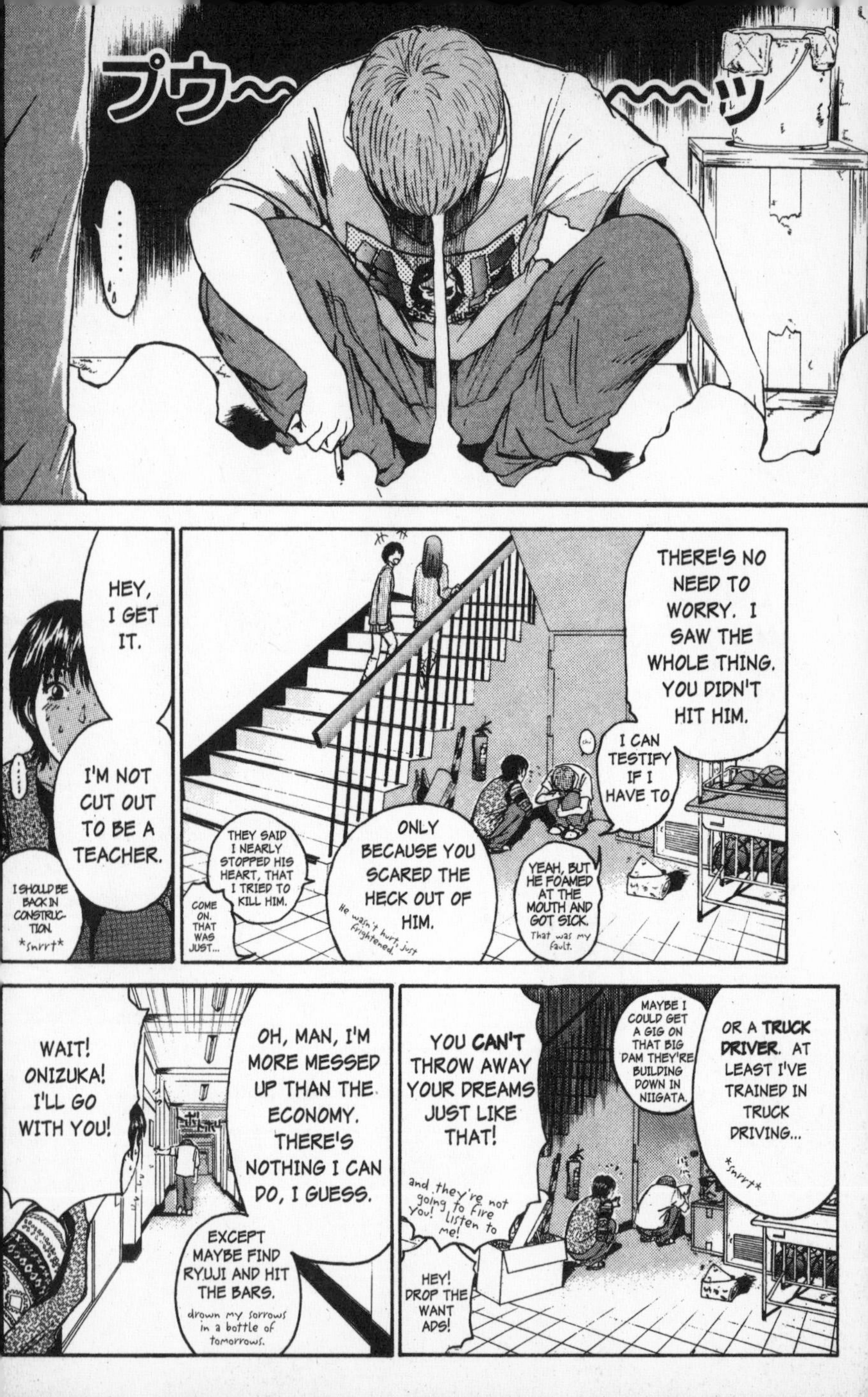
プウ〜〜〜〜ッ
......
THERE'S NO NEED TO WORRY. I SAW THE WHOLE THING. YOU DIDN'T HIT HIM.
I CAN TESTIFY IF I HAVE TO.
YEAH, BUT HE FOAMED AT THE MOUTH AND GOT SICK.
That was my fault.
ONLY BECAUSE YOU SCARED THE HECK OUT OF HIM.
He wasn't hurt, just frightened.
THEY SAID I NEARLY STOPPED HIS HEART, THAT I TRIED TO KILL HIM.
COME ON. THAT WAS JUST...
HEY, I GET IT.
I'M NOT CUT OUT TO BE A TEACHER.
I SHOULD BE BACK IN CONSTRUCTION.
snrrt
OR A **TRUCK DRIVER**. AT LEAST I'VE TRAINED IN TRUCK DRIVING...
snrrt
MAYBE I COULD GET A GIG ON THAT BIG DAM THEY'RE BUILDING DOWN IN NIIGATA.
YOU **CAN'T** THROW AWAY YOUR DREAMS JUST LIKE THAT!
and they're not going to fire you! listen to me!
HEY! DROP THE WANT ADS!
OH, MAN, I'M MORE MESSED UP THAN THE ECONOMY. THERE'S NOTHING I CAN DO, I GUESS.
WAIT! ONIZUKA! I'LL GO WITH YOU!
EXCEPT MAYBE FIND RYUJI AND HIT THE BARS.
drown my sorrows in a bottle of tomorrows.

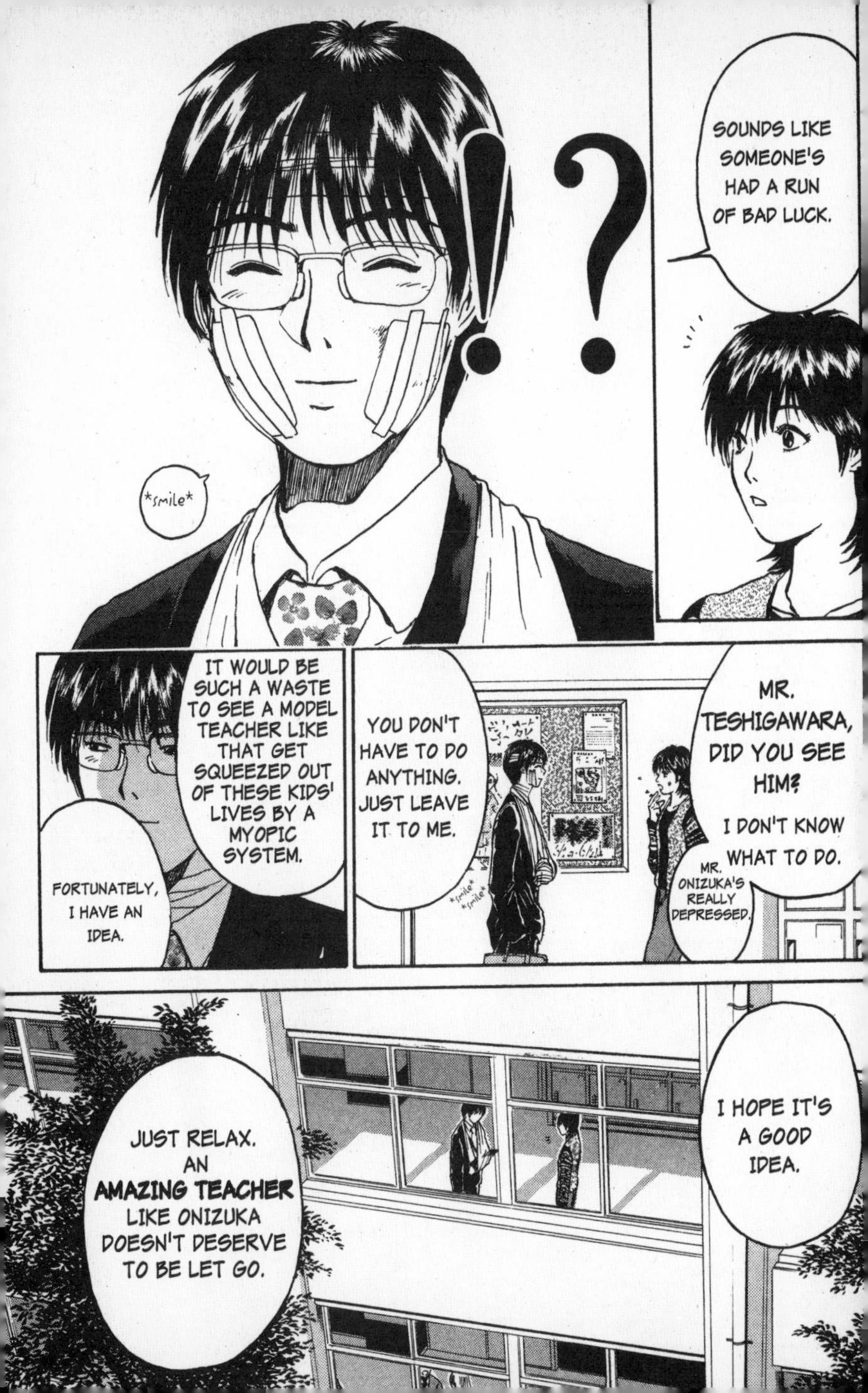
SOUNDS LIKE SOMEONE'S HAD A RUN OF BAD LUCK.
!?
smile
MR. TESHIGAWARA, DID YOU SEE HIM?
I DON'T KNOW WHAT TO DO.
MR. ONIZUKA'S REALLY DEPRESSED.
YOU DON'T HAVE TO DO ANYTHING. JUST LEAVE IT TO ME.
smile *smile*
IT WOULD BE SUCH A WASTE TO SEE A MODEL TEACHER LIKE THAT GET SQUEEZED OUT OF THESE KIDS' LIVES BY A MYOPIC SYSTEM.
FORTUNATELY, I HAVE AN IDEA.
I HOPE IT'S A GOOD IDEA.
JUST RELAX. AN **AMAZING TEACHER** LIKE ONIZUKA DOESN'T DESERVE TO BE LET GO.

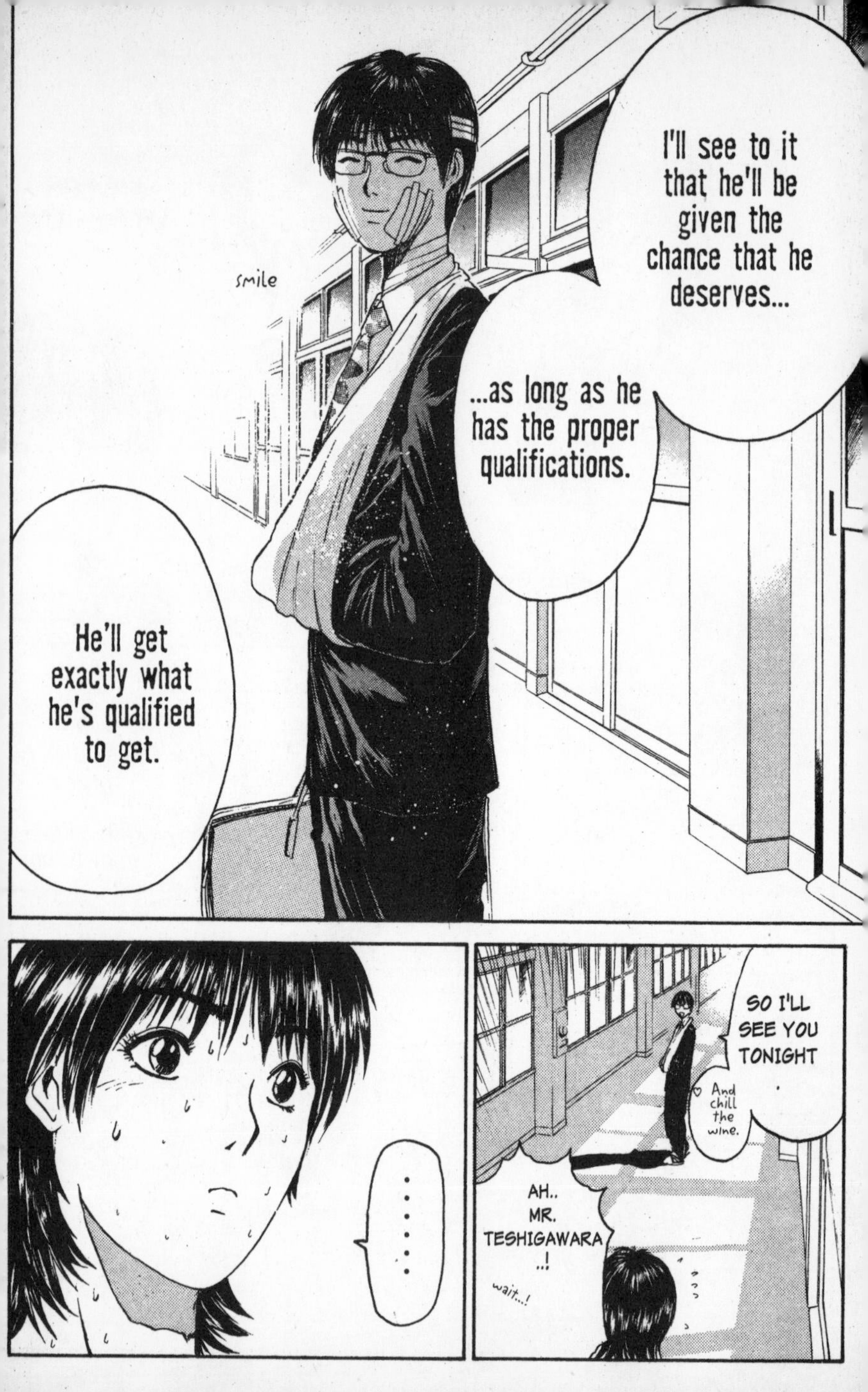
I'll see to it that he'll be given the chance that he deserves...
...as long as he has the proper qualifications.
smile
He'll get exactly what he's qualified to get.
SO I'LL SEE YOU TONIGHT.
And chill the wine.
AH.. MR. TESHIGAWARA ..!
wait...!
......

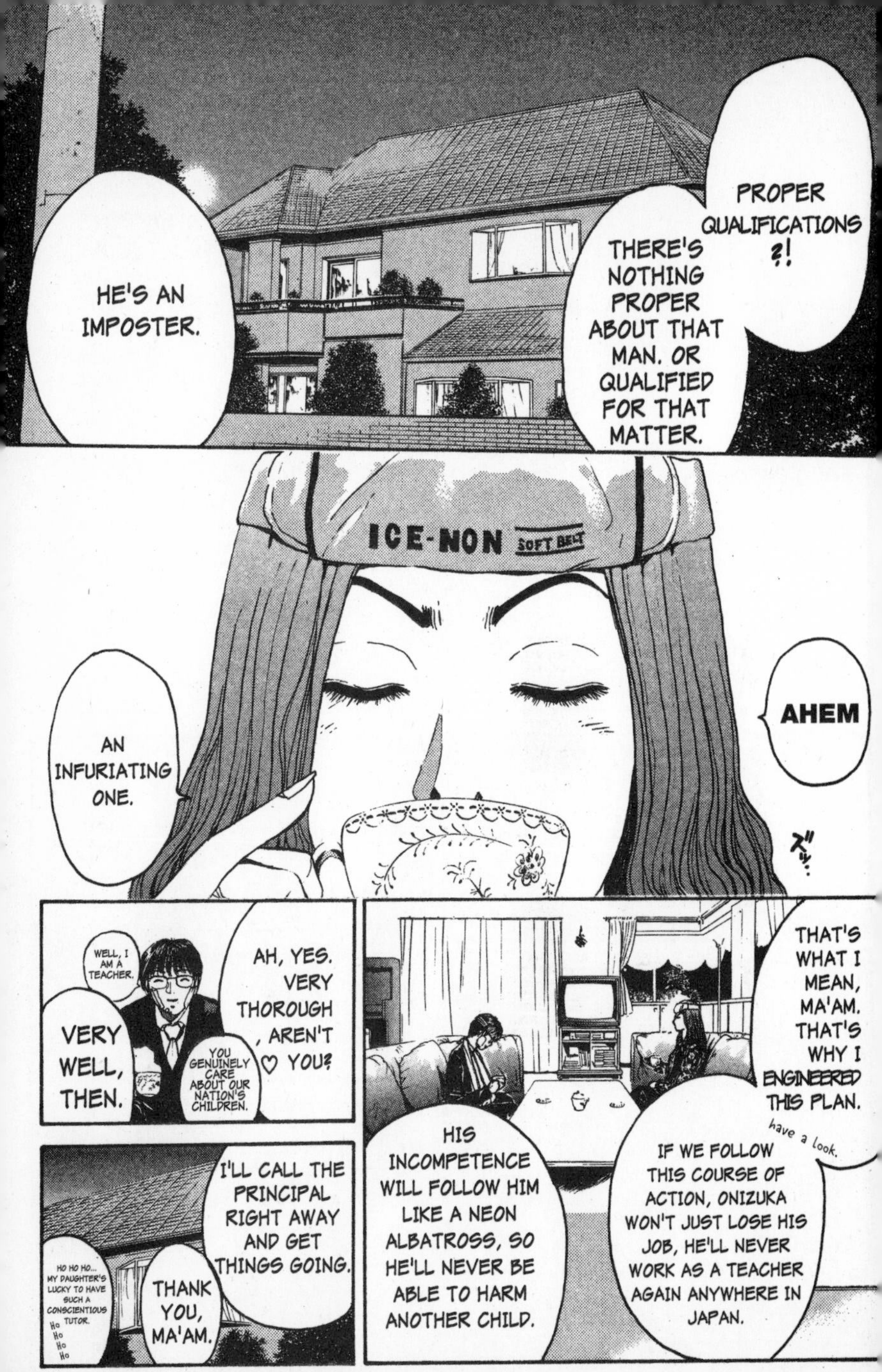
PROPER QUALIFICATIONS ?!
THERE'S NOTHING PROPER ABOUT THAT MAN. OR QUALIFIED FOR THAT MATTER.
HE'S AN IMPOSTER.
ICE-NON SOFT BELT
AHEM
AN INFURIATING ONE.
ズッ..
THAT'S WHAT I MEAN, MA'AM. THAT'S WHY I ENGINEERED THIS PLAN.
have a look.
IF WE FOLLOW THIS COURSE OF ACTION, ONIZUKA WON'T JUST LOSE HIS JOB, HE'LL NEVER WORK AS A TEACHER AGAIN ANYWHERE IN JAPAN.
HIS INCOMPETENCE WILL FOLLOW HIM LIKE A NEON ALBATROSS, SO HE'LL NEVER BE ABLE TO HARM ANOTHER CHILD.
AH, YES. VERY THOROUGH, AREN'T ♡ YOU?
YOU GENUINELY CARE ABOUT OUR NATION'S CHILDREN.
WELL, I AM A TEACHER.
VERY WELL, THEN.
I'LL CALL THE PRINCIPAL RIGHT AWAY AND GET THINGS GOING.
THANK YOU, MA'AM.
HO HO HO... MY DAUGHTER'S LUCKY TO HAVE SUCH A CONSCIENTIOUS TUTOR.
Ho Ho Ho Ho

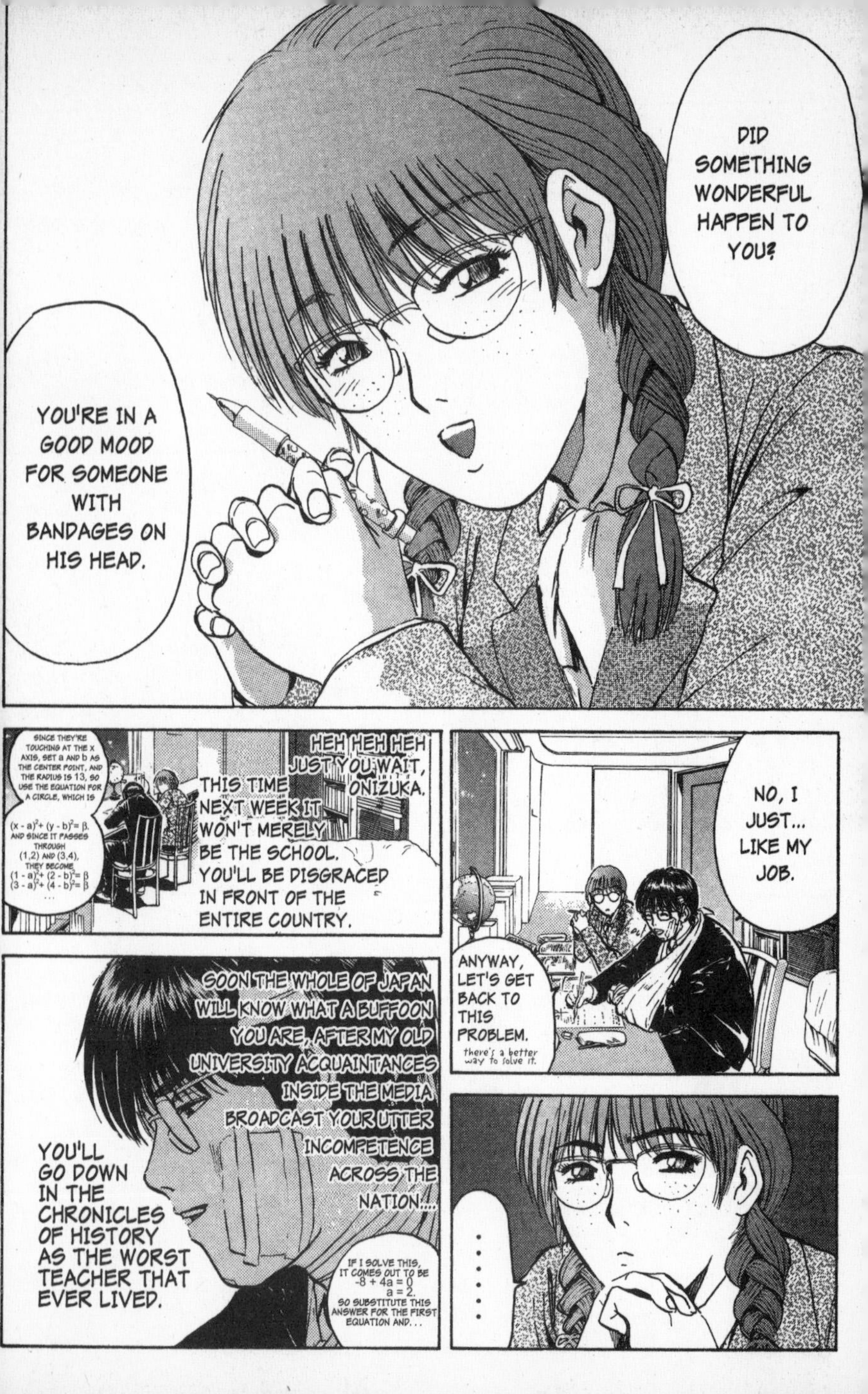
DID SOMETHING WONDERFUL HAPPEN TO YOU?
YOU'RE IN A GOOD MOOD FOR SOMEONE WITH BANDAGES ON HIS HEAD.
NO, I JUST... LIKE MY JOB.
ANYWAY, LET'S GET BACK TO THIS PROBLEM.
there's a better way to solve it.
HEH HEH HEH JUST YOU WAIT, ONIZUKA.
THIS TIME NEXT WEEK IT WON'T MERELY BE THE SCHOOL. YOU'LL BE DISGRACED IN FRONT OF THE ENTIRE COUNTRY.
SINCE THEY'RE TOUCHING AT THE X AXIS, SET a AND b AS THE CENTER POINT, AND THE RADIUS IS 13, SO USE THE EQUATION FOR A CIRCLE, WHICH IS $(x - a)^2 + (y - b)^2 = \beta$. AND SINCE IT PASSES THROUGH (1,2) AND (3,4), THEY BECOME $(1 - a)^2 + (2 - b)^2 = \beta$ $(3 - a)^2 + (4 - b)^2 = \beta$ ...
.....
SOON THE WHOLE OF JAPAN WILL KNOW WHAT A BUFFOON YOU ARE, AFTER MY OLD UNIVERSITY ACQUAINTANCES INSIDE THE MEDIA BROADCAST YOUR UTTER INCOMPETENCE ACROSS THE NATION...
YOU'LL GO DOWN IN THE CHRONICLES OF HISTORY AS THE WORST TEACHER THAT EVER LIVED.
IF I SOLVE THIS, IT COMES OUT TO BE $-8 + 4a = 0$ $a = 2$. SO SUBSTITUTE THIS ANSWER FOR THE FIRST EQUATION AND. . .

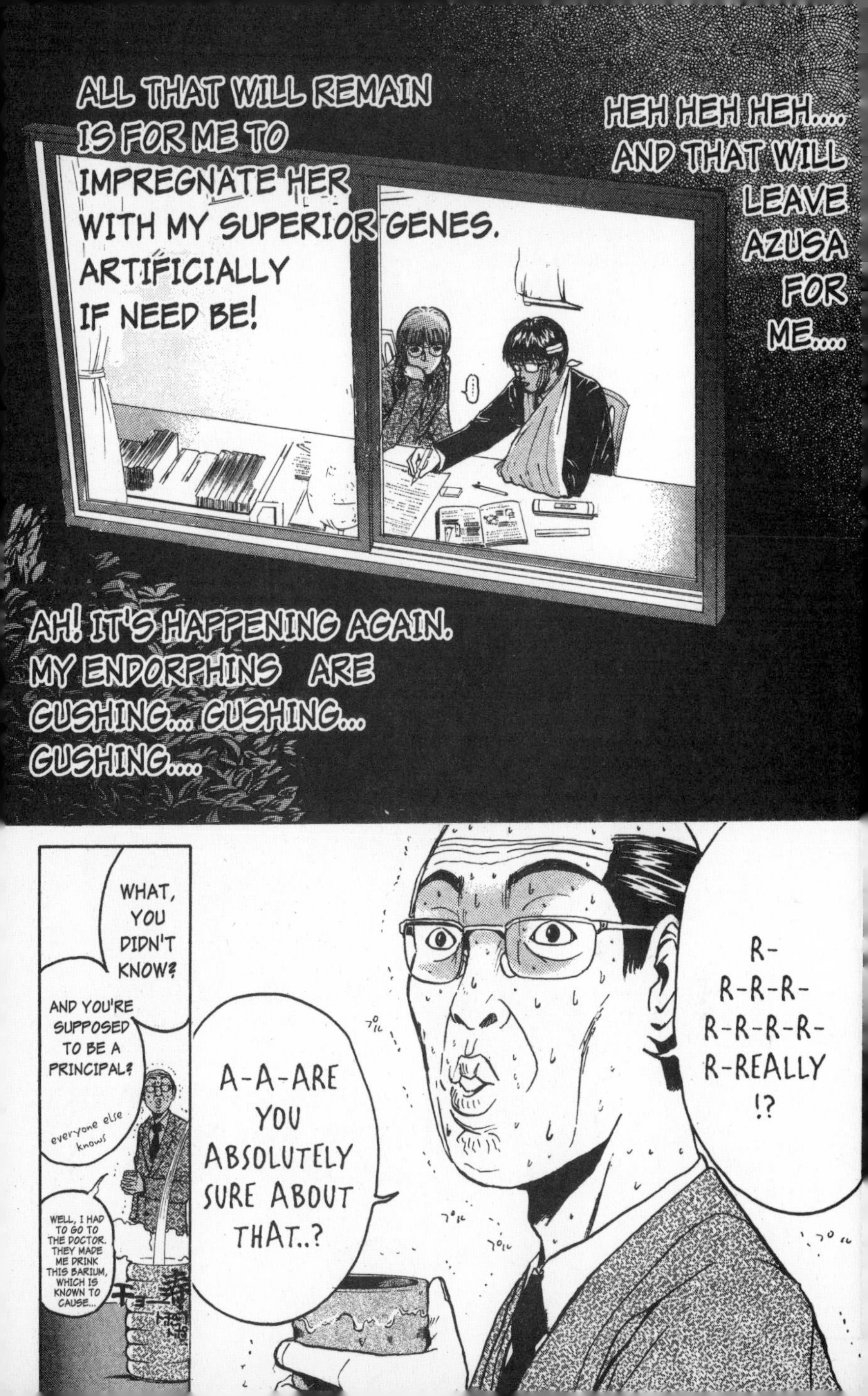
HEH HEH HEH.... AND THAT WILL LEAVE AZUSA FOR ME....
ALL THAT WILL REMAIN IS FOR ME TO IMPREGNATE HER WITH MY SUPERIOR GENES. ARTIFICIALLY IF NEED BE!
AH! IT'S HAPPENING AGAIN. MY ENDORPHINS ARE GUSHING... GUSHING... GUSHING....
R- R-R-R- R-R-R-R- R-REALLY !?
A-A-ARE YOU ABSOLUTELY SURE ABOUT THAT..?
WHAT, YOU DIDN'T KNOW?
AND YOU'RE SUPPOSED TO BE A PRINCIPAL?
everyone else knows
WELL, I HAD TO GO TO THE DOCTOR. THEY MADE ME DRINK THIS BARIUM, WHICH IS KNOWN TO CAUSE...

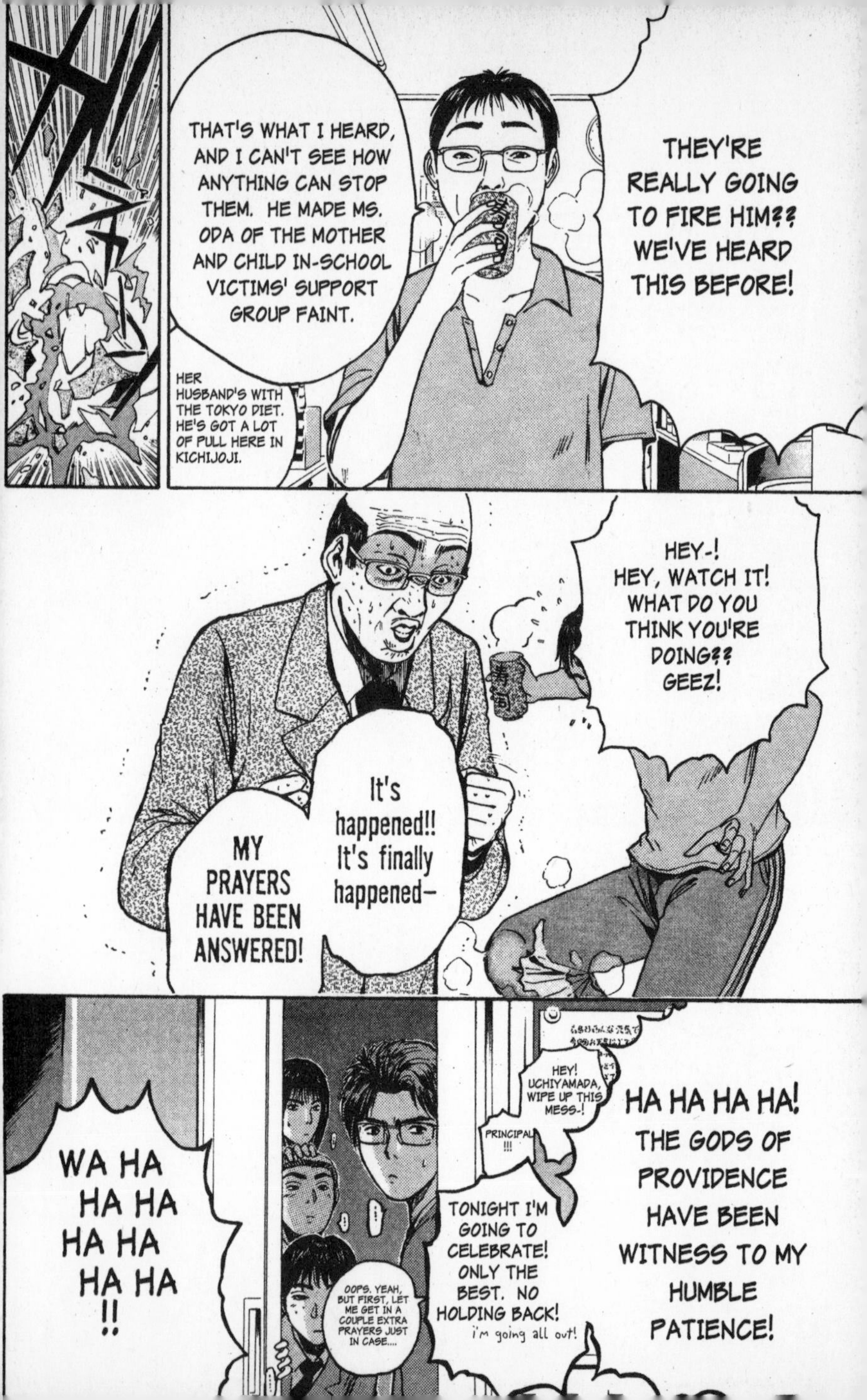
THEY'RE REALLY GOING TO FIRE HIM?? WE'VE HEARD THIS BEFORE!
THAT'S WHAT I HEARD, AND I CAN'T SEE HOW ANYTHING CAN STOP THEM. HE MADE MS. ODA OF THE MOTHER AND CHILD IN-SCHOOL VICTIMS' SUPPORT GROUP FAINT.
HER HUSBAND'S WITH THE TOKYO DIET. HE'S GOT A LOT OF PULL HERE IN KICHIJOJI.
HEY-! HEY, WATCH IT! WHAT DO YOU THINK YOU'RE DOING?? GEEZ!
It's happened!! It's finally happened–
MY PRAYERS HAVE BEEN ANSWERED!
HA HA HA HA! THE GODS OF PROVIDENCE HAVE BEEN WITNESS TO MY HUMBLE PATIENCE!
HEY! UCHIYAMADA, WIPE UP THIS MESS-!
PRINCIPAL!!!
TONIGHT I'M GOING TO CELEBRATE! ONLY THE BEST. NO HOLDING BACK!
i'm going all out!
OOPS. YEAH, BUT FIRST, LET ME GET IN A COUPLE EXTRA PRAYERS JUST IN CASE....
WA HA HA HA HA HA HA HA !!

SUGURU TESHIGAWARA

Age 24, Blood-Type AB
Born Year of the Snake

Second son of a wealthy Nakameguro bureaucrat
Attended state primary, middle and high schools
Accepted into prestigious
Tokyo University First Department of Science
directly from high school
Disappointed his family's expectations and became a teacher
virgin
Enjoys reading, collecting insects, game programming,
PEOPLE WATCHING, studying, studying, studying. .
Favorite music, Wagner, Mahler, Maria Callas
(That's Maria Callas, the singer. Not Mil Mascaras, the Mexican wrestler.)

Respects **father** above all people

Ideal qualities in a woman: Mild pheromones, seems to be virgin, hair shouldn't be too long, not too skinny, fat is also a negative, breasts should be small (no larger than B-Cup) She should be of high moral standing and properly educated at a top ranking university, such as Waseda, Ke... ...ouchi, etc.

In other words, Azus... ...a Fuy...tsuki Az...
...utsuki Azusa Fuyutsu... ...Fuyutsuki
...yutsuki Azusa Fuy... ...yutsu...
Azusa Fuyutsuki A... ...sa
a Fuyutsuki Azusa ...
Azusa Fuyutsuki ...
...sa Fuyutsuki Azus...
...i Azusa Fuyutsuk...
...uyutsuki Azusa F...
Azusa Fuyutsuki
Fuyutsu...

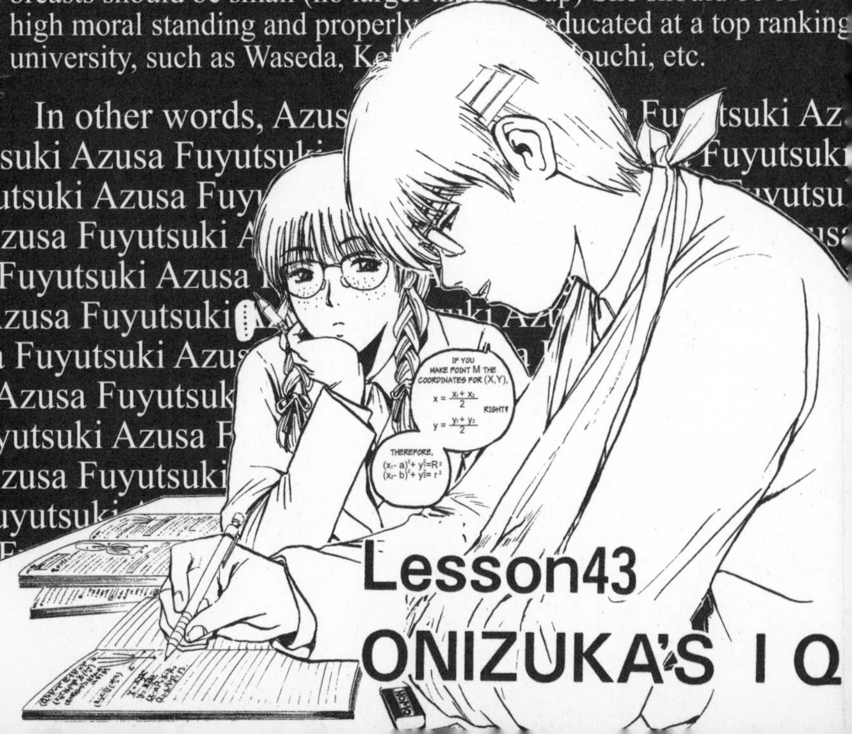

IF YOU MAKE POINT M THE COORDINATES FOR (X,Y),
$x = \frac{x_1 + x_2}{2}$
$y = \frac{y_1 + y_2}{2}$
RIGHT?
THEREFORE,
$(x_1 - a)^2 + y_1^2 = R^2$
$(x_2 - b)^2 + y_2^2 = r^2$

Lesson43
ONIZUKA'S I Q

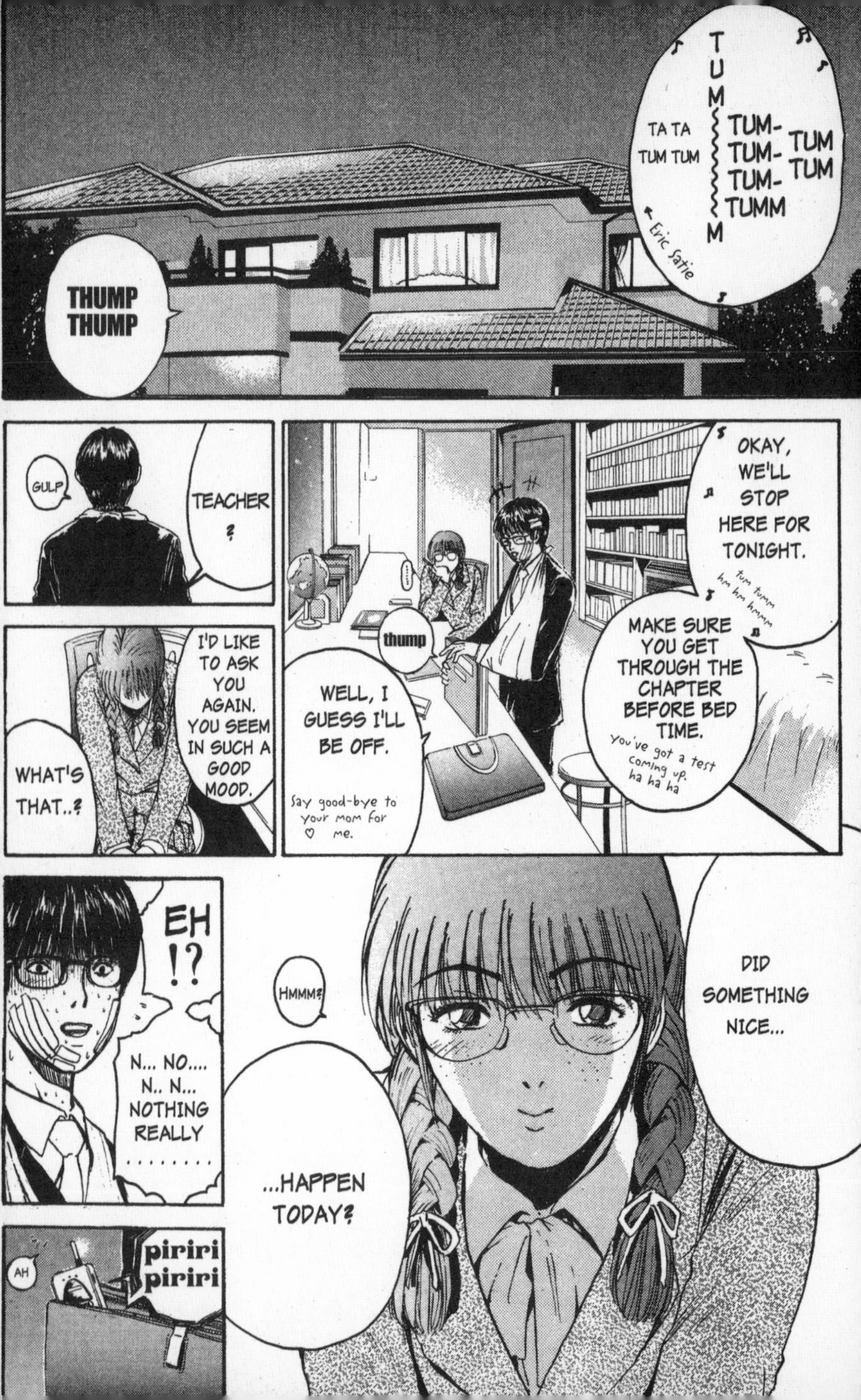

TUMMM
TUM- TUM- TUM- TUMM
TUM TUM
TA TA TUM TUM
Eric Satie
THUMP THUMP
OKAY, WE'LL STOP HERE FOR TONIGHT.
tum tumm hm hm hmmm
MAKE SURE YOU GET THROUGH THE CHAPTER BEFORE BED TIME.
You've got a test coming up. ha ha ha
thump
WELL, I GUESS I'LL BE OFF.
Say good-bye to your mom for ♡ me.
TEACHER?
GULP
I'D LIKE TO ASK YOU AGAIN. YOU SEEM IN SUCH A GOOD MOOD.
WHAT'S THAT..?
DID SOMETHING NICE...
...HAPPEN TODAY?
HMMM?
EH !?
N... NO.... N.. N... NOTHING REALLY ....
piriri piriri
AH

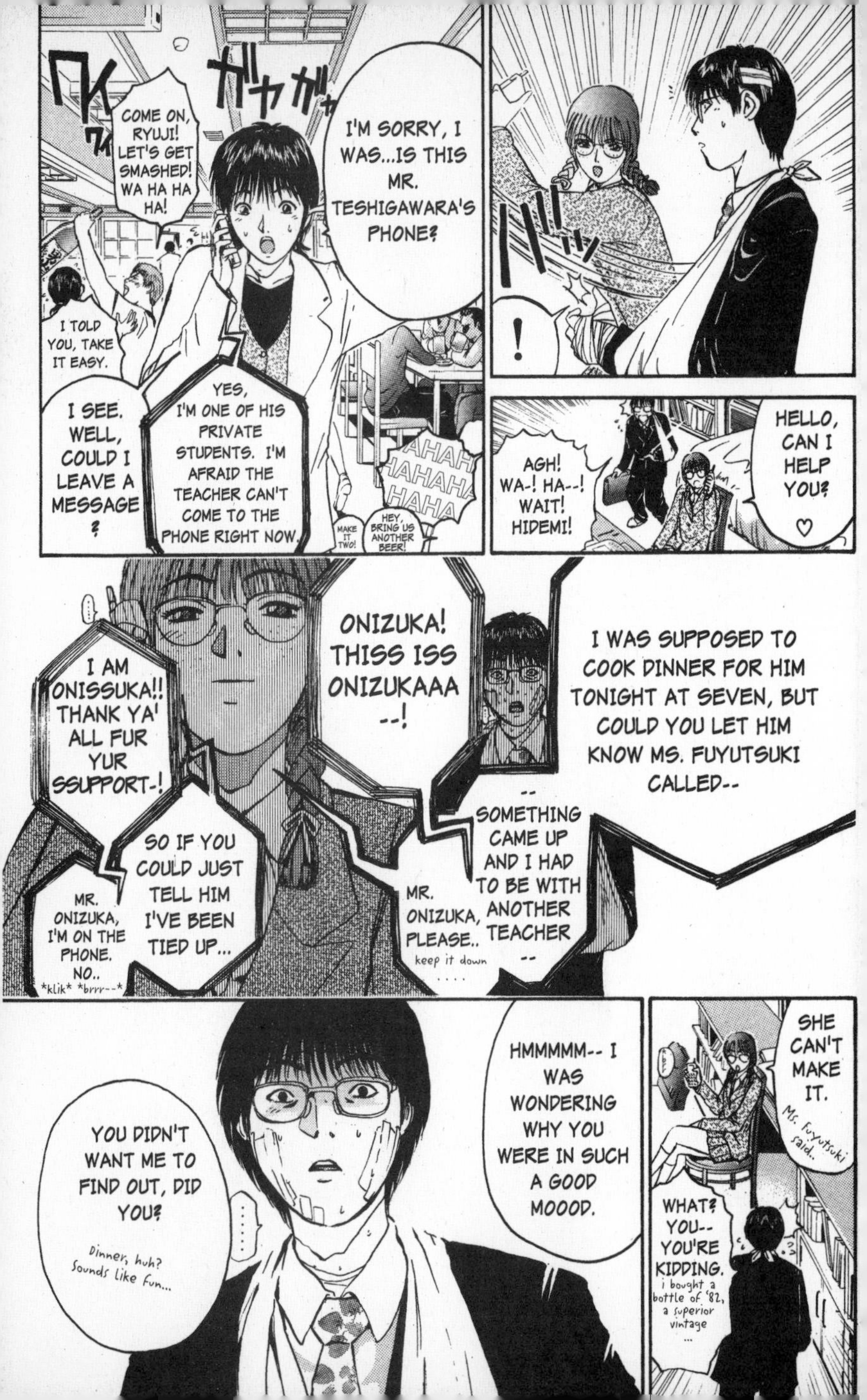
!
HELLO, CAN I HELP YOU? ♡
AGH! WA-! HA--! WAIT! HIDEMI!
I'M SORRY, I WAS...IS THIS MR. TESHIGAWARA'S PHONE?
COME ON, RYUJI! LET'S GET SMASHED! WA HA HA HA!
I TOLD YOU, TAKE IT EASY.
HAHAHAHAHAHA
HEY, BRING US ANOTHER BEER!
MAKE IT TWO!
YES, I'M ONE OF HIS PRIVATE STUDENTS. I'M AFRAID THE TEACHER CAN'T COME TO THE PHONE RIGHT NOW.
I SEE. WELL, COULD I LEAVE A MESSAGE?
I WAS SUPPOSED TO COOK DINNER FOR HIM TONIGHT AT SEVEN, BUT COULD YOU LET HIM KNOW MS. FUYUTSUKI CALLED--
--SOMETHING CAME UP AND I HAD TO BE WITH ANOTHER TEACHER--
ONIZUKA! THISS ISS ONIZUKAAA--!
MR. ONIZUKA, PLEASE..
keep it down ....
I AM ONISSUKA!! THANK YA' ALL FUR YUR SSUPPORT-!
SO IF YOU COULD JUST TELL HIM I'VE BEEN TIED UP...
MR. ONIZUKA, I'M ON THE PHONE. NO..
klik *brrr--*
SHE CAN'T MAKE IT.
Ms. Fuyutsuki said..
WHAT? YOU-- YOU'RE KIDDING.
i bought a bottle of '82, a superior vintage ...
HMMMMM-- I WAS WONDERING WHY YOU WERE IN SUCH A GOOD MOOOD.
YOU DIDN'T WANT ME TO FIND OUT, DID YOU?
......
Dinner, huh? Sounds like fun...

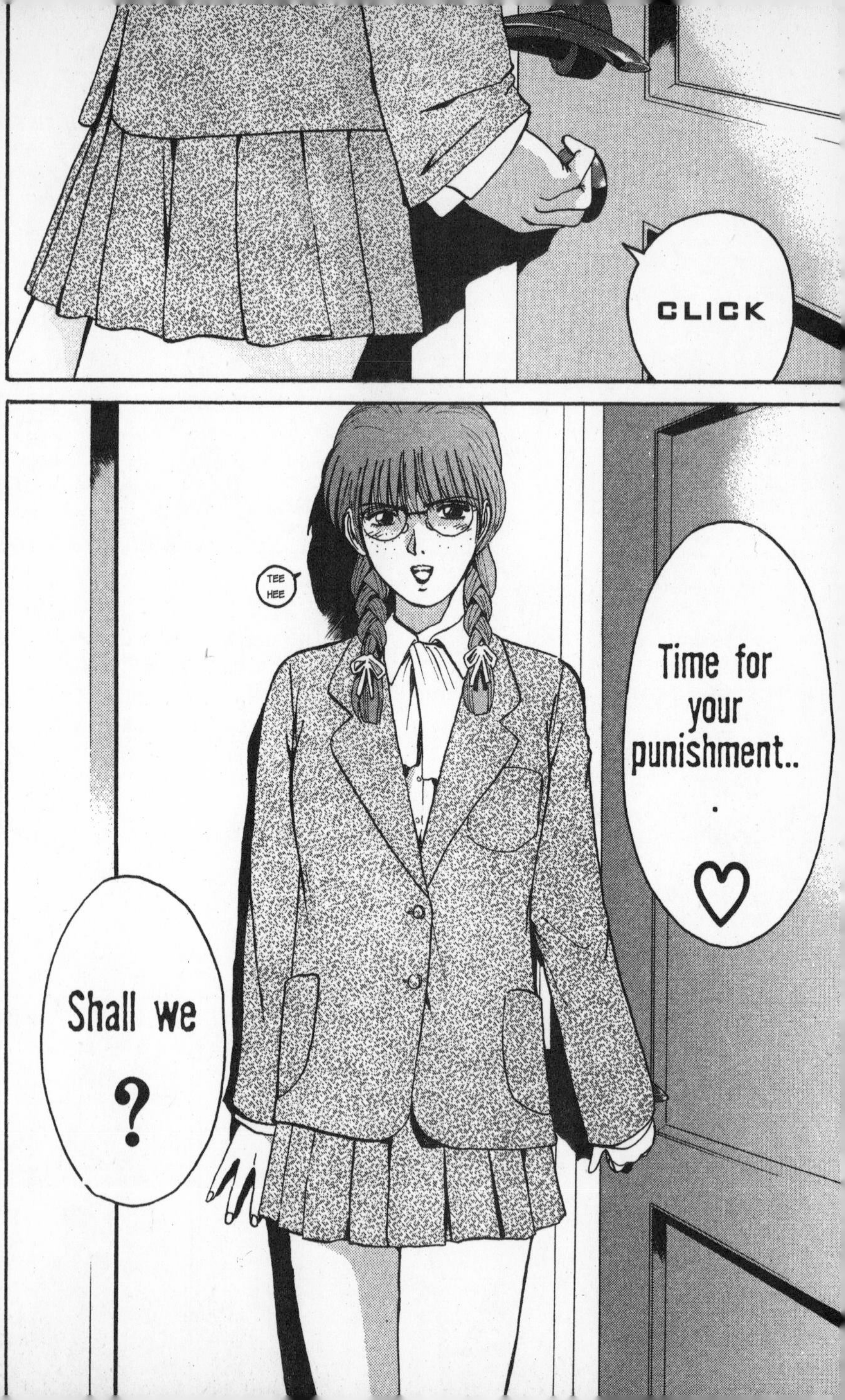
CLICK
Time for your punishment.. . ♡
TEE HEE
Shall we ?

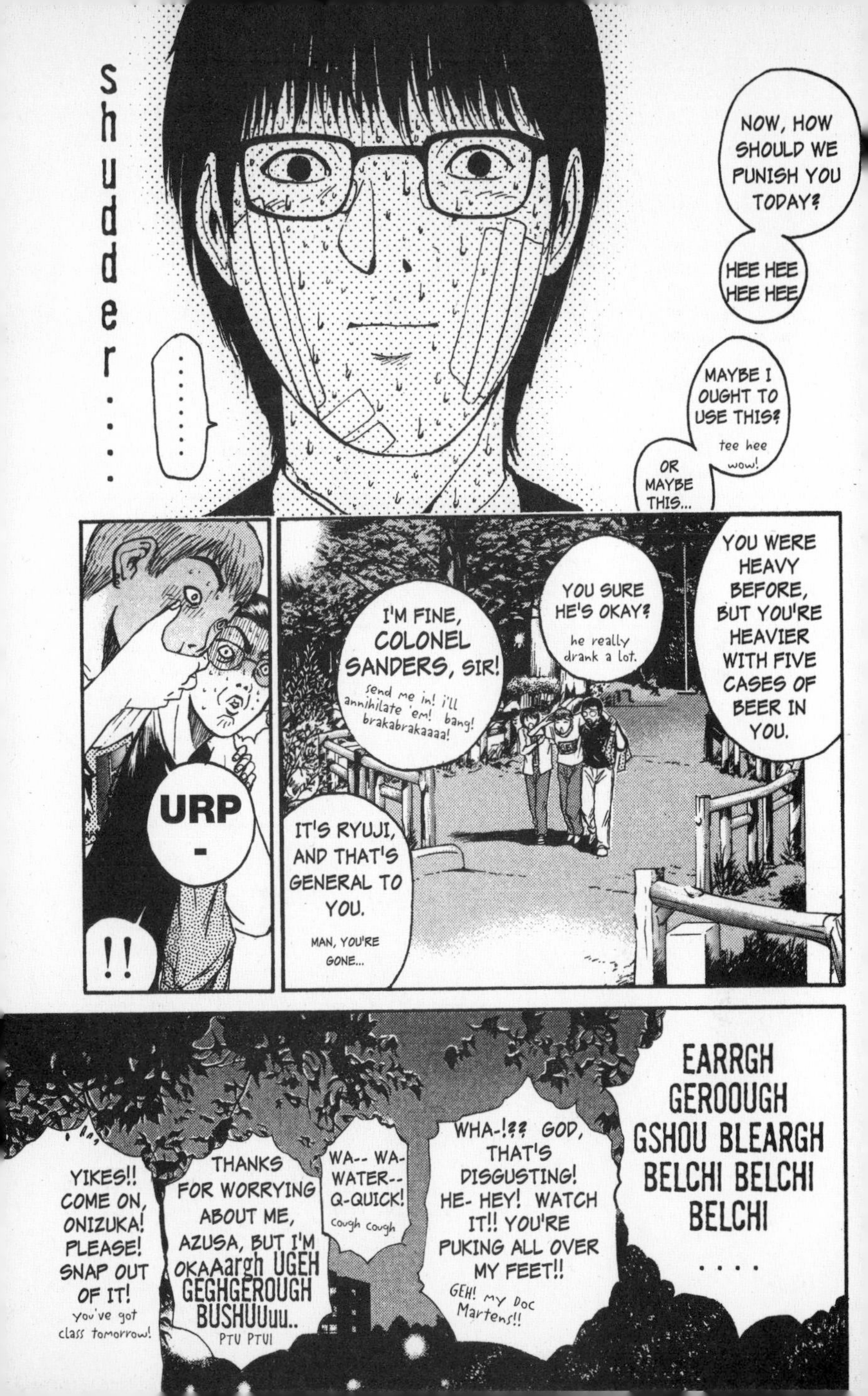
NOW, HOW SHOULD WE PUNISH YOU TODAY?
HEE HEE HEE HEE
MAYBE I OUGHT TO USE THIS?
tee hee wow!
OR MAYBE THIS...
......
shudder...
YOU WERE HEAVY BEFORE, BUT YOU'RE HEAVIER WITH FIVE CASES OF BEER IN YOU.
YOU SURE HE'S OKAY?
he really drank a lot.
I'M FINE, COLONEL SANDERS, SIR!
send me in! i'll annihilate 'em! bang! brakabrakaaaa!
IT'S RYUJI, AND THAT'S GENERAL TO YOU.
MAN, YOU'RE GONE...
URP -
!!
EARRGH GEROOUGH GSHOU BLEARGH BELCHI BELCHI BELCHI
....
WHA-!?? GOD, THAT'S DISGUSTING! HE- HEY! WATCH IT!! YOU'RE PUKING ALL OVER MY FEET!!
GEH! MY DOC Martens!!
WA-- WA- WATER-- Q-QUICK!
cough cough
THANKS FOR WORRYING ABOUT ME, AZUSA, BUT I'M OKAAargh UGEH GEGHGEROUGH BUSHUUuu..
PTU PTUI
YIKES!! COME ON, ONIZUKA! PLEASE! SNAP OUT OF IT!
You've got class tomorrow!

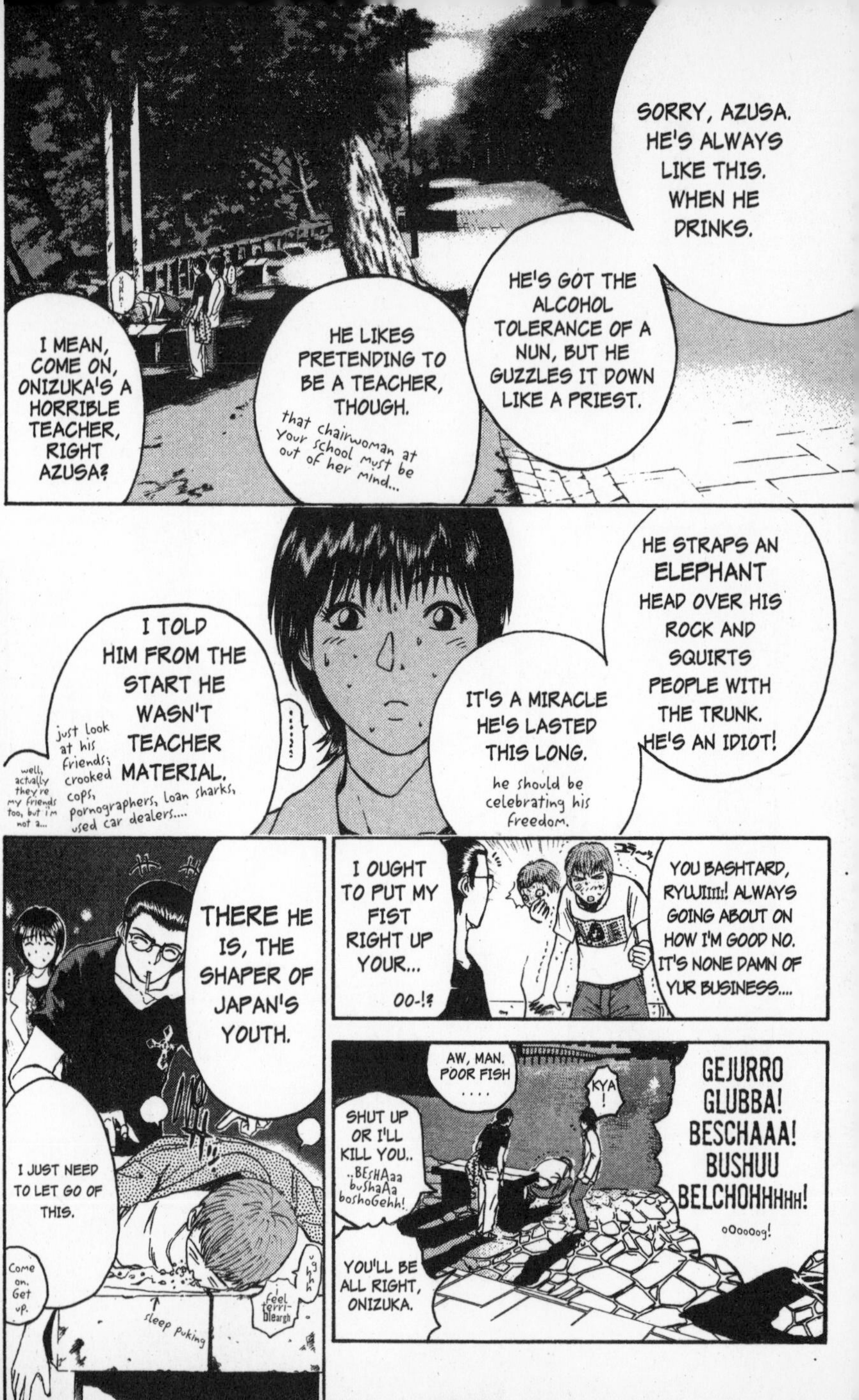
SORRY, AZUSA. HE'S ALWAYS LIKE THIS. WHEN HE DRINKS.
HE'S GOT THE ALCOHOL TOLERANCE OF A NUN, BUT HE GUZZLES IT DOWN LIKE A PRIEST.
HE LIKES PRETENDING TO BE A TEACHER, THOUGH.
that chairwoman at your school must be out of her mind...
I MEAN, COME ON, ONIZUKA'S A HORRIBLE TEACHER, RIGHT AZUSA?
HE STRAPS AN ELEPHANT HEAD OVER HIS ROCK AND SQUIRTS PEOPLE WITH THE TRUNK. HE'S AN IDIOT!
IT'S A MIRACLE HE'S LASTED THIS LONG.
he should be celebrating his freedom.
......
I TOLD HIM FROM THE START HE WASN'T TEACHER MATERIAL.
just look at his friends; crooked cops, pornographers, loan sharks, used car dealers....
well, actually they're my friends too, but i'm not a...
YOU BASHTARD, RYUJIiiii! ALWAYS GOING ABOUT ON HOW I'M GOOD NO. IT'S NONE DAMN OF YUR BUSINESS....
I OUGHT TO PUT MY FIST RIGHT UP YOUR...
OO-!?
GEJURRO GLUBBA! BESCHAAA! BUSHUU BELCHOHHhhh!
oOooOog!
AW, MAN. POOR FISH ....
KYA!
SHUT UP OR I'LL KILL YOU..
..BESHAaa buShaAa boshoGehh!
YOU'LL BE ALL RIGHT, ONIZUKA.
THERE HE IS, THE SHAPER OF JAPAN'S YOUTH.
I JUST NEED TO LET GO OF THIS.
Come on. Get up.
ughhh
i feel terri-bleargh
sleep puking

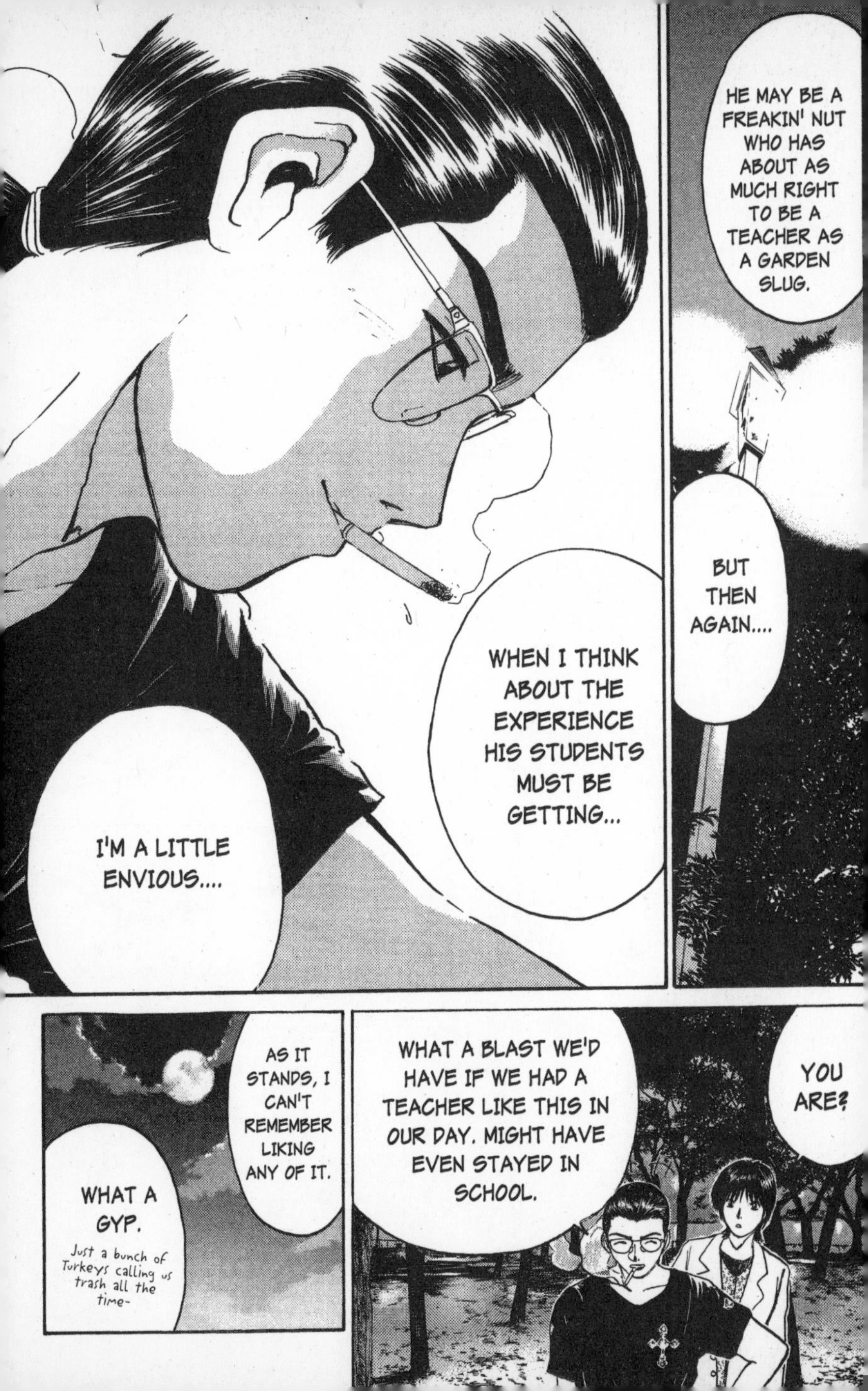
HE MAY BE A FREAKIN' NUT WHO HAS ABOUT AS MUCH RIGHT TO BE A TEACHER AS A GARDEN SLUG.
BUT THEN AGAIN....
WHEN I THINK ABOUT THE EXPERIENCE HIS STUDENTS MUST BE GETTING...
I'M A LITTLE ENVIOUS....
YOU ARE?
WHAT A BLAST WE'D HAVE IF WE HAD A TEACHER LIKE THIS IN OUR DAY. MIGHT HAVE EVEN STAYED IN SCHOOL.
AS IT STANDS, I CAN'T REMEMBER LIKING ANY OF IT.
WHAT A GYP.
Just a bunch of Turkeys calling us trash all the time-

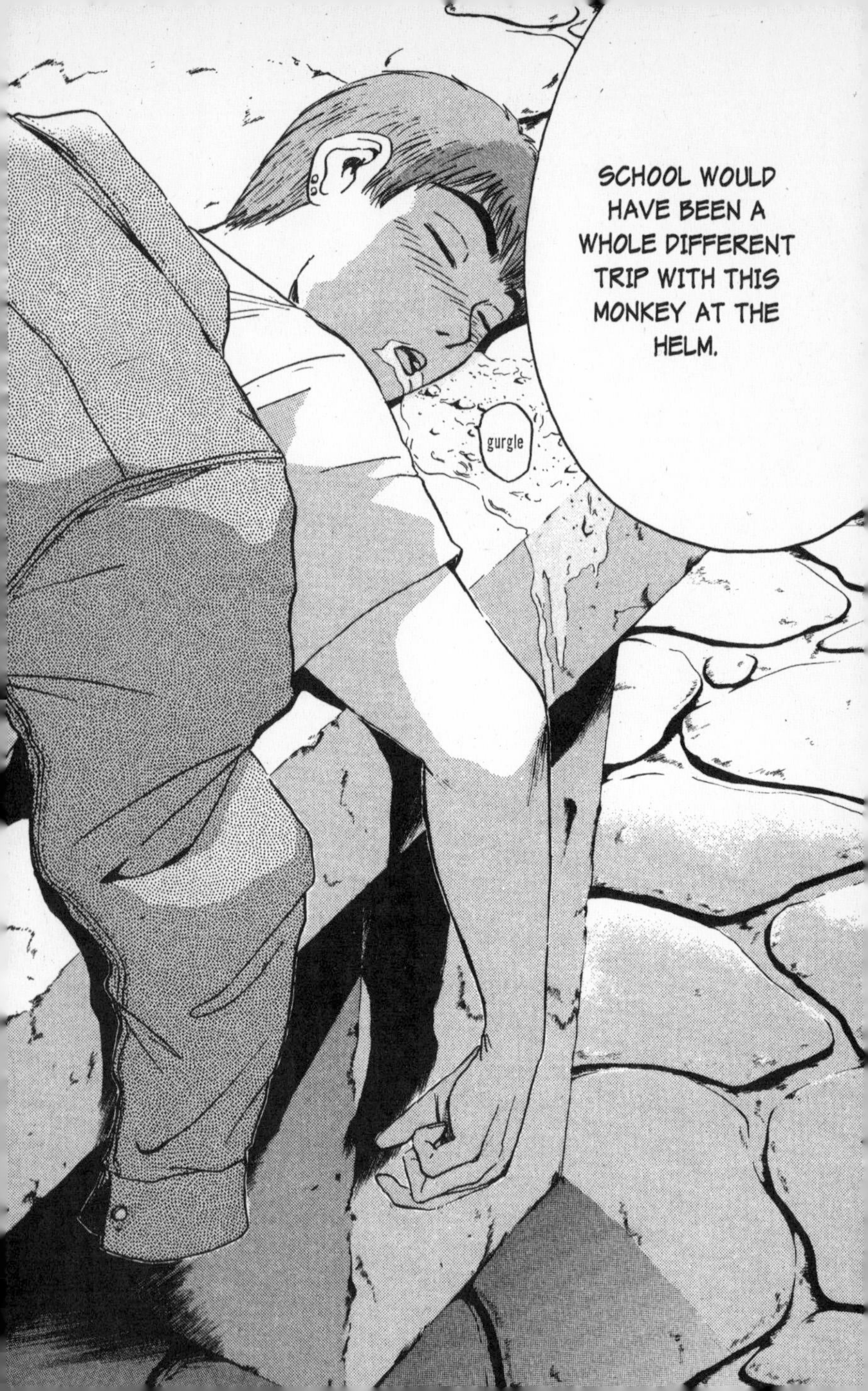
SCHOOL WOULD HAVE BEEN A WHOLE DIFFERENT TRIP WITH THIS MONKEY AT THE HELM.
gurgle

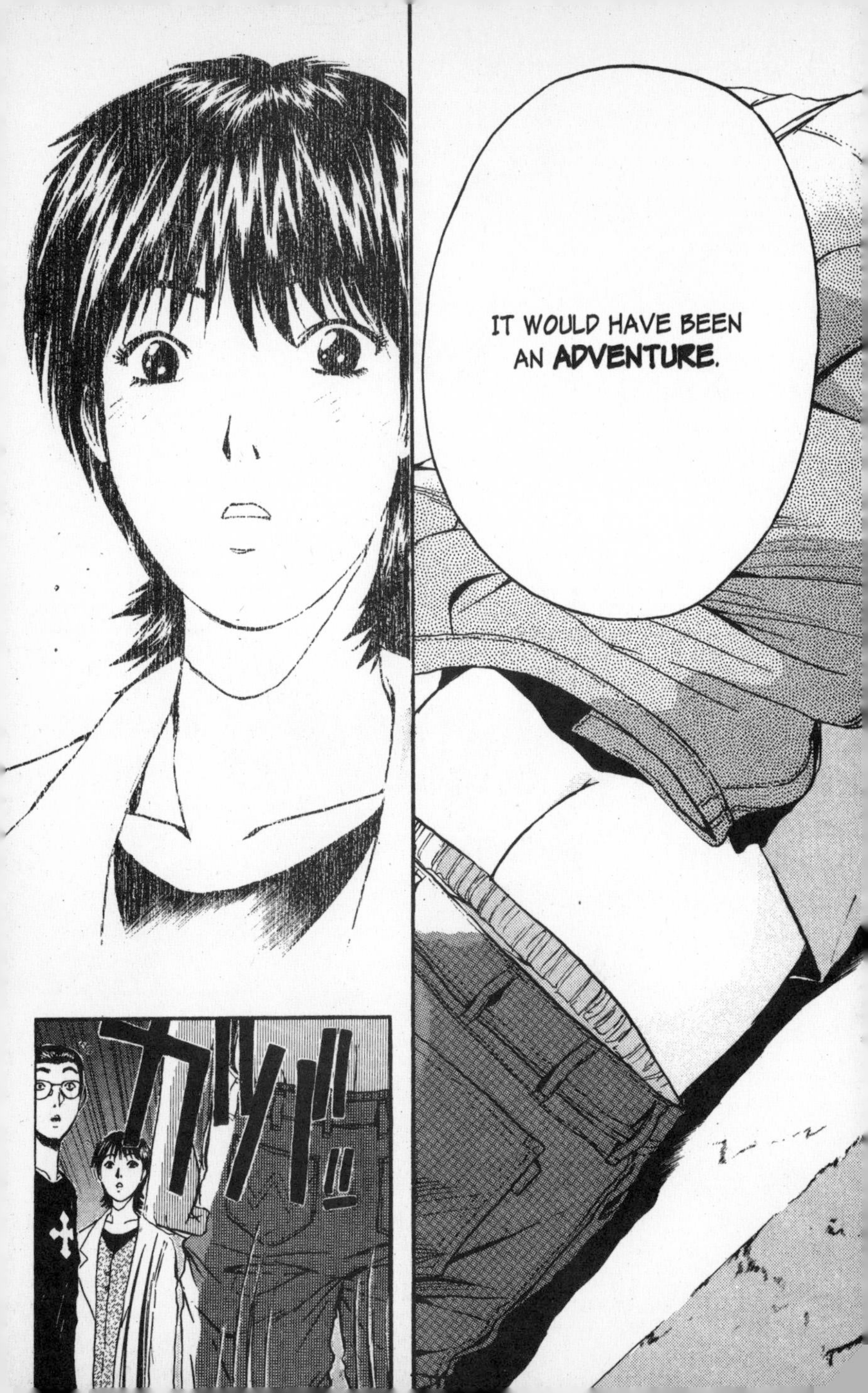
IT WOULD HAVE BEEN AN **ADVENTURE.**
カツ!!

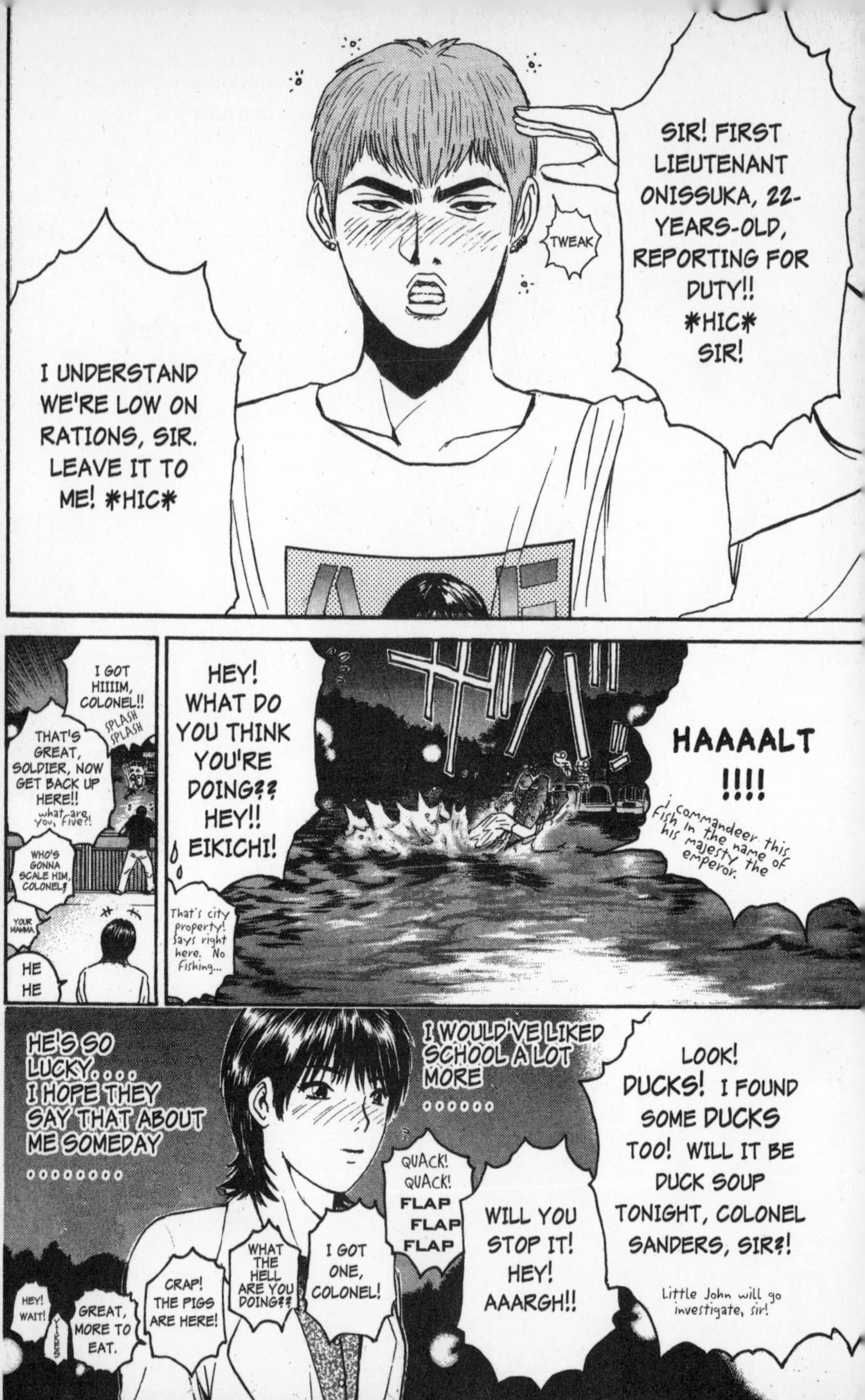

SIR! FIRST LIEUTENANT ONISSUKA, 22-YEARS-OLD, REPORTING FOR DUTY!! *HIC* SIR!
TWEAK
I UNDERSTAND WE'RE LOW ON RATIONS, SIR. LEAVE IT TO ME! *HIC*
HAAAALT !!!!
i commandeer this fish in the name of his majesty the emperor.
HEY! WHAT DO YOU THINK YOU'RE DOING?? HEY!! EIKICHI!
That's city property! Says right here. No fishing...
I GOT HIIIIM, COLONEL!!
SPLASH SPLASH
THAT'S GREAT, SOLDIER, NOW GET BACK UP HERE!!
what are you, five?!
WHO'S GONNA SCALE HIM, COLONEL?
YOUR MAMMA
HE HE
LOOK! DUCKS! I FOUND SOME DUCKS TOO! WILL IT BE DUCK SOUP TONIGHT, COLONEL SANDERS, SIR?!
Little John will go investigate, sir!
I WOULD'VE LIKED SCHOOL A LOT MORE ......
WILL YOU STOP IT! HEY! AAARGH!!
QUACK! QUACK!
FLAP FLAP FLAP
I GOT ONE, COLONEL!
WHAT THE HELL ARE YOU DOING??
HE'S SO LUCKY.... I HOPE THEY SAY THAT ABOUT ME SOMEDAY ....
CRAP! THE PIGS ARE HERE!
GREAT, MORE TO EAT.
HEY! WAIT!

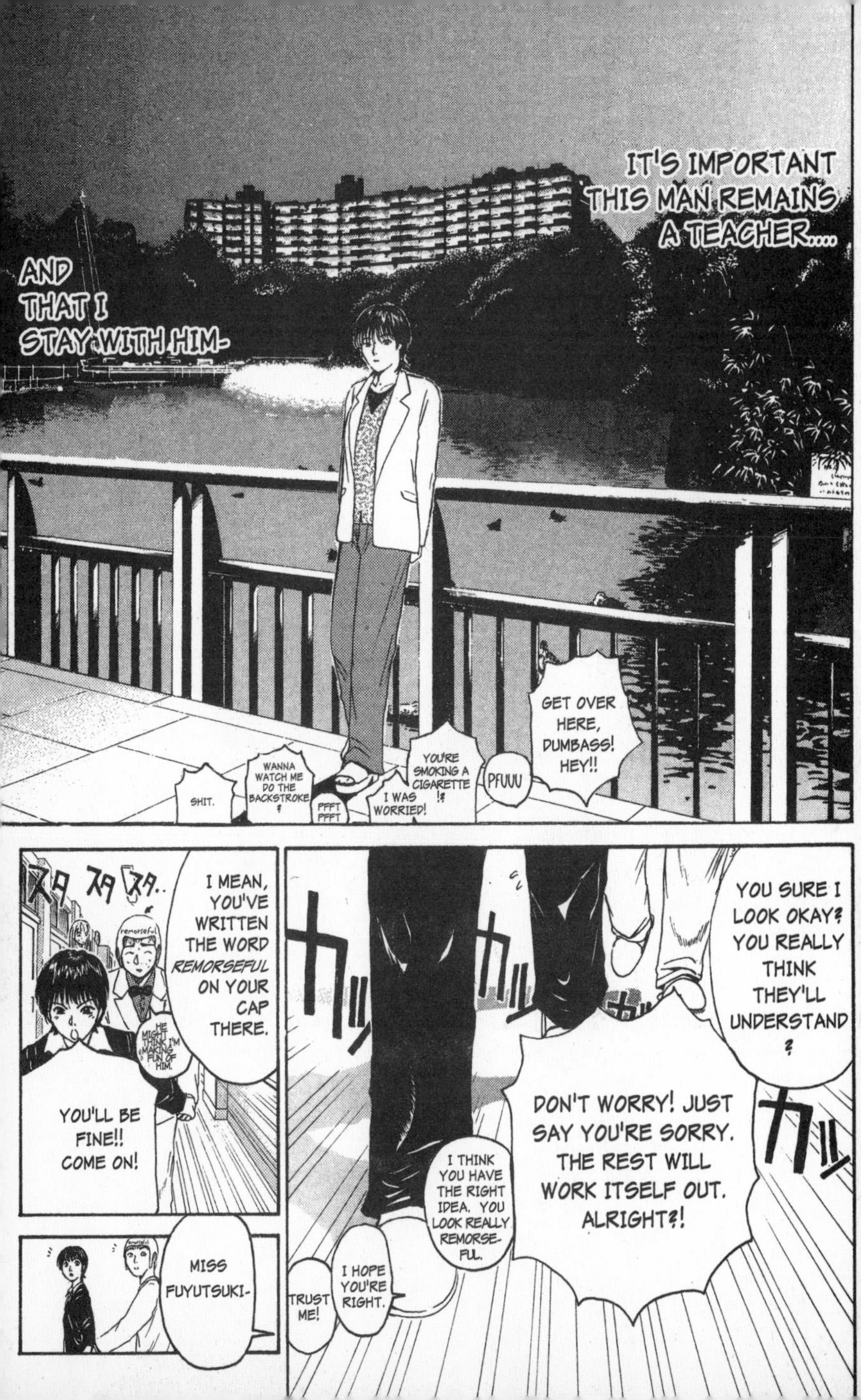
IT'S IMPORTANT THIS MAN REMAINS A TEACHER....
AND THAT I STAY WITH HIM-
GET OVER HERE, DUMBASS! HEY!!
PFUUU
YOU'RE SMOKING A CIGARETTE !?
I WAS WORRIED!
PFFT PFFT
WANNA WATCH ME DO THE BACKSTROKE?
SHIT.
カツ
カツ
カツ
YOU SURE I LOOK OKAY? YOU REALLY THINK THEY'LL UNDERSTAND?
DON'T WORRY! JUST SAY YOU'RE SORRY. THE REST WILL WORK ITSELF OUT. ALRIGHT?!
I THINK YOU HAVE THE RIGHT IDEA. YOU LOOK REALLY REMORSE-FUL.
I HOPE YOU'RE RIGHT.
TRUST ME!
スタ スタ スタ..
I MEAN, YOU'VE WRITTEN THE WORD *REMORSEFUL* ON YOUR CAP THERE.
remorseful
HE MIGHT THINK I'M MAKING FUN OF HIM.
YOU'LL BE FINE!! COME ON!
MISS FUYUTSUKI-

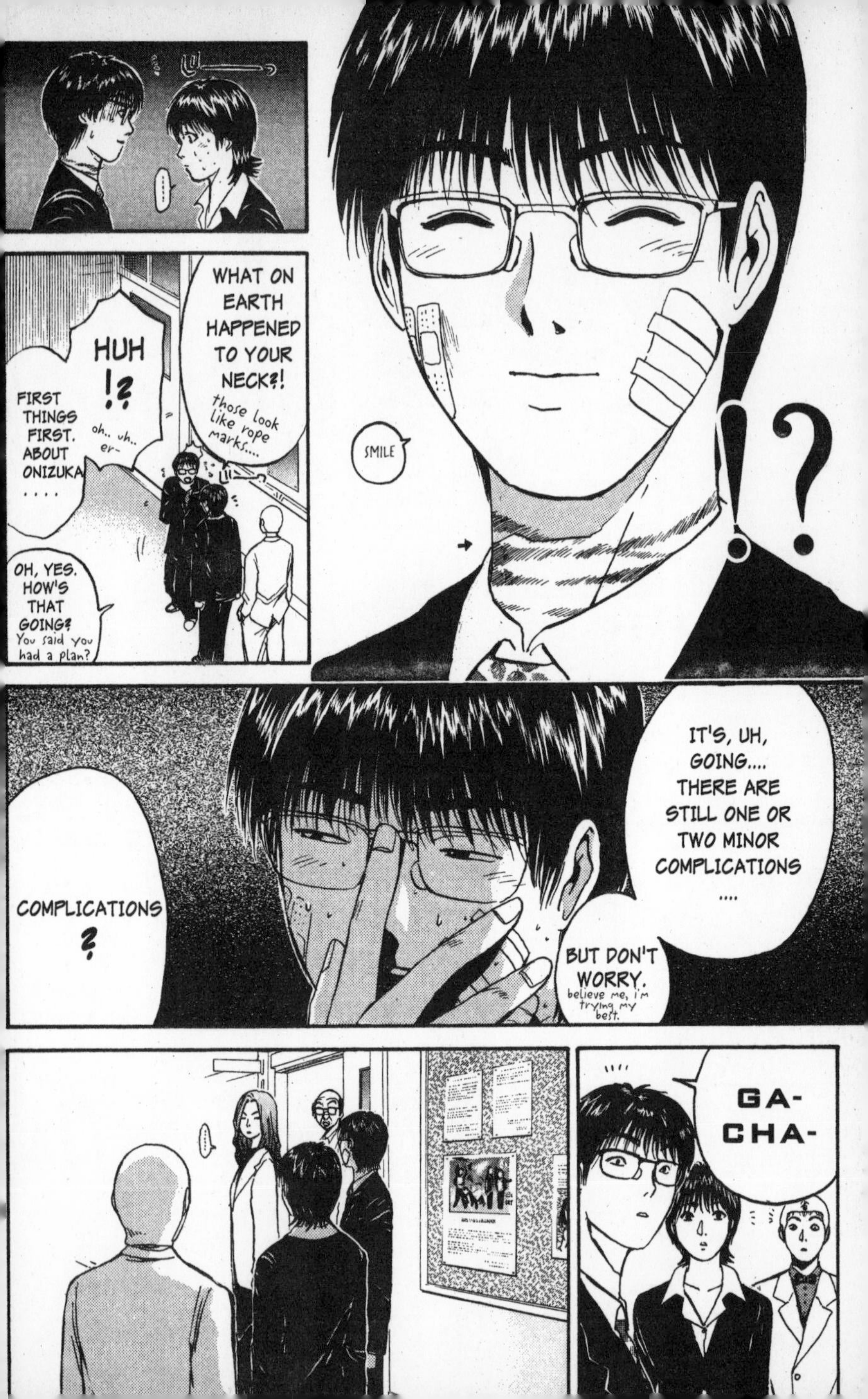
SMILE
!?
WHAT ON EARTH HAPPENED TO YOUR NECK?!
those look like rope marks....
HUH !?
oh.. uh.. er-
FIRST THINGS FIRST. ABOUT ONIZUKA....
OH, YES. HOW'S THAT GOING?
You said you had a plan?
IT'S, UH, GOING.... THERE ARE STILL ONE OR TWO MINOR COMPLICATIONS ....
BUT DON'T WORRY.
believe me, i'm trying my best.
COMPLICATIONS ?
GA-
CHA-

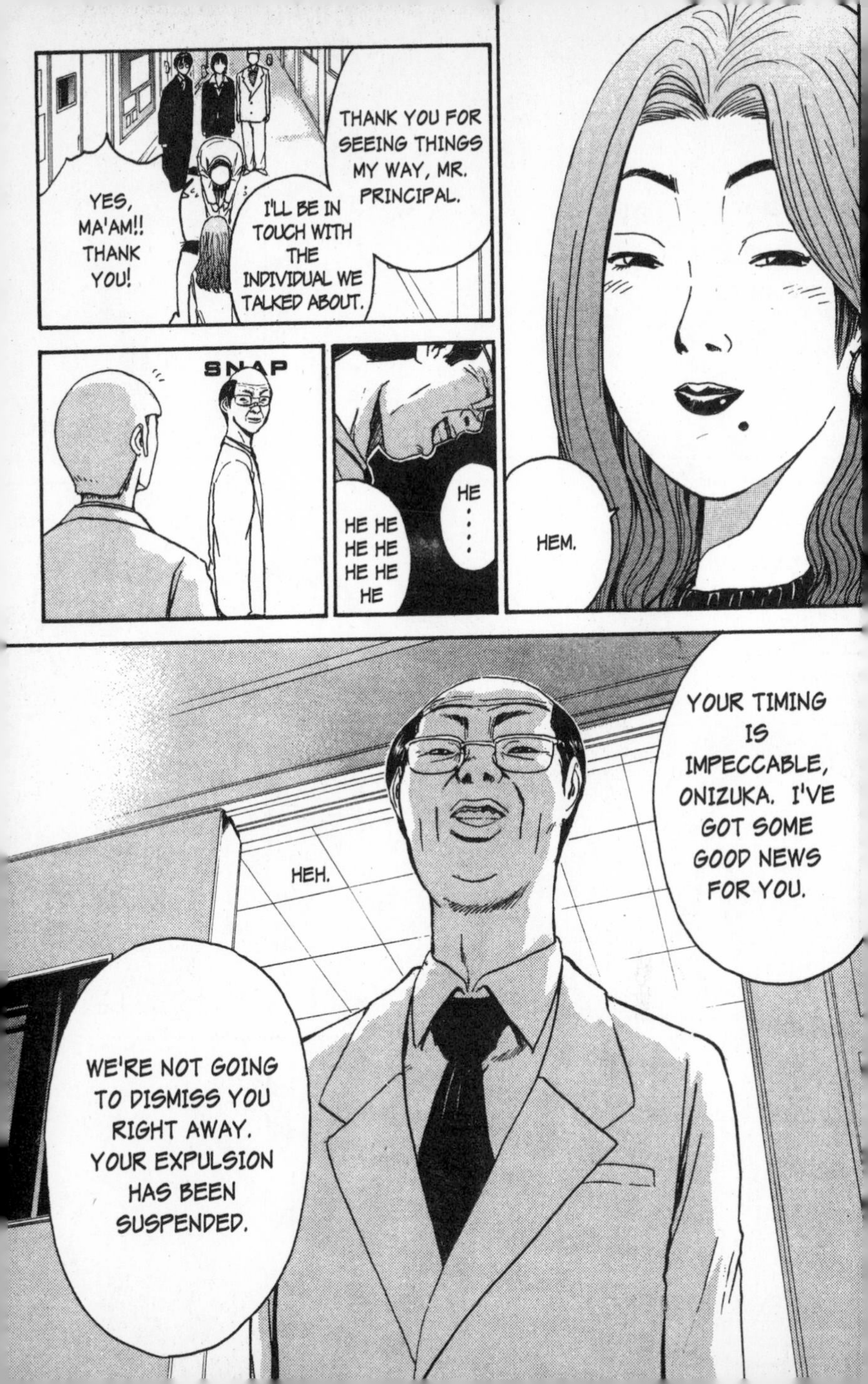
HEM.
THANK YOU FOR SEEING THINGS MY WAY, MR. PRINCIPAL.
I'LL BE IN TOUCH WITH THE INDIVIDUAL WE TALKED ABOUT.
YES, MA'AM!! THANK YOU!
HE ....
HE HE HE HE HE HE HE
SNAP
YOUR TIMING IS IMPECCABLE, ONIZUKA. I'VE GOT SOME GOOD NEWS FOR YOU.
HEH.
WE'RE NOT GOING TO DISMISS YOU RIGHT AWAY. YOUR EXPULSION HAS BEEN SUSPENDED.

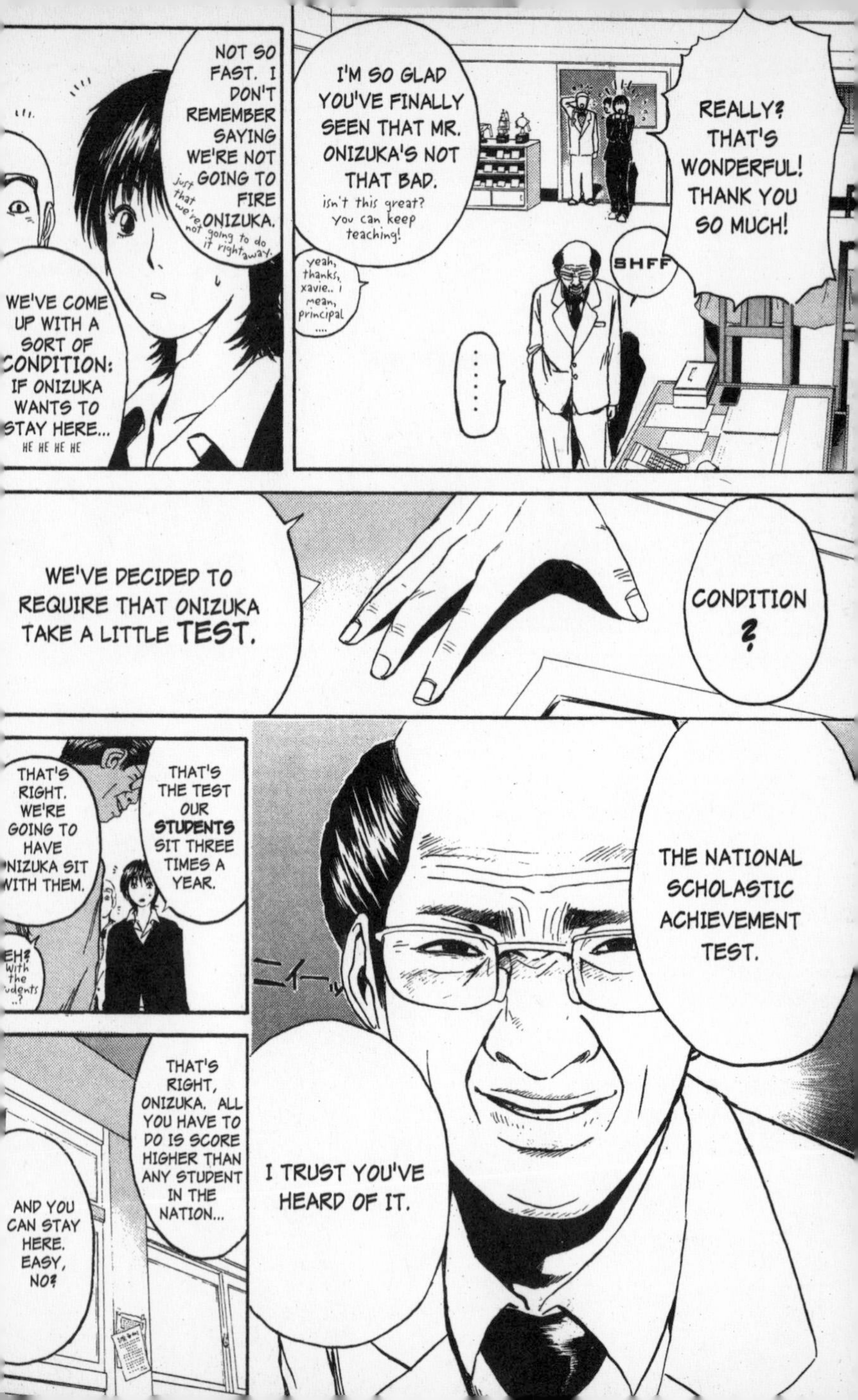
REALLY? THAT'S WONDERFUL! THANK YOU SO MUCH!
SHFF
I'M SO GLAD YOU'VE FINALLY SEEN THAT MR. ONIZUKA'S NOT THAT BAD.
isn't this great? you can keep teaching!
yeah, thanks, xavie.. i mean, principal ....
......
NOT SO FAST. I DON'T REMEMBER SAYING WE'RE NOT GOING TO FIRE ONIZUKA.
just that we're not going to do it rightaway.
WE'VE COME UP WITH A SORT OF CONDITION: IF ONIZUKA WANTS TO STAY HERE...
HE HE HE HE
CONDITION?
WE'VE DECIDED TO REQUIRE THAT ONIZUKA TAKE A LITTLE TEST.
THE NATIONAL SCHOLASTIC ACHIEVEMENT TEST.
I TRUST YOU'VE HEARD OF IT.
THAT'S THE TEST OUR STUDENTS SIT THREE TIMES A YEAR.
THAT'S RIGHT. WE'RE GOING TO HAVE NIZUKA SIT WITH THEM.
EH? with the udents ..?
THAT'S RIGHT, ONIZUKA. ALL YOU HAVE TO DO IS SCORE HIGHER THAN ANY STUDENT IN THE NATION...
AND YOU CAN STAY HERE. EASY, NO?

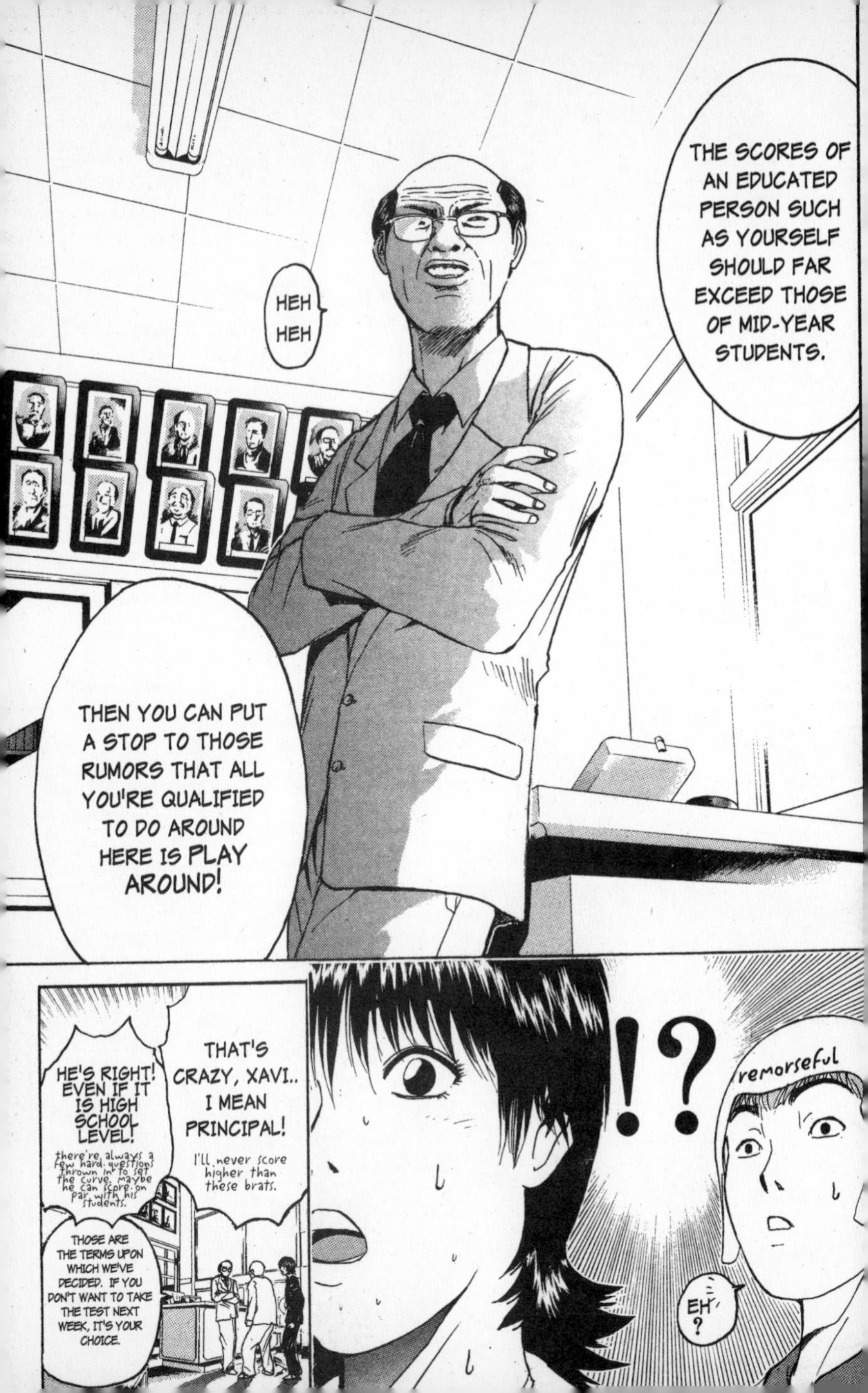
THE SCORES OF AN EDUCATED PERSON SUCH AS YOURSELF SHOULD FAR EXCEED THOSE OF MID-YEAR STUDENTS.
HEH HEH
THEN YOU CAN PUT A STOP TO THOSE RUMORS THAT ALL YOU'RE QUALIFIED TO DO AROUND HERE IS PLAY AROUND!
remorseful
!?
EH?
THAT'S CRAZY, XAVI.. I MEAN PRINCIPAL!
I'll never score higher than these brats.
HE'S RIGHT! EVEN IF IT IS HIGH SCHOOL LEVEL!
there're always a few hard questions thrown in to set the curve, maybe he can score on par with his students.
THOSE ARE THE TERMS UPON WHICH WE'VE DECIDED. IF YOU DON'T WANT TO TAKE THE TEST NEXT WEEK, IT'S YOUR CHOICE.

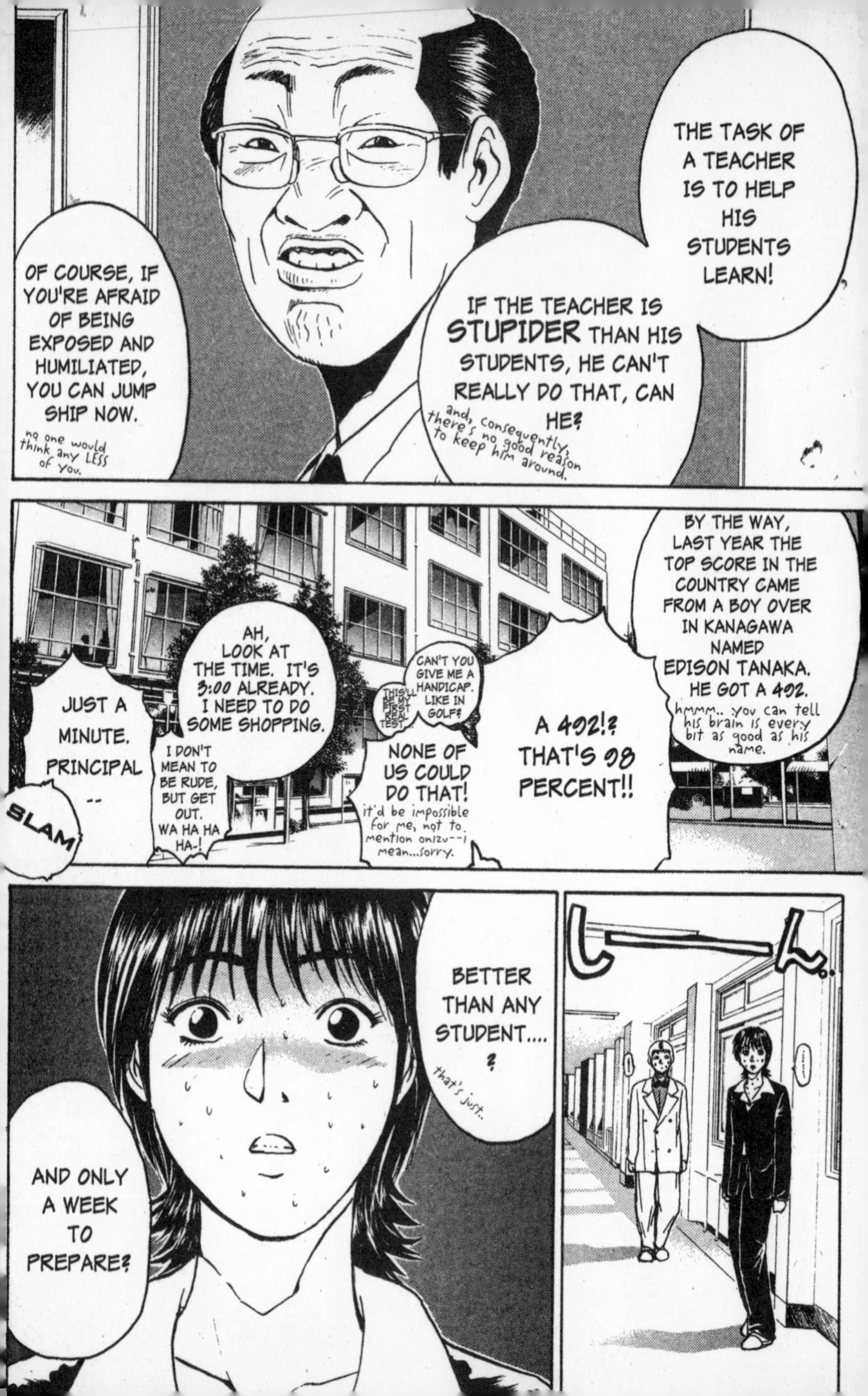
THE TASK OF A TEACHER IS TO HELP HIS STUDENTS LEARN!
IF THE TEACHER IS STUPIDER THAN HIS STUDENTS, HE CAN'T REALLY DO THAT, CAN HE?
and, consequently, there's no good reason to keep him around.
OF COURSE, IF YOU'RE AFRAID OF BEING EXPOSED AND HUMILIATED, YOU CAN JUMP SHIP NOW.
no one would think any LESS of you.
BY THE WAY, LAST YEAR THE TOP SCORE IN THE COUNTRY CAME FROM A BOY OVER IN KANAGAWA NAMED EDISON TANAKA. HE GOT A 492.
hmmm.. you can tell his brain is every bit as good as his name.
A 492!? THAT'S 98 PERCENT!!
NONE OF US COULD DO THAT!
it'd be impossible for me, not to mention onizu--I mean...sorry.
CAN'T YOU GIVE ME A HANDICAP. LIKE IN GOLF?
THIS'LL BE MY FIRST REAL TEST.
AH, LOOK AT THE TIME. IT'S 3:00 ALREADY. I NEED TO DO SOME SHOPPING.
I DON'T MEAN TO BE RUDE, BUT GET OUT. WA HA HA HA-!
JUST A MINUTE. PRINCIPAL --
SLAM
しーん。
!!
......
BETTER THAN ANY STUDENT....?
that's just.
AND ONLY A WEEK TO PREPARE?

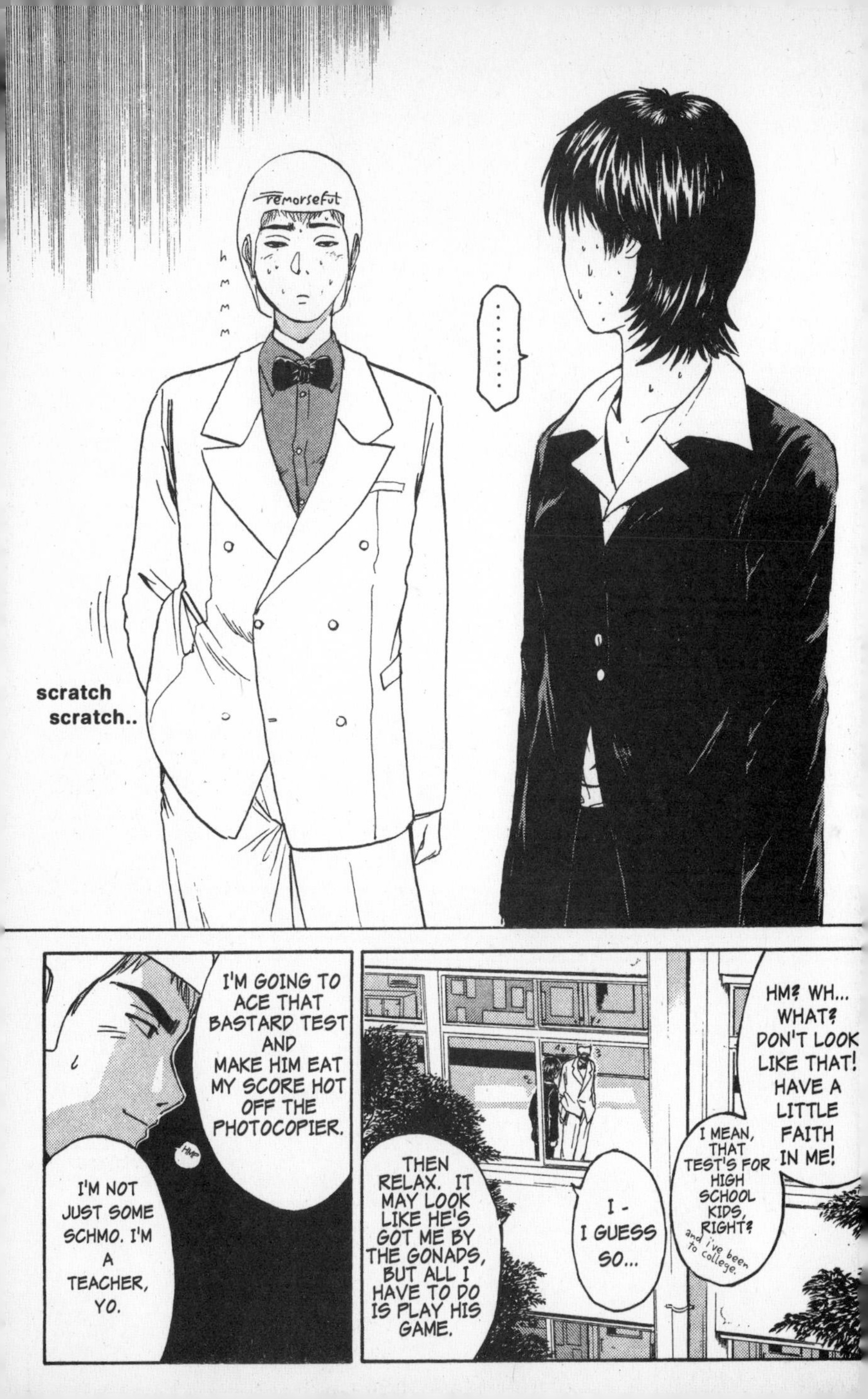
remorseful
hmmm
....
scratch scratch..
HM? WH... WHAT? DON'T LOOK LIKE THAT! HAVE A LITTLE FAITH IN ME!
I MEAN, THAT TEST'S FOR HIGH SCHOOL KIDS, RIGHT?
and i've been to college.
I - I GUESS SO...
THEN RELAX. IT MAY LOOK LIKE HE'S GOT ME BY THE GONADS, BUT ALL I HAVE TO DO IS PLAY HIS GAME.
I'M GOING TO ACE THAT BASTARD TEST AND MAKE HIM EAT MY SCORE HOT OFF THE PHOTOCOPIER.
HMP
I'M NOT JUST SOME SCHMO. I'M A TEACHER, YO.

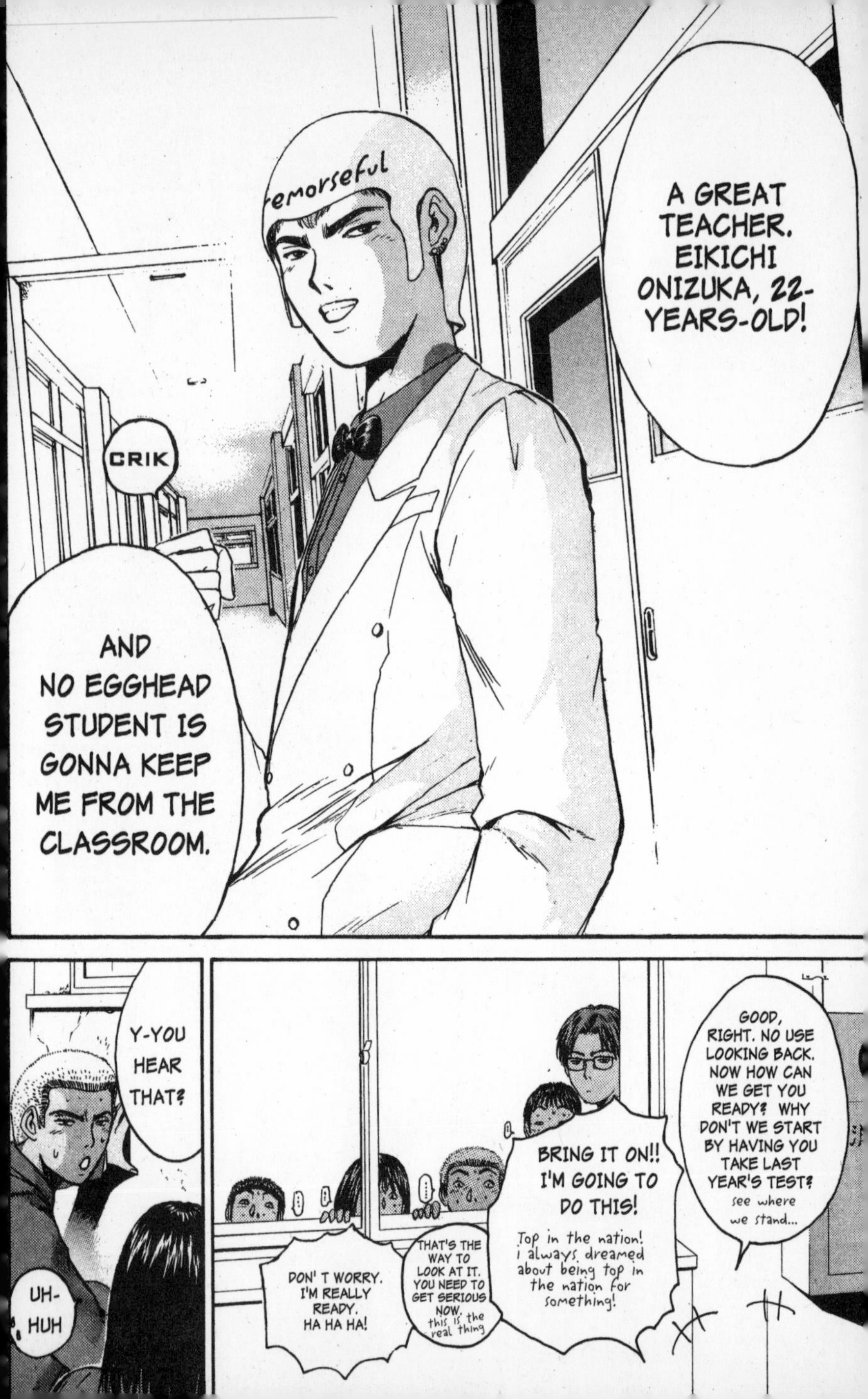
A GREAT TEACHER. EIKICHI ONIZUKA, 22-YEARS-OLD!
remorseful
CRIK
AND NO EGGHEAD STUDENT IS GONNA KEEP ME FROM THE CLASSROOM.
GOOD, RIGHT. NO USE LOOKING BACK. NOW HOW CAN WE GET YOU READY? WHY DON'T WE START BY HAVING YOU TAKE LAST YEAR'S TEST?
see where we stand...
BRING IT ON!! I'M GOING TO DO THIS!
Top in the nation! i always dreamed about being top in the nation for something!
THAT'S THE WAY TO LOOK AT IT. YOU NEED TO GET SERIOUS NOW.
this is the real thing
DON' T WORRY. I'M REALLY READY. HA HA HA!
Y-YOU HEAR THAT?
UH-HUH

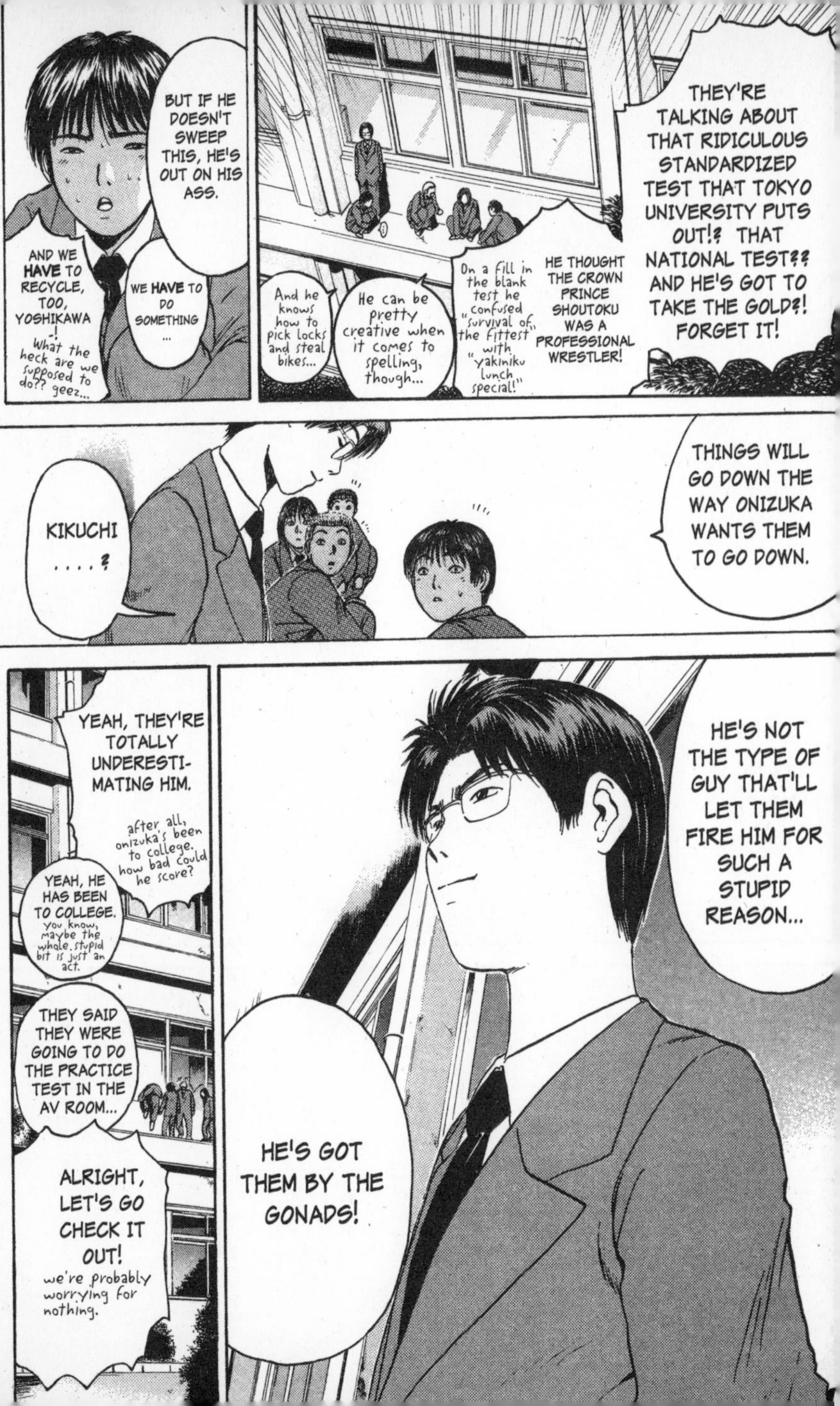
THEY'RE TALKING ABOUT THAT RIDICULOUS STANDARDIZED TEST THAT TOKYO UNIVERSITY PUTS OUT!? THAT NATIONAL TEST?? AND HE'S GOT TO TAKE THE GOLD?! FORGET IT!
HE THOUGHT THE CROWN PRINCE SHOUTOKU WAS A PROFESSIONAL WRESTLER!
On a fill in the blank test he confused "survival of the fittest" with "yakiniku lunch special!"
He can be pretty creative when it comes to spelling, though...
And he knows how to pick locks and steal bikes...
BUT IF HE DOESN'T SWEEP THIS, HE'S OUT ON HIS ASS.
WE HAVE TO DO SOMETHING ...
AND WE HAVE TO RECYCLE, TOO, YOSHIKAWA-! What the heck are we supposed to do?? geez...
THINGS WILL GO DOWN THE WAY ONIZUKA WANTS THEM TO GO DOWN.
KIKUCHI ....?
HE'S NOT THE TYPE OF GUY THAT'LL LET THEM FIRE HIM FOR SUCH A STUPID REASON...
HE'S GOT THEM BY THE GONADS!
YEAH, THEY'RE TOTALLY UNDERESTIMATING HIM.
after all, onizuka's been to college. how bad could he score?
YEAH, HE HAS BEEN TO COLLEGE. You know, maybe the whole stupid bit is just an act.
THEY SAID THEY WERE GOING TO DO THE PRACTICE TEST IN THE AV ROOM...
ALRIGHT, LET'S GO CHECK IT OUT! we're probably worrying for nothing.

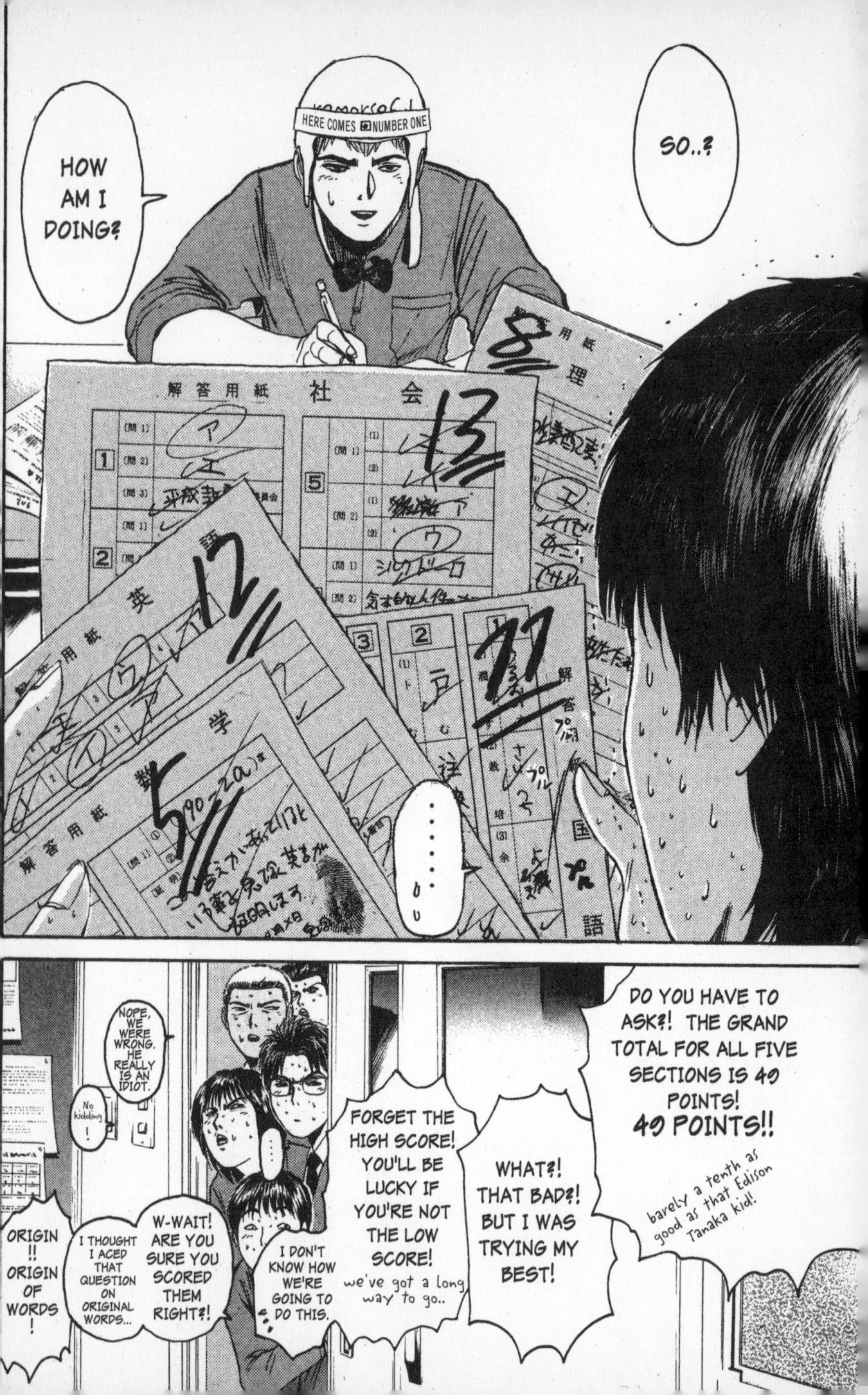
SO..?
HERE COMES NUMBER ONE
HOW AM I DOING?
......
DO YOU HAVE TO ASK?! THE GRAND TOTAL FOR ALL FIVE SECTIONS IS 49 POINTS! 49 POINTS!!
barely a tenth as good as that Edison Tanaka kid!
WHAT?! THAT BAD?! BUT I WAS TRYING MY BEST!
FORGET THE HIGH SCORE! YOU'LL BE LUCKY IF YOU'RE NOT THE LOW SCORE!
we've got a long way to go..
NOPE, WE WERE WRONG. HE REALLY IS AN IDIOT.
No kidding!
I DON'T KNOW HOW WE'RE GOING TO DO THIS.
W-WAIT! ARE YOU SURE YOU SCORED THEM RIGHT?!
I THOUGHT I ACED THAT QUESTION ON ORIGINAL WORDS...
ORIGIN!! ORIGIN OF WORDS!

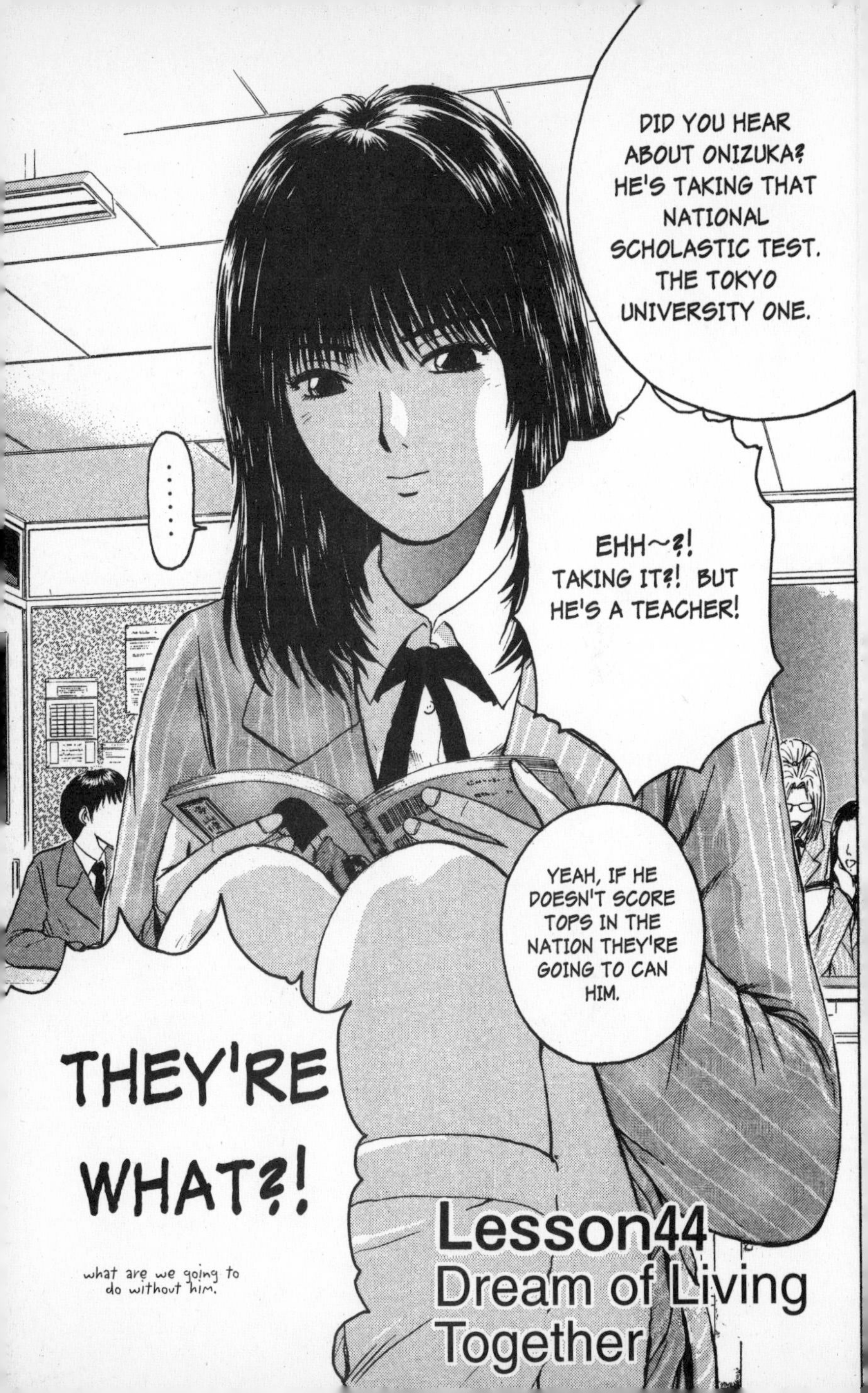
DID YOU HEAR ABOUT ONIZUKA? HE'S TAKING THAT NATIONAL SCHOLASTIC TEST. THE TOKYO UNIVERSITY ONE.
......
EHH~?! TAKING IT?! BUT HE'S A TEACHER!
YEAH, IF HE DOESN'T SCORE TOPS IN THE NATION THEY'RE GOING TO CAN HIM.
THEY'RE WHAT?!
what are we going to do without him.
Lesson44
Dream of Living Together

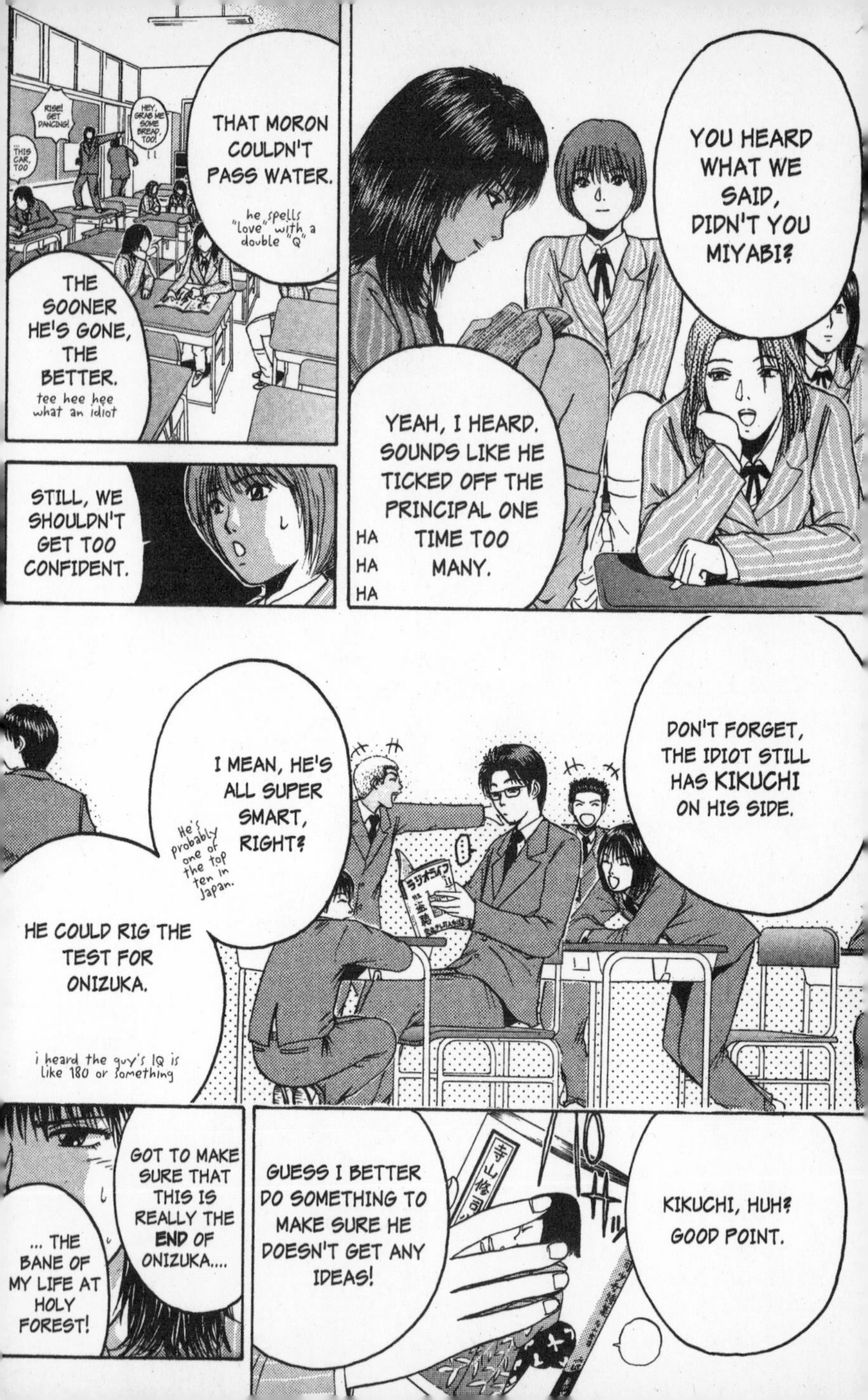
YOU HEARD WHAT WE SAID, DIDN'T YOU MIYABI?
YEAH, I HEARD. SOUNDS LIKE HE TICKED OFF THE PRINCIPAL ONE TIME TOO MANY.
HA HA HA
THAT MORON COULDN'T PASS WATER.
he spells "love" with a double "Q"
HEY, GRAB ME SOME BREAD, TOO!
RISE! GET DANCING!
... THIS CAR, TOO
THE SOONER HE'S GONE, THE BETTER.
tee hee hee what an idiot
STILL, WE SHOULDN'T GET TOO CONFIDENT.
DON'T FORGET, THE IDIOT STILL HAS KIKUCHI ON HIS SIDE.
I MEAN, HE'S ALL SUPER SMART, RIGHT?
He's probably one of the top ten in Japan.
HE COULD RIG THE TEST FOR ONIZUKA.
i heard the guy's IQ is like 180 or something
KIKUCHI, HUH? GOOD POINT.
寺山修司
GUESS I BETTER DO SOMETHING TO MAKE SURE HE DOESN'T GET ANY IDEAS!
GOT TO MAKE SURE THAT THIS IS REALLY THE END OF ONIZUKA....
... THE BANE OF MY LIFE AT HOLY FOREST!

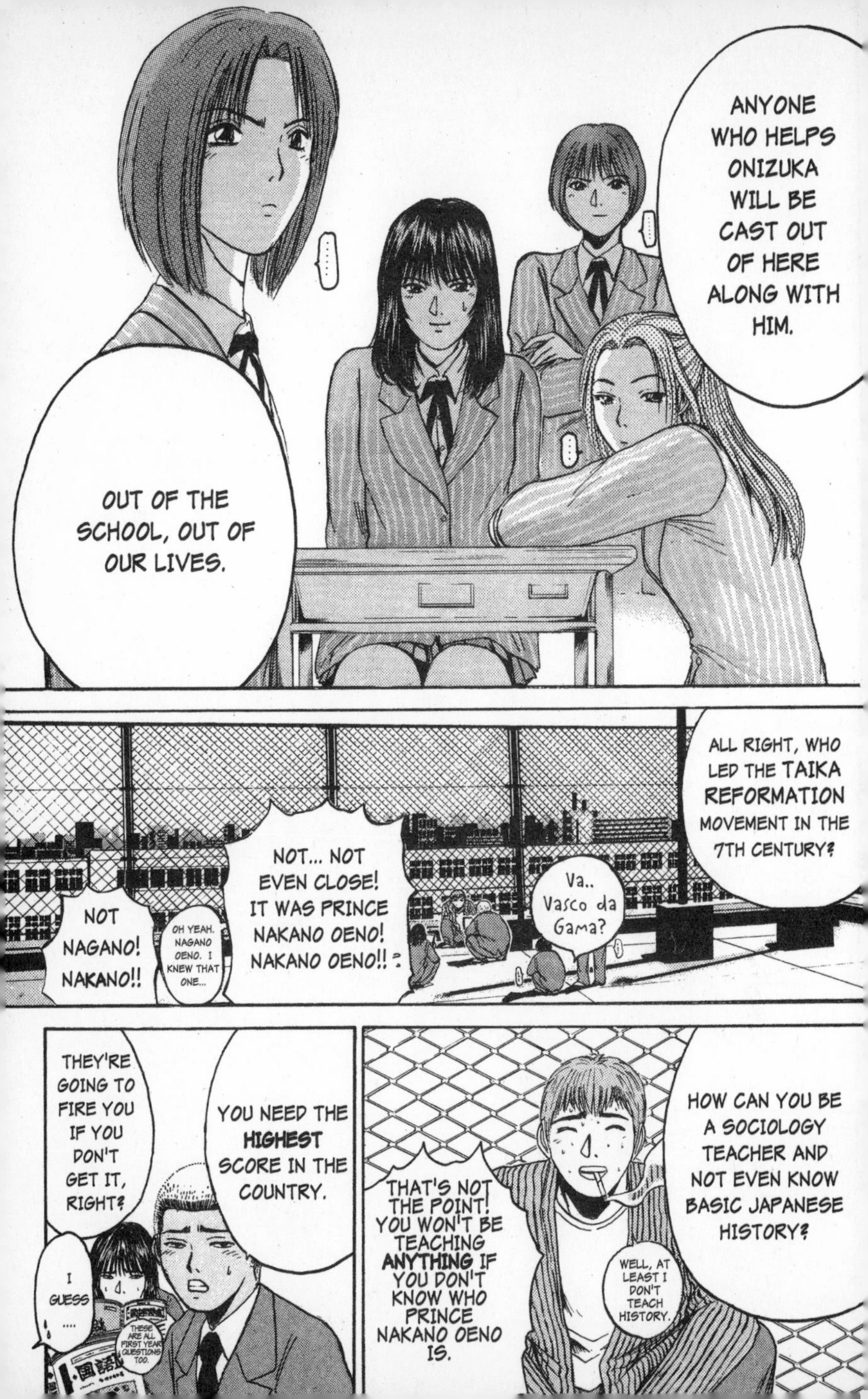
ANYONE WHO HELPS ONIZUKA WILL BE CAST OUT OF HERE ALONG WITH HIM.
OUT OF THE SCHOOL, OUT OF OUR LIVES.
ALL RIGHT, WHO LED THE TAIKA REFORMATION MOVEMENT IN THE 7TH CENTURY?
Va.. Vasco da Gama?
NOT... NOT EVEN CLOSE! IT WAS PRINCE NAKANO OENO! NAKANO OENO!!
OH YEAH. NAGANO OENO. I KNEW THAT ONE...
NOT NAGANO! NAKANO!!
HOW CAN YOU BE A SOCIOLOGY TEACHER AND NOT EVEN KNOW BASIC JAPANESE HISTORY?
WELL, AT LEAST I DON'T TEACH HISTORY.
THAT'S NOT THE POINT! YOU WON'T BE TEACHING ANYTHING IF YOU DON'T KNOW WHO PRINCE NAKANO OENO IS.
YOU NEED THE HIGHEST SCORE IN THE COUNTRY.
THEY'RE GOING TO FIRE YOU IF YOU DON'T GET IT, RIGHT?
I GUESS....
THESE ARE ALL FIRST YEAR QUESTIONS TOO.

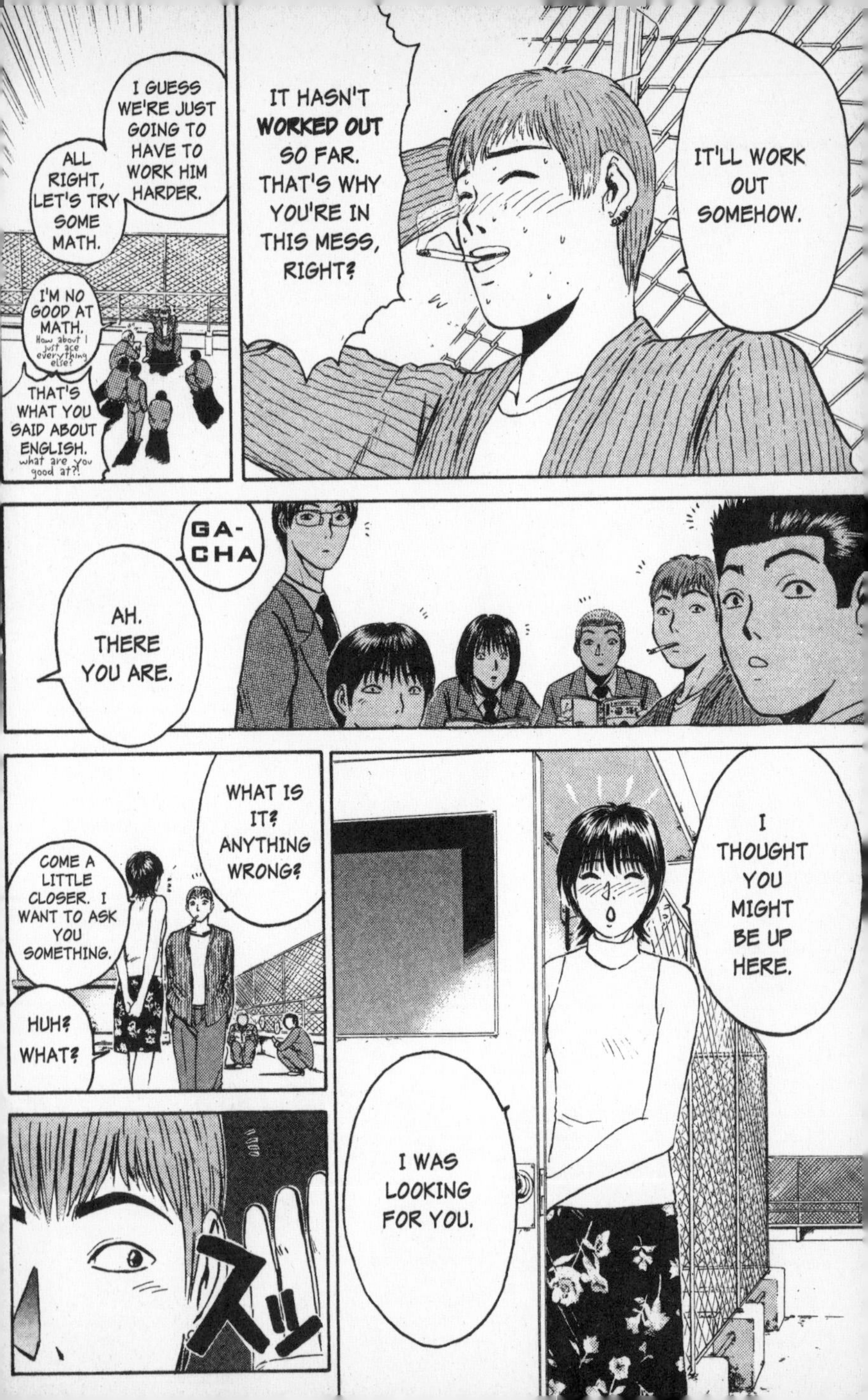
IT'LL WORK OUT SOMEHOW.
IT HASN'T **WORKED OUT** SO FAR. THAT'S WHY YOU'RE IN THIS MESS, RIGHT?
I GUESS WE'RE JUST GOING TO HAVE TO WORK HIM HARDER.
ALL RIGHT, LET'S TRY SOME MATH.
I'M NO GOOD AT MATH. How about I just ace everything else?
THAT'S WHAT YOU SAID ABOUT ENGLISH. what are you good at?!
GA-CHA
AH. THERE YOU ARE.
I THOUGHT YOU MIGHT BE UP HERE.
I WAS LOOKING FOR YOU.
WHAT IS IT? ANYTHING WRONG?
COME A LITTLE CLOSER. I WANT TO ASK YOU SOMETHING.
HUH? WHAT?

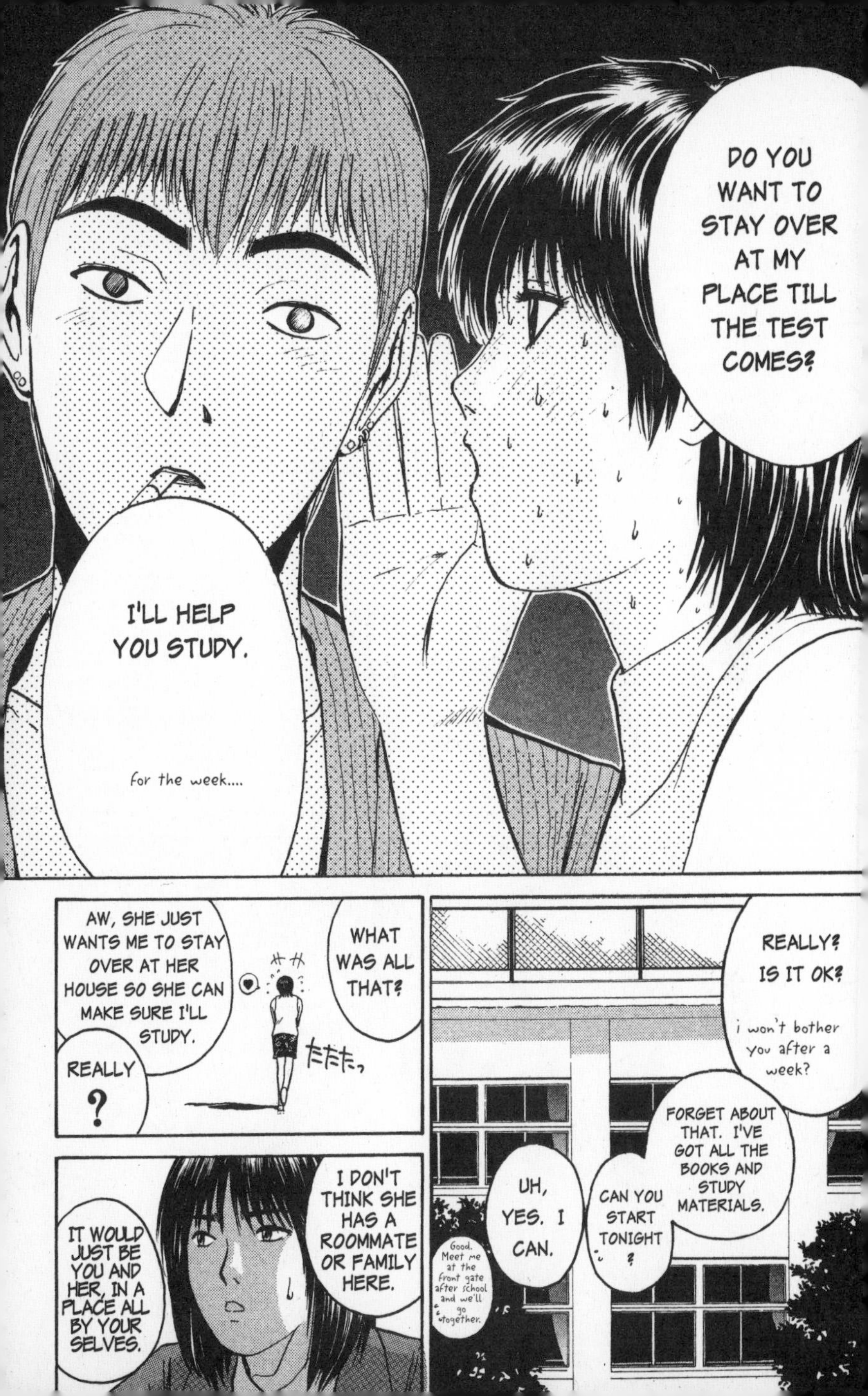
DO YOU WANT TO STAY OVER AT MY PLACE TILL THE TEST COMES?
I'LL HELP YOU STUDY.
for the week....
REALLY? IS IT OK?
i won't bother you after a week?
FORGET ABOUT THAT. I'VE GOT ALL THE BOOKS AND STUDY MATERIALS.
CAN YOU START TONIGHT?
UH, YES. I CAN.
Good. Meet me at the front gate after school and we'll go together.
WHAT WAS ALL THAT?
AW, SHE JUST WANTS ME TO STAY OVER AT HER HOUSE SO SHE CAN MAKE SURE I'LL STUDY.
REALLY ?
たたたっ
I DON'T THINK SHE HAS A ROOMMATE OR FAMILY HERE.
IT WOULD JUST BE YOU AND HER, IN A PLACE ALL BY YOUR SELVES.

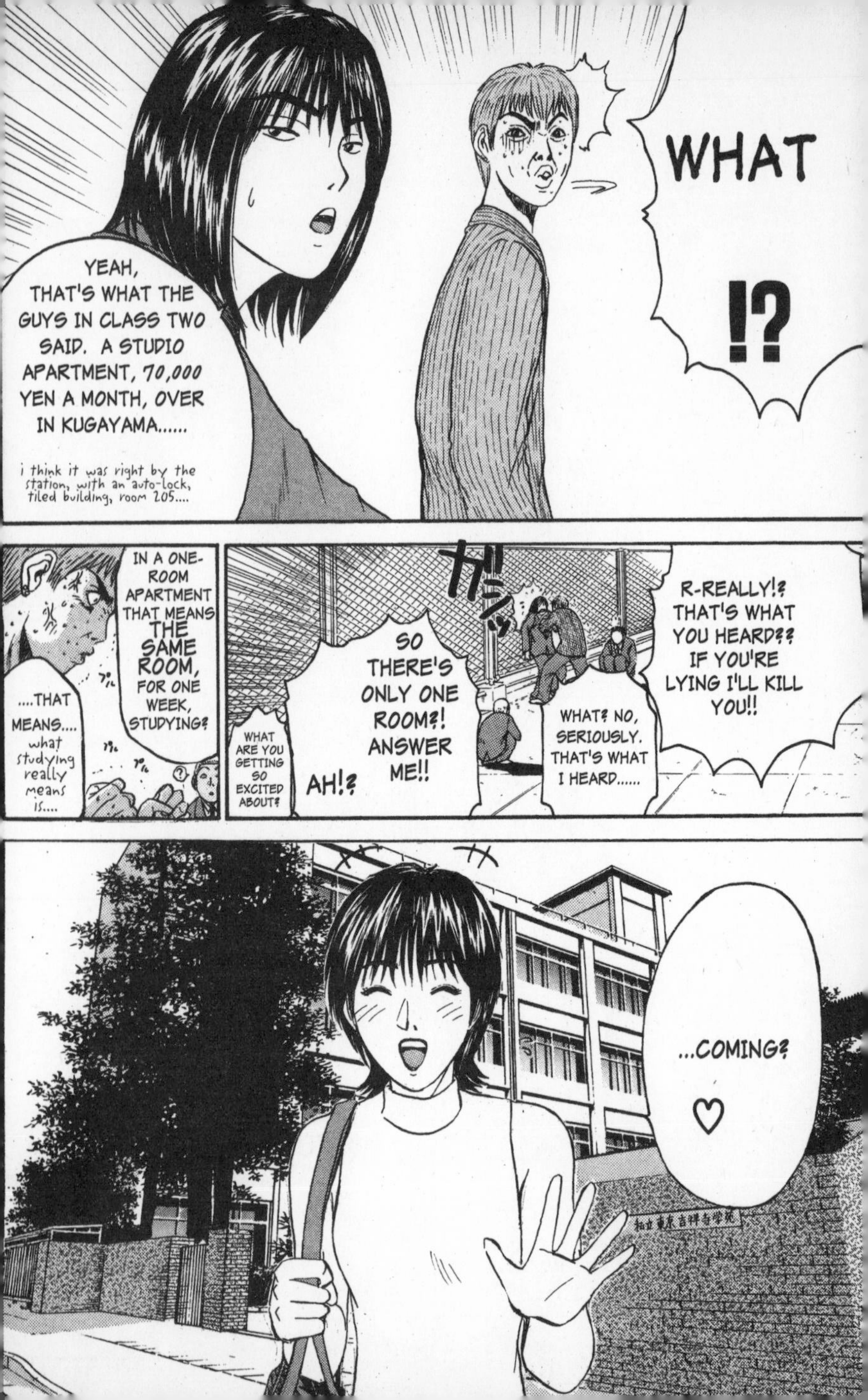
WHAT !?
YEAH, THAT'S WHAT THE GUYS IN CLASS TWO SAID. A STUDIO APARTMENT, 70,000 YEN A MONTH, OVER IN KUGAYAMA......
i think it was right by the station, with an auto-lock, tiled building, room 205....
R-REALLY!? THAT'S WHAT YOU HEARD?? IF YOU'RE LYING I'LL KILL YOU!!
WHAT? NO, SERIOUSLY. THAT'S WHAT I HEARD......
SO THERE'S ONLY ONE ROOM?! ANSWER ME!!
AH!?
WHAT ARE YOU GETTING SO EXCITED ABOUT?
IN A ONE-ROOM APARTMENT THAT MEANS THE SAME ROOM, FOR ONE WEEK, STUDYING?
....THAT MEANS.... what studying really means is....
...COMING? ♡

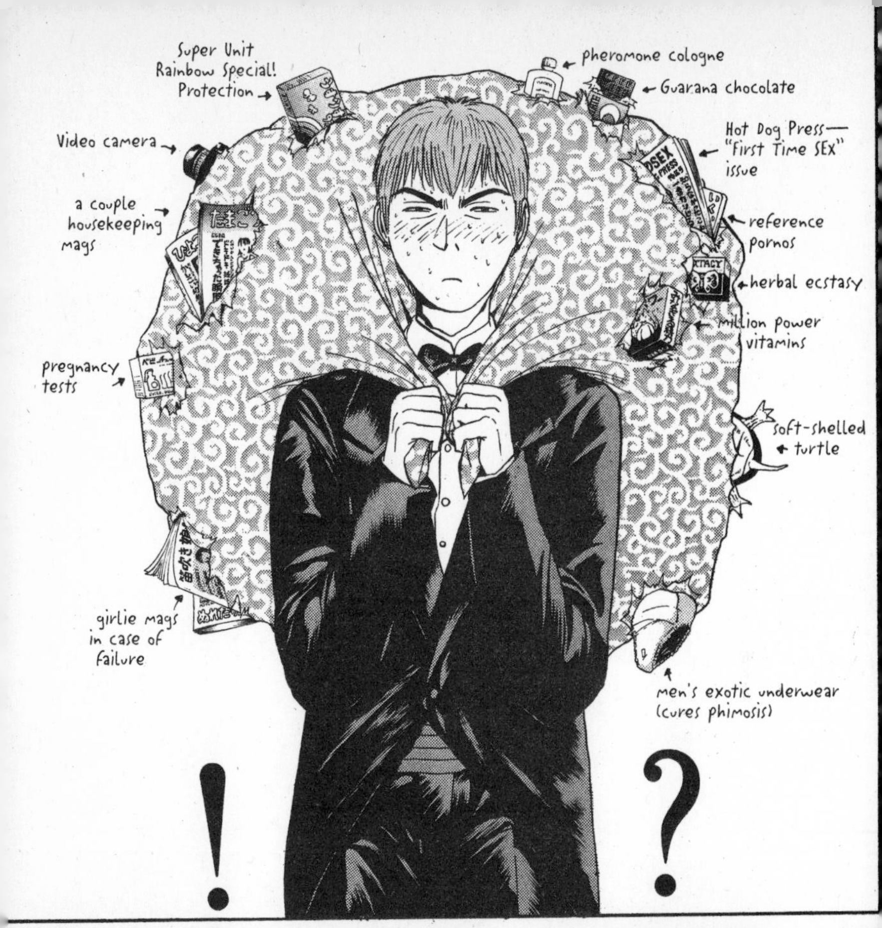
pheromone cologne
Guarana chocolate
Super Unit Rainbow Special! Protection
Hot Dog Press— "First Time SEX" issue
Video camera
reference pornos
a couple housekeeping mags
herbal ecstasy
million power vitamins
pregnancy tests
soft-shelled turtle
girlie mags in case of failure
men's exotic underwear (cures phimosis)
!
?
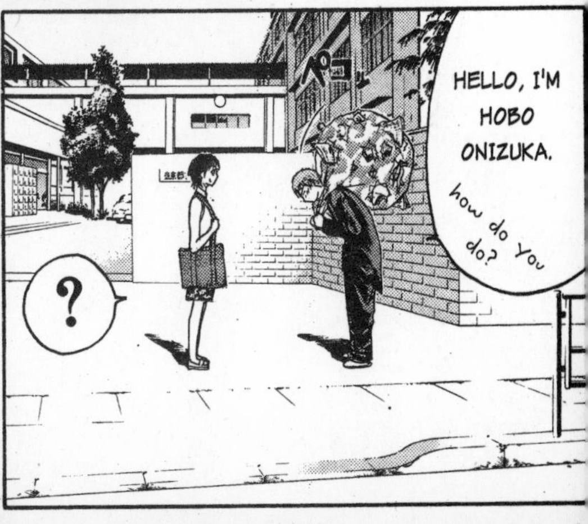
HELLO, I'M HOBO ONIZUKA.
how do you do?
?
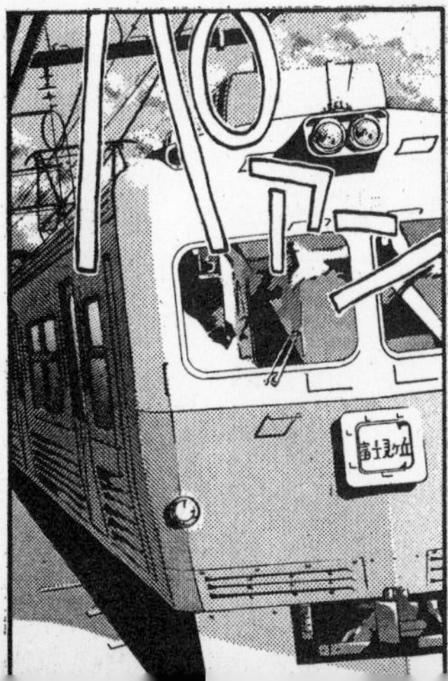

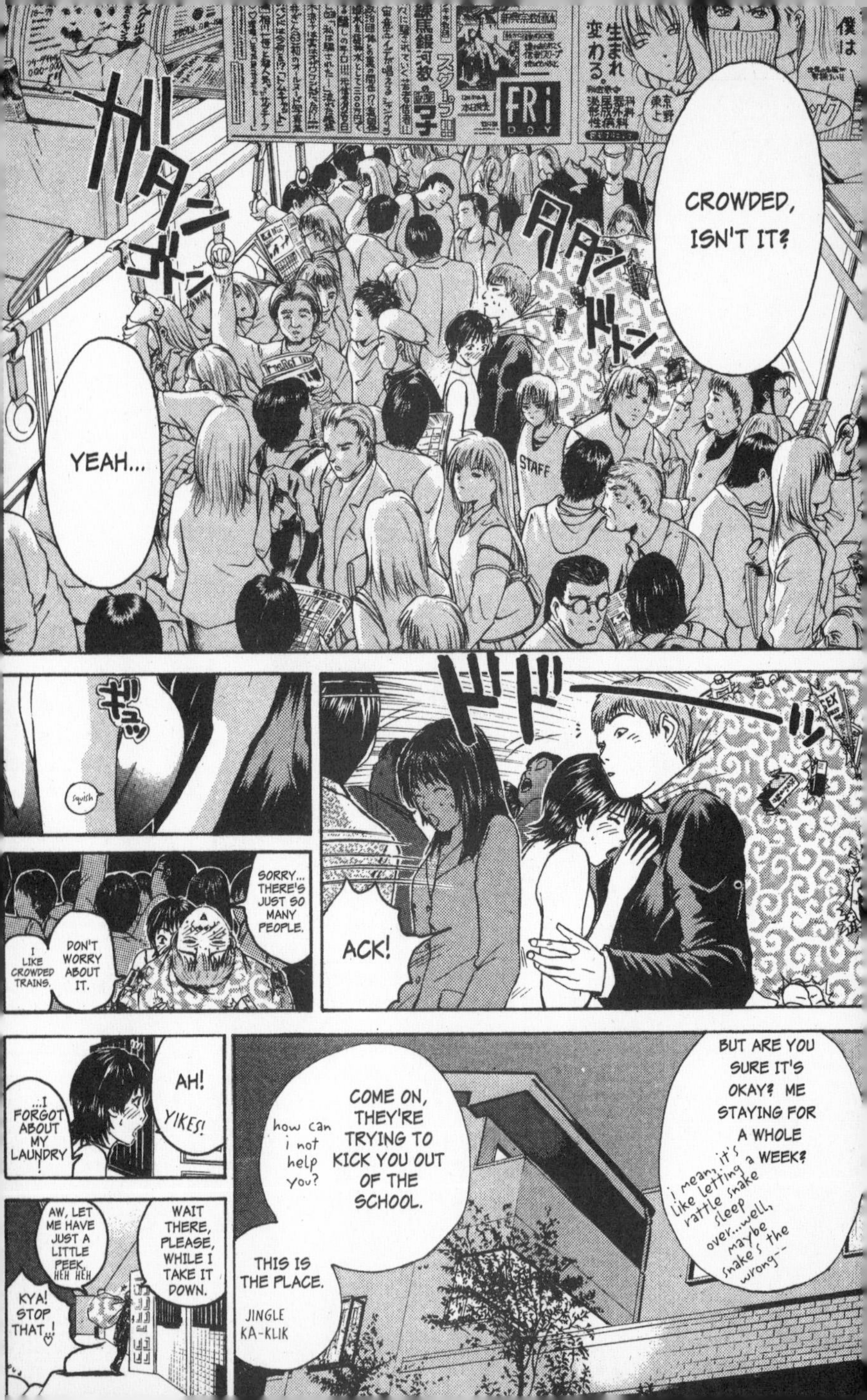
CROWDED, ISN'T IT?
YEAH...
ドドーッ
ACK!
ギュッ
squish
SORRY... THERE'S JUST SO MANY PEOPLE.
DON'T WORRY ABOUT IT.
I LIKE CROWDED TRAINS.
BUT ARE YOU SURE IT'S OKAY? ME STAYING FOR A WHOLE WEEK?
i mean, it's like letting a rattle snake sleep over...well, maybe snake's the wrong--
COME ON, THEY'RE TRYING TO KICK YOU OUT OF THE SCHOOL.
how can i not help you?
THIS IS THE PLACE.
JINGLE KA-KLIK
AH!
YIKES!
...I FORGOT ABOUT MY LAUNDRY!
WAIT THERE, PLEASE, WHILE I TAKE IT DOWN.
AW, LET ME HAVE JUST A LITTLE PEEK, HEH HEH
KYA! STOP THAT..! ♡

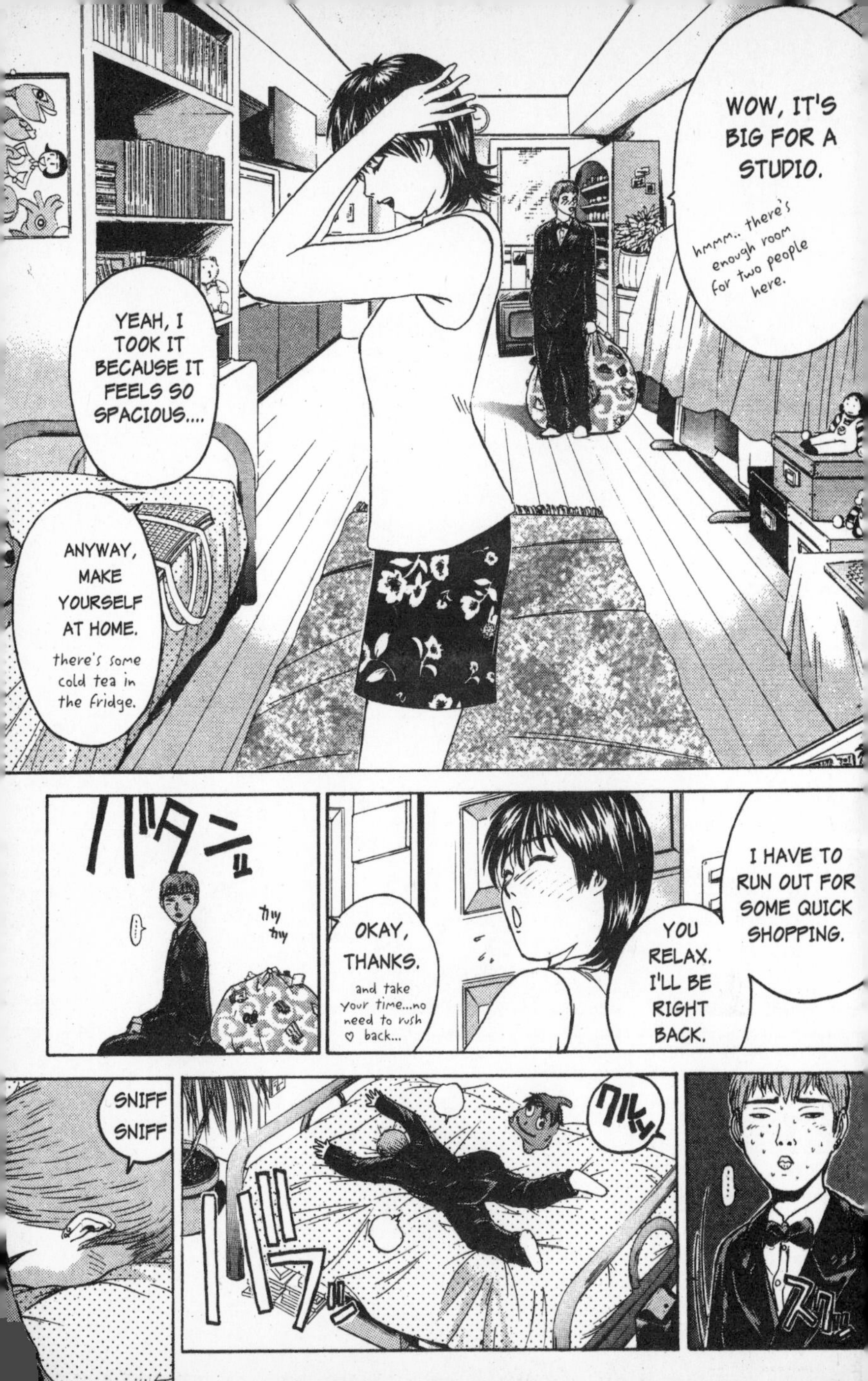
WOW, IT'S BIG FOR A STUDIO.
hmmm.. there's enough room for two people here.
YEAH, I TOOK IT BECAUSE IT FEELS SO SPACIOUS....
ANYWAY, MAKE YOURSELF AT HOME.
there's some cold tea in the fridge.
I HAVE TO RUN OUT FOR SOME QUICK SHOPPING.
YOU RELAX. I'LL BE RIGHT BACK.
OKAY, THANKS.
and take your time...no need to rush ♡ back...
バタン
...
カツカツ
...
SNIFF SNIFF

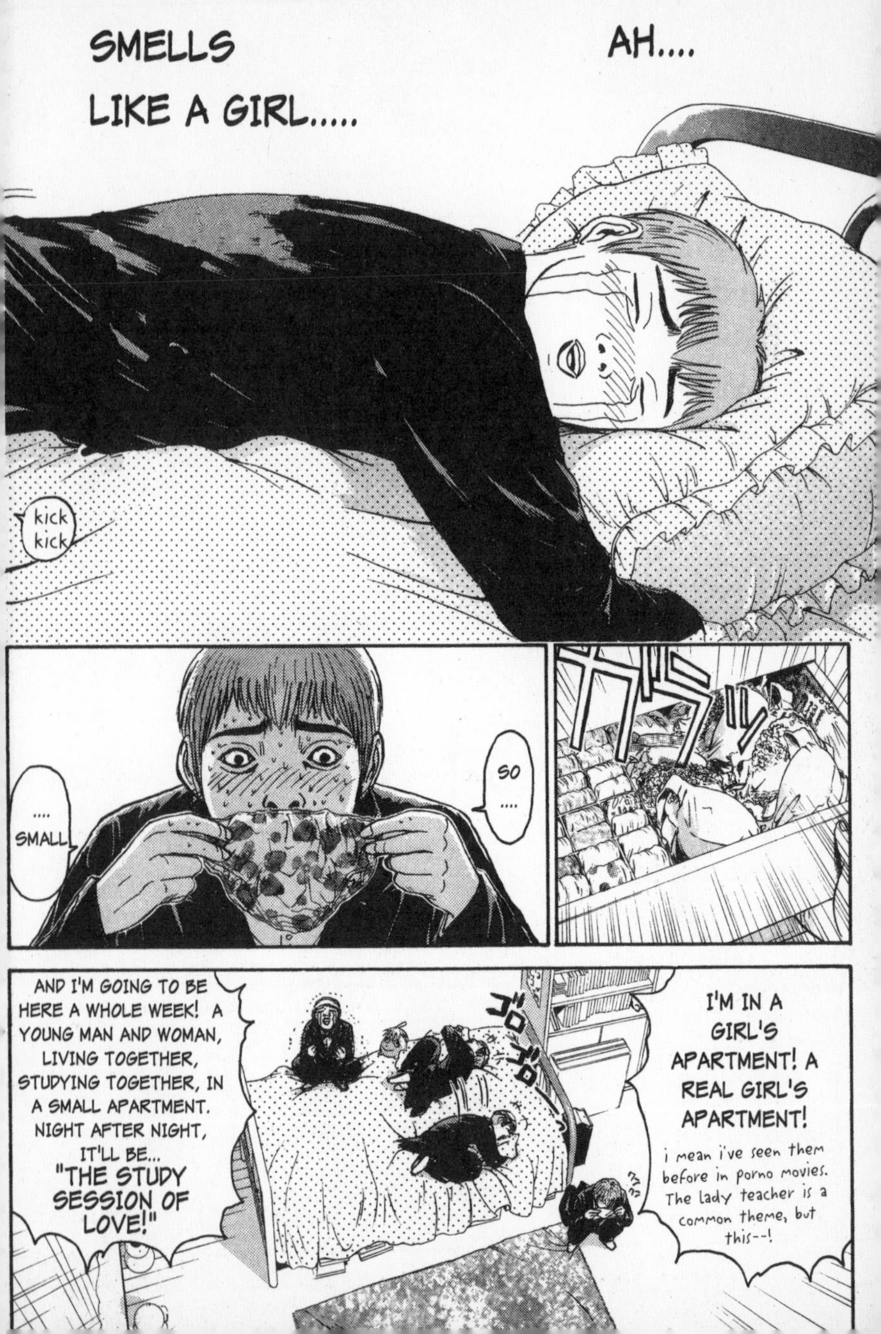
AH....
SMELLS LIKE A GIRL.....
kick kick
ガラッ
SO ....
.... SMALL
I'M IN A GIRL'S APARTMENT! A REAL GIRL'S APARTMENT!
i mean i've seen them before in porno movies. The lady teacher is a common theme, but this--!
ゴロゴロ
AND I'M GOING TO BE HERE A WHOLE WEEK! A YOUNG MAN AND WOMAN, LIVING TOGETHER, STUDYING TOGETHER, IN A SMALL APARTMENT. NIGHT AFTER NIGHT, IT'LL BE... "THE STUDY SESSION OF LOVE!"

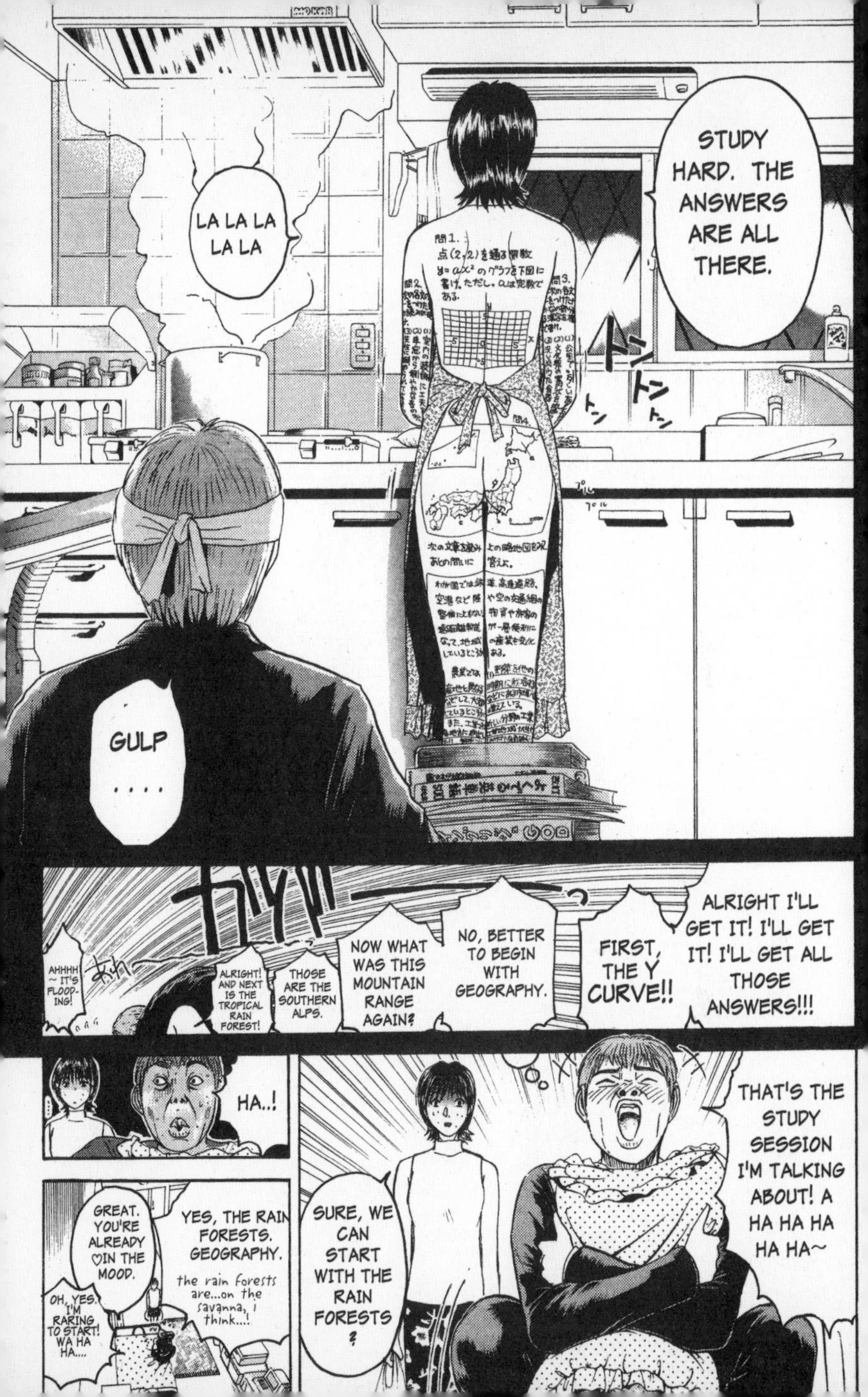
STUDY HARD. THE ANSWERS ARE ALL THERE.
トン
トン
トン
トン
LA LA LA LA LA
問1.
点(2,2)を通る関数
y=ax² のグラフを下図に書け。ただし、aは定数である。
次の文章を読み あとの問いに
上の略地図を見 答えよ。
GULP
....
ALRIGHT I'LL GET IT! I'LL GET IT! I'LL GET ALL THOSE ANSWERS!!!
FIRST, THE Y CURVE!!
NO, BETTER TO BEGIN WITH GEOGRAPHY.
NOW WHAT WAS THIS MOUNTAIN RANGE AGAIN?
THOSE ARE THE SOUTHERN ALPS.
ALRIGHT! AND NEXT IS THE TROPICAL RAIN FOREST!
AHHHH ~ IT'S FLOODING!
THAT'S THE STUDY SESSION I'M TALKING ABOUT! A HA HA HA HA HA~
SURE, WE CAN START WITH THE RAIN FORESTS?
HA..!
YES, THE RAIN FORESTS. GEOGRAPHY.
the rain forests are...on the savanna, I think...!
GREAT. YOU'RE ALREADY ♡IN THE MOOD.
OH, YES. I'M RARING TO START! WA HA HA....

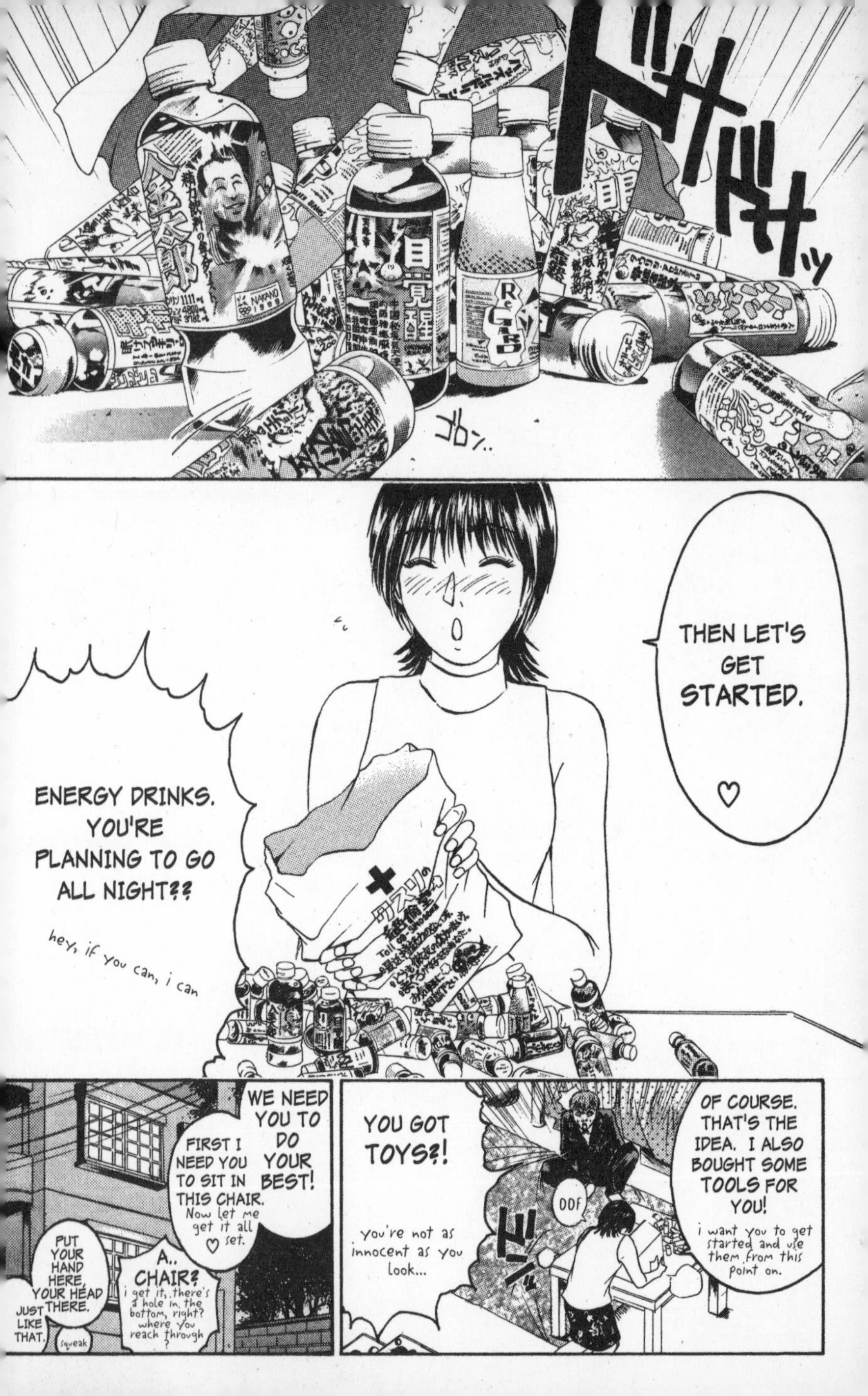
ドサドサッ
ゴロン..
THEN LET'S GET STARTED. ♡
ENERGY DRINKS. YOU'RE PLANNING TO GO ALL NIGHT??
hey, if you can, i can
OF COURSE. THAT'S THE IDEA. I ALSO BOUGHT SOME TOOLS FOR YOU!
i want you to get started and use them from this point on.
YOU GOT TOYS?!
you're not as innocent as you look...
OOF
WE NEED YOU TO DO YOUR BEST!
FIRST I NEED YOU TO SIT IN THIS CHAIR.
Now let me get it all set. ♡
A.. CHAIR?
i get it, there's a hole in the bottom, right? where you reach through?
PUT YOUR HAND HERE, YOUR HEAD THERE.
JUST LIKE THAT.
squeak

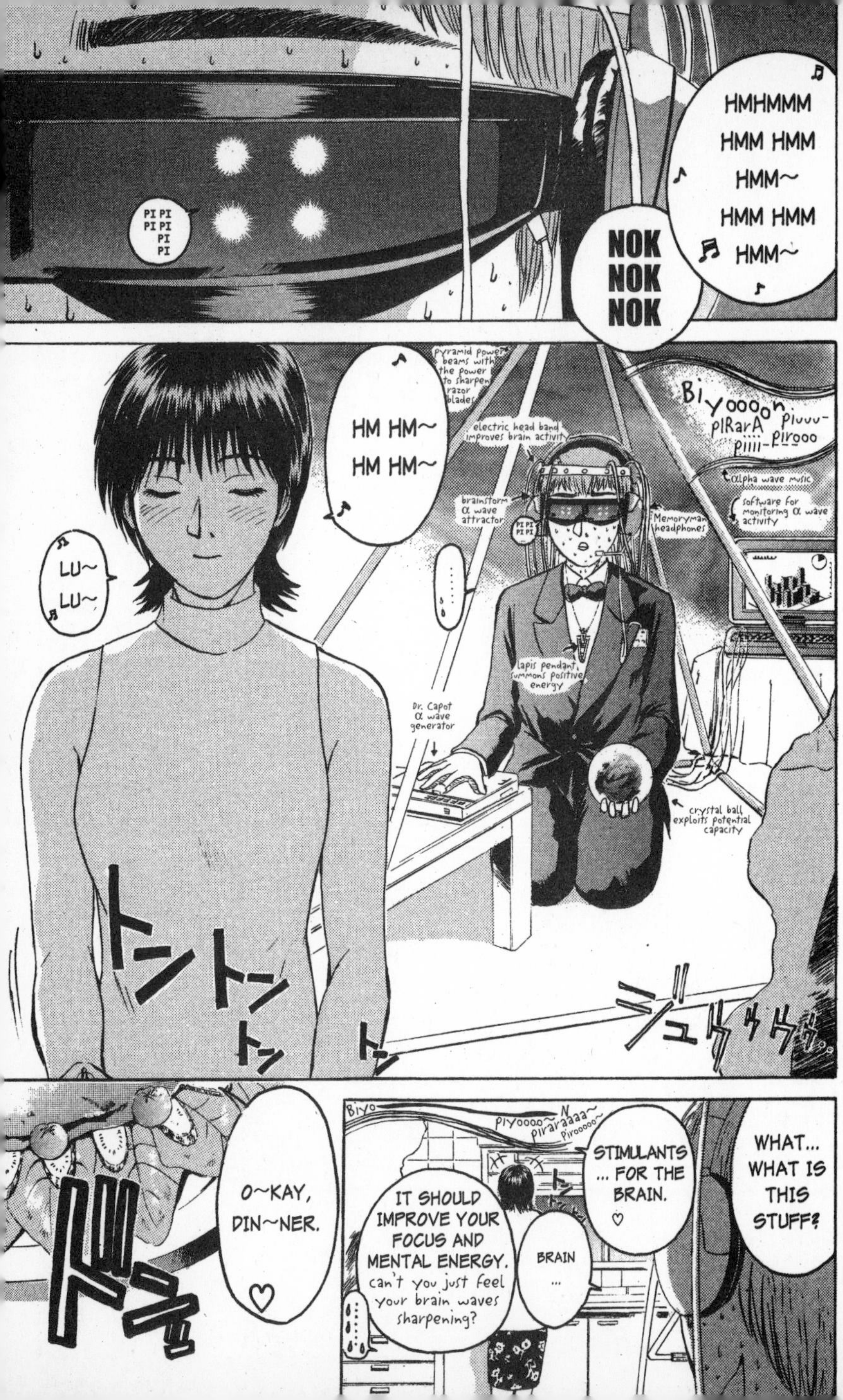
HMHMMM HMM HMM HMM~ HMM HMM HMM~
NOK NOK NOK
PI PI PI PI PI PI
Biyoooon pIRarA pluuu- piiii-pirooo
alpha wave music
software for monitoring α wave activity
Memoryman headphones
crystal ball exploits potential capacity
electric head band improves brain activity
pyramid power beams with the power to sharpen razor blades
HM HM~ HM HM~
brainstorm α wave attractor
PI PI PI PI
lapis pendant summons positive energy
Dr. Capot α wave generator
......
LU~ LU~
トン トン トン トン
WHAT... WHAT IS THIS STUFF?
STIMULANTS ... FOR THE BRAIN. ♡
Biyo N piyoooo~ piraraaaa~ Piroooo~
BRAIN ...
IT SHOULD IMPROVE YOUR FOCUS AND MENTAL ENERGY. can't you just feel your brain waves sharpening?
O~KAY, DIN~NER. ♡
ドン

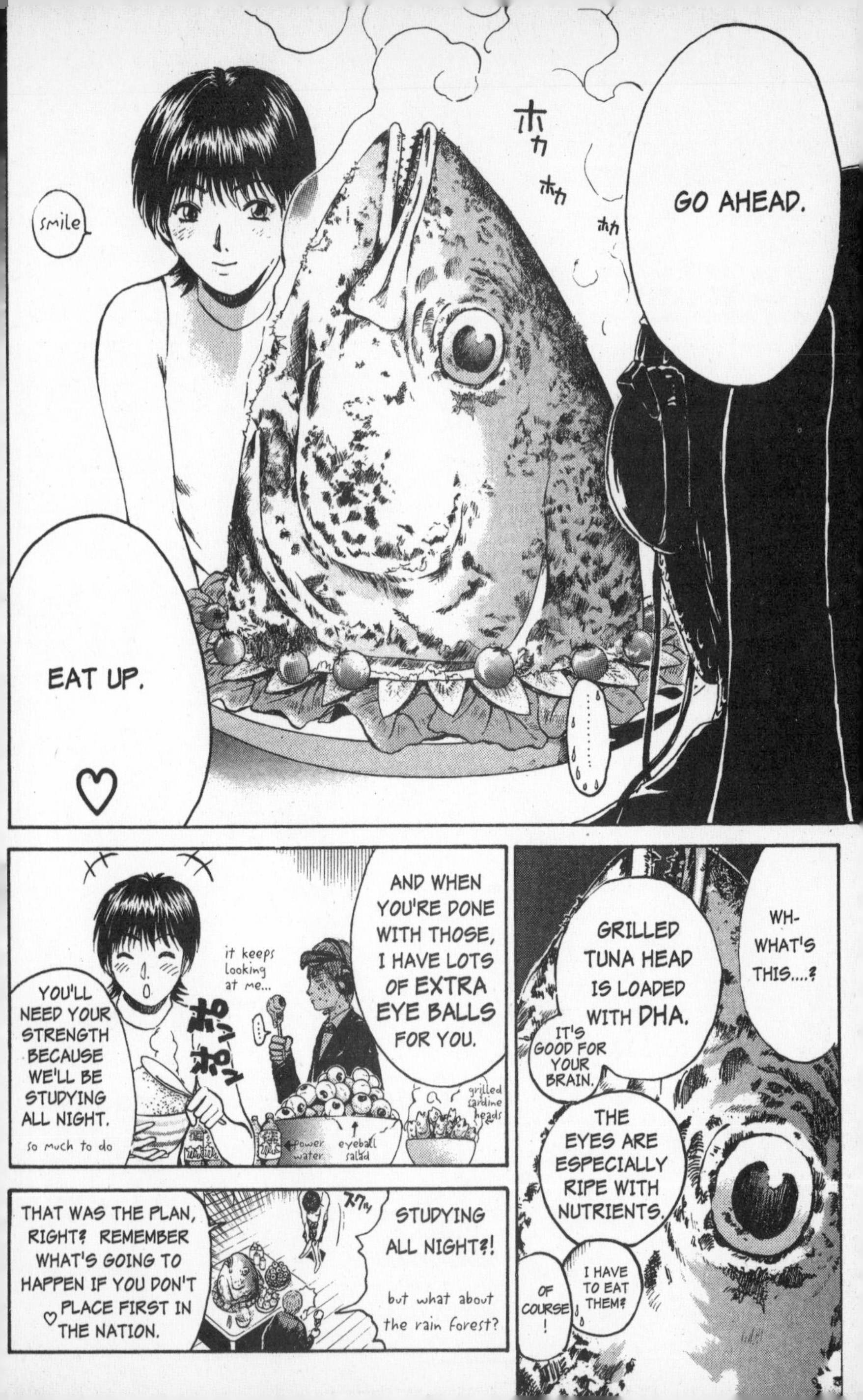

GO AHEAD.
ホカ
ホカ
ホカ
smile
EAT UP. ♡
....
WH- WHAT'S THIS....?
GRILLED TUNA HEAD IS LOADED WITH DHA.
IT'S GOOD FOR YOUR BRAIN.
THE EYES ARE ESPECIALLY RIPE WITH NUTRIENTS.
I HAVE TO EAT THEM?
OF COURSE!
AND WHEN YOU'RE DONE WITH THOSE, I HAVE LOTS OF EXTRA EYE BALLS FOR YOU.
it keeps looking at me...
...
YOU'LL NEED YOUR STRENGTH BECAUSE WE'LL BE STUDYING ALL NIGHT.
so much to do
grilled sardine heads
eyeball salad
power water
STUDYING ALL NIGHT?!
but what about the rain forest?
THAT WAS THE PLAN, RIGHT? REMEMBER WHAT'S GOING TO HAPPEN IF YOU DON'T PLACE FIRST IN THE NATION. ♡

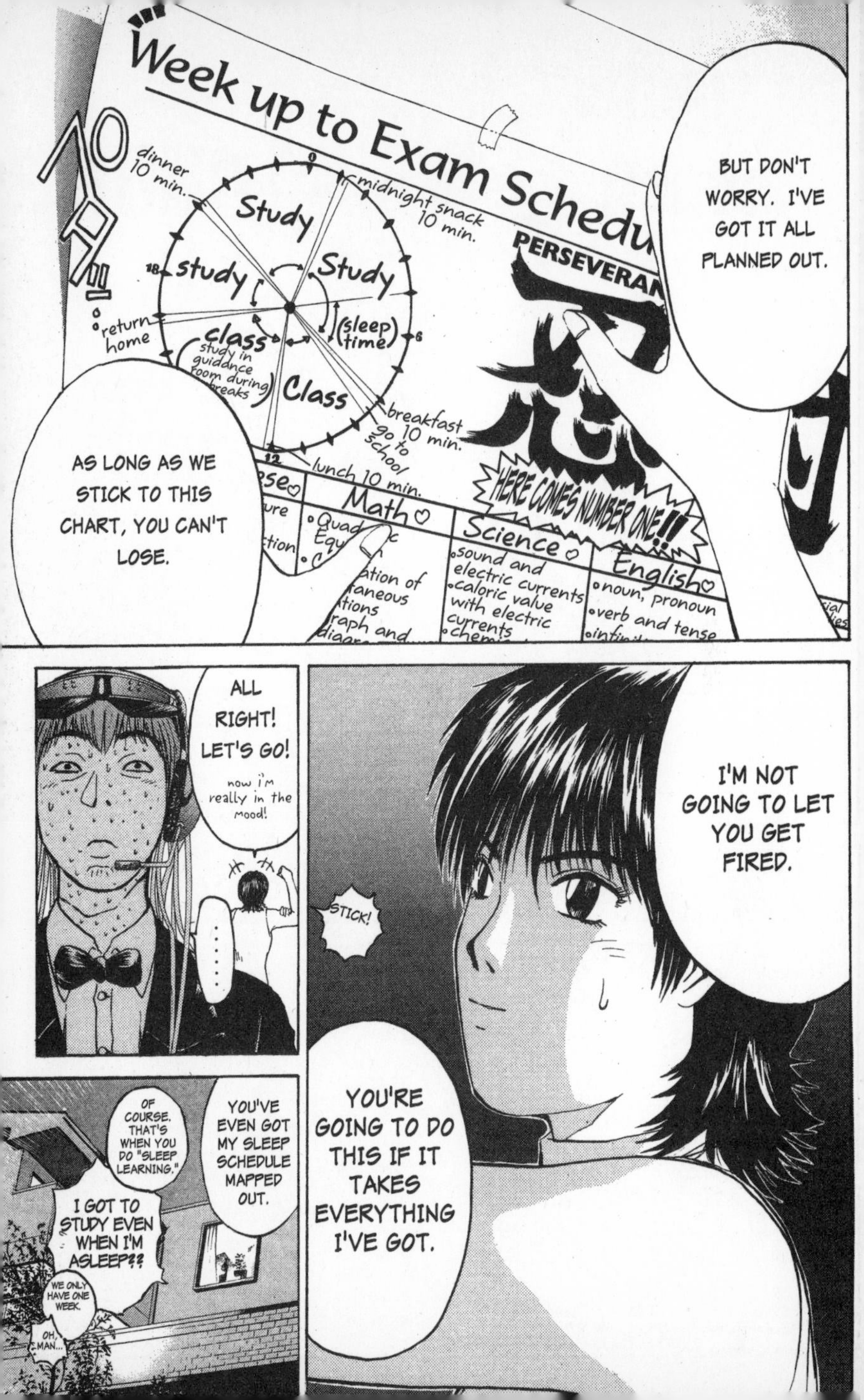
BUT DON'T WORRY. I'VE GOT IT ALL PLANNED OUT.
Week up to Exam Schedu
PERSEVERAN
dinner 10 min.
midnight snack 10 min.
Study
study
Study
(sleep time)
return home
class
study in guidance room during breaks
Class
breakfast 10 min.
go to school
lunch 10 min.
Math
Science
English
sound and electric currents
caloric value with electric currents
noun, pronoun
verb and tense
HERE COMES NUMBER ONE!!
AS LONG AS WE STICK TO THIS CHART, YOU CAN'T LOSE.
I'M NOT GOING TO LET YOU GET FIRED.
STICK!
YOU'RE GOING TO DO THIS IF IT TAKES EVERYTHING I'VE GOT.
ALL RIGHT! LET'S GO!
now i'm really in the mood!
……
YOU'VE EVEN GOT MY SLEEP SCHEDULE MAPPED OUT.
OF COURSE. THAT'S WHEN YOU DO "SLEEP LEARNING."
I GOT TO STUDY EVEN WHEN I'M ASLEEP??
WE ONLY HAVE ONE WEEK.
OH, MAN...

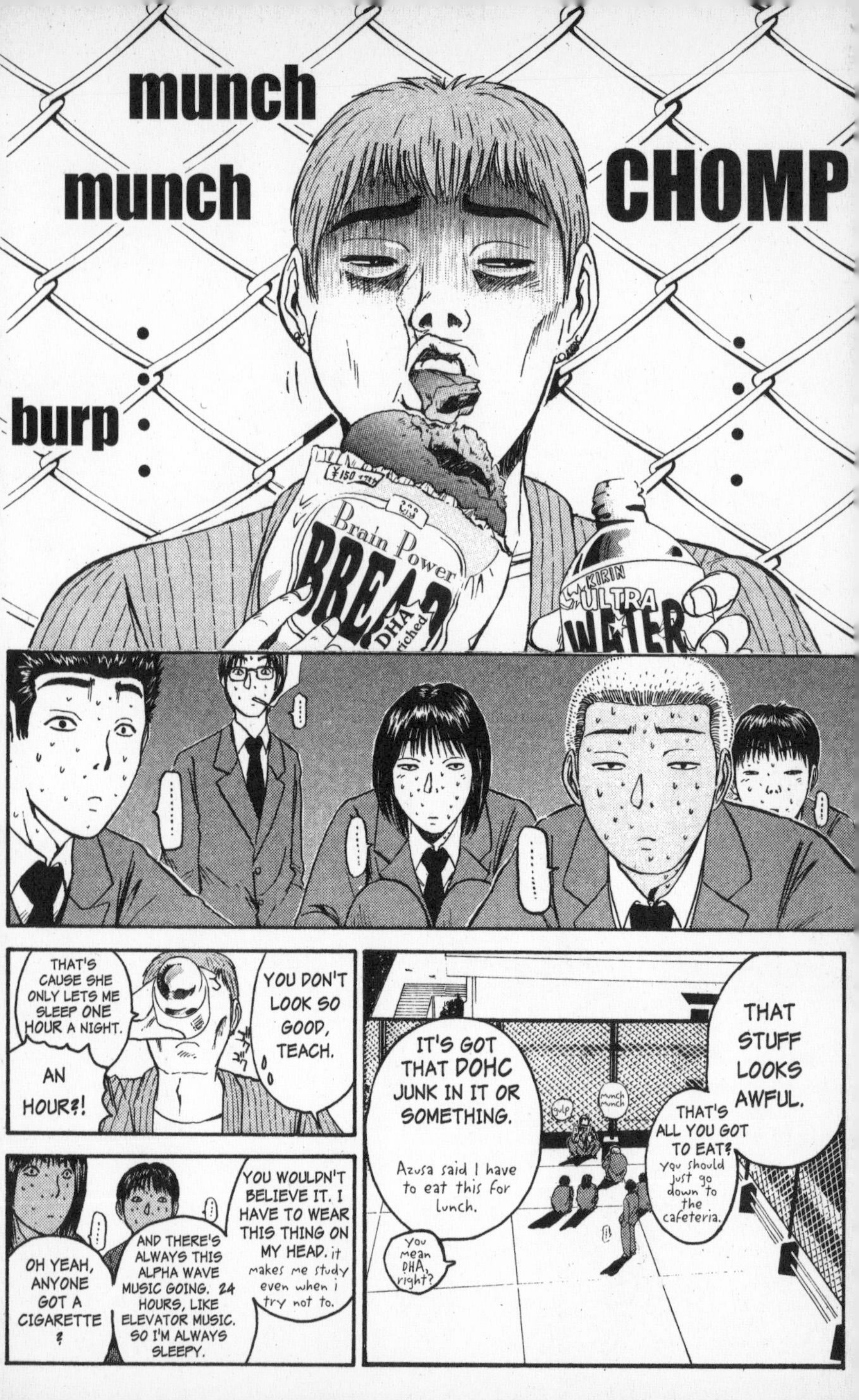
CHOMP
munch
munch
burp
Brain Power
BREAD
DHA
KIRIN
ULTRA
THAT STUFF LOOKS AWFUL.
THAT'S ALL YOU GOT TO EAT? You should just go down to the cafeteria.
IT'S GOT THAT DOHC JUNK IN IT OR SOMETHING. Azusa said I have to eat this for lunch.
You mean DHA, right?
YOU DON'T LOOK SO GOOD, TEACH.
THAT'S CAUSE SHE ONLY LETS ME SLEEP ONE HOUR A NIGHT.
AN HOUR?!
YOU WOULDN'T BELIEVE IT. I HAVE TO WEAR THIS THING ON MY HEAD. it makes me study even when i try not to.
AND THERE'S ALWAYS THIS ALPHA WAVE MUSIC GOING. 24 HOURS, LIKE ELEVATOR MUSIC. SO I'M ALWAYS SLEEPY.
OH YEAH, ANYONE GOT A CIGARETTE?

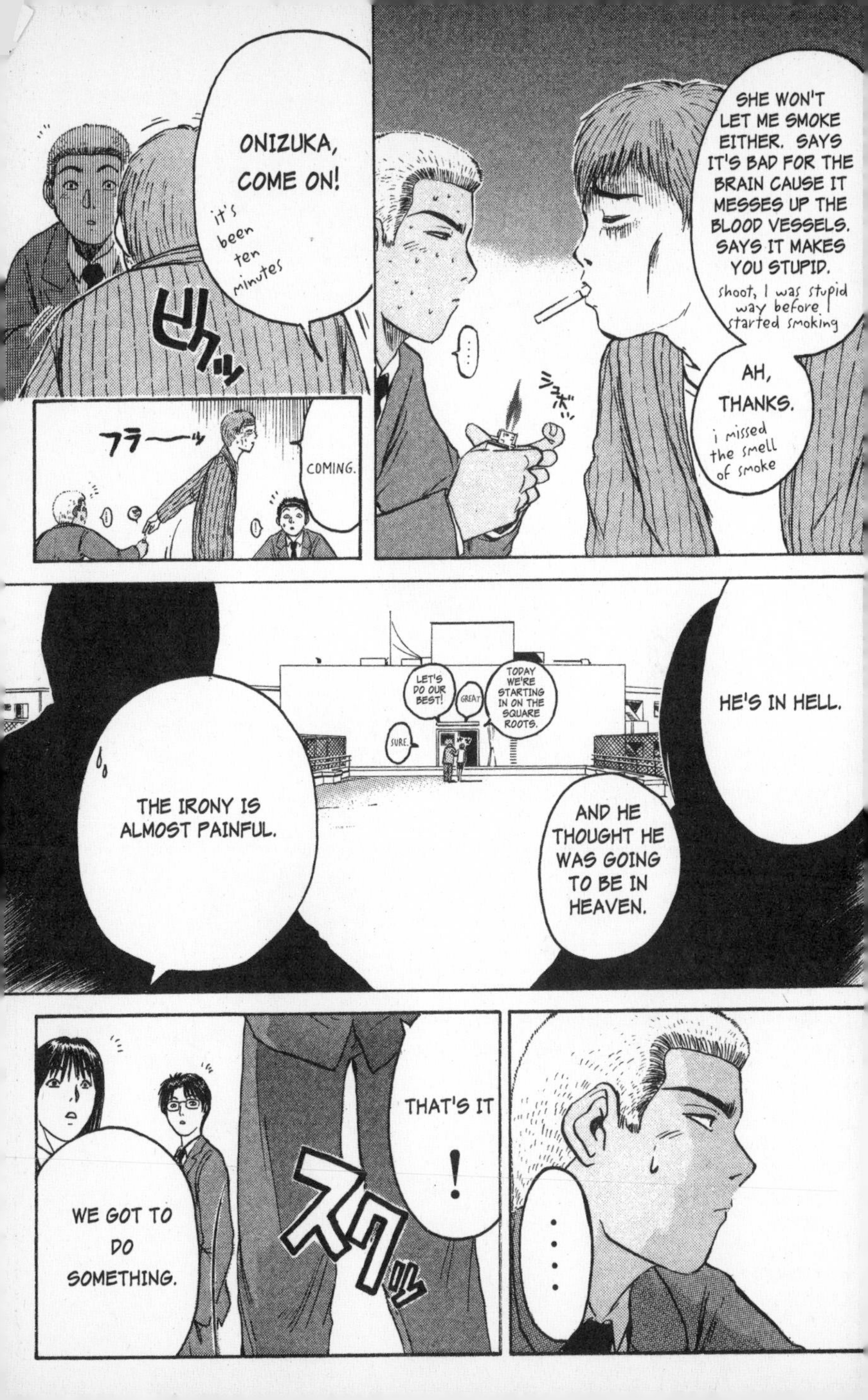
SHE WON'T LET ME SMOKE EITHER. SAYS IT'S BAD FOR THE BRAIN CAUSE IT MESSES UP THE BLOOD VESSELS. SAYS IT MAKES YOU STUPID.
shoot, I was stupid way before I started smoking
...
シュボッ
AH, THANKS.
i missed the smell of smoke
ONIZUKA, COME ON!
it's been ten minutes
ビクッ
COMING.
フラ〜〜ッ
HE'S IN HELL.
AND HE THOUGHT HE WAS GOING TO BE IN HEAVEN.
TODAY WE'RE STARTING IN ON THE SQUARE ROOTS.
GREAT.
LET'S DO OUR BEST!
SURE.
THE IRONY IS ALMOST PAINFUL.
...
THAT'S IT !
スクッ
WE GOT TO DO SOMETHING.

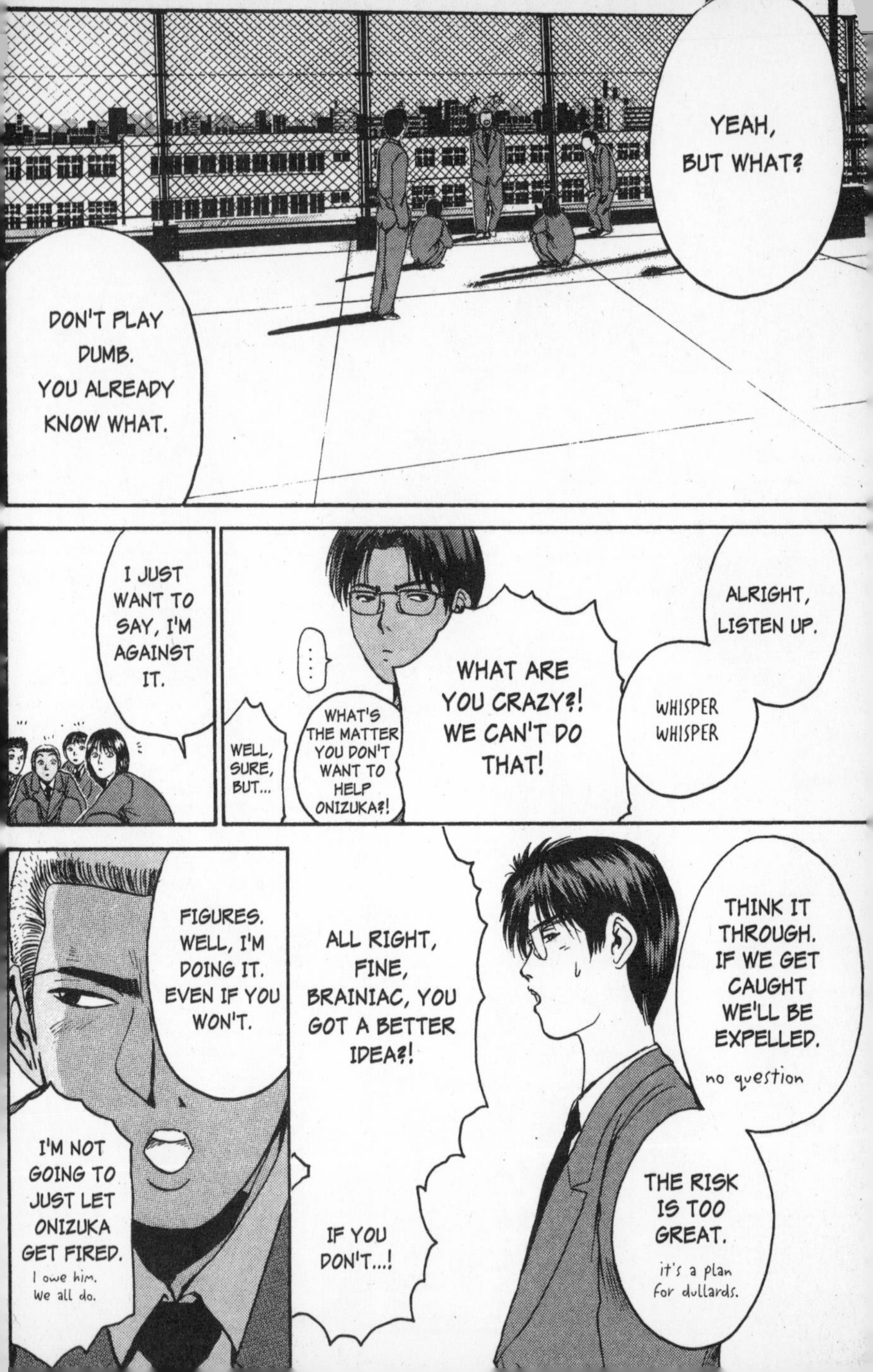
YEAH, BUT WHAT?
DON'T PLAY DUMB. YOU ALREADY KNOW WHAT.
ALRIGHT, LISTEN UP.
WHISPER WHISPER
WHAT ARE YOU CRAZY?! WE CAN'T DO THAT!
....
WHAT'S THE MATTER YOU DON'T WANT TO HELP ONIZUKA?!
WELL, SURE, BUT...
I JUST WANT TO SAY, I'M AGAINST IT.
THINK IT THROUGH. IF WE GET CAUGHT WE'LL BE EXPELLED.
no question
THE RISK IS TOO GREAT.
it's a plan for dullards.
ALL RIGHT, FINE, BRAINIAC, YOU GOT A BETTER IDEA?!
IF YOU DON'T...!
FIGURES. WELL, I'M DOING IT. EVEN IF YOU WON'T.
I'M NOT GOING TO JUST LET ONIZUKA GET FIRED.
I owe him. We all do.

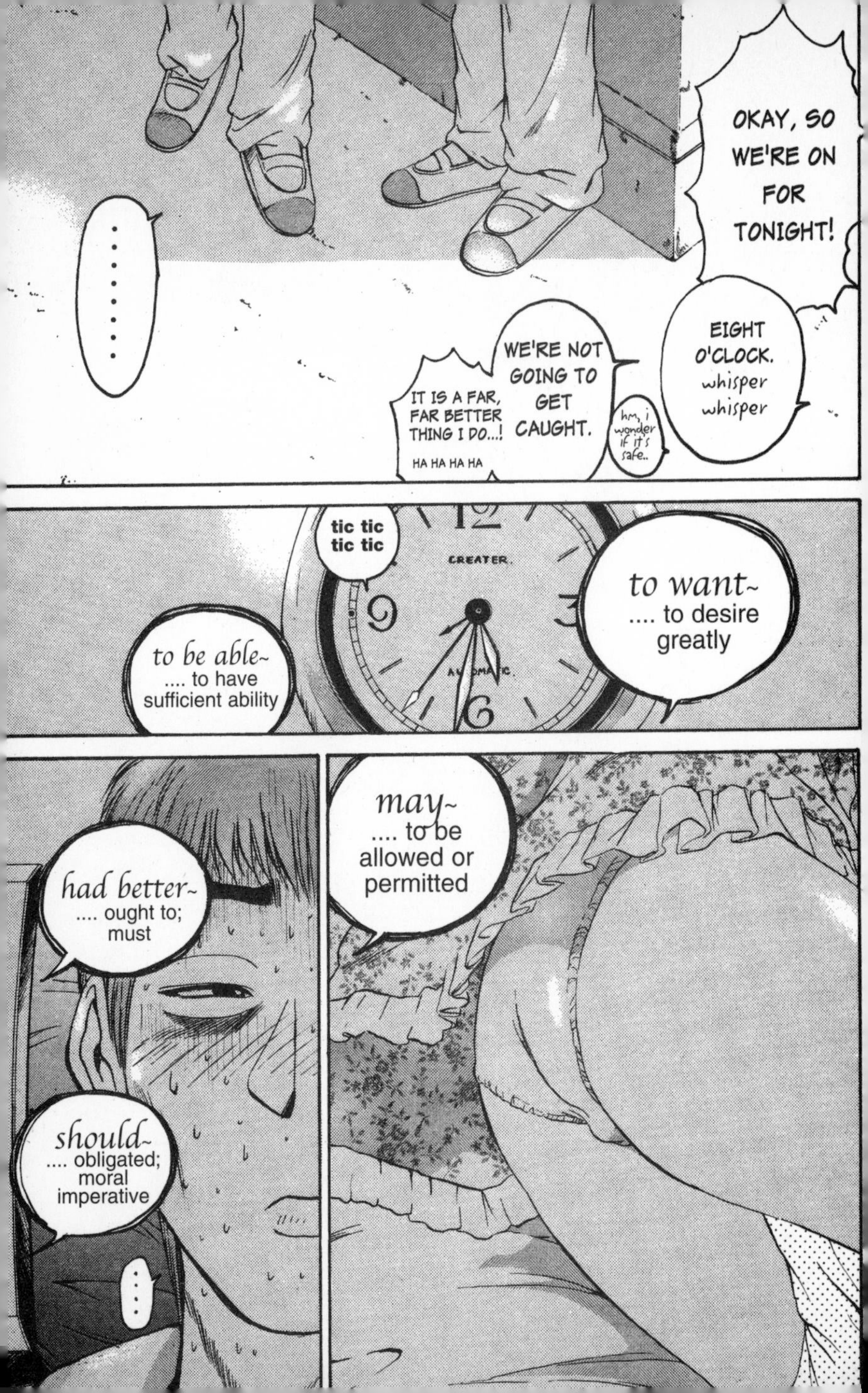
OKAY, SO WE'RE ON FOR TONIGHT!
EIGHT O'CLOCK. whisper whisper
hm, i wonder if it's safe..
WE'RE NOT GOING TO GET CAUGHT.
IT IS A FAR, FAR BETTER THING I DO...!
HA HA HA HA
....
tic tic tic tic
to want~ .... to desire greatly
to be able~ .... to have sufficient ability
may~ .... to be allowed or permitted
had better~ .... ought to; must
should~ .... obligated; moral imperative
....

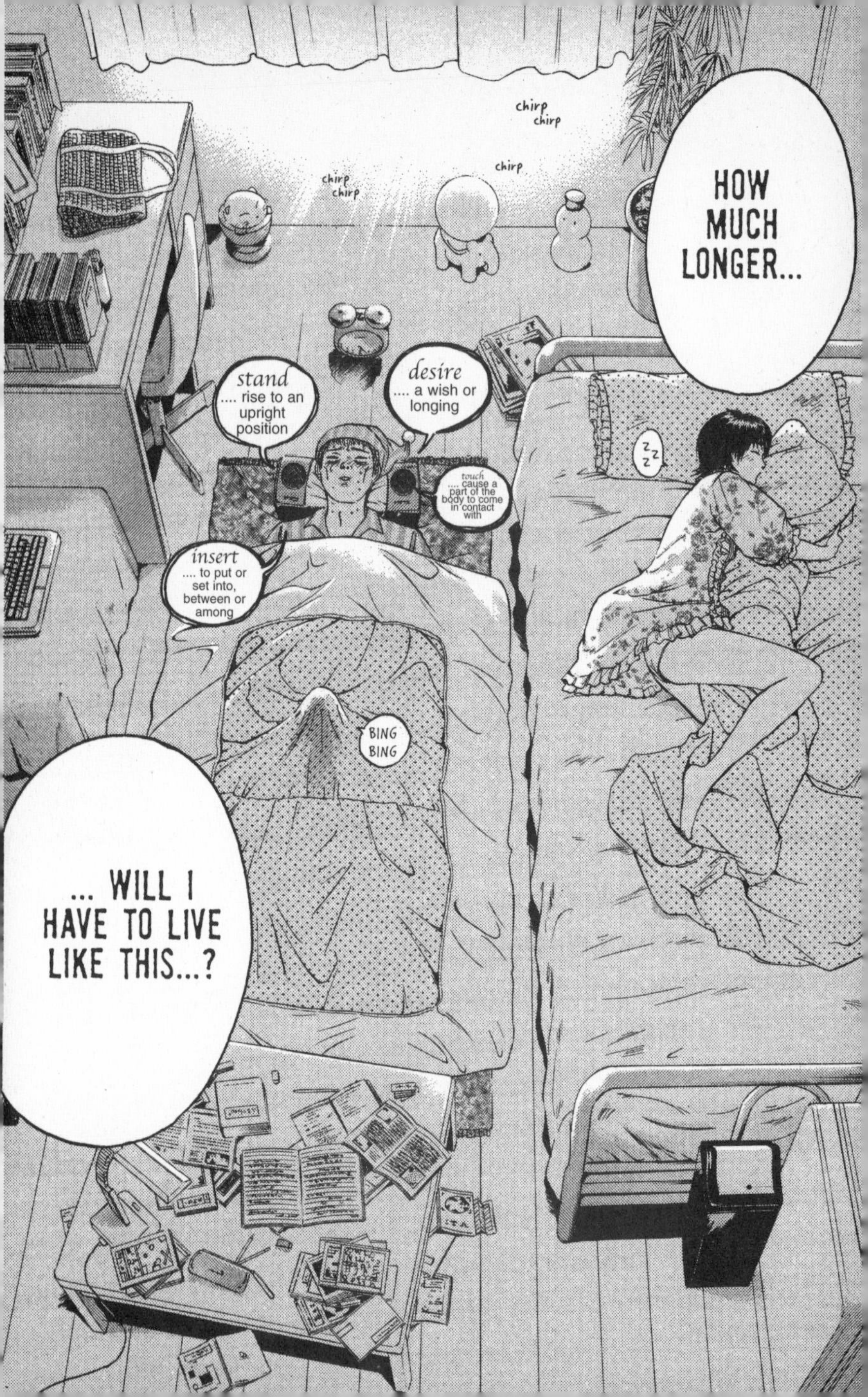

HOW MUCH LONGER...
chirp chirp
chirp
chirp chirp
desire .... a wish or longing
stand .... rise to an upright position
z z z
touch .... cause a part of the body to come in contact with
insert .... to put or set into, between or among
BING BING
... WILL I HAVE TO LIVE LIKE THIS...?

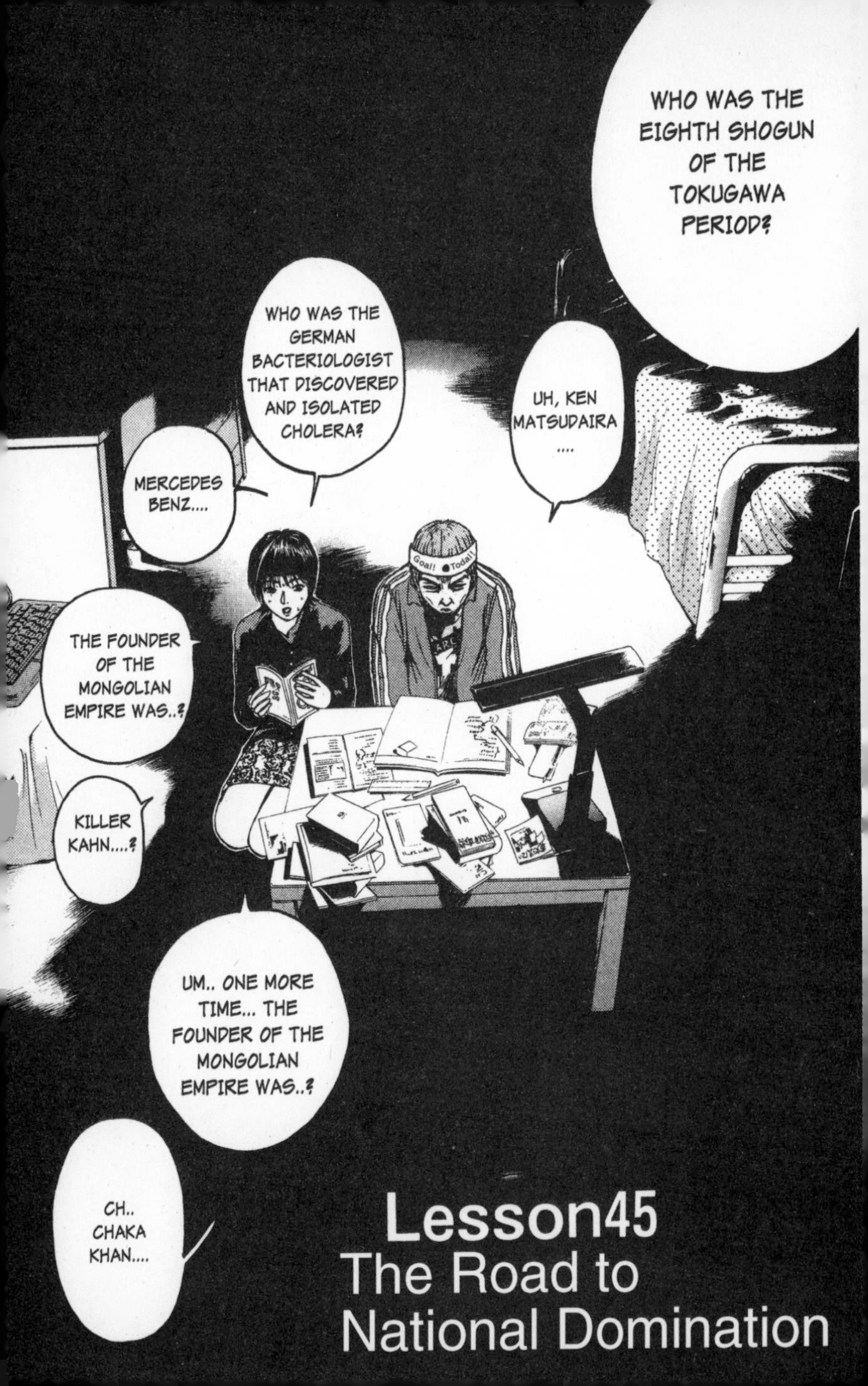
WHO WAS THE EIGHTH SHOGUN OF THE TOKUGAWA PERIOD?
UH, KEN MATSUDAIRA ....
WHO WAS THE GERMAN BACTERIOLOGIST THAT DISCOVERED AND ISOLATED CHOLERA?
MERCEDES BENZ....
THE FOUNDER OF THE MONGOLIAN EMPIRE WAS..?
KILLER KAHN....?
UM.. ONE MORE TIME... THE FOUNDER OF THE MONGOLIAN EMPIRE WAS..?
CH.. CHAKA KHAN....
Lesson45
The Road to National Domination

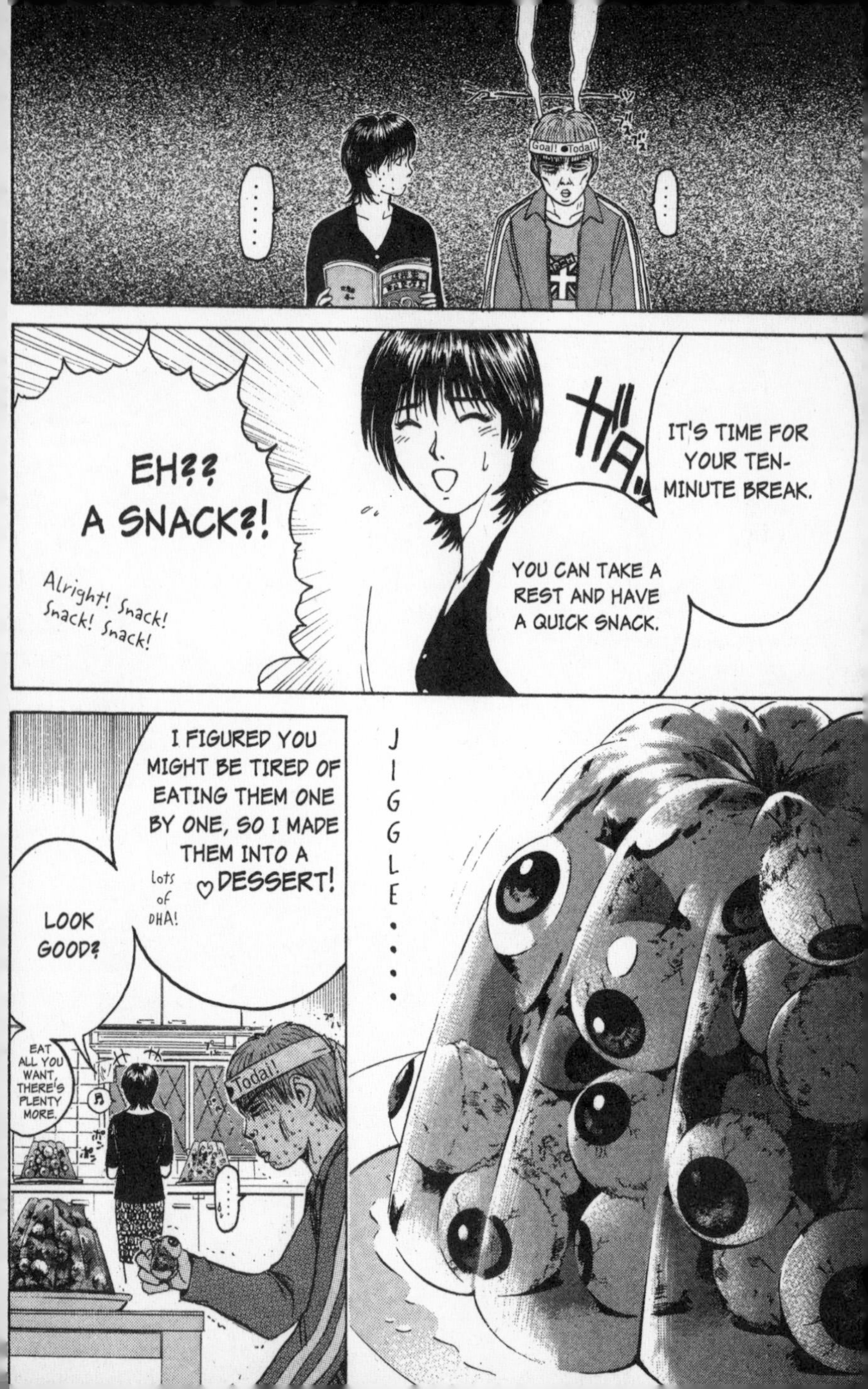
Goal! Todai!
......
......
IT'S TIME FOR YOUR TEN-MINUTE BREAK.
YOU CAN TAKE A REST AND HAVE A QUICK SNACK.
EH?? A SNACK?!
Alright! Snack! Snack! Snack!
JIGGLE...
I FIGURED YOU MIGHT BE TIRED OF EATING THEM ONE BY ONE, SO I MADE THEM INTO A ♡ DESSERT!
lots of DHA!
LOOK GOOD?
EAT ALL YOU WANT, THERE'S PLENTY MORE.
Todai!
......

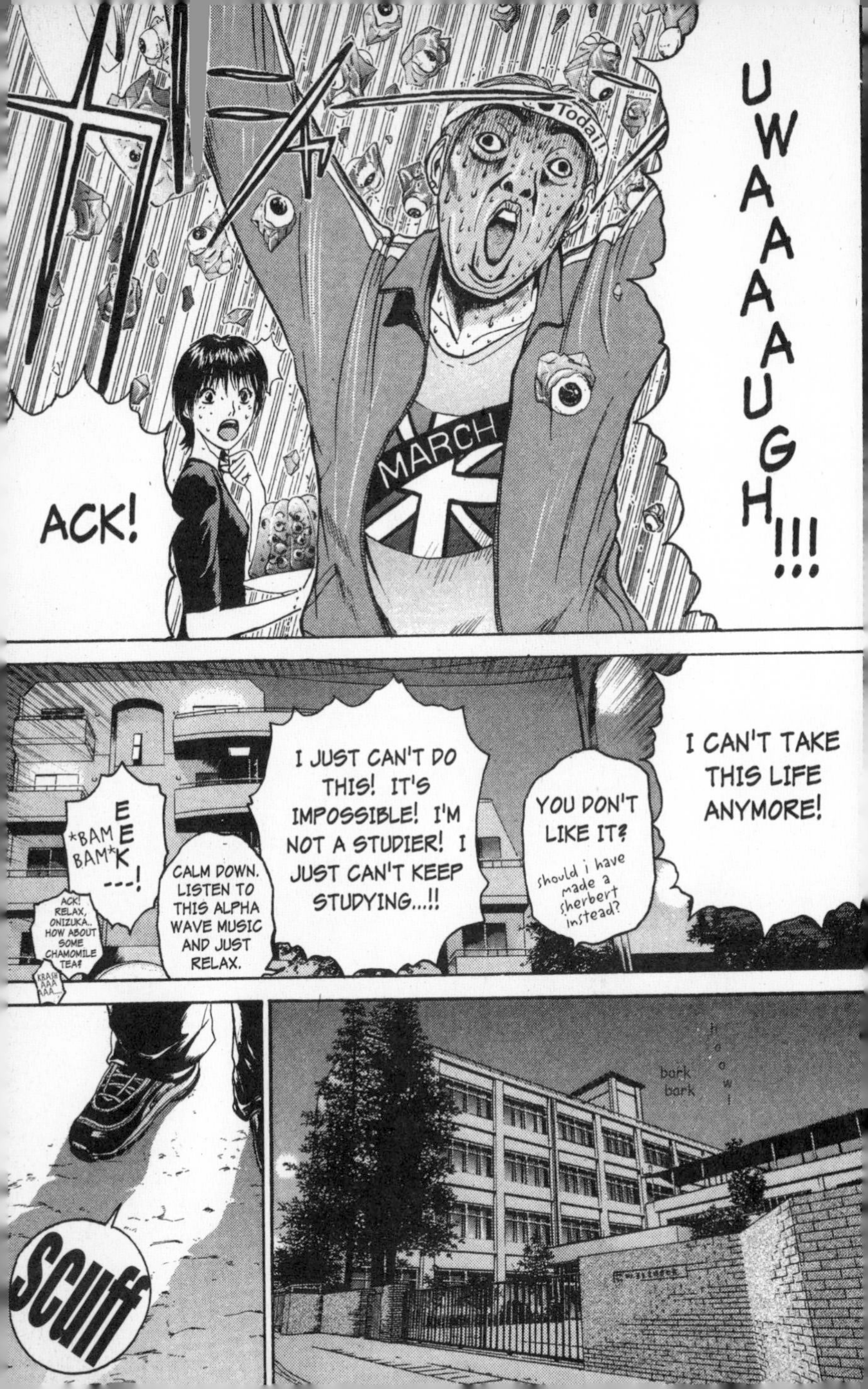
UWAAAAAUGH!!!
ACK!
I CAN'T TAKE THIS LIFE ANYMORE!
YOU DON'T LIKE IT?
should i have made a sherbert instead?
I JUST CAN'T DO THIS! IT'S IMPOSSIBLE! I'M NOT A STUDIER! I JUST CAN'T KEEP STUDYING...!!
CALM DOWN. LISTEN TO THIS ALPHA WAVE MUSIC AND JUST RELAX.
EEEK---!
BAM BAM
ACK! RELAX, ONIZUKA.. HOW ABOUT SOME CHAMOMILE TEA?
KRASH AAA AAA...
bark bark
hoow!
scuff

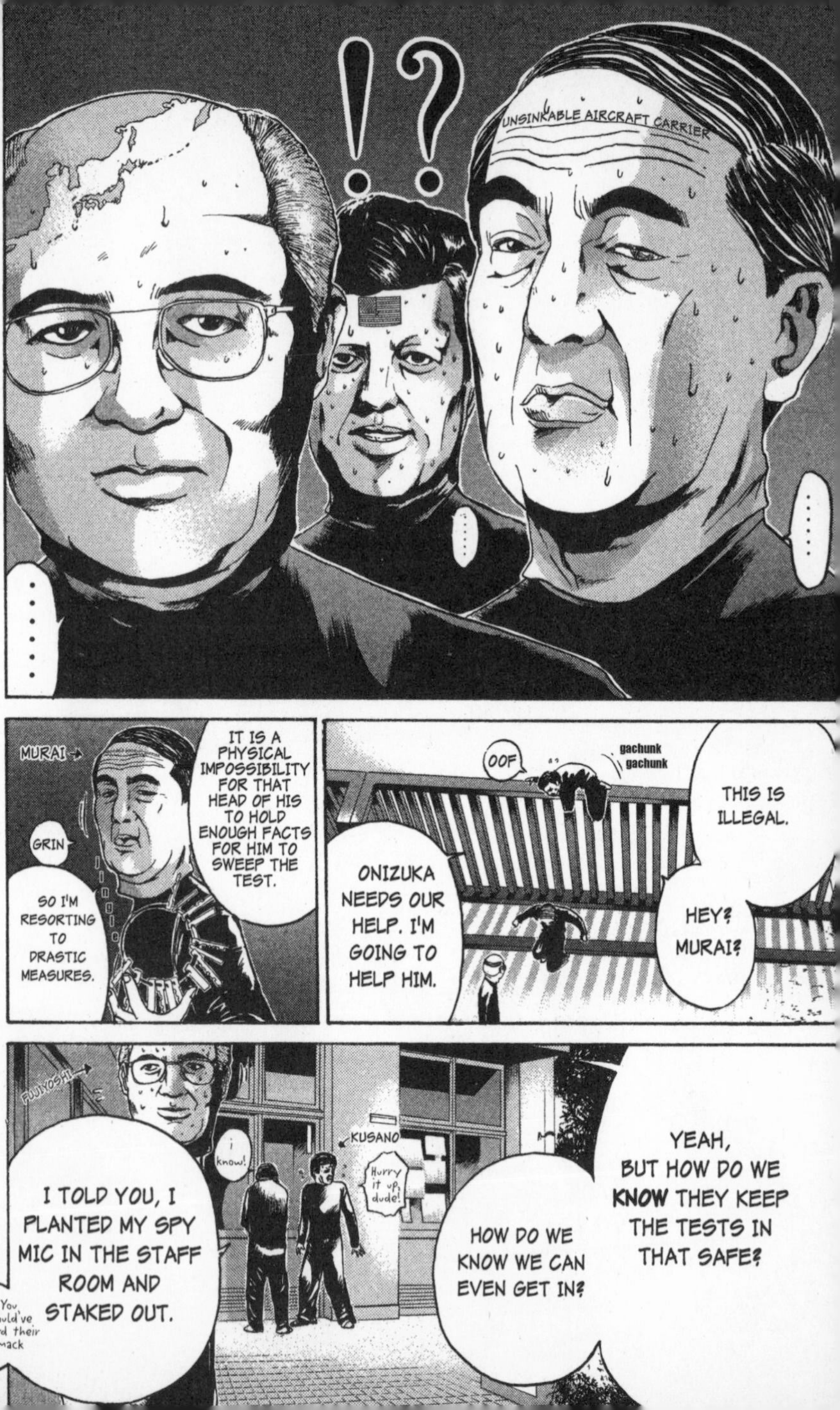
!?
UNSINKABLE AIRCRAFT CARRIER
......
......
......
gachunk gachunk
OOF
THIS IS ILLEGAL.
HEY? MURAI?
ONIZUKA NEEDS OUR HELP. I'M GOING TO HELP HIM.
MURAI
IT IS A PHYSICAL IMPOSSIBILITY FOR THAT HEAD OF HIS TO HOLD ENOUGH FACTS FOR HIM TO SWEEP THE TEST.
GRIN
jingle
SO I'M RESORTING TO DRASTIC MEASURES.
YEAH, BUT HOW DO WE **KNOW** THEY KEEP THE TESTS IN THAT SAFE?
HOW DO WE KNOW WE CAN EVEN GET IN?
KUSANO
Hurry it up, dude!
FUJIYOSHI
I know!
I TOLD YOU, I PLANTED MY SPY MIC IN THE STAFF ROOM AND STAKED OUT.
You should've heard their smack

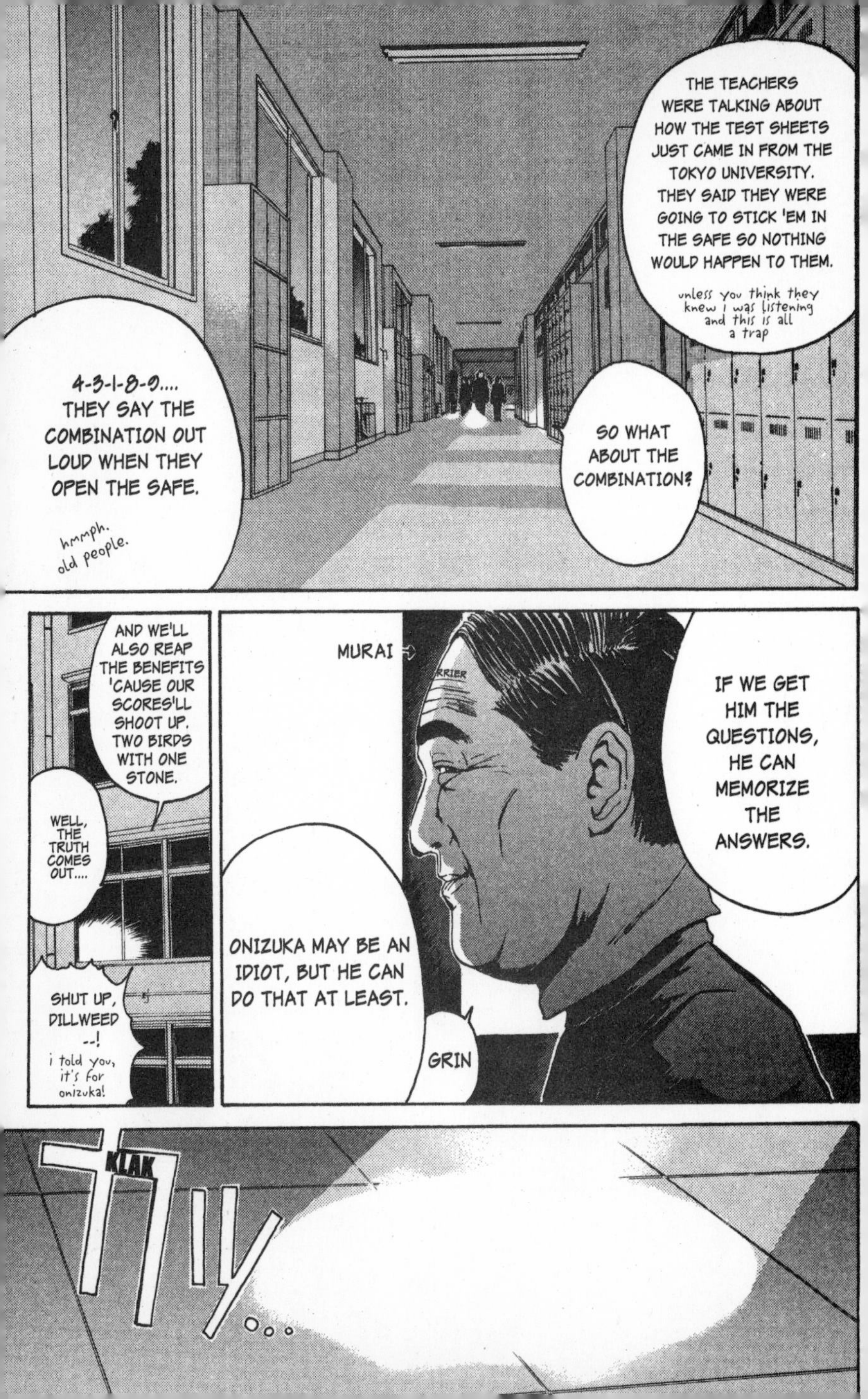

THE TEACHERS WERE TALKING ABOUT HOW THE TEST SHEETS JUST CAME IN FROM THE TOKYO UNIVERSITY. THEY SAID THEY WERE GOING TO STICK 'EM IN THE SAFE SO NOTHING WOULD HAPPEN TO THEM.
unless you think they knew i was listening and this is all a trap
SO WHAT ABOUT THE COMBINATION?
4-3-1-8-9.... THEY SAY THE COMBINATION OUT LOUD WHEN THEY OPEN THE SAFE.
hmmph. old people.
IF WE GET HIM THE QUESTIONS, HE CAN MEMORIZE THE ANSWERS.
MURAI
ONIZUKA MAY BE AN IDIOT, BUT HE CAN DO THAT AT LEAST.
GRIN
AND WE'LL ALSO REAP THE BENEFITS 'CAUSE OUR SCORES'LL SHOOT UP. TWO BIRDS WITH ONE STONE.
WELL, THE TRUTH COMES OUT....
SHUT UP, DILLWEED --!
i told you, it's for onizuka!
KLAK

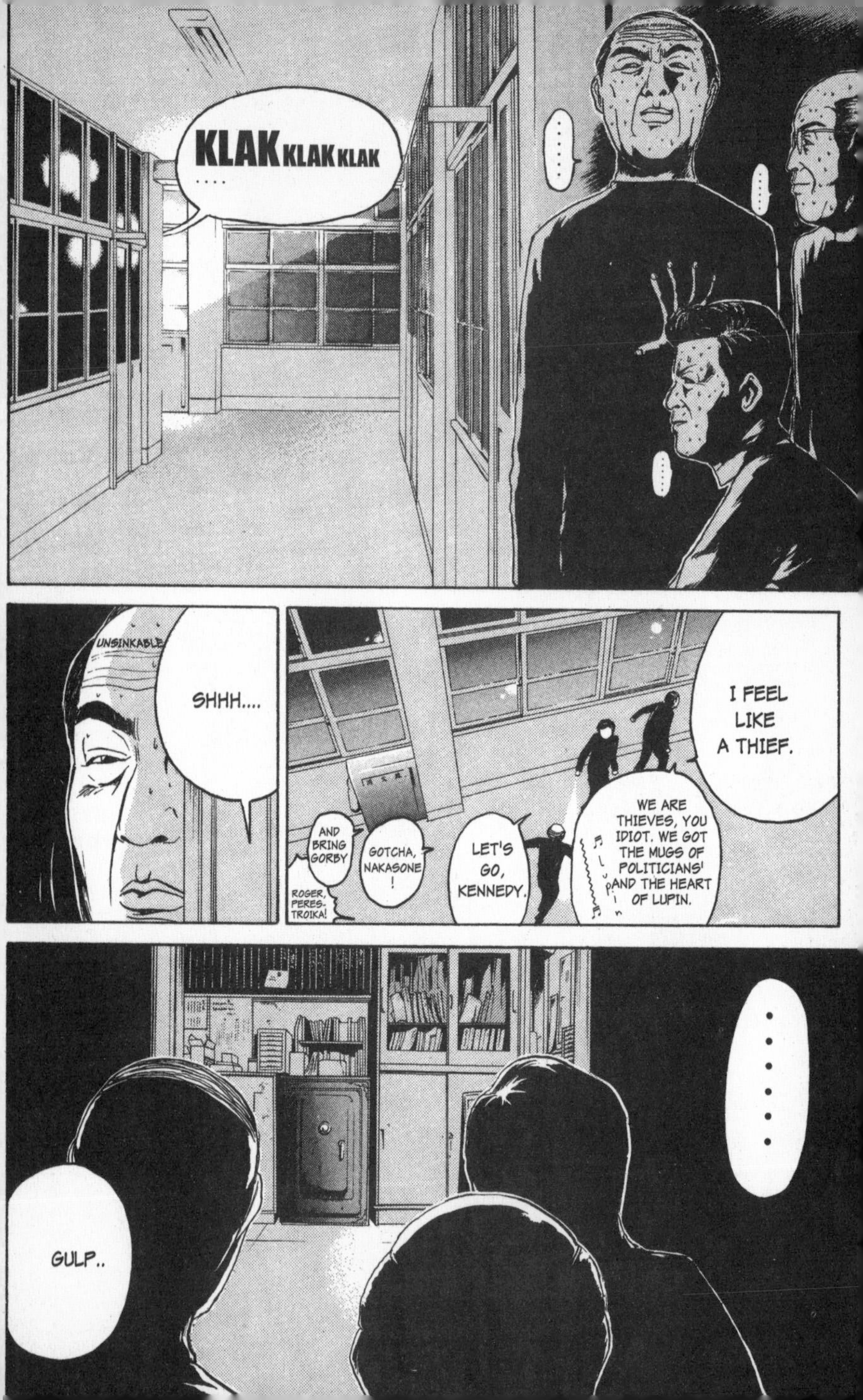
......
......
......
KLAK KLAK KLAK
....
I FEEL LIKE A THIEF.
WE ARE THIEVES, YOU IDIOT. WE GOT THE MUGS OF POLITICIANS' AND THE HEART OF LUPIN.
LET'S GO, KENNEDY.
GOTCHA, NAKASONE!
AND BRING GORBY
ROGER, PERES-TROIKA!
UNSINKABLE
SHHH....
......
GULP..

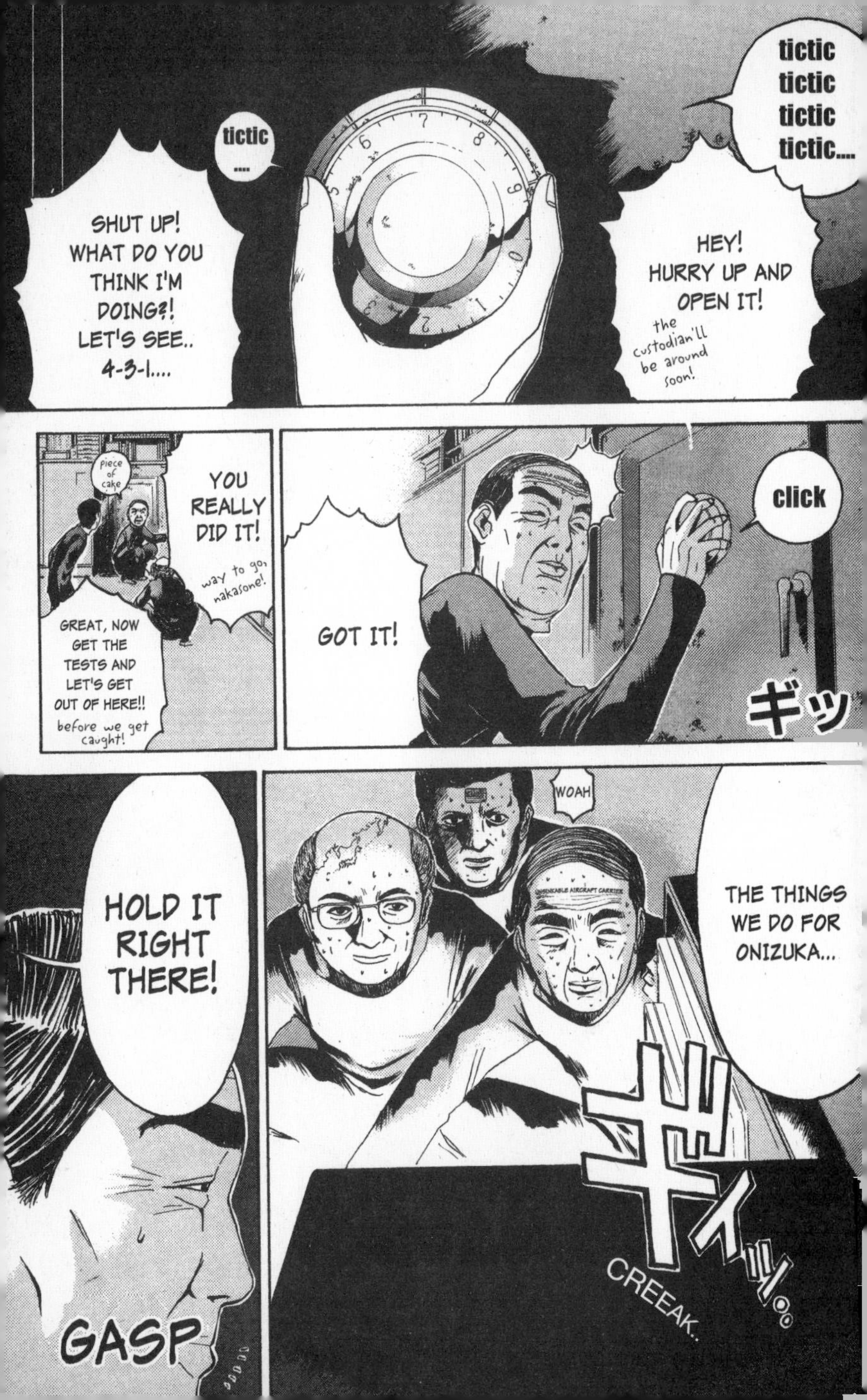
tictic tictic tictic tictic....
HEY! HURRY UP AND OPEN IT!
the custodian'll be around soon!
tictic ....
SHUT UP! WHAT DO YOU THINK I'M DOING?! LET'S SEE.. 4-3-1....
click
GOT IT!
ギッ
YOU REALLY DID IT!
way to go, nakasone!
piece of cake
GREAT, NOW GET THE TESTS AND LET'S GET OUT OF HERE!!
before we get caught!
THE THINGS WE DO FOR ONIZUKA...
WOAH
ギィッ。。
CREEAK..
HOLD IT RIGHT THERE!
GASP

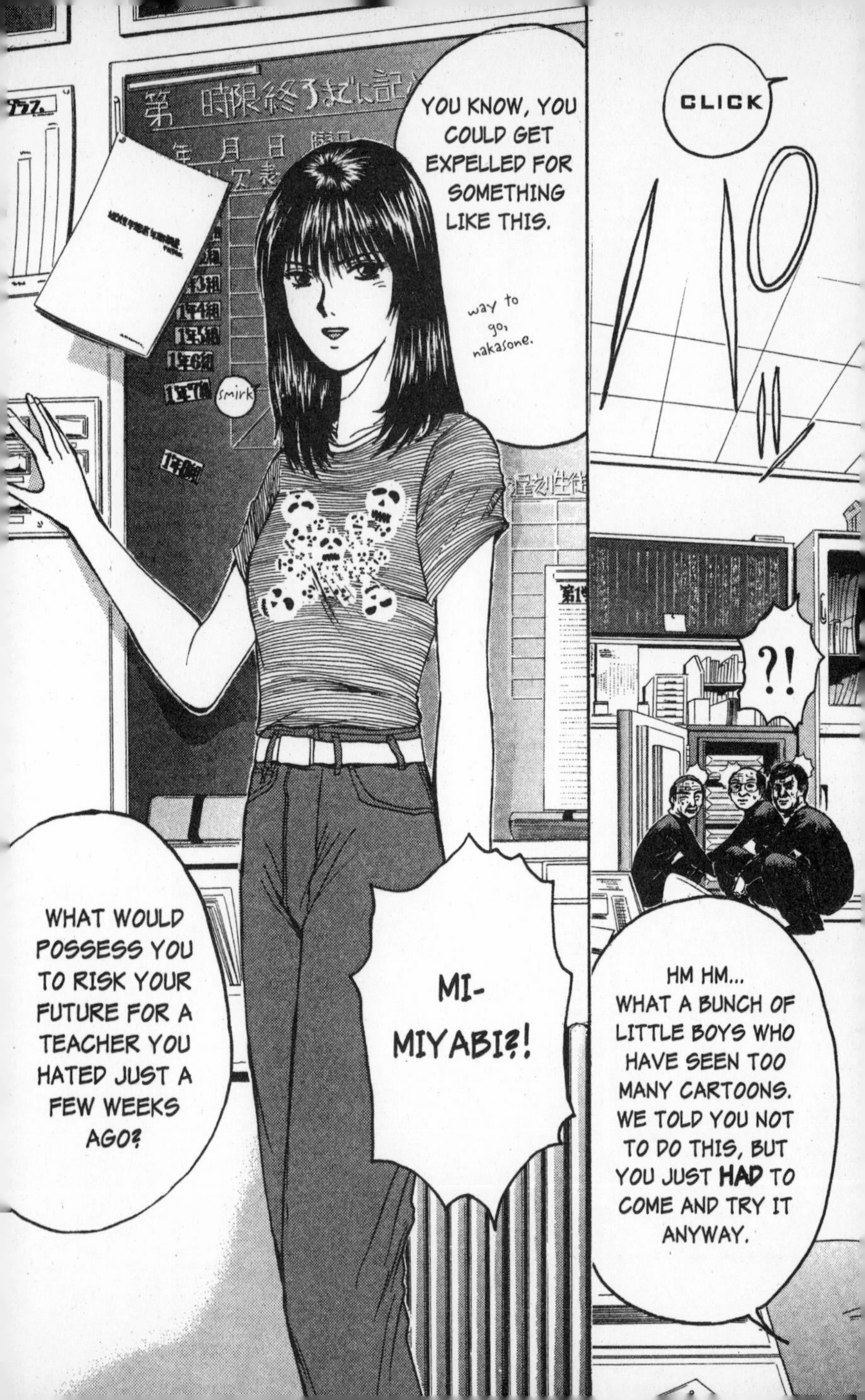
CLICK
?!
HM HM...
WHAT A BUNCH OF LITTLE BOYS WHO HAVE SEEN TOO MANY CARTOONS. WE TOLD YOU NOT TO DO THIS, BUT YOU JUST **HAD** TO COME AND TRY IT ANYWAY.
YOU KNOW, YOU COULD GET EXPELLED FOR SOMETHING LIKE THIS.
way to go, nakasone.
smirk
MI-MIYABI?!
WHAT WOULD POSSESS YOU TO RISK YOUR FUTURE FOR A TEACHER YOU HATED JUST A FEW WEEKS AGO?

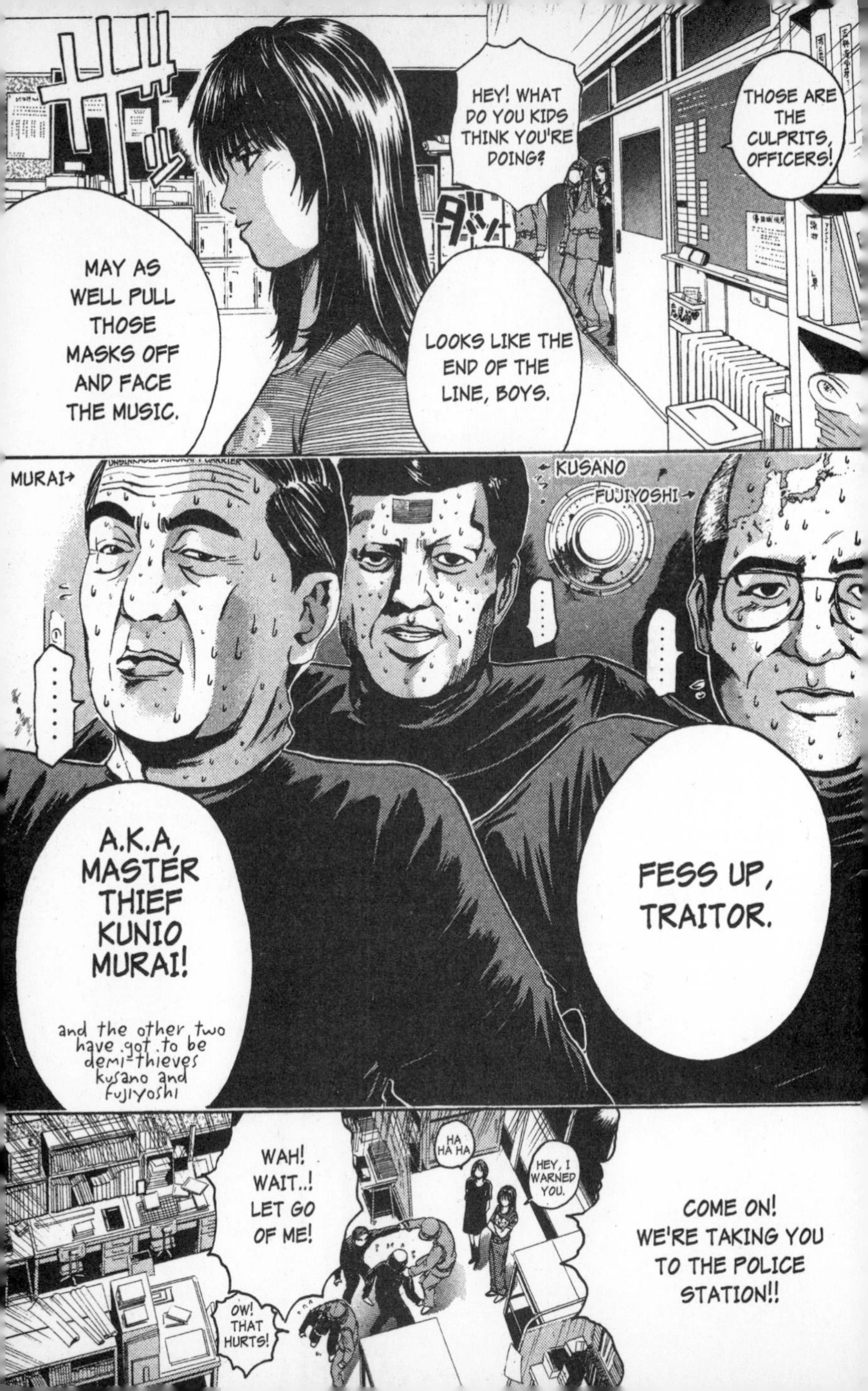
THOSE ARE THE CULPRITS, OFFICERS!
HEY! WHAT DO YOU KIDS THINK YOU'RE DOING?
LOOKS LIKE THE END OF THE LINE, BOYS.
MAY AS WELL PULL THOSE MASKS OFF AND FACE THE MUSIC.
← KUSANO
FUJIYOSHI →
MURAI →
......
......
......
FESS UP, TRAITOR.
A.K.A, MASTER THIEF KUNIO MURAI!
and the other two have got to be demi-thieves kusano and fujiyoshi
COME ON! WE'RE TAKING YOU TO THE POLICE STATION!!
HEY, I WARNED YOU.
HA HA HA
WAH! WAIT..! LET GO OF ME!
OW! THAT HURTS!

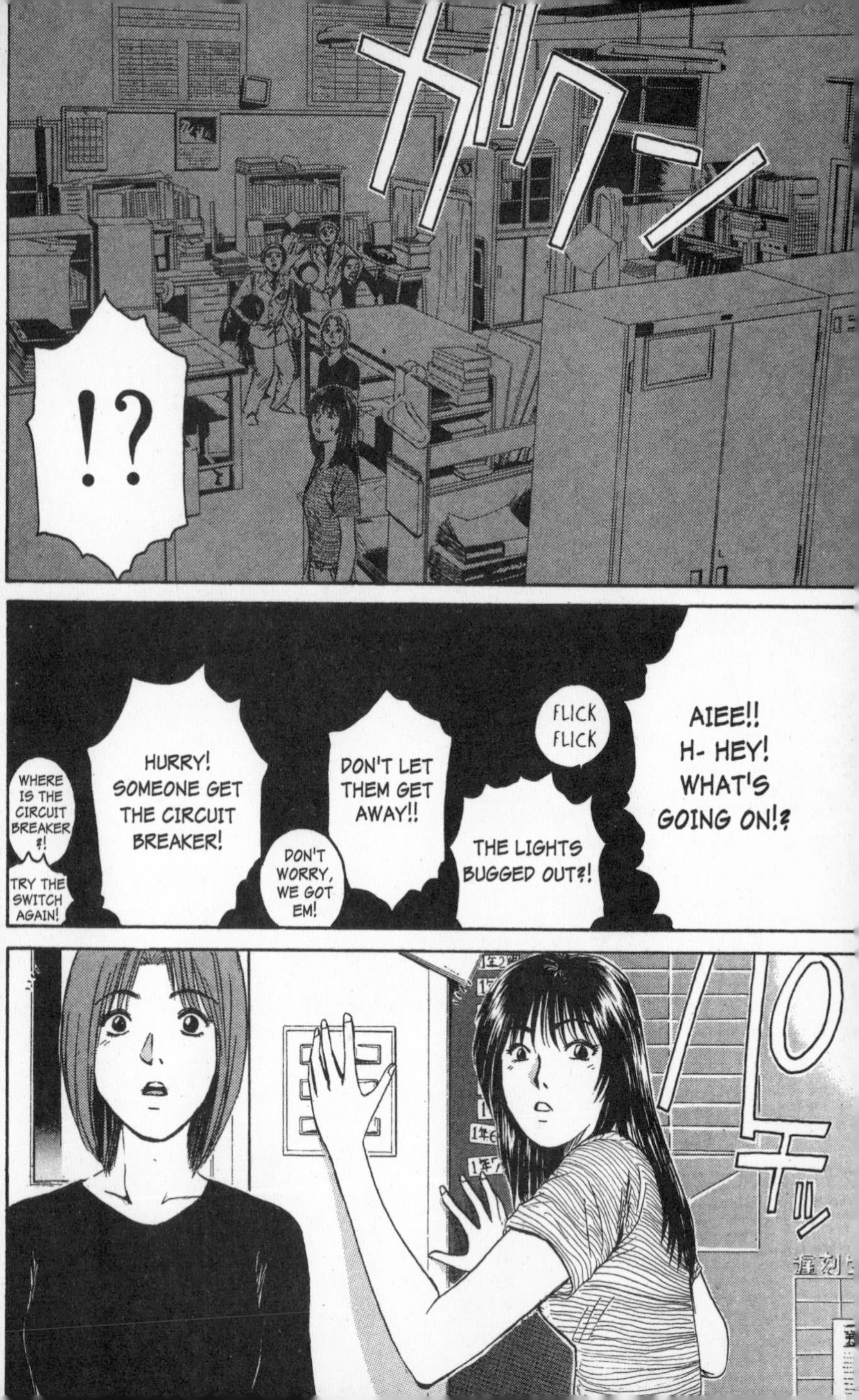
ガクーン
!?
AIEE!! H- HEY! WHAT'S GOING ON!?
FLICK FLICK
THE LIGHTS BUGGED OUT?!
DON'T LET THEM GET AWAY!!
DON'T WORRY, WE GOT EM!
HURRY! SOMEONE GET THE CIRCUIT BREAKER!
WHERE IS THE CIRCUIT BREAKER?!
TRY THE SWITCH AGAIN!

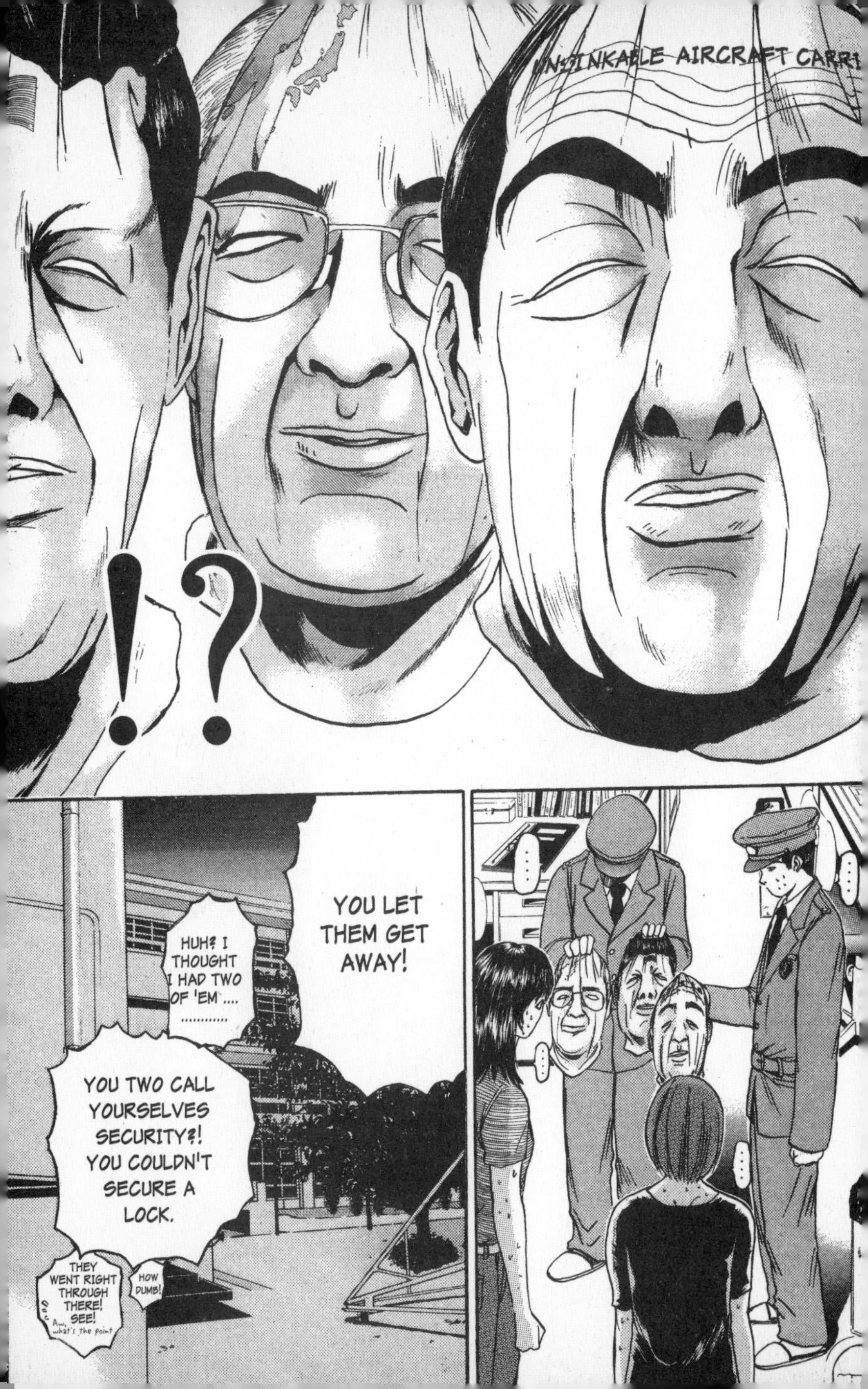
!?
...
...
...
...
YOU LET THEM GET AWAY!
HUH?! I THOUGHT I HAD TWO OF 'EM ....
YOU TWO CALL YOURSELVES SECURITY?! YOU COULDN'T SECURE A LOCK.
HOW DUMB!
THEY WENT RIGHT THROUGH THERE! SEE!
Aw, what's the point

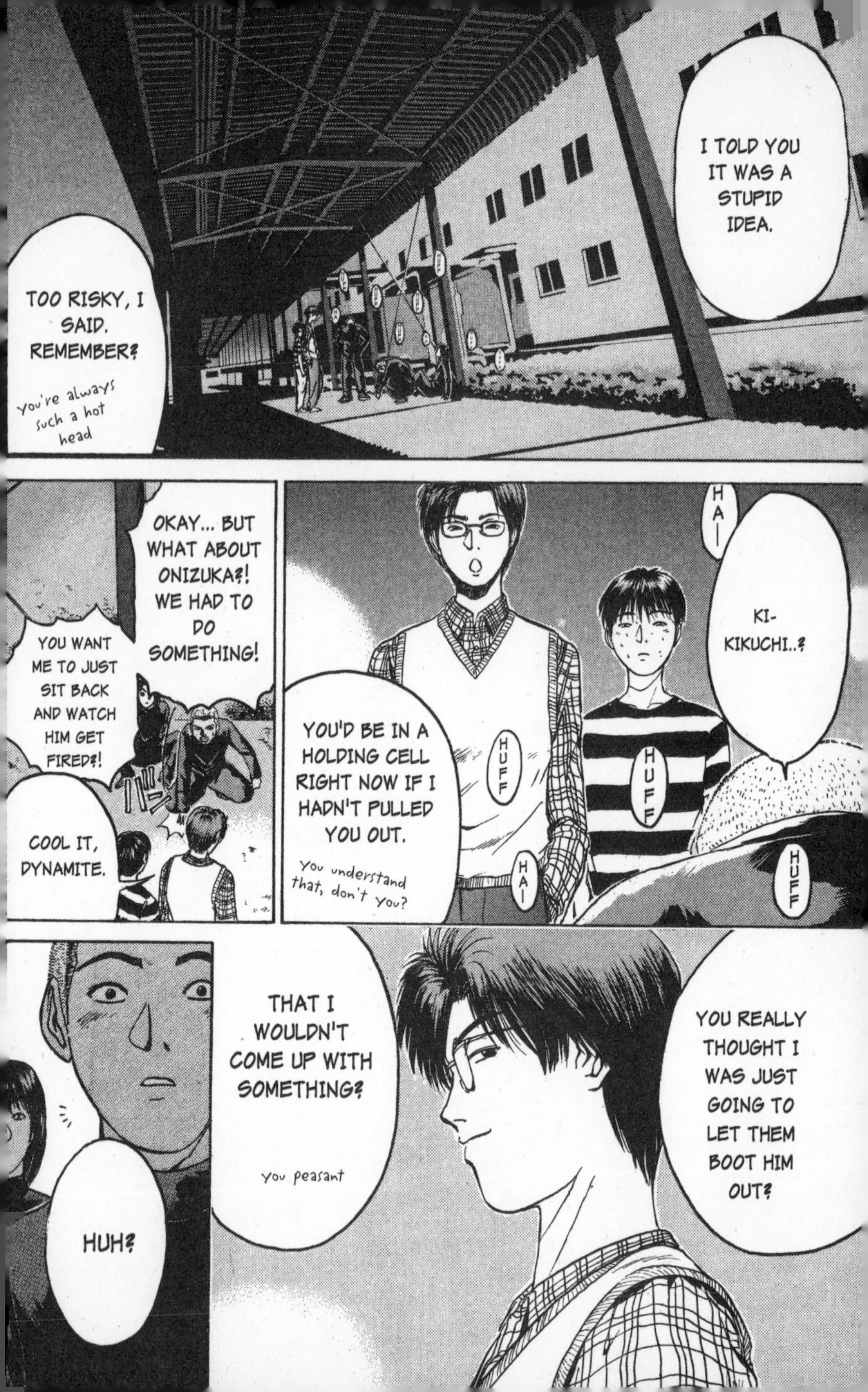
I TOLD YOU IT WAS A STUPID IDEA.
TOO RISKY, I SAID. REMEMBER?
you're always such a hot head
HA
KI- KIKUCHI..?
HUFF
HUFF
HA
HUFF
YOU'D BE IN A HOLDING CELL RIGHT NOW IF I HADN'T PULLED YOU OUT.
You understand that, don't you?
OKAY... BUT WHAT ABOUT ONIZUKA?! WE HAD TO DO SOMETHING!
YOU WANT ME TO JUST SIT BACK AND WATCH HIM GET FIRED?!
COOL IT, DYNAMITE.
YOU REALLY THOUGHT I WAS JUST GOING TO LET THEM BOOT HIM OUT?
THAT I WOULDN'T COME UP WITH SOMETHING?
You peasant
HUH?

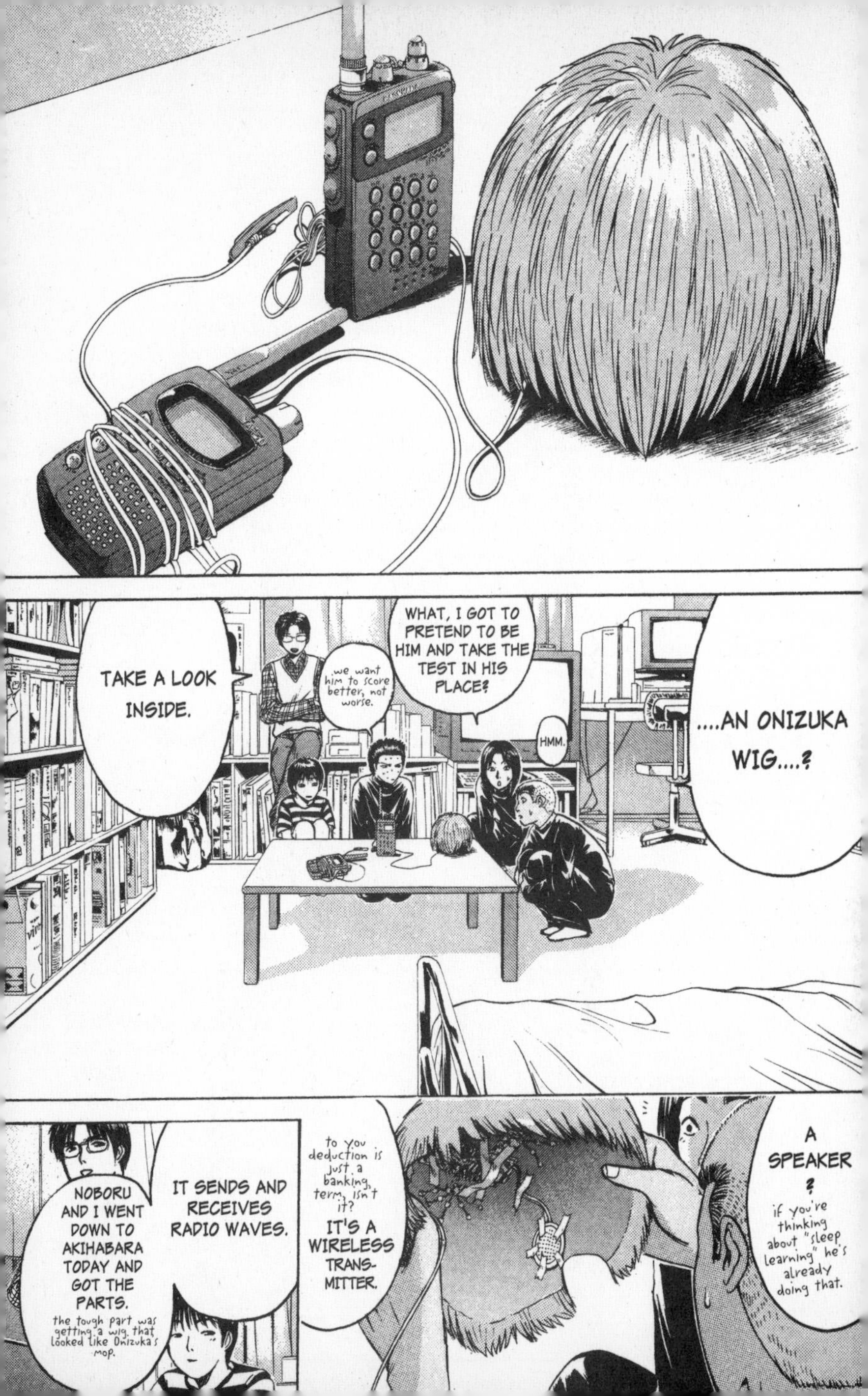
....AN ONIZUKA WIG....?
HMM.
WHAT, I GOT TO PRETEND TO BE HIM AND TAKE THE TEST IN HIS PLACE?
we want him to score better, not worse.
TAKE A LOOK INSIDE.
A SPEAKER?
if you're thinking about "sleep learning" he's already doing that.
to you deduction is just a banking term, isn't it?
IT'S A WIRELESS TRANS-MITTER.
IT SENDS AND RECEIVES RADIO WAVES.
NOBORU AND I WENT DOWN TO AKIHABARA TODAY AND GOT THE PARTS.
the tough part was getting a wig that looked like Onizuka's mop.

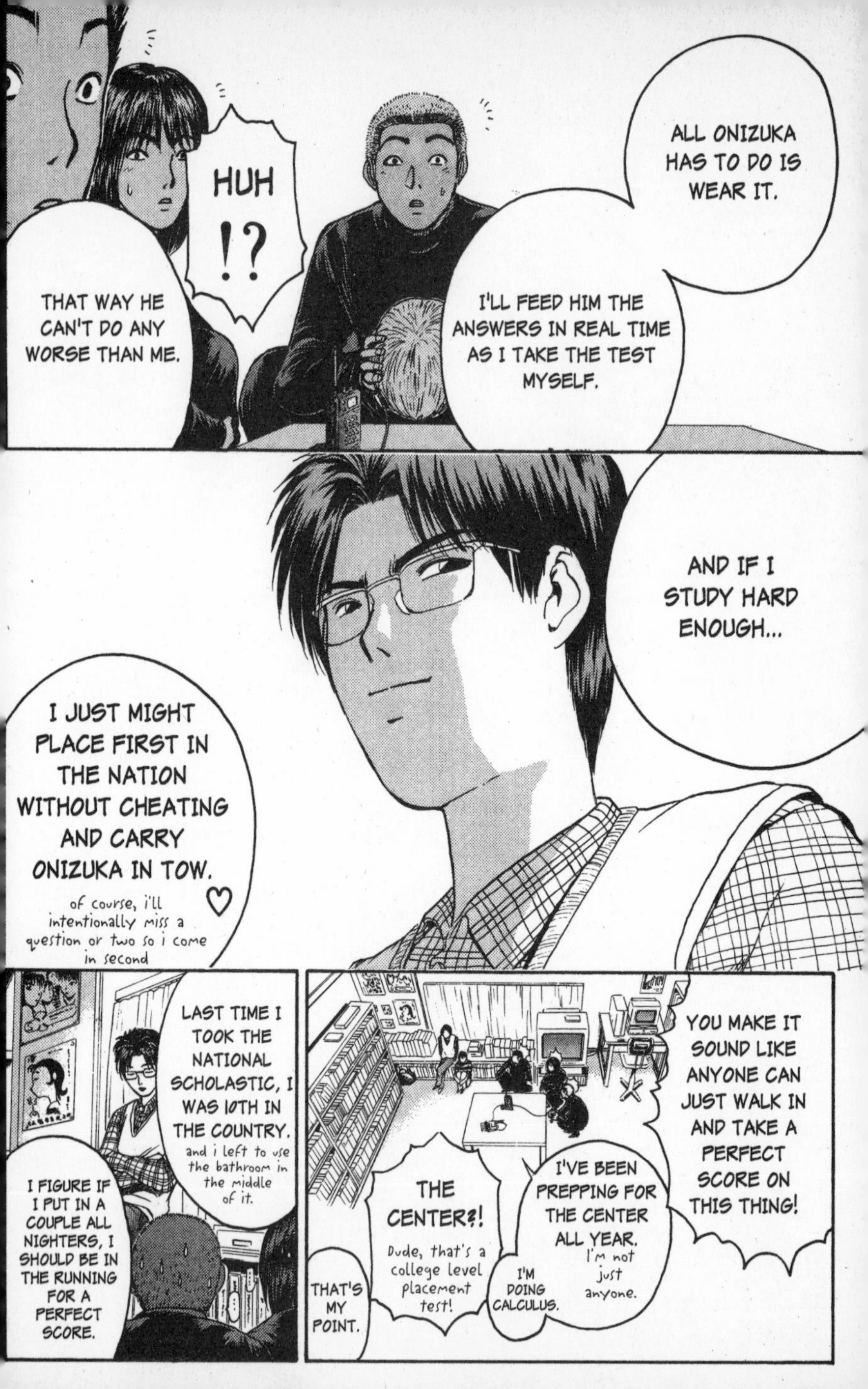
ALL ONIZUKA HAS TO DO IS WEAR IT.
I'LL FEED HIM THE ANSWERS IN REAL TIME AS I TAKE THE TEST MYSELF.
HUH !?
THAT WAY HE CAN'T DO ANY WORSE THAN ME.
AND IF I STUDY HARD ENOUGH...
I JUST MIGHT PLACE FIRST IN THE NATION WITHOUT CHEATING AND CARRY ONIZUKA IN TOW. ♡
of course, i'll intentionally miss a question or two so i come in second
YOU MAKE IT SOUND LIKE ANYONE CAN JUST WALK IN AND TAKE A PERFECT SCORE ON THIS THING!
I'VE BEEN PREPPING FOR THE CENTER ALL YEAR.
I'm not just anyone.
I'M DOING CALCULUS.
THE CENTER?!
Dude, that's a college level placement test!
THAT'S MY POINT.
LAST TIME I TOOK THE NATIONAL SCHOLASTIC, I WAS 10TH IN THE COUNTRY.
and i left to use the bathroom in the middle of it.
I FIGURE IF I PUT IN A COUPLE ALL NIGHTERS, I SHOULD BE IN THE RUNNING FOR A PERFECT SCORE.

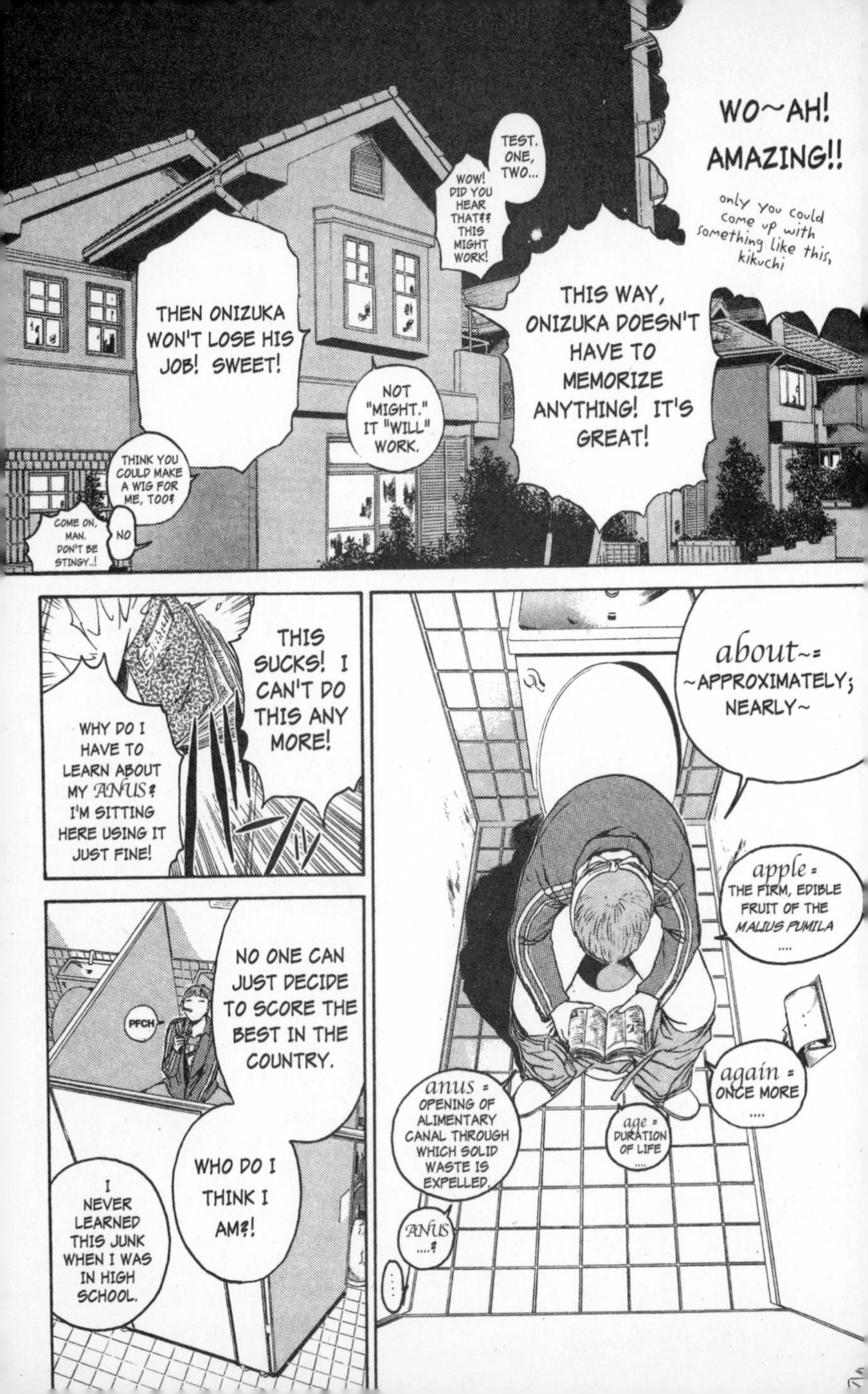
WO~AH! AMAZING!!
only you could come up with something like this, kikuchi
TEST. ONE, TWO...
WOW! DID YOU HEAR THAT?? THIS MIGHT WORK!
THIS WAY, ONIZUKA DOESN'T HAVE TO MEMORIZE ANYTHING! IT'S GREAT!
NOT "MIGHT." IT "WILL" WORK.
THEN ONIZUKA WON'T LOSE HIS JOB! SWEET!
THINK YOU COULD MAKE A WIG FOR ME, TOO?
NO
COME ON, MAN. DON'T BE STINGY..!
about~= ~APPROXIMATELY; NEARLY~
apple = THE FIRM, EDIBLE FRUIT OF THE MALIUS PUMILA ....
again = ONCE MORE ....
age = DURATION OF LIFE ....
anus = OPENING OF ALIMENTARY CANAL THROUGH WHICH SOLID WASTE IS EXPELLED.
ANUS ....?
...
THIS SUCKS! I CAN'T DO THIS ANY MORE!
WHY DO I HAVE TO LEARN ABOUT MY ANUS? I'M SITTING HERE USING IT JUST FINE!
NO ONE CAN JUST DECIDE TO SCORE THE BEST IN THE COUNTRY.
PFCH
WHO DO I THINK I AM?!
I NEVER LEARNED THIS JUNK WHEN I WAS IN HIGH SCHOOL.

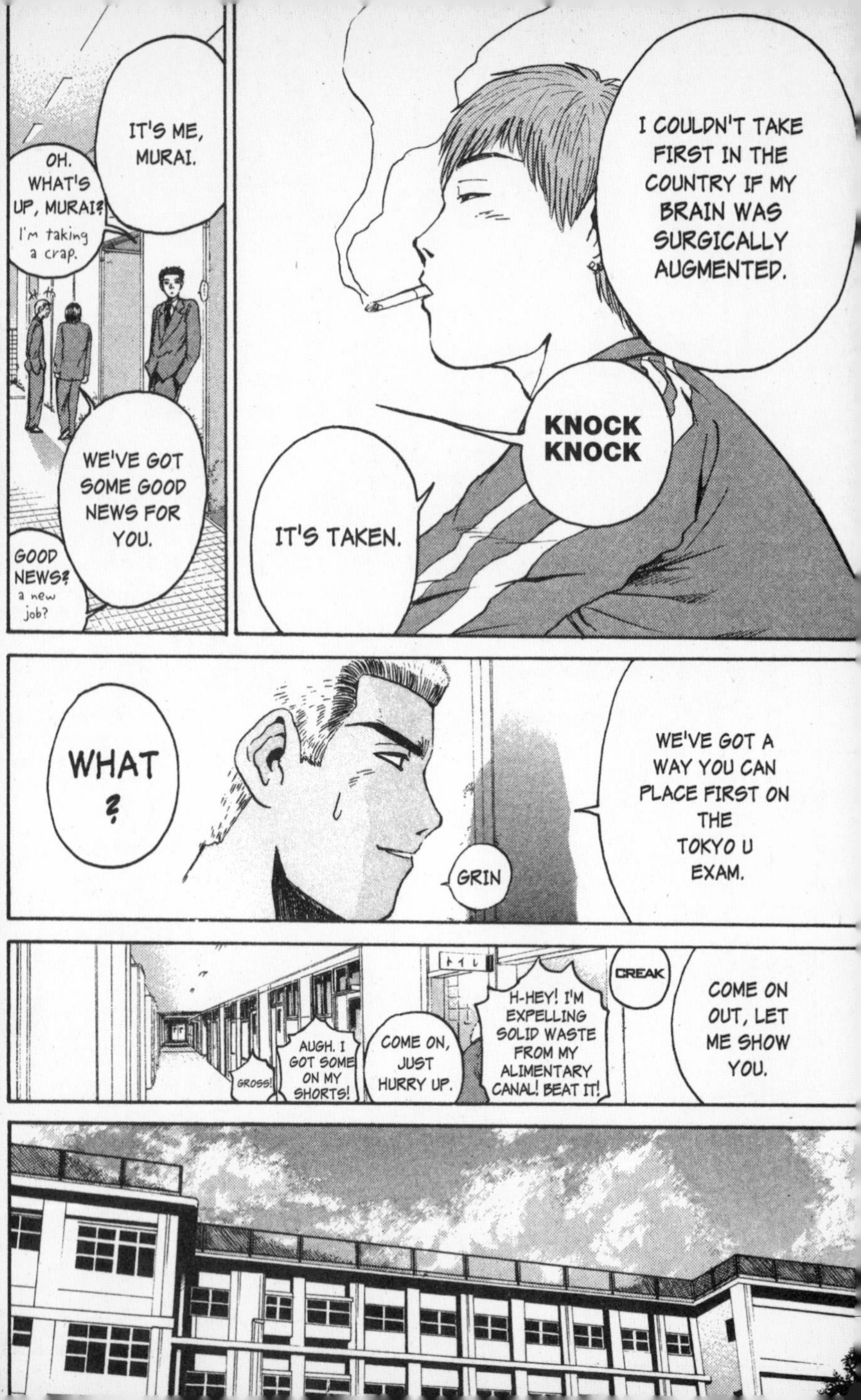
I COULDN'T TAKE FIRST IN THE COUNTRY IF MY BRAIN WAS SURGICALLY AUGMENTED.
KNOCK KNOCK
IT'S TAKEN.
IT'S ME, MURAI.
OH. WHAT'S UP, MURAI?
I'm taking a crap.
WE'VE GOT SOME GOOD NEWS FOR YOU.
GOOD NEWS?
a new job?
WE'VE GOT A WAY YOU CAN PLACE FIRST ON THE TOKYO U EXAM.
GRIN
WHAT?
COME ON OUT, LET ME SHOW YOU.
CREAK
H-HEY! I'M EXPELLING SOLID WASTE FROM MY ALIMENTARY CANAL! BEAT IT!
COME ON, JUST HURRY UP.
AUGH. I GOT SOME ON MY SHORTS!
GROSS!

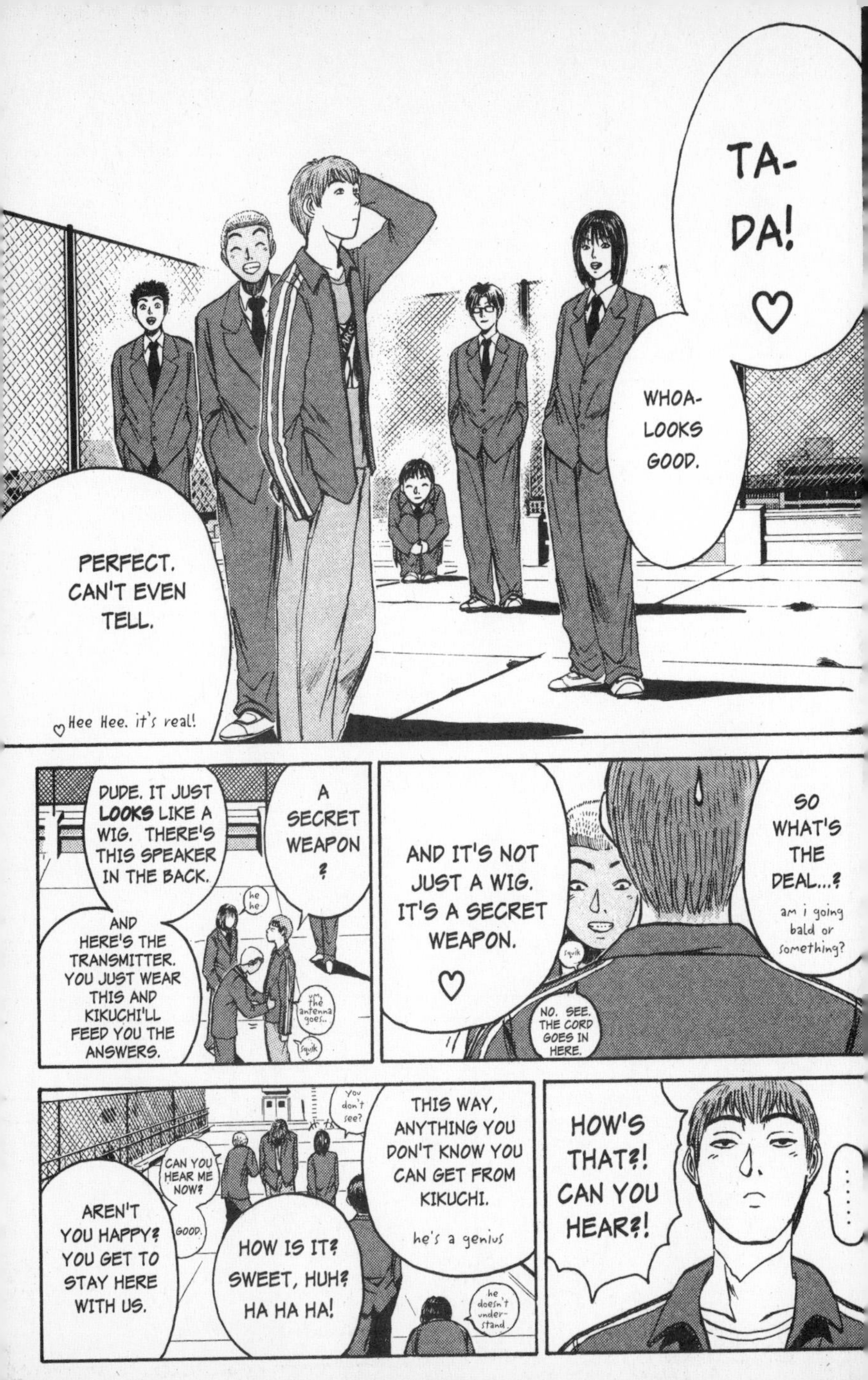
TA-DA! ♡
WHOA- LOOKS GOOD.
PERFECT. CAN'T EVEN TELL.
♡Hee Hee. it's real!
SO WHAT'S THE DEAL...?
am i going bald or something?
AND IT'S NOT JUST A WIG. IT'S A SECRET WEAPON. ♡
squik
NO. SEE. THE CORD GOES IN HERE.
A SECRET WEAPON?
DUDE. IT JUST **LOOKS** LIKE A WIG. THERE'S THIS SPEAKER IN THE BACK.
he he
AND HERE'S THE TRANSMITTER. YOU JUST WEAR THIS AND KIKUCHI'LL FEED YOU THE ANSWERS.
um, the antenna goes...
squik
...
HOW'S THAT?! CAN YOU HEAR?!
THIS WAY, ANYTHING YOU DON'T KNOW YOU CAN GET FROM KIKUCHI.
he's a genius
You don't see?
CAN YOU HEAR ME NOW?
GOOD.
HOW IS IT? SWEET, HUH? HA HA HA!
AREN'T YOU HAPPY? YOU GET TO STAY HERE WITH US.
he doesn't under-stand

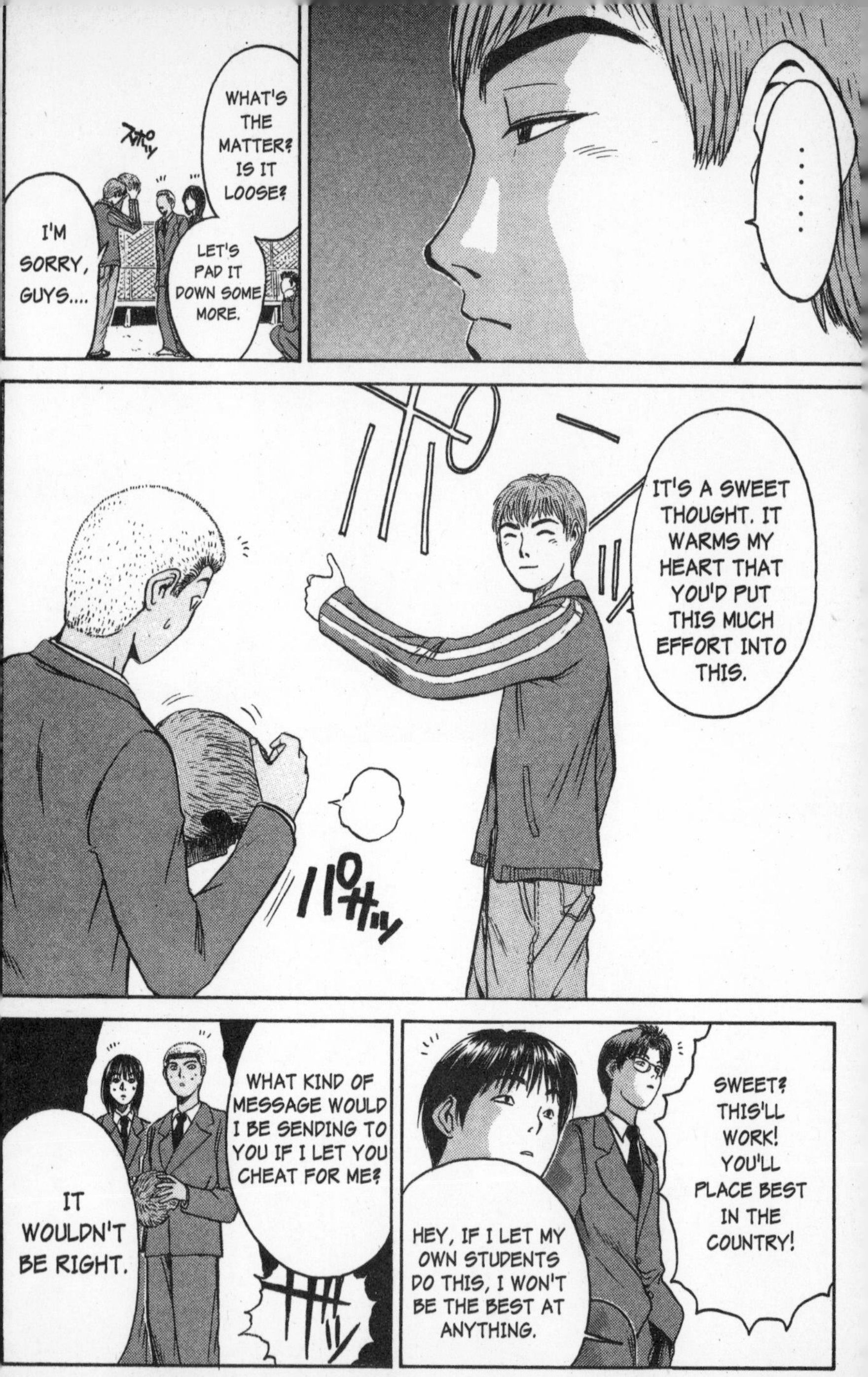
......
WHAT'S THE MATTER? IS IT LOOSE?
LET'S PAD IT DOWN SOME MORE.
I'M SORRY, GUYS....
IT'S A SWEET THOUGHT. IT WARMS MY HEART THAT YOU'D PUT THIS MUCH EFFORT INTO THIS.
SWEET? THIS'LL WORK! YOU'LL PLACE BEST IN THE COUNTRY!
HEY, IF I LET MY OWN STUDENTS DO THIS, I WON'T BE THE BEST AT ANYTHING.
WHAT KIND OF MESSAGE WOULD I BE SENDING TO YOU IF I LET YOU CHEAT FOR ME?
IT WOULDN'T BE RIGHT.

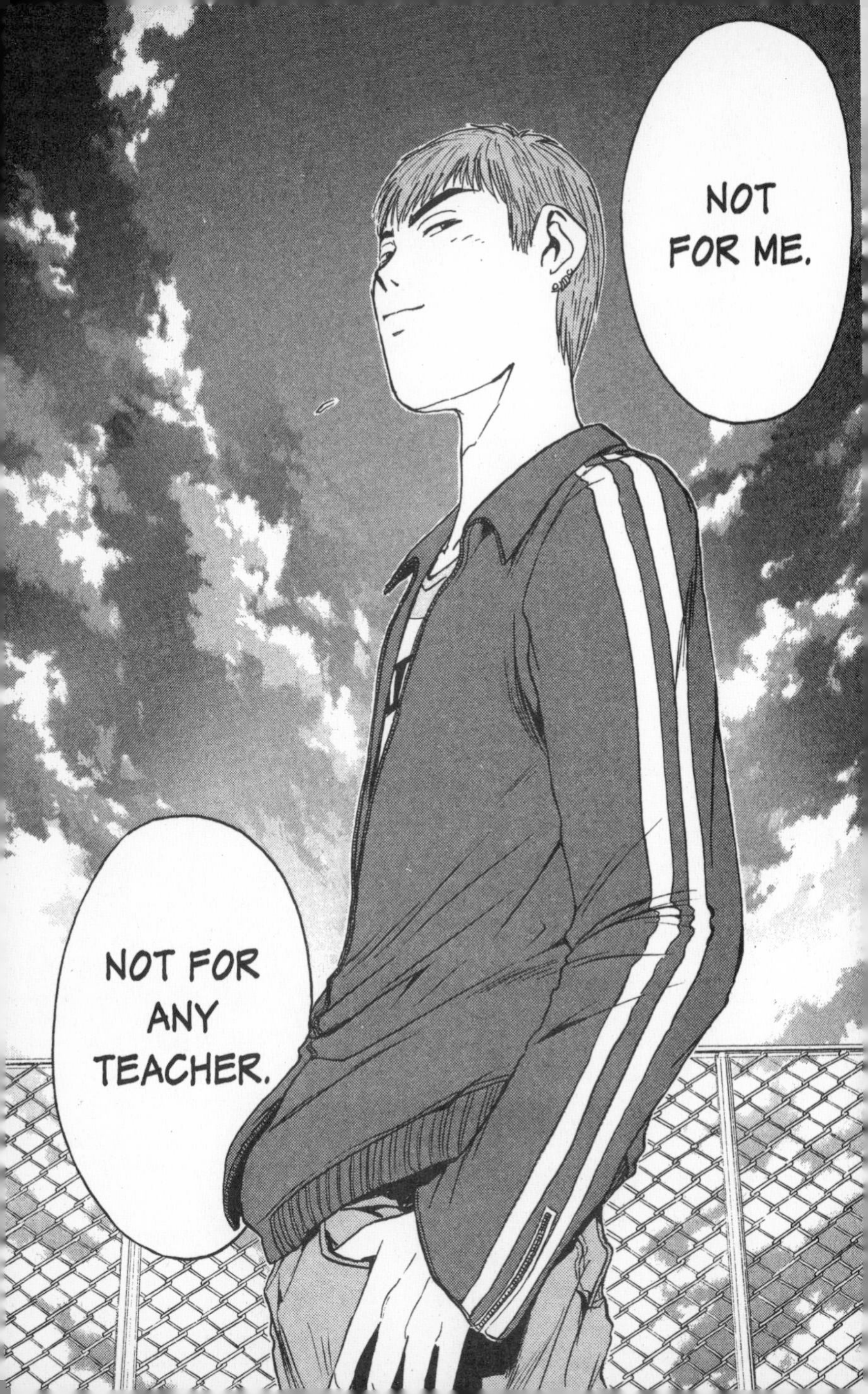
NOT FOR ME.
NOT FOR ANY TEACHER.

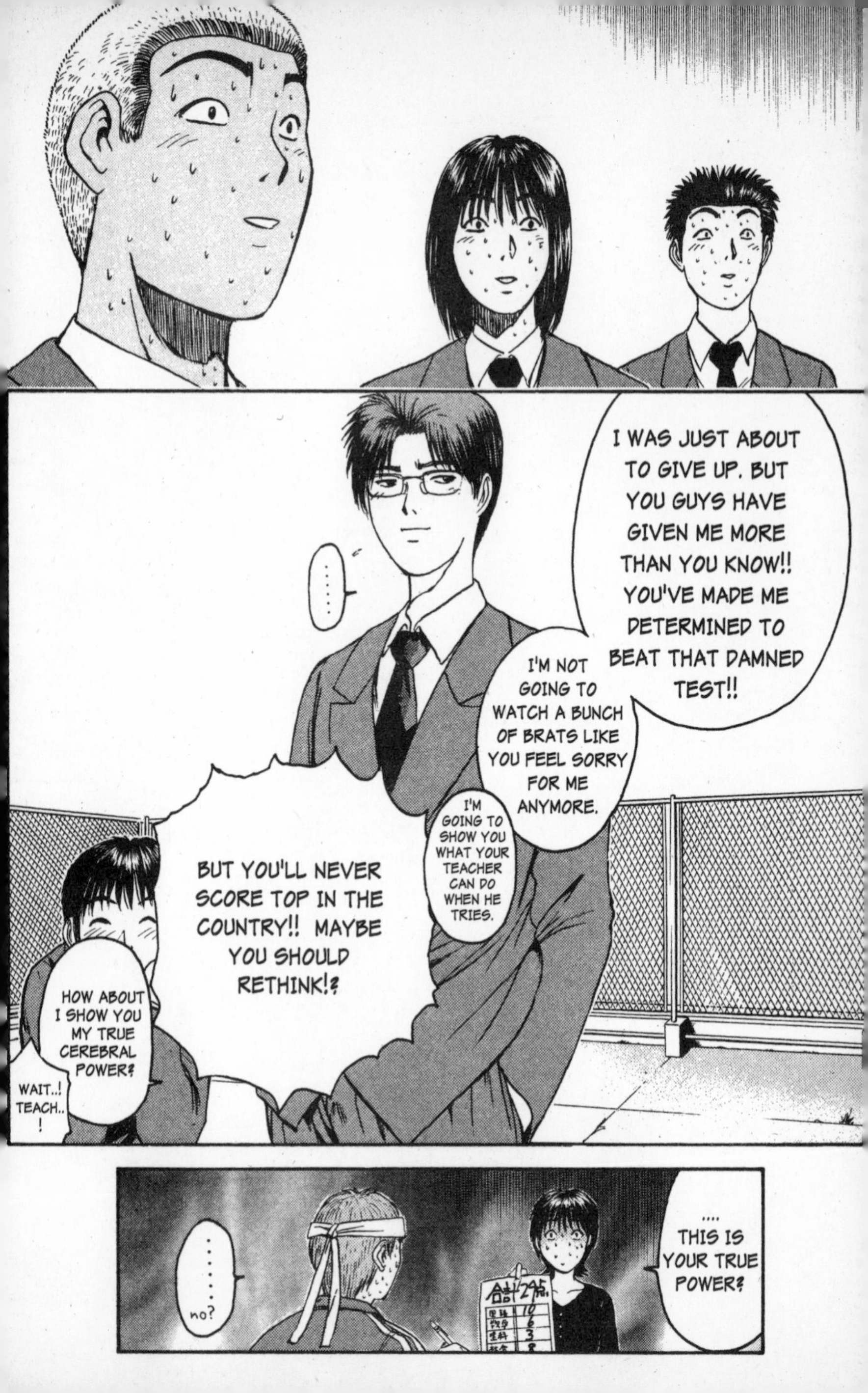
I WAS JUST ABOUT TO GIVE UP. BUT YOU GUYS HAVE GIVEN ME MORE THAN YOU KNOW!! YOU'VE MADE ME DETERMINED TO BEAT THAT DAMNED TEST!!
I'M NOT GOING TO WATCH A BUNCH OF BRATS LIKE YOU FEEL SORRY FOR ME ANYMORE.
I'M GOING TO SHOW YOU WHAT YOUR TEACHER CAN DO WHEN HE TRIES.
......
BUT YOU'LL NEVER SCORE TOP IN THE COUNTRY!! MAYBE YOU SHOULD RETHINK!?
HOW ABOUT I SHOW YOU MY TRUE CEREBRAL POWER?
WAIT..! TEACH..!
.... THIS IS YOUR TRUE POWER?
...... no?

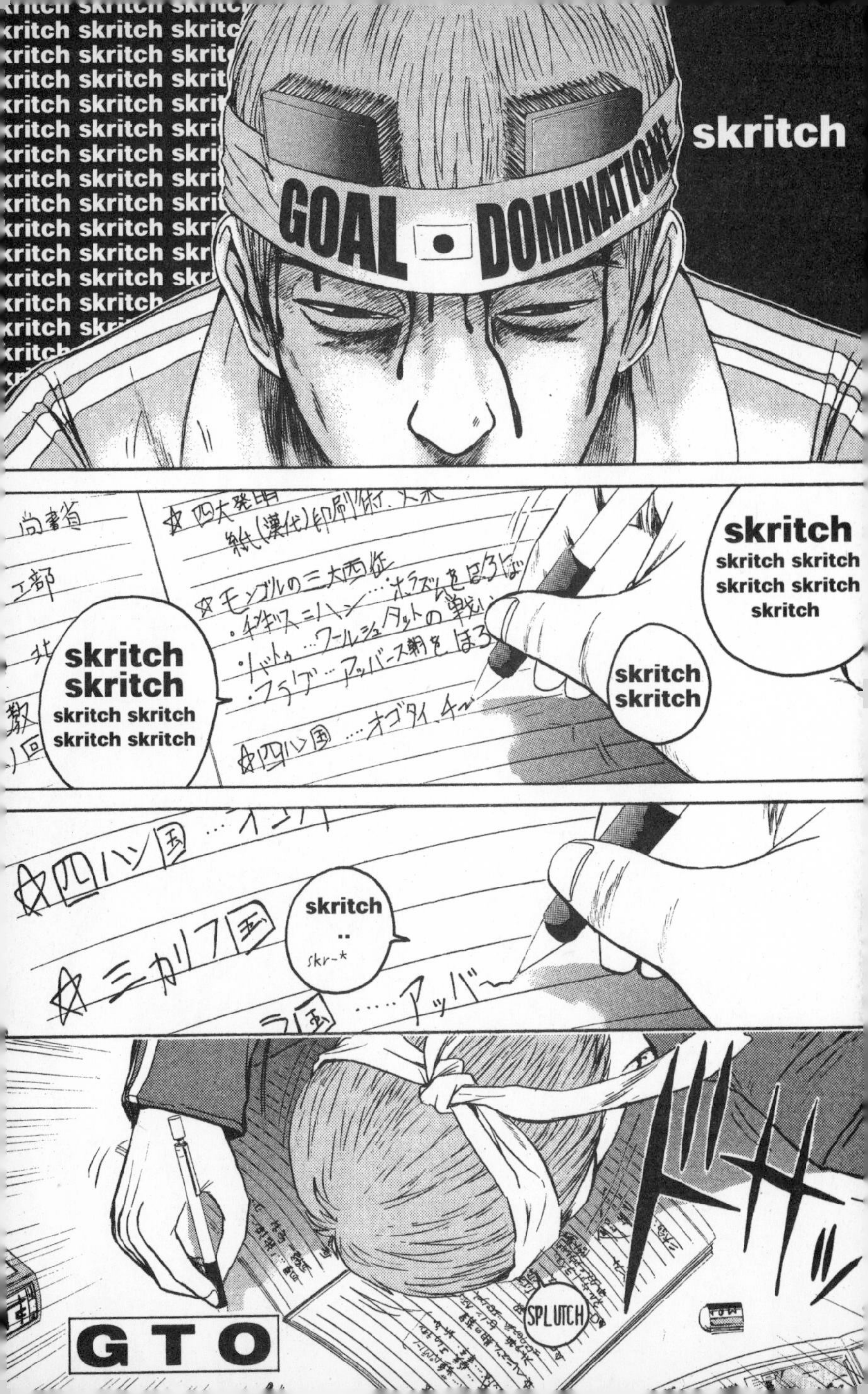
skritch
skritch skritch skritch
GOAL · DOMINATION!
skritch skritch skritch skritch skritch skritch
skritch skritch
skritch skritch skritch skritch skritch skritch
☆四大発明
☆モンゴルの三大西征
skritch .. skr-*
SPLUTCH
GTO

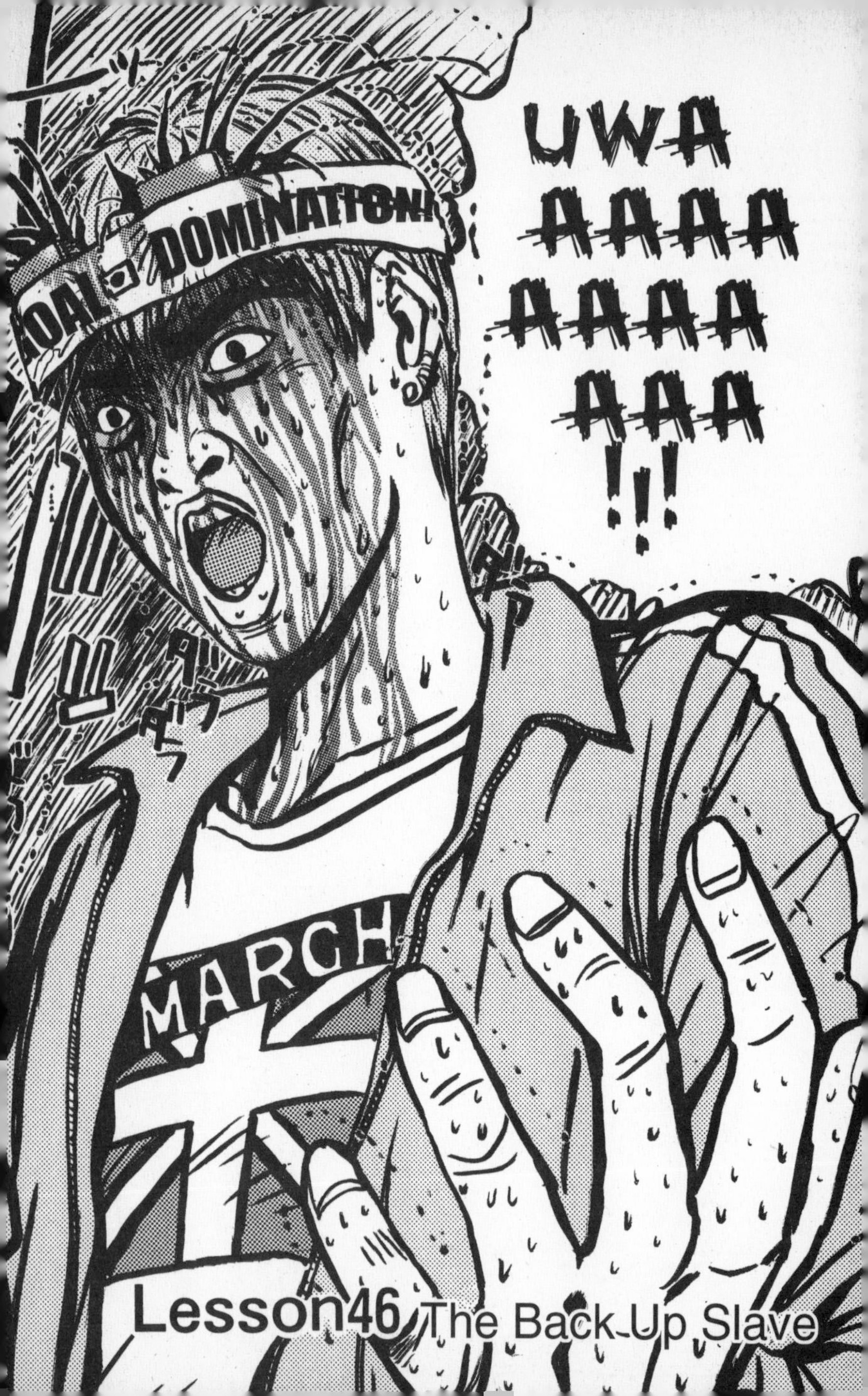
DOMINATION!
UWAAAAAAAAAAAA!!
MARCH

Lesson46 The Back Up Slave

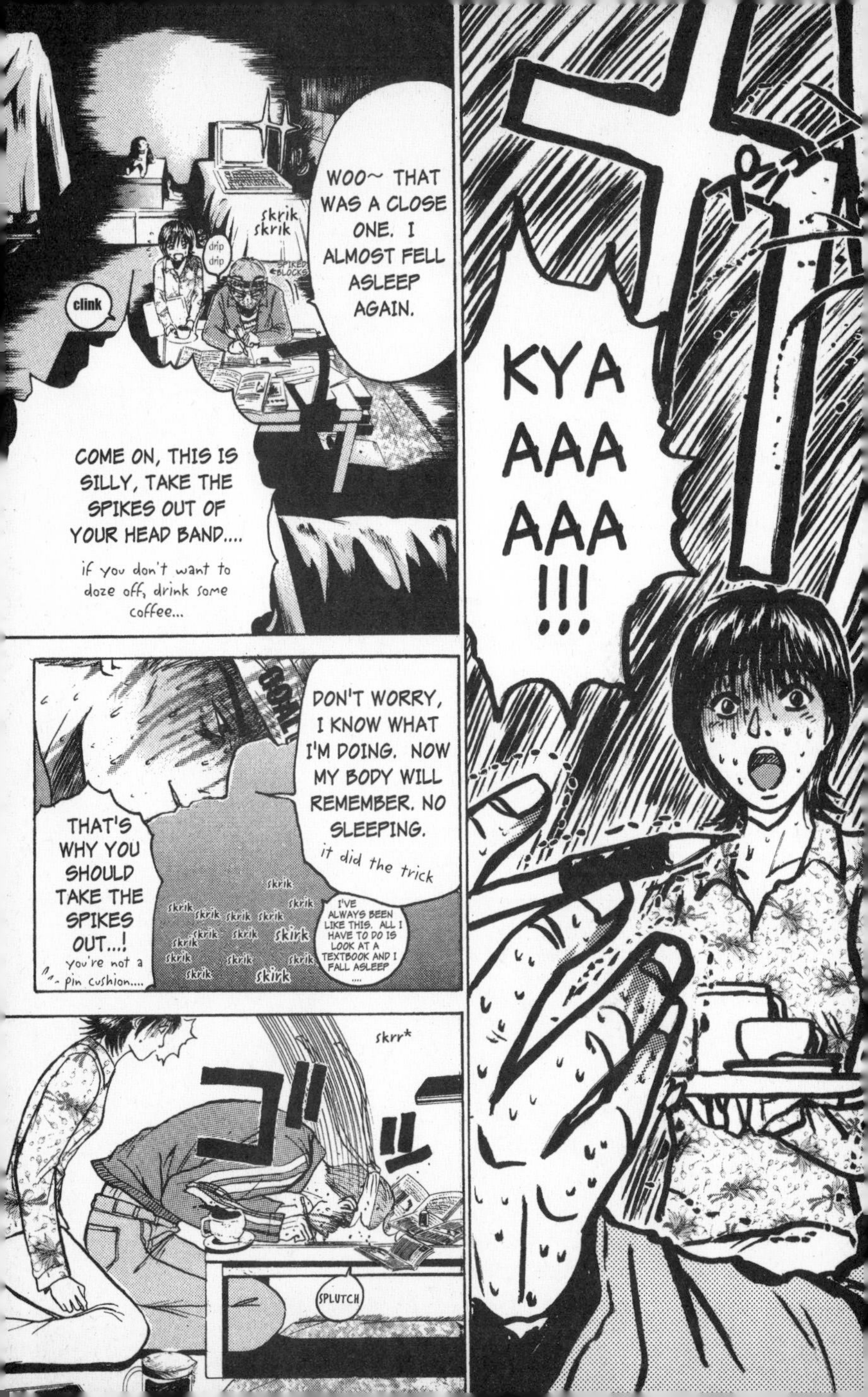
KYAAAAAAA!!!
WOO~ THAT WAS A CLOSE ONE. I ALMOST FELL ASLEEP AGAIN.
skrik skrik
drip drip
SPIKED BLOCKS
clink
COME ON, THIS IS SILLY, TAKE THE SPIKES OUT OF YOUR HEAD BAND....
if you don't want to doze off, drink some coffee...
DON'T WORRY, I KNOW WHAT I'M DOING. NOW MY BODY WILL REMEMBER. NO SLEEPING.
it did the trick
THAT'S WHY YOU SHOULD TAKE THE SPIKES OUT...!
you're not a pin cushion....
skrik skrik skrik skrik skrik skrik skrik skrik skirk skrik skrik skrik skrik skirk
I'VE ALWAYS BEEN LIKE THIS. ALL I HAVE TO DO IS LOOK AT A TEXTBOOK AND I FALL ASLEEP ....
skrr*
SPLUTCH

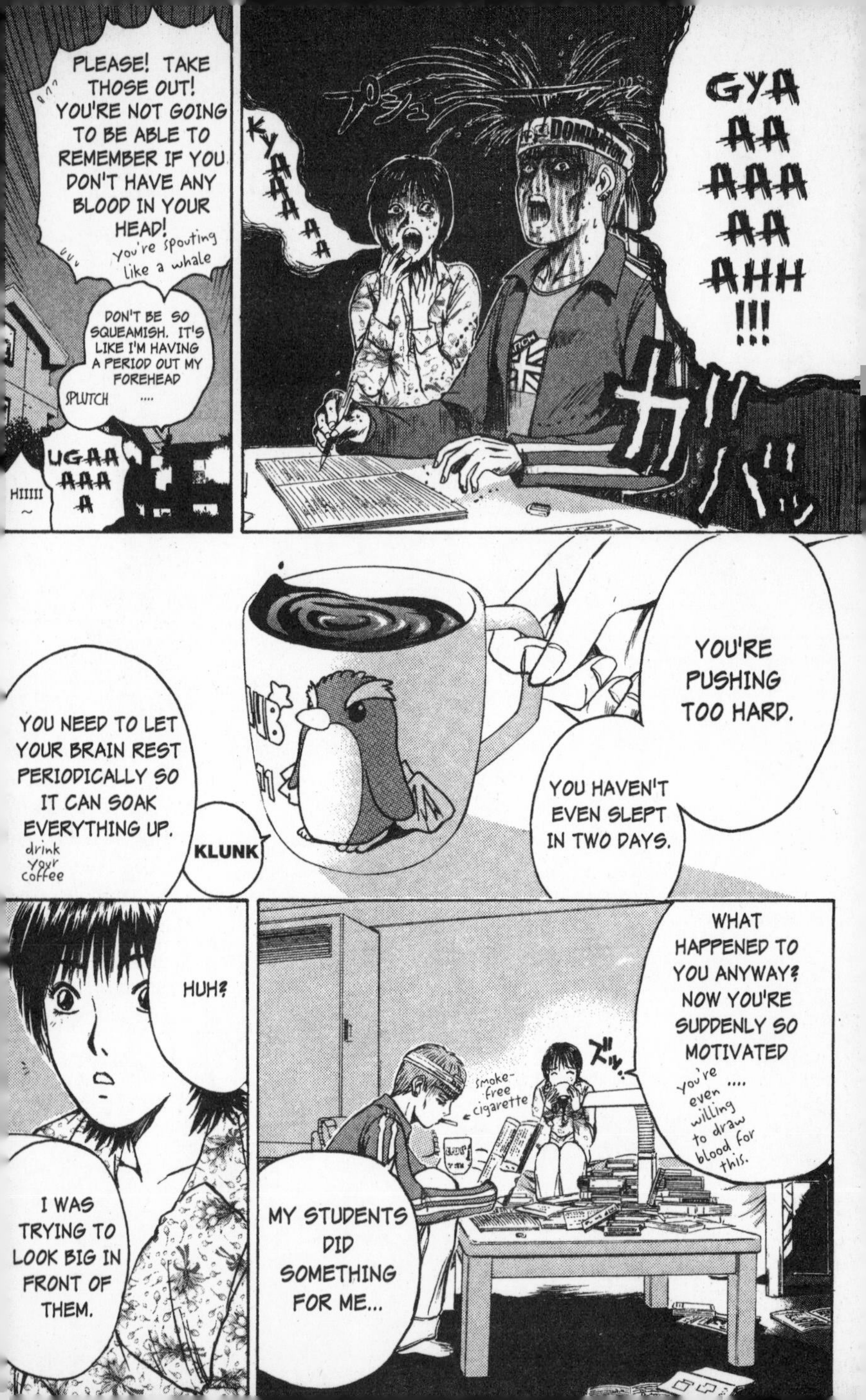
KYAAAAAA
GYAAAAAAAAAAAHH!!!
PLEASE! TAKE THOSE OUT! YOU'RE NOT GOING TO BE ABLE TO REMEMBER IF YOU DON'T HAVE ANY BLOOD IN YOUR HEAD!
you're spouting like a whale
DON'T BE SO SQUEAMISH. IT'S LIKE I'M HAVING A PERIOD OUT MY FOREHEAD ....
SPLUTCH
UGAAAAAA
HIIIII~
YOU'RE PUSHING TOO HARD.
YOU HAVEN'T EVEN SLEPT IN TWO DAYS.
KLUNK
YOU NEED TO LET YOUR BRAIN REST PERIODICALLY SO IT CAN SOAK EVERYTHING UP.
drink your coffee
WHAT HAPPENED TO YOU ANYWAY? NOW YOU'RE SUDDENLY SO MOTIVATED
you're even willing to draw blood for this. ....
smoke-free cigarette
MY STUDENTS DID SOMETHING FOR ME...
HUH?
I WAS TRYING TO LOOK BIG IN FRONT OF THEM.

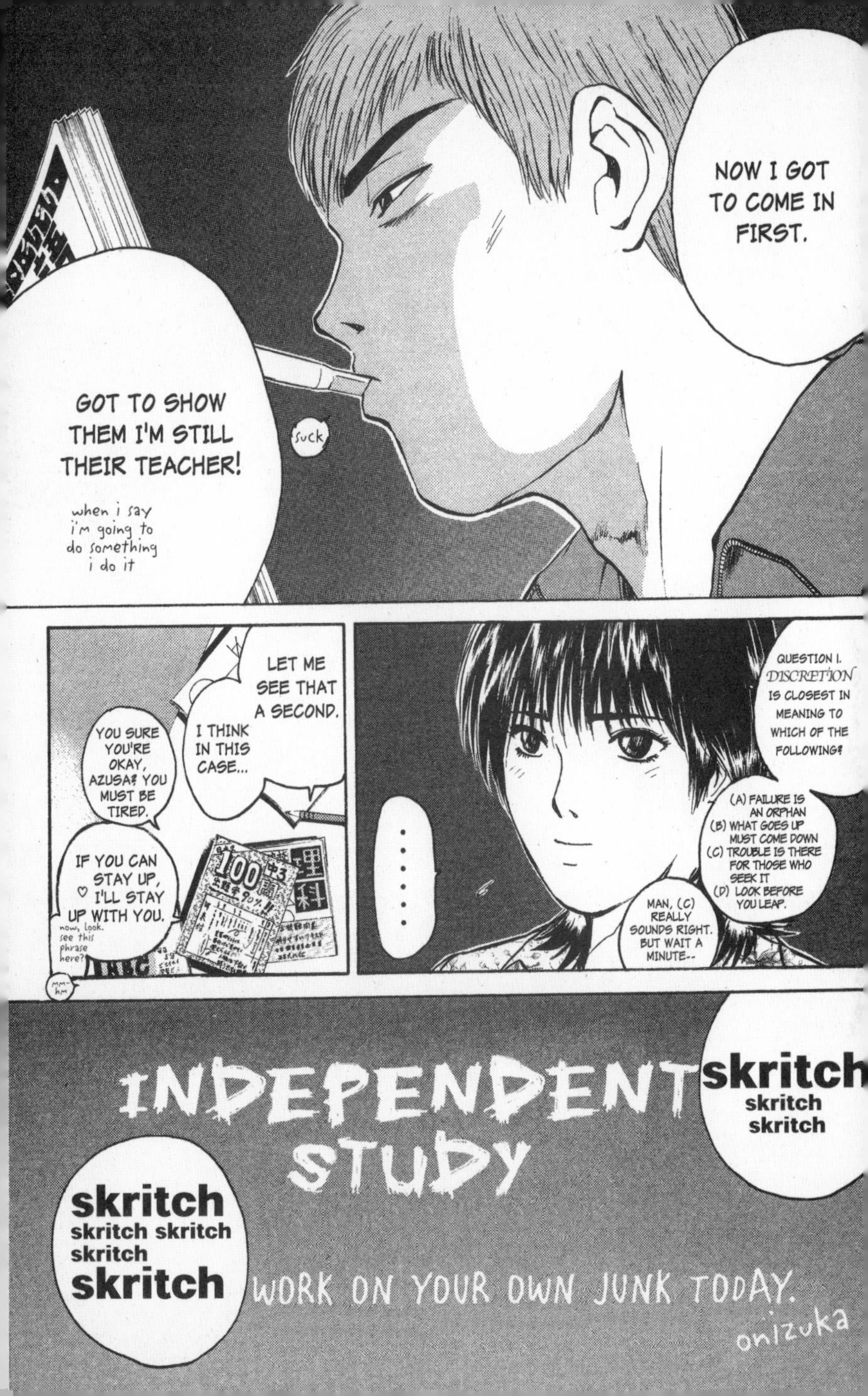
NOW I GOT TO COME IN FIRST.
GOT TO SHOW THEM I'M STILL THEIR TEACHER!
suck
when i say i'm going to do something i do it
QUESTION 1. DISCRETION IS CLOSEST IN MEANING TO WHICH OF THE FOLLOWING?
(A) FAILURE IS AN ORPHAN (B) WHAT GOES UP MUST COME DOWN (C) TROUBLE IS THERE FOR THOSE WHO SEEK IT (D) LOOK BEFORE YOU LEAP.
MAN, (C) REALLY SOUNDS RIGHT. BUT WAIT A MINUTE--
......
LET ME SEE THAT A SECOND.
I THINK IN THIS CASE...
YOU SURE YOU'RE OKAY, AZUSA? YOU MUST BE TIRED.
IF YOU CAN STAY UP, ♡ I'LL STAY UP WITH YOU.
now, look. see this phrase here?
mm-hm
skritch skritch skritch
INDEPENDENT STUDY
skritch skritch skritch skritch skritch
WORK ON YOUR OWN JUNK TODAY.
onizuka

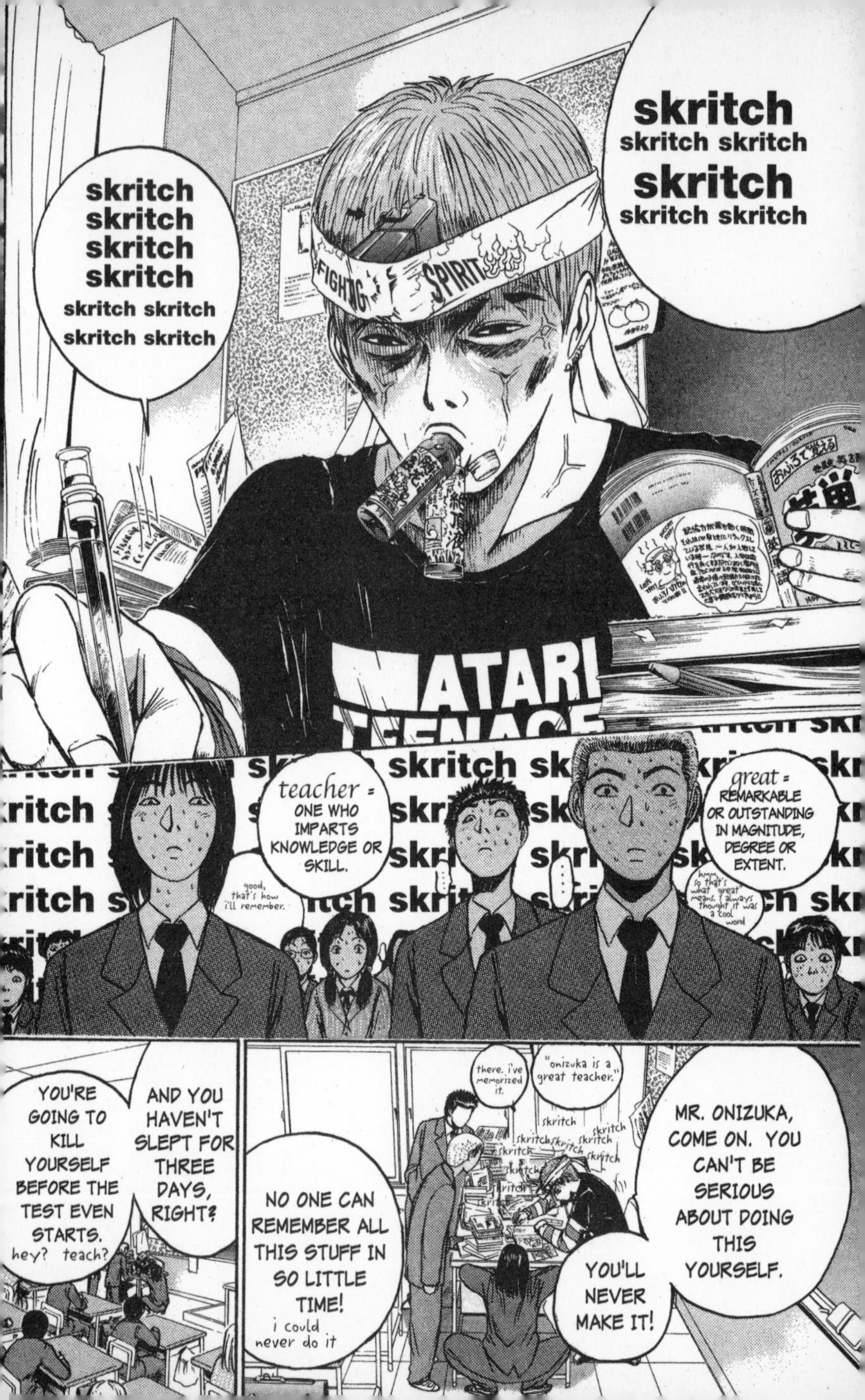
skritch skritch skritch skritch skritch skritch
skritch skritch skritch skritch skritch skritch skritch skritch
great = REMARKABLE OR OUTSTANDING IN MAGNITUDE, DEGREE OR EXTENT.
hmm, so that's what "great" means. i always thought it was a cool word
...
...
teacher = ONE WHO IMPARTS KNOWLEDGE OR SKILL.
good, that's how i'll remember.
MR. ONIZUKA, COME ON. YOU CAN'T BE SERIOUS ABOUT DOING THIS YOURSELF.
YOU'LL NEVER MAKE IT!
"onizuka is a great teacher."
there. i've memorized it.
skritch skritch skritch skritch skritch skritch skritch skritch skritch skritch
NO ONE CAN REMEMBER ALL THIS STUFF IN SO LITTLE TIME!
i could never do it
AND YOU HAVEN'T SLEPT FOR THREE DAYS, RIGHT?
YOU'RE GOING TO KILL YOURSELF BEFORE THE TEST EVEN STARTS.
hey? teach?

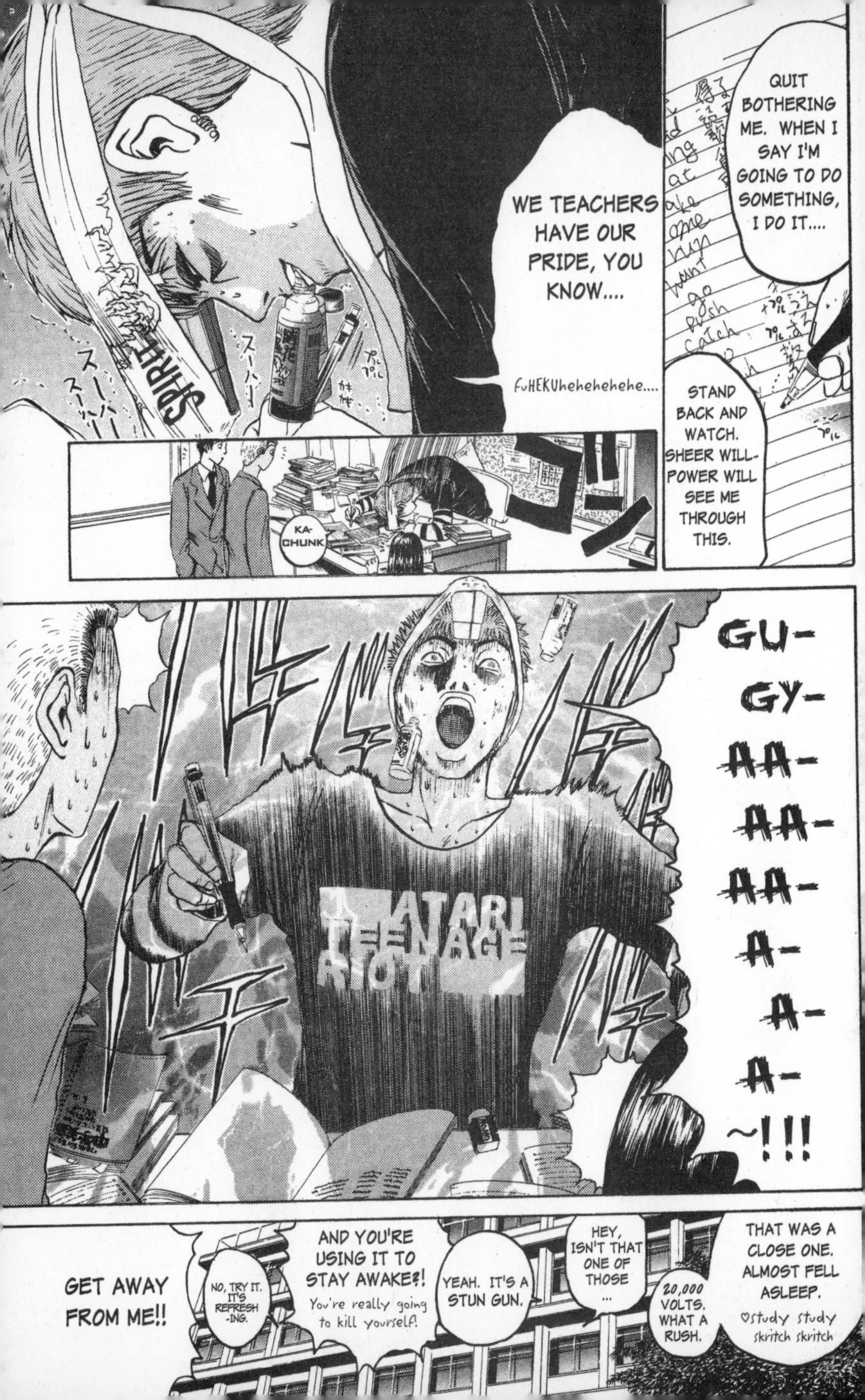
QUIT BOTHERING ME. WHEN I SAY I'M GOING TO DO SOMETHING, I DO IT....
STAND BACK AND WATCH. SHEER WILL-POWER WILL SEE ME THROUGH THIS.
WE TEACHERS HAVE OUR PRIDE, YOU KNOW....
FuHEKUhehehehehe....
SPIRIT
KA-CHUNK
GU-GY-AA-AA-AA-A-A-A-~!!!
THAT WAS A CLOSE ONE. ALMOST FELL ASLEEP.
♡study study skritch skritch
20,000 VOLTS. WHAT A RUSH.
HEY, ISN'T THAT ONE OF THOSE ...
YEAH. IT'S A STUN GUN.
AND YOU'RE USING IT TO STAY AWAKE?!
You're really going to kill yourself
NO, TRY IT. IT'S REFRESH-ING.
GET AWAY FROM ME!!

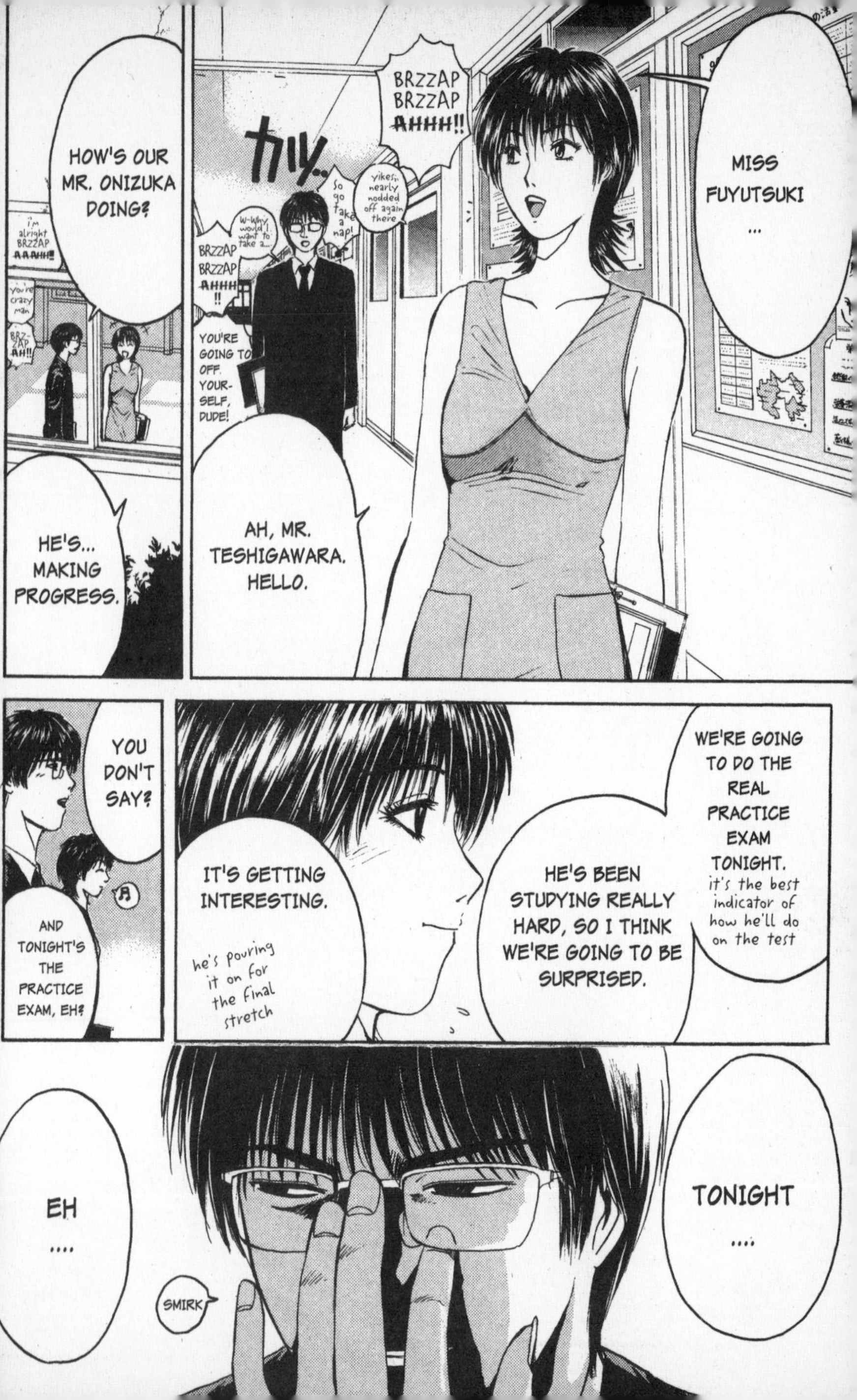
MISS FUYUTSUKI ...
AH, MR. TESHIGAWARA. HELLO.
BRZZAP BRZZAP AHHH!!
yikes, nearly nodded off again there
So go take a nap!
W-Why would I want to take a...
BRZZAP BRZZAP AHHH!!
YOU'RE GOING TO OFF. YOURSELF, DUDE!
HOW'S OUR MR. ONIZUKA DOING?
i'm alright BRZZAP AHHH!!
you're crazy man
BRZ-ZAP AH!!
HE'S... MAKING PROGRESS.
WE'RE GOING TO DO THE REAL PRACTICE EXAM TONIGHT.
it's the best indicator of how he'll do on the test
HE'S BEEN STUDYING REALLY HARD, SO I THINK WE'RE GOING TO BE SURPRISED.
IT'S GETTING INTERESTING.
he's pouring it on for the final stretch
YOU DON'T SAY?
AND TONIGHT'S THE PRACTICE EXAM, EH?
TONIGHT ....
SMIRK
EH ....

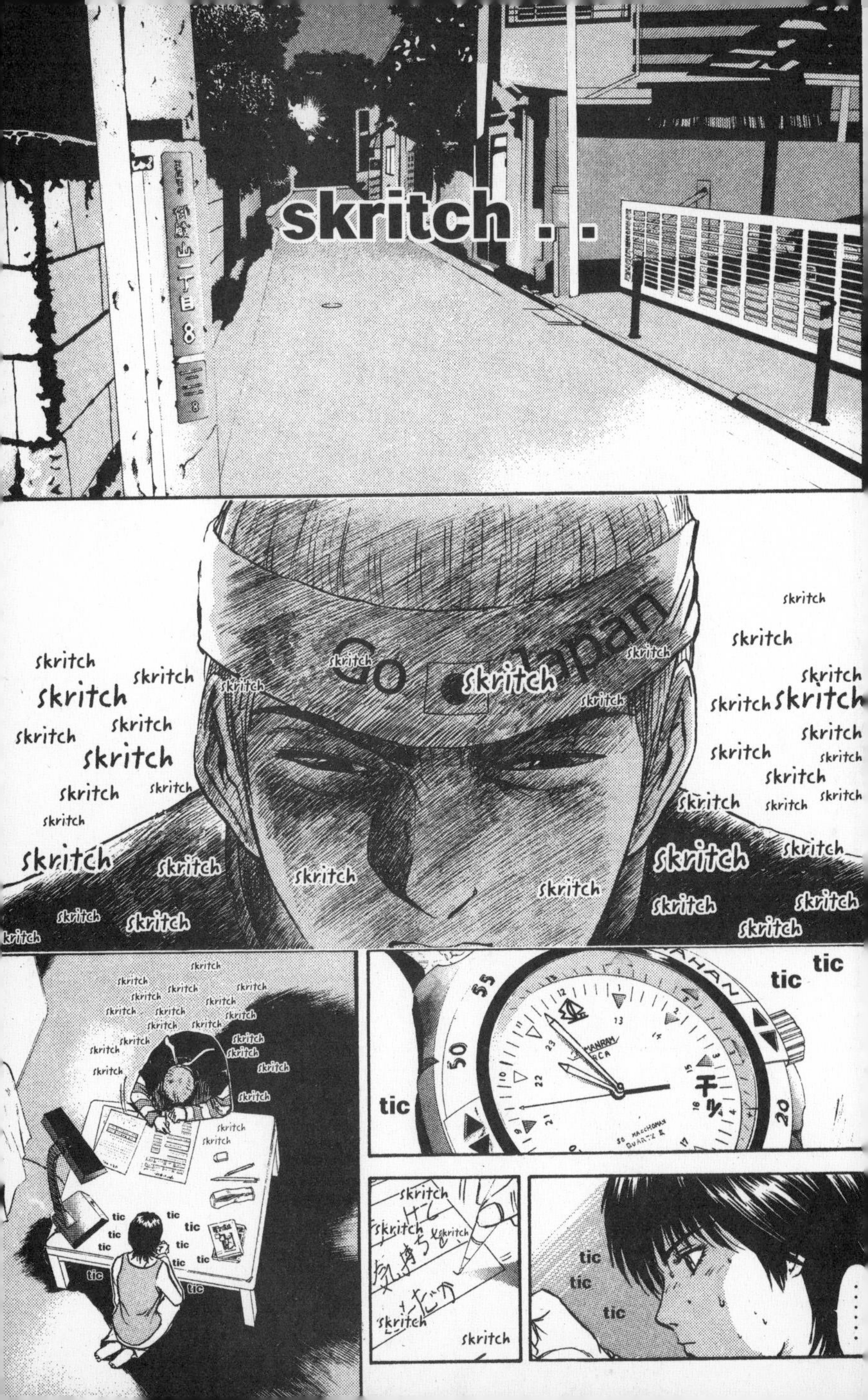
skritch . . .
Go Japan
skritch skritch skritch skritch skritch skritch skritch
tic tic tic
skritch skritch skritch
tic tic tic tic
tic tic tic
skritch skritch skritch skritch

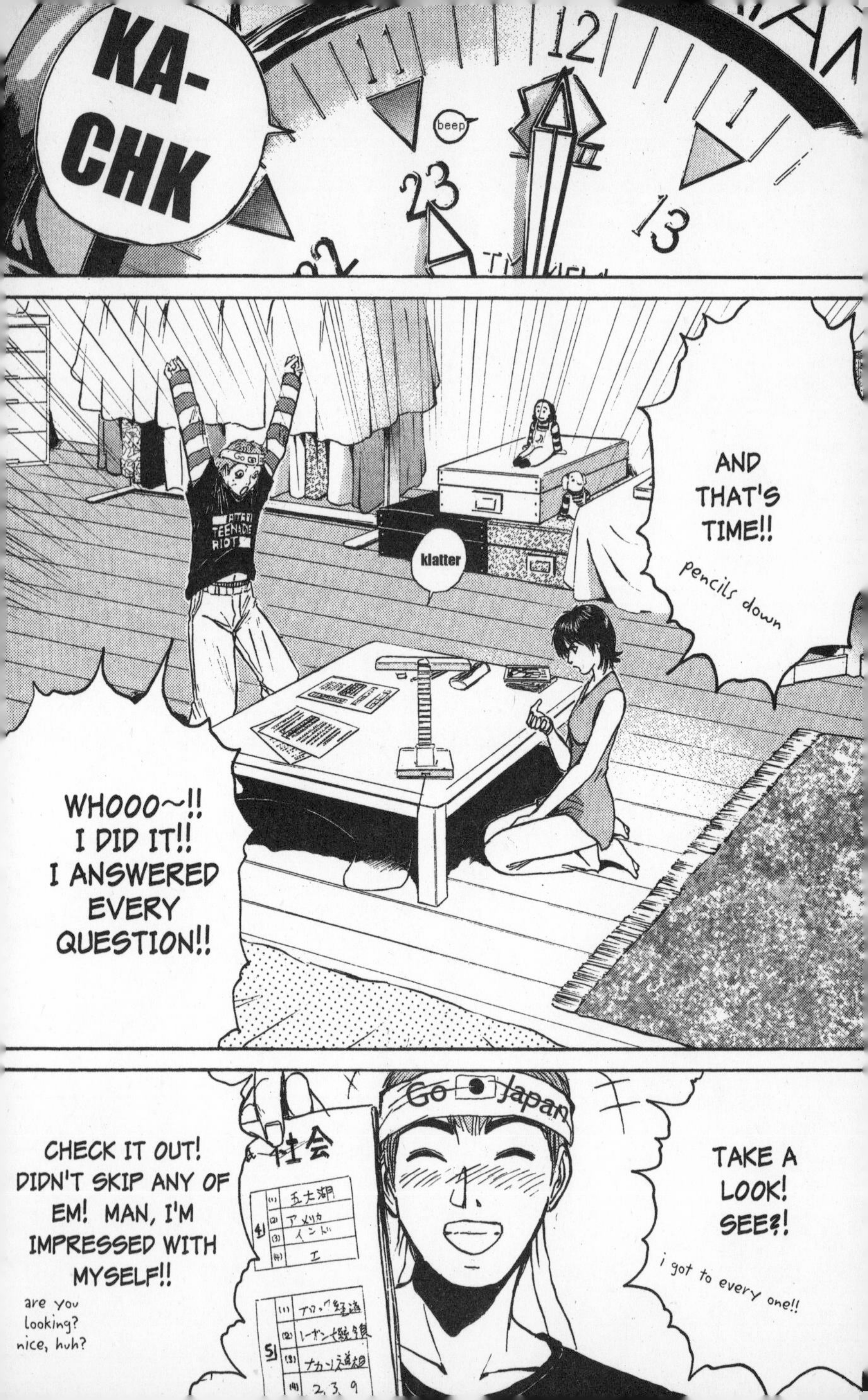
KA-CHK
beep
AND THAT'S TIME!!
pencils down
klatter
WHOOO~!! I DID IT!! I ANSWERED EVERY QUESTION!!
Go Japan
TAKE A LOOK! SEE?!
i got to every one!!
社会
CHECK IT OUT! DIDN'T SKIP ANY OF EM! MAN, I'M IMPRESSED WITH MYSELF!!
are you looking? nice, huh?

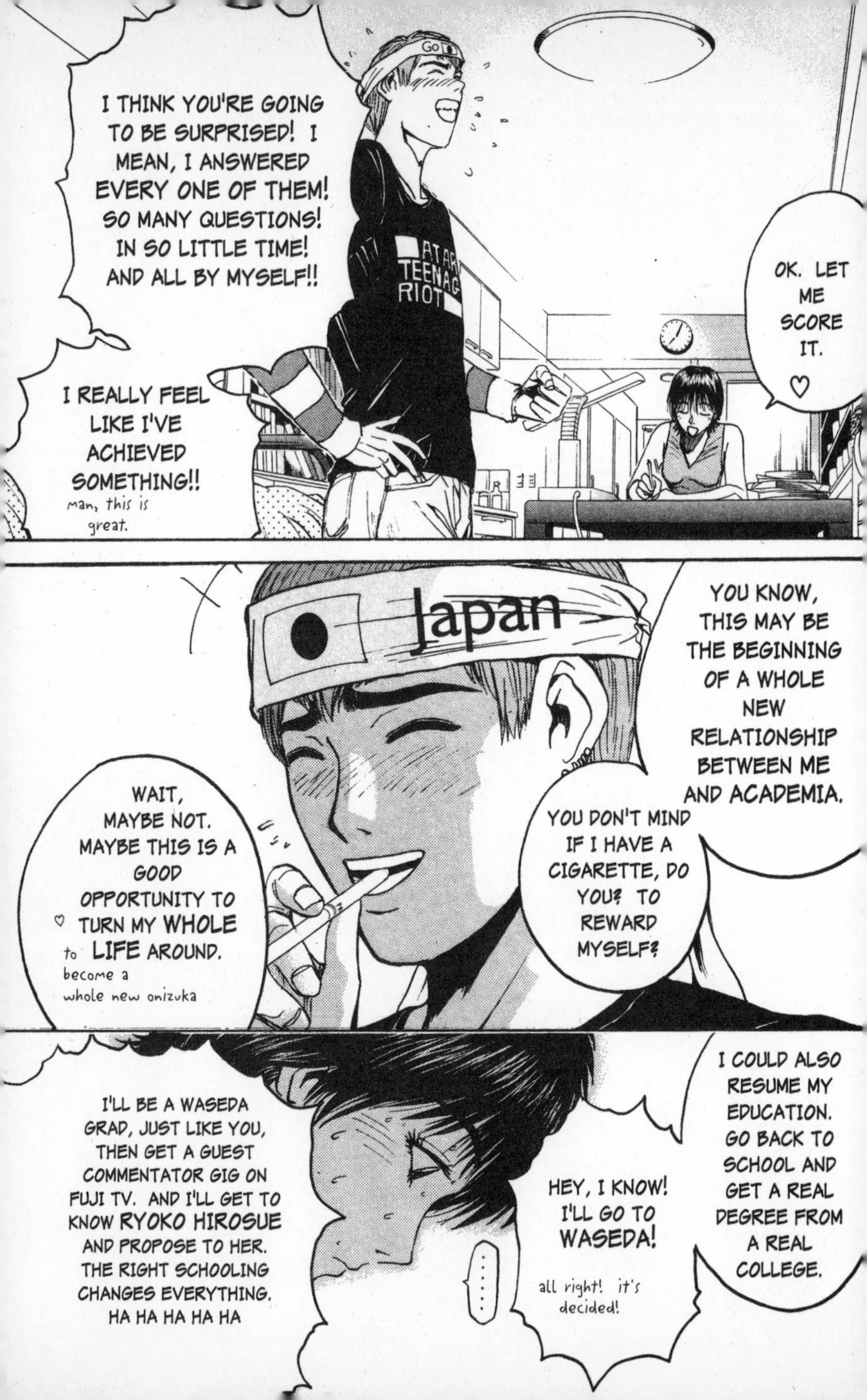
I THINK YOU'RE GOING TO BE SURPRISED! I MEAN, I ANSWERED EVERY ONE OF THEM! SO MANY QUESTIONS! IN SO LITTLE TIME! AND ALL BY MYSELF!!
I REALLY FEEL LIKE I'VE ACHIEVED SOMETHING!!
man, this is great.
OK. LET ME SCORE IT. ♡
YOU KNOW, THIS MAY BE THE BEGINNING OF A WHOLE NEW RELATIONSHIP BETWEEN ME AND ACADEMIA.
YOU DON'T MIND IF I HAVE A CIGARETTE, DO YOU? TO REWARD MYSELF?
WAIT, MAYBE NOT. MAYBE THIS IS A GOOD OPPORTUNITY TO TURN MY WHOLE LIFE AROUND. ♡
to become a whole new onizuka
I COULD ALSO RESUME MY EDUCATION. GO BACK TO SCHOOL AND GET A REAL DEGREE FROM A REAL COLLEGE.
HEY, I KNOW! I'LL GO TO WASEDA!
all right! it's decided!
......
I'LL BE A WASEDA GRAD, JUST LIKE YOU, THEN GET A GUEST COMMENTATOR GIG ON FUJI TV. AND I'LL GET TO KNOW RYOKO HIROSUE AND PROPOSE TO HER. THE RIGHT SCHOOLING CHANGES EVERYTHING. HA HA HA HA HA

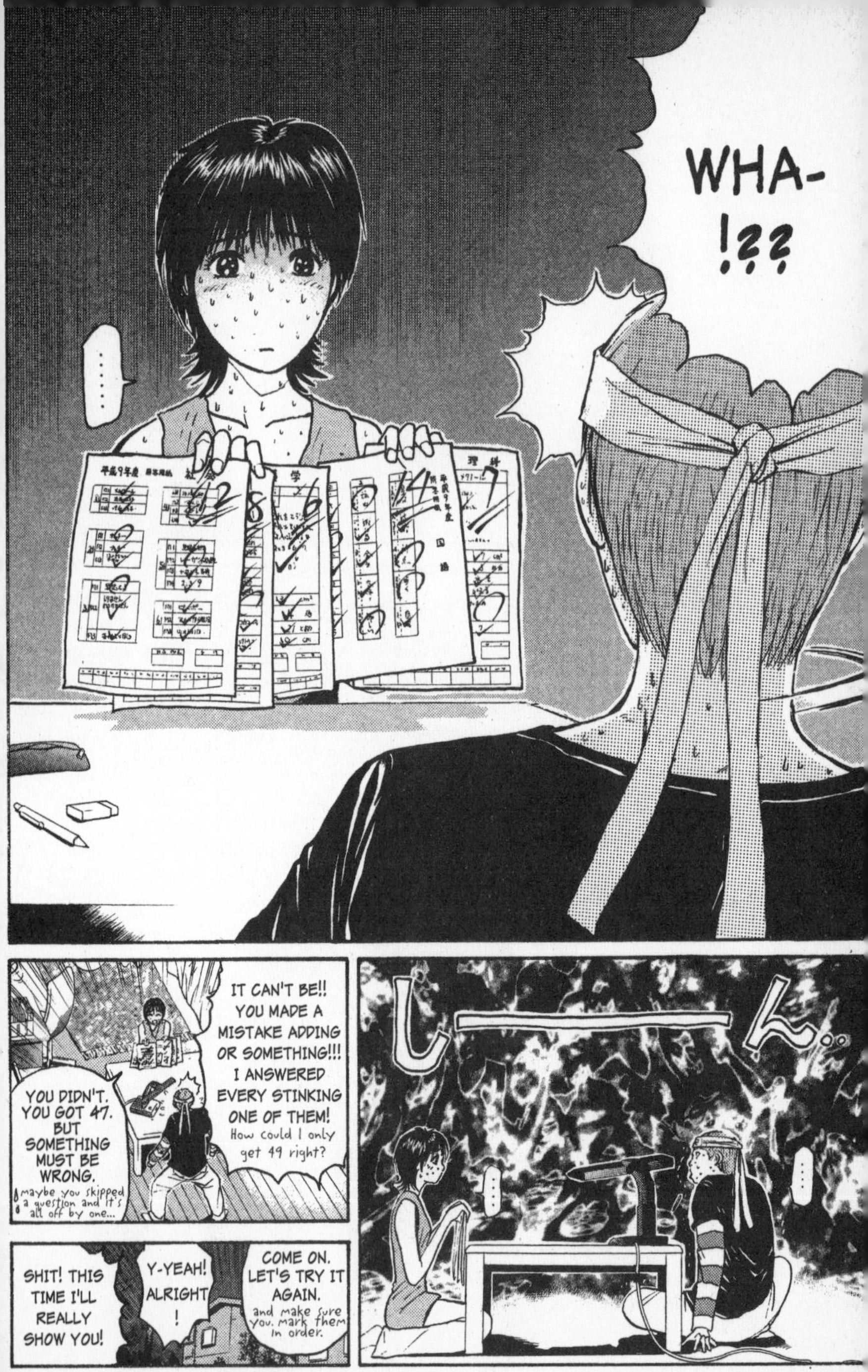

WHA-!???
......
し―――ん..
...
...
IT CAN'T BE!! YOU MADE A MISTAKE ADDING OR SOMETHING!!! I ANSWERED EVERY STINKING ONE OF THEM! How could I only get 49 right?
YOU DIDN'T. YOU GOT 47. BUT SOMETHING MUST BE WRONG. maybe you skipped a question and it's all off by one...
COME ON. LET'S TRY IT AGAIN. and make sure you mark them in order.
Y-YEAH! ALRIGHT!
SHIT! THIS TIME I'LL REALLY SHOW YOU!

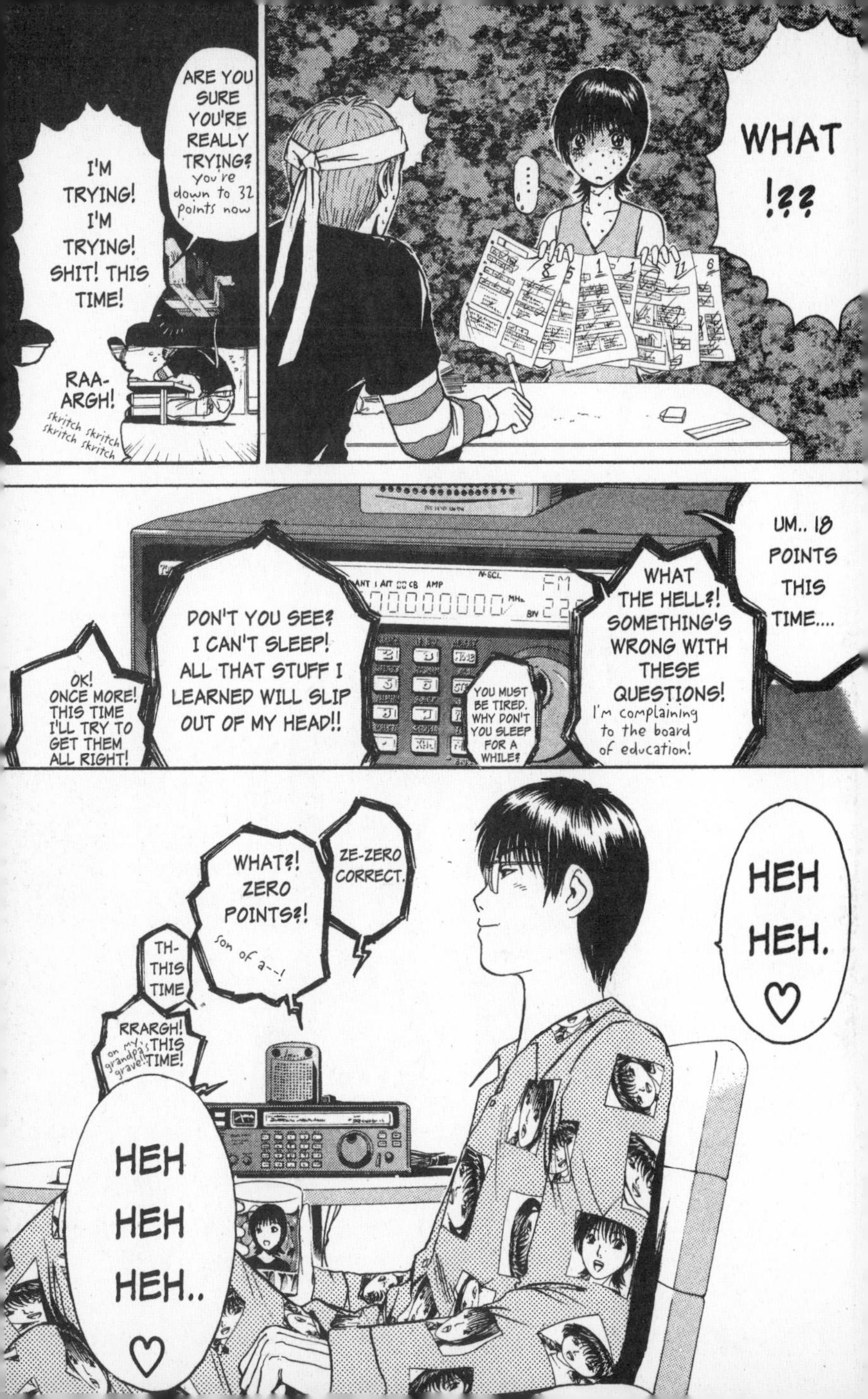
WHAT !??
ARE YOU SURE YOU'RE REALLY TRYING? you're down to 32 points now
I'M TRYING! I'M TRYING! SHIT! THIS TIME!
RAA-ARGH!
skritch skritch skritch skritch
UM.. 18 POINTS THIS TIME....
WHAT THE HELL?! SOMETHING'S WRONG WITH THESE QUESTIONS! I'm complaining to the board of education!
YOU MUST BE TIRED. WHY DON'T YOU SLEEP FOR A WHILE?
DON'T YOU SEE? I CAN'T SLEEP! ALL THAT STUFF I LEARNED WILL SLIP OUT OF MY HEAD!!
OK! ONCE MORE! THIS TIME I'LL TRY TO GET THEM ALL RIGHT!
HEH HEH. ♡
ZE-ZERO CORRECT.
WHAT?! ZERO POINTS?! son of a--!
TH- THIS TIME
RRARGH! THIS TIME! on my grandpa's grave!
HEH HEH HEH.. ♡

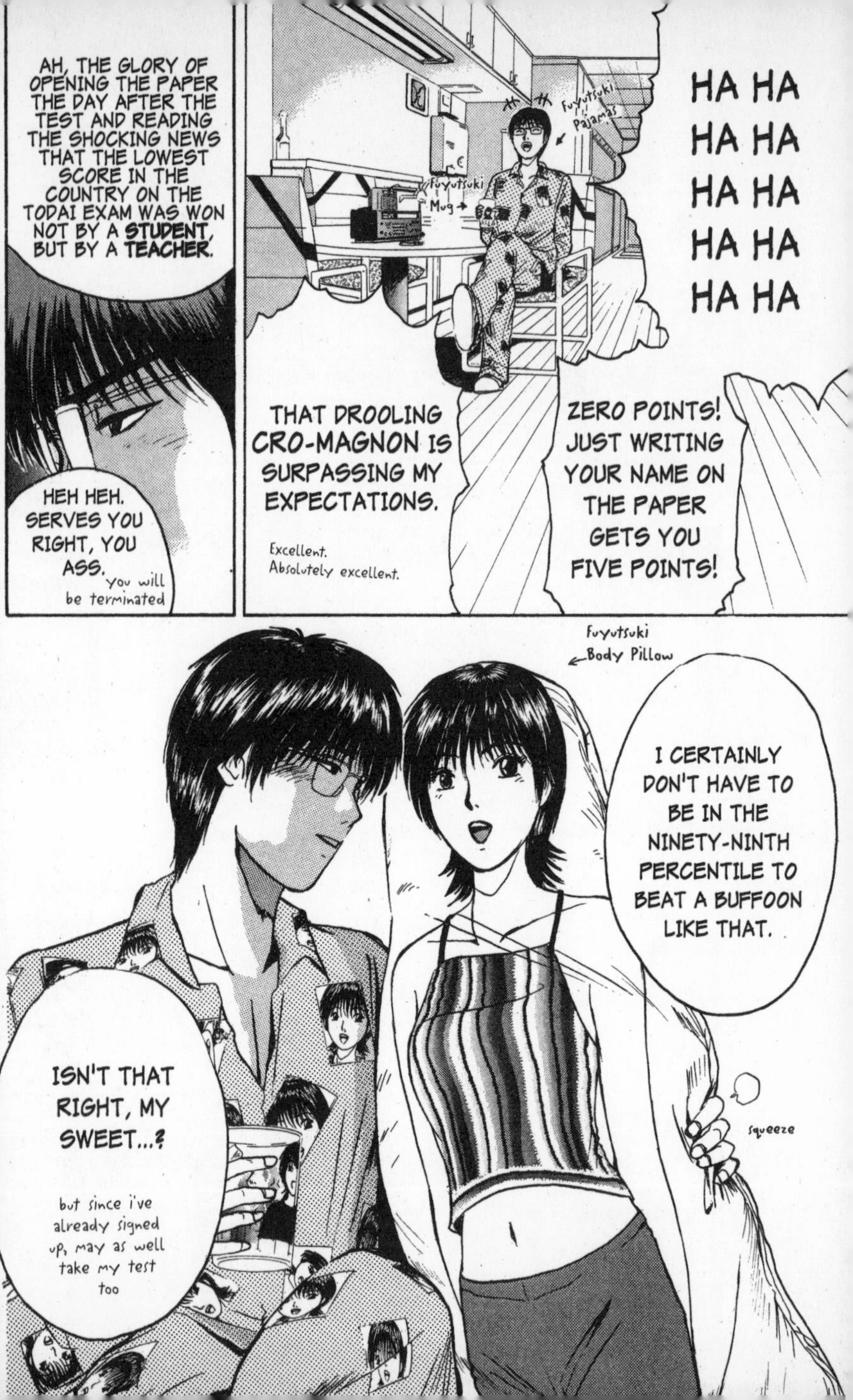
HA HA HA HA HA HA HA HA HA HA
Fuyutsuki Pajamas
Fuyutsuki Mug
ZERO POINTS! JUST WRITING YOUR NAME ON THE PAPER GETS YOU FIVE POINTS!
THAT DROOLING CRO-MAGNON IS SURPASSING MY EXPECTATIONS.
Excellent. Absolutely excellent.
AH, THE GLORY OF OPENING THE PAPER THE DAY AFTER THE TEST AND READING THE SHOCKING NEWS THAT THE LOWEST SCORE IN THE COUNTRY ON THE TODAI EXAM WAS WON NOT BY A **STUDENT**, BUT BY A **TEACHER**.
HEH HEH. SERVES YOU RIGHT, YOU ASS.
you will be terminated
Fuyutsuki Body Pillow
I CERTAINLY DON'T HAVE TO BE IN THE NINETY-NINTH PERCENTILE TO BEAT A BUFFOON LIKE THAT.
squeeze
ISN'T THAT RIGHT, MY SWEET...?
but since i've already signed up, may as well take my test too

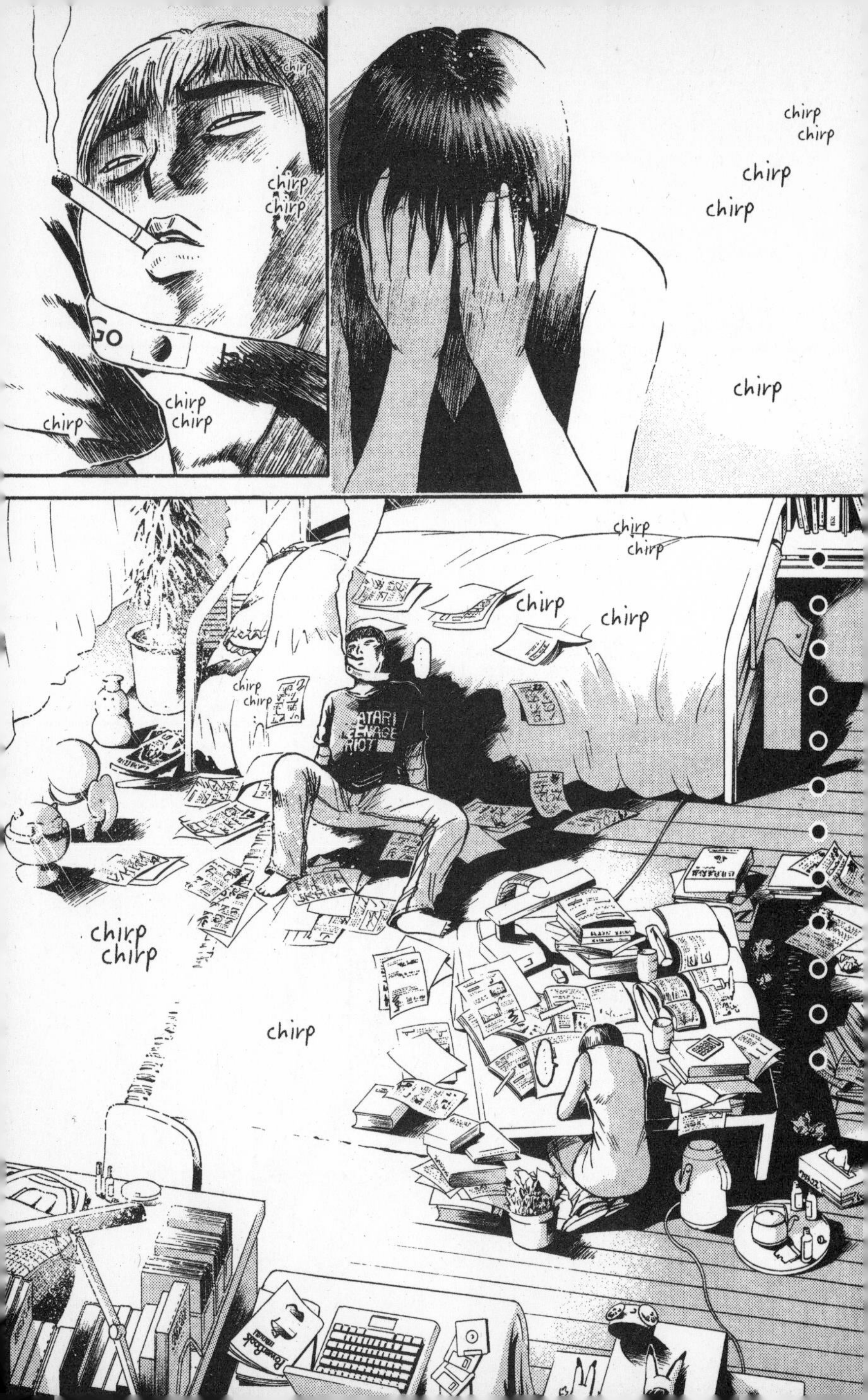
chirp
chirp
chirp
chirp
chirp
chirp
chirp
chirp
GO
chirp
chirp
chirp
chirp
chirp
chirp
chirp
chirp
chirp
ATARI
RIOT
chirp
chirp
chirp
PowerBook

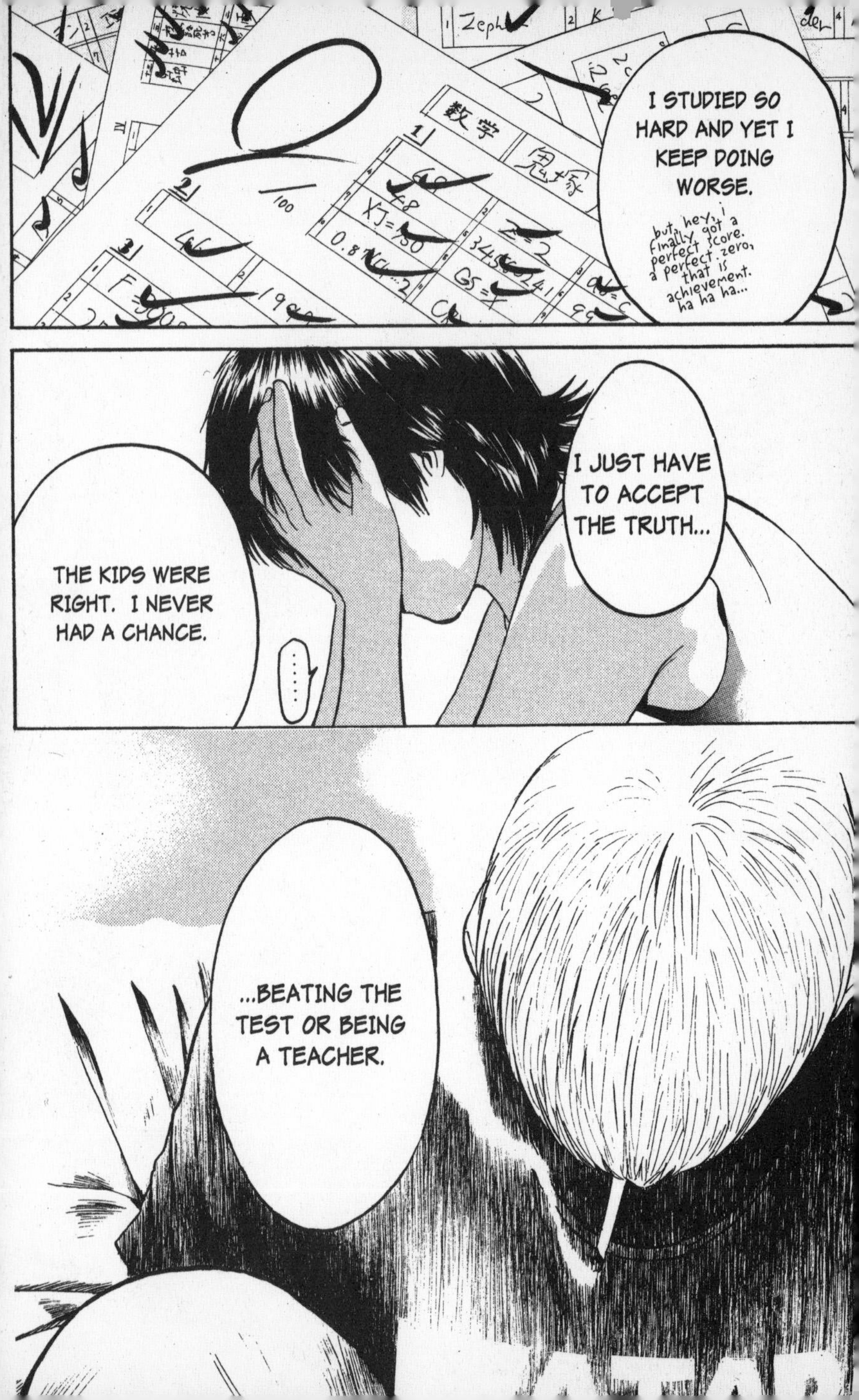
I STUDIED SO HARD AND YET I KEEP DOING WORSE.
but, hey, I finally got a perfect score. a perfect zero, that is achievement. ha ha ha...
I JUST HAVE TO ACCEPT THE TRUTH...
THE KIDS WERE RIGHT. I NEVER HAD A CHANCE.
......
...BEATING THE TEST OR BEING A TEACHER.

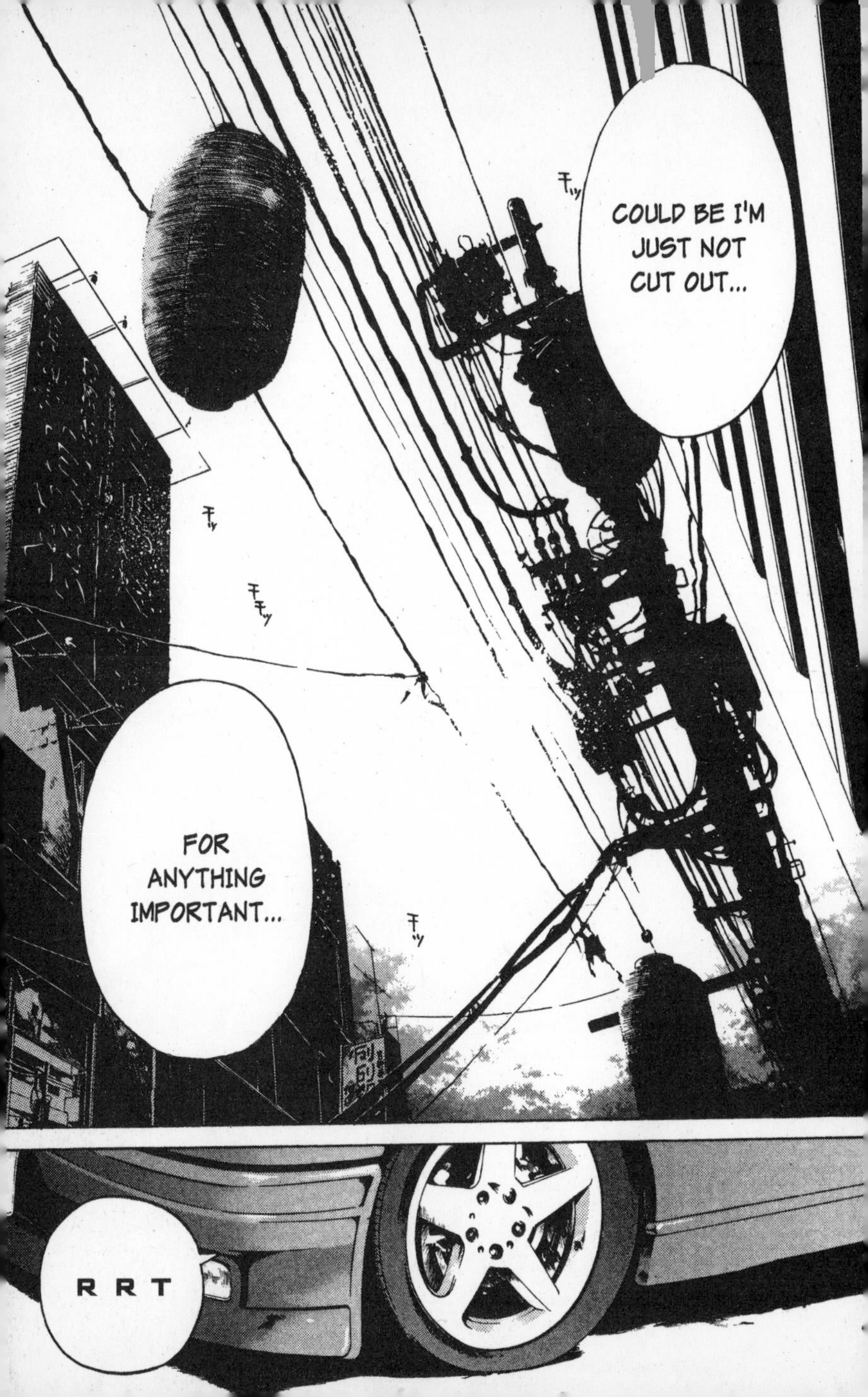
COULD BE I'M JUST NOT CUT OUT...
FOR ANYTHING IMPORTANT...
R R T

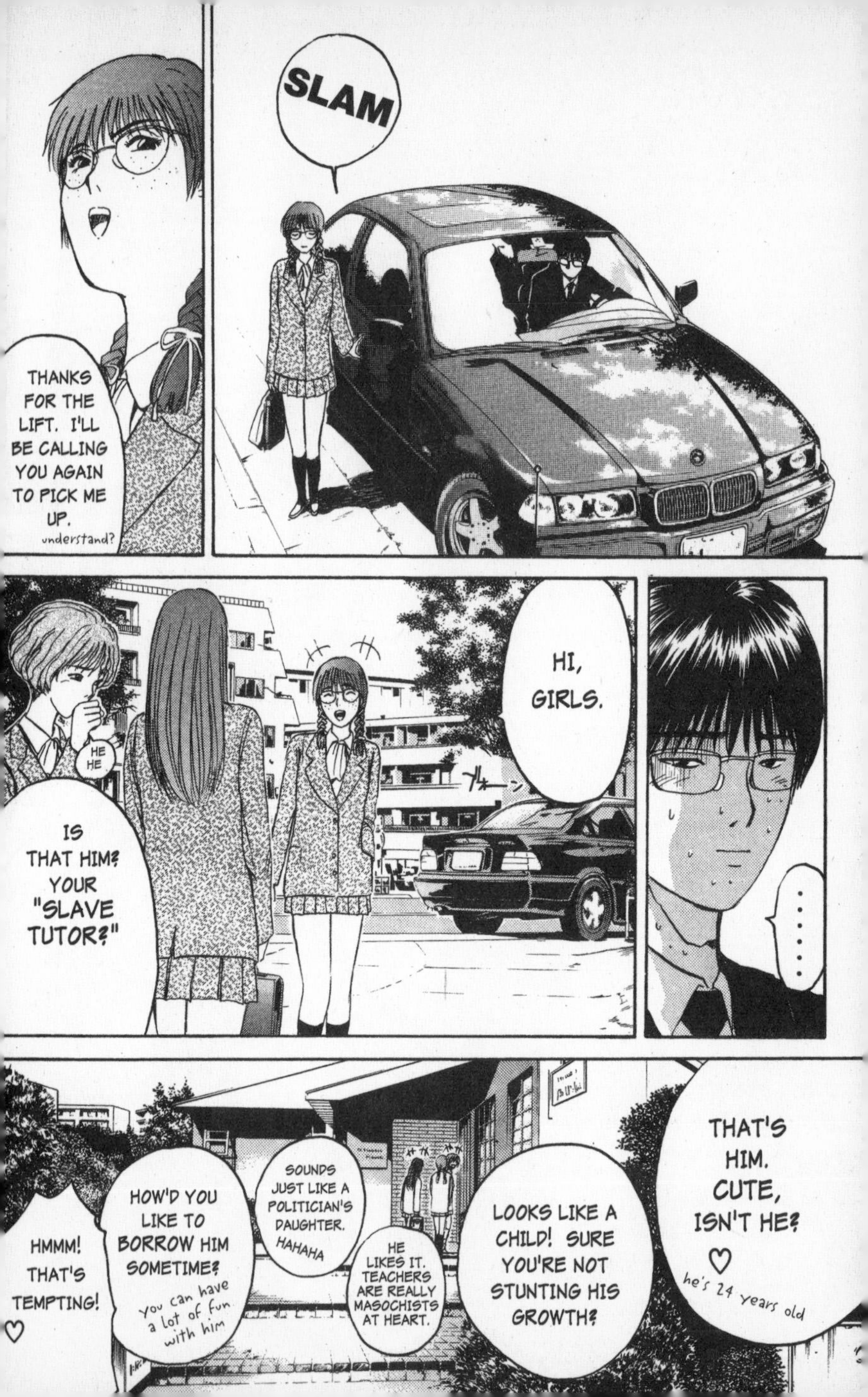
SLAM
THANKS FOR THE LIFT. I'LL BE CALLING YOU AGAIN TO PICK ME UP.
understand?
......
HI, GIRLS.
HE HE
IS THAT HIM? YOUR "SLAVE TUTOR?"
THAT'S HIM. CUTE, ISN'T HE? ♡
he's 24 years old
LOOKS LIKE A CHILD! SURE YOU'RE NOT STUNTING HIS GROWTH?
HE LIKES IT. TEACHERS ARE REALLY MASOCHISTS AT HEART.
SOUNDS JUST LIKE A POLITICIAN'S DAUGHTER.
HAHAHA
HOW'D YOU LIKE TO BORROW HIM SOMETIME?
You can have a lot of fun with him
HMMM! THAT'S TEMPTING! ♡

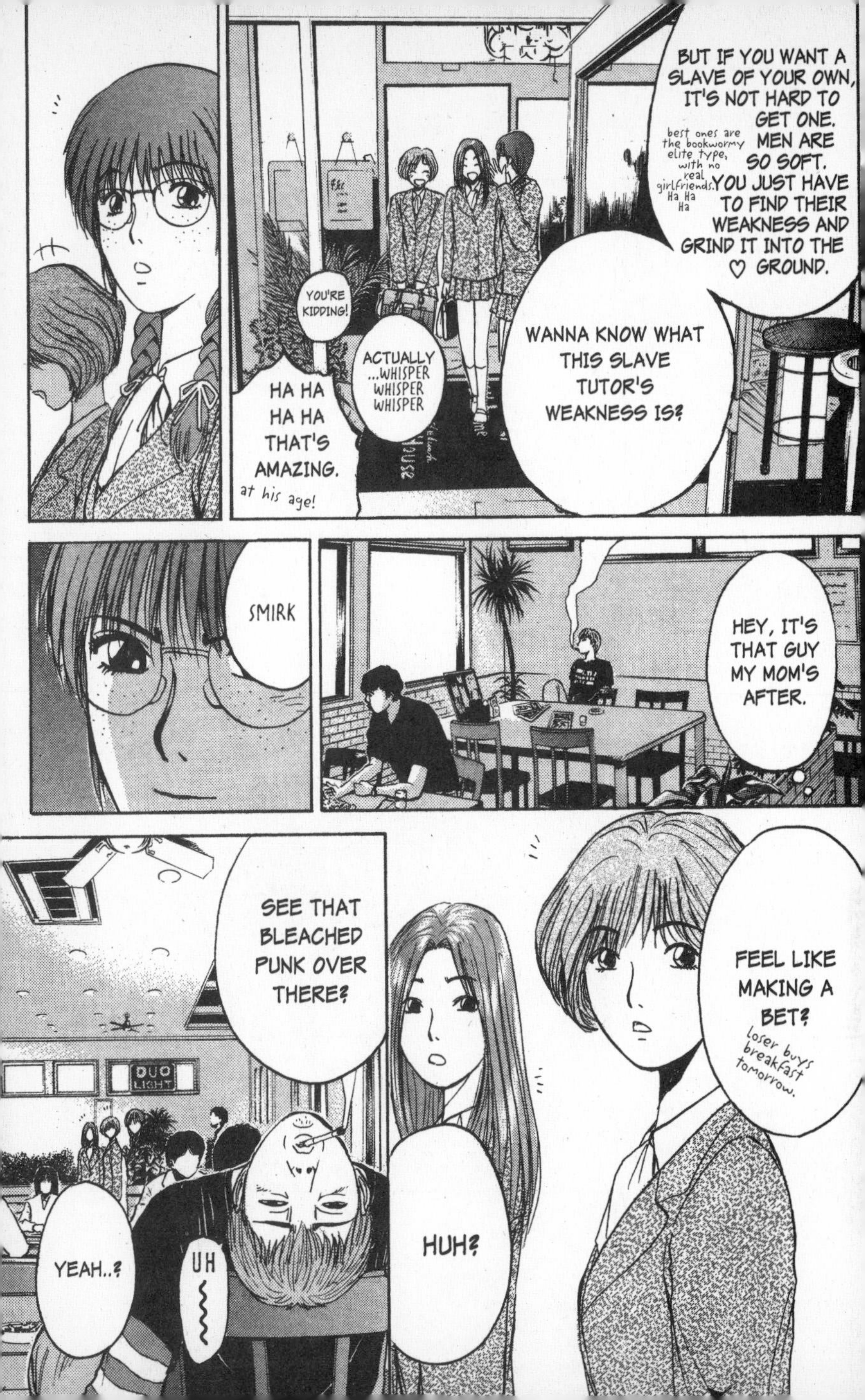
BUT IF YOU WANT A SLAVE OF YOUR OWN, IT'S NOT HARD TO GET ONE. MEN ARE SO SOFT. YOU JUST HAVE TO FIND THEIR WEAKNESS AND GRIND IT INTO THE ♡ GROUND.
best ones are the bookwormy elite type, with no real girlfriends. Ha Ha Ha
WANNA KNOW WHAT THIS SLAVE TUTOR'S WEAKNESS IS?
ACTUALLY ...WHISPER WHISPER WHISPER
YOU'RE KIDDING!
HA HA HA HA THAT'S AMAZING.
at his age!
HEY, IT'S THAT GUY MY MOM'S AFTER.
SMIRK
FEEL LIKE MAKING A BET?
loser buys breakfast tomorrow.
SEE THAT BLEACHED PUNK OVER THERE?
HUH?
UH~
YEAH..?

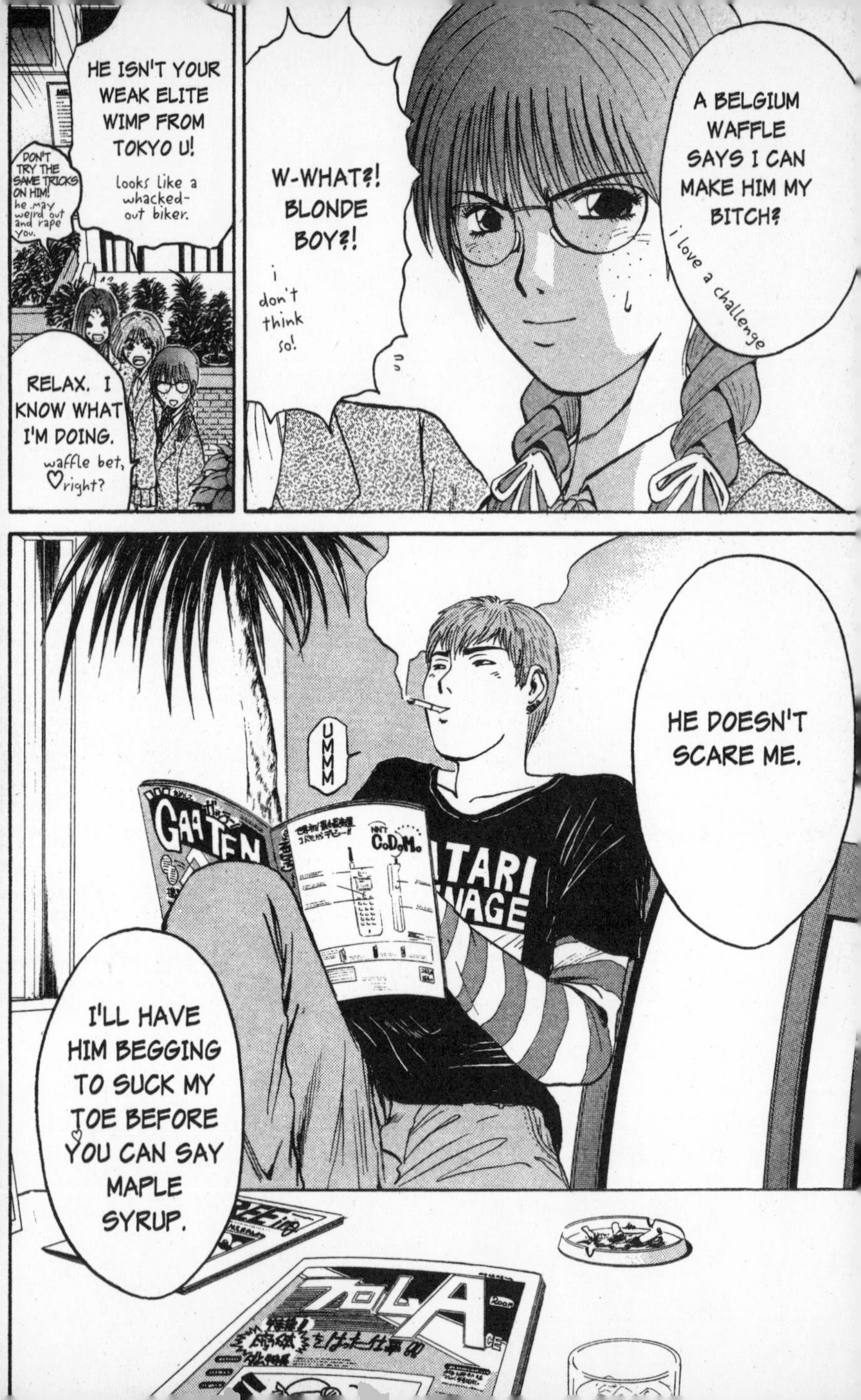
A BELGIUM WAFFLE SAYS I CAN MAKE HIM MY BITCH?
i love a challenge
W-WHAT?! BLONDE BOY?!
i don't think so!
HE ISN'T YOUR WEAK ELITE WIMP FROM TOKYO U!
looks like a whacked-out biker.
DON'T TRY THE SAME TRICKS ON HIM! he may weird out and rape you.
RELAX. I KNOW WHAT I'M DOING.
waffle bet, ♡right?
HE DOESN'T SCARE ME.
UMMM
I'LL HAVE HIM BEGGING TO SUCK MY TOE BEFORE ♡YOU CAN SAY MAPLE SYRUP.

Lesson47 Lick Me ♡

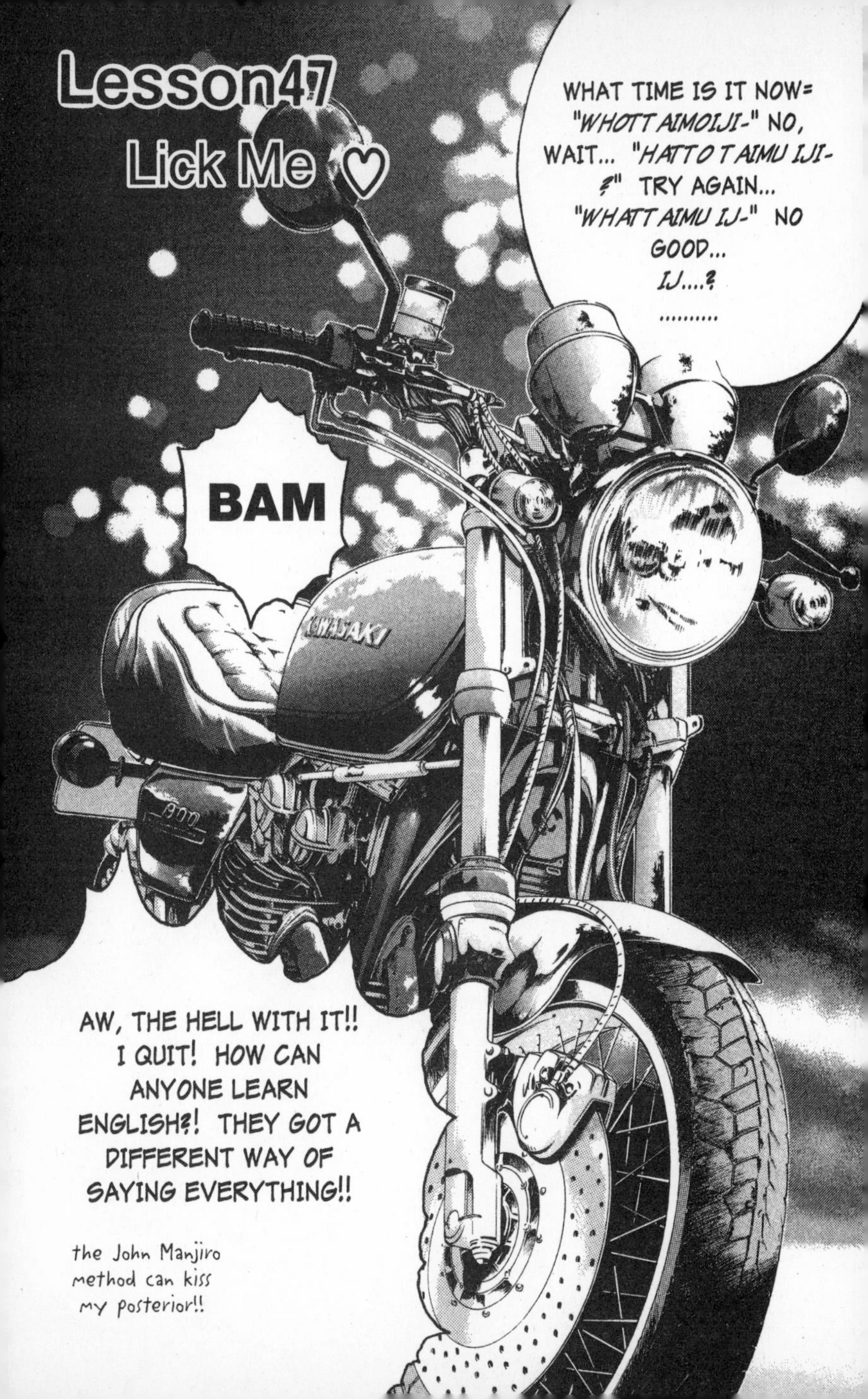
WHAT TIME IS IT NOW= "WHOTT AIMOIJI-" NO, WAIT... "HATTO T AIMU IJI-?" TRY AGAIN... "WHATT AIMU IJ-" NO GOOD... IJ....? ....
BAM
AW, THE HELL WITH IT!! I QUIT! HOW CAN ANYONE LEARN ENGLISH?! THEY GOT A DIFFERENT WAY OF SAYING EVERYTHING!!
the John Manjiro method can kiss my posterior!!

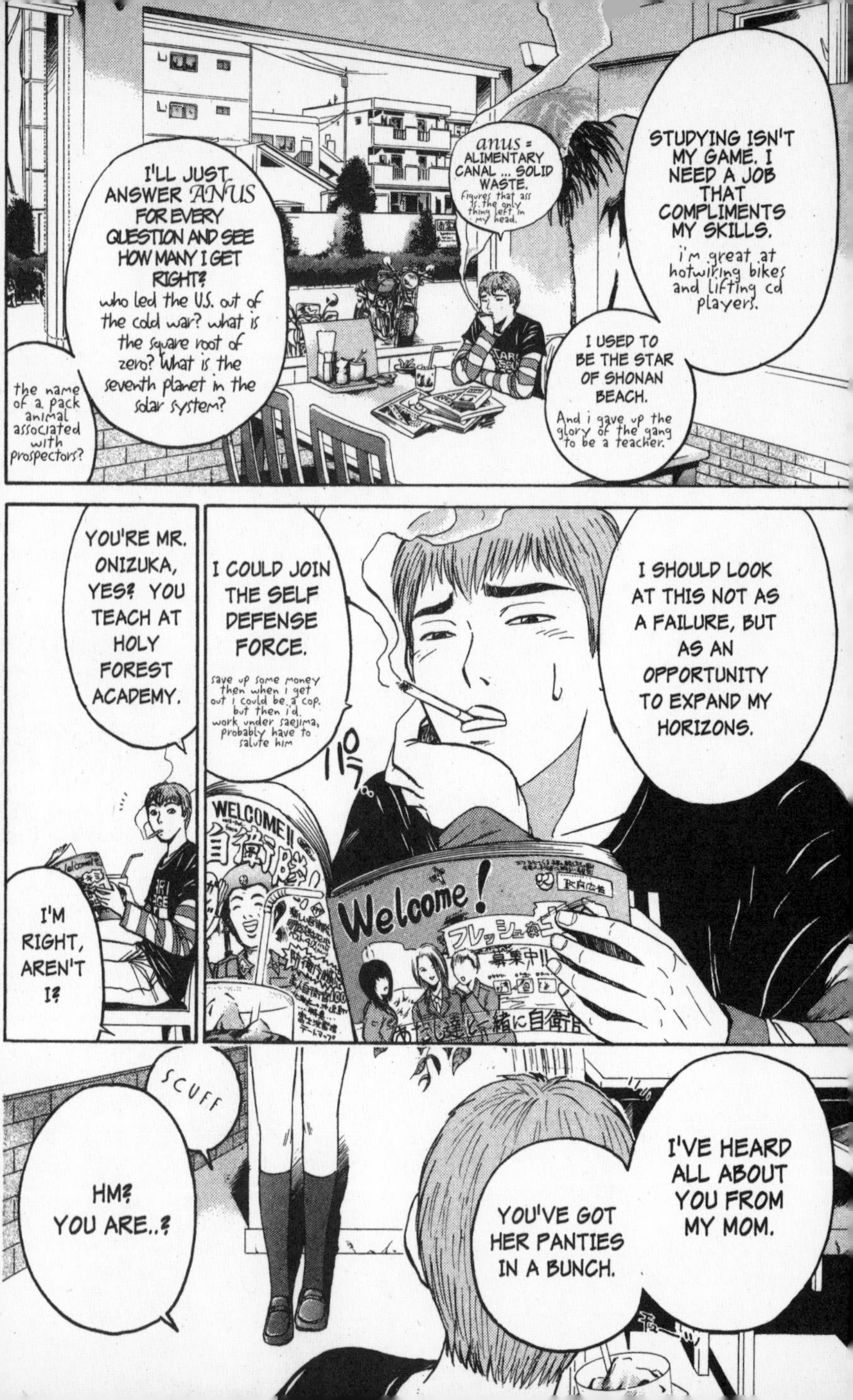
STUDYING ISN'T MY GAME. I NEED A JOB THAT COMPLIMENTS MY SKILLS.
i'm great at hotwiring bikes and lifting cd players.
I USED TO BE THE STAR OF SHONAN BEACH.
And i gave up the glory of the gang to be a teacher.
anus = ALIMENTARY CANAL ... SOLID WASTE.
Figures that ass is the only thing left in my head.
I'LL JUST ANSWER ANUS FOR EVERY QUESTION AND SEE HOW MANY I GET RIGHT?
who led the U.S. out of the cold war? what is the square root of zero? What is the seventh planet in the solar system?
the name of a pack animal associated with prospectors?
I SHOULD LOOK AT THIS NOT AS A FAILURE, BUT AS AN OPPORTUNITY TO EXPAND MY HORIZONS.
I COULD JOIN THE SELF DEFENSE FORCE.
save up some money then when i get out i could be a cop. but then i'd work under saejima, probably have to salute him
Welcome!
WELCOME!!
YOU'RE MR. ONIZUKA, YES? YOU TEACH AT HOLY FOREST ACADEMY.
I'M RIGHT, AREN'T I?
I'VE HEARD ALL ABOUT YOU FROM MY MOM.
YOU'VE GOT HER PANTIES IN A BUNCH.
SCUFF
HM? YOU ARE..?

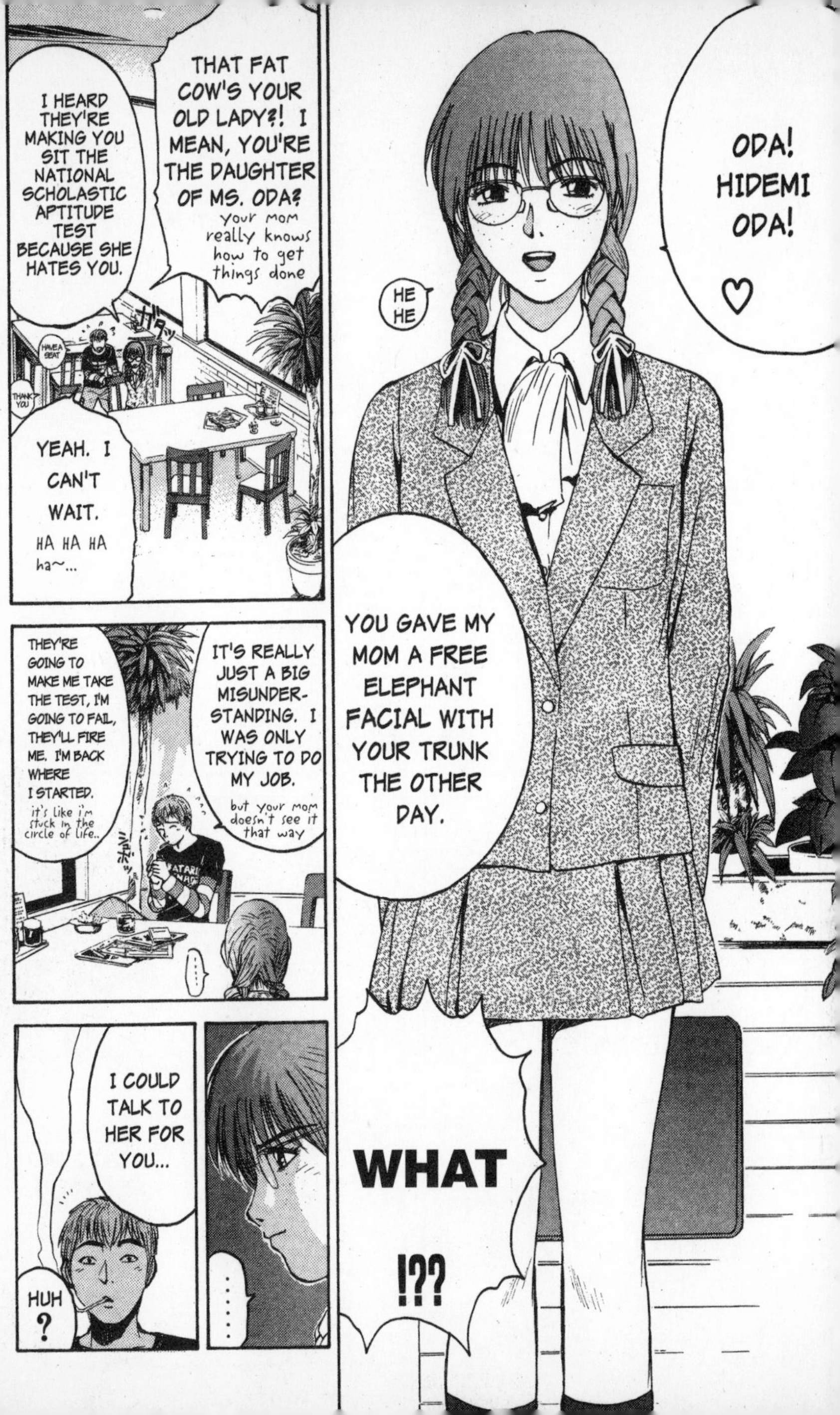
ODA! HIDEMI ODA! ♡
HE HE
YOU GAVE MY MOM A FREE ELEPHANT FACIAL WITH YOUR TRUNK THE OTHER DAY.
WHAT !??
THAT FAT COW'S YOUR OLD LADY?! I MEAN, YOU'RE THE DAUGHTER OF MS. ODA?
your mom really knows how to get things done
I HEARD THEY'RE MAKING YOU SIT THE NATIONAL SCHOLASTIC APTITUDE TEST BECAUSE SHE HATES YOU.
HAVE A SEAT
THANK YOU
YEAH. I CAN'T WAIT.
HA HA HA ha~...
IT'S REALLY JUST A BIG MISUNDER-STANDING. I WAS ONLY TRYING TO DO MY JOB.
but your mom doesn't see it that way
THEY'RE GOING TO MAKE ME TAKE THE TEST, I'M GOING TO FAIL, THEY'LL FIRE ME. I'M BACK WHERE I STARTED.
it's like i'm stuck in the circle of life..
......
......
I COULD TALK TO HER FOR YOU...
HUH ?

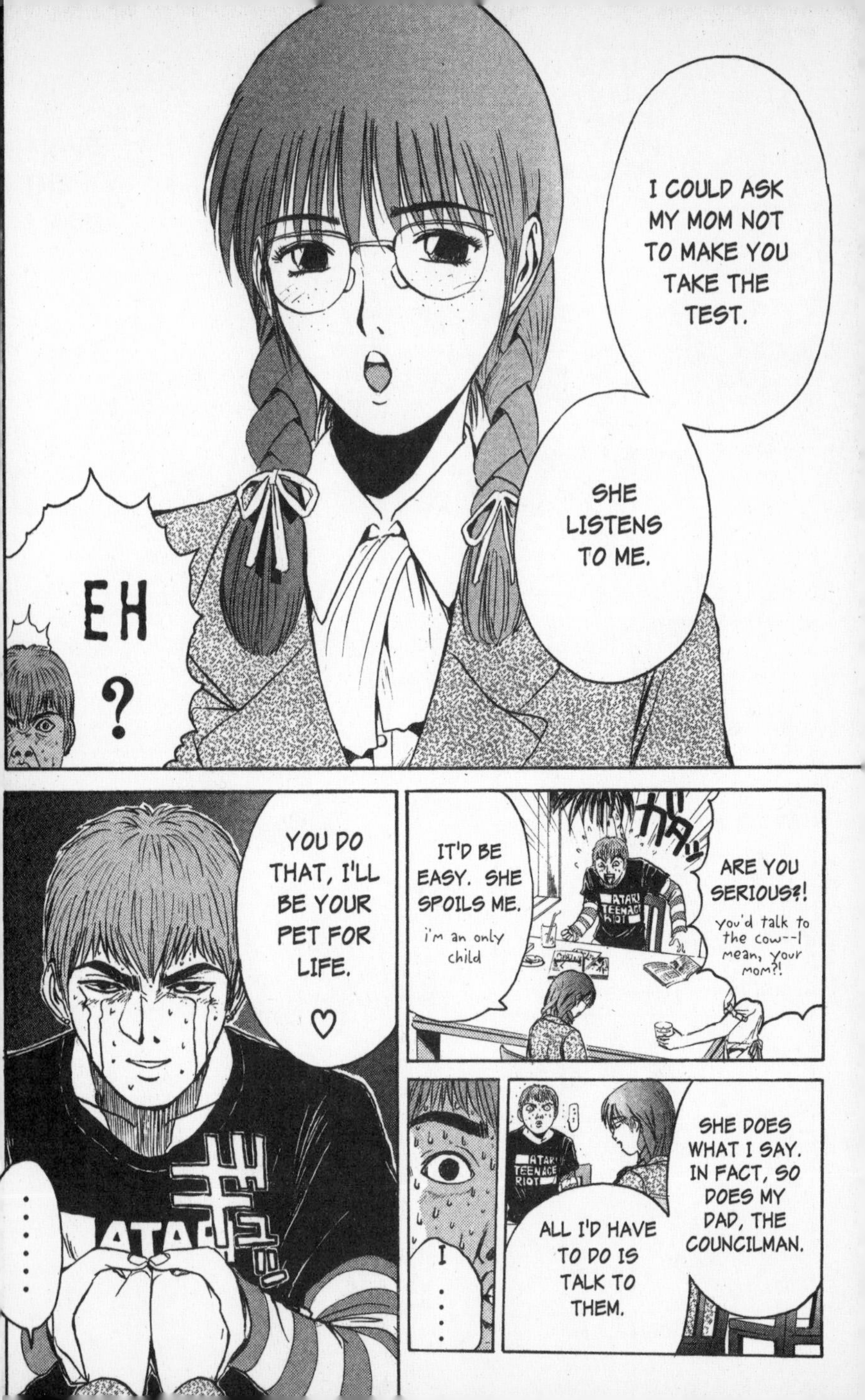
I COULD ASK MY MOM NOT TO MAKE YOU TAKE THE TEST.
SHE LISTENS TO ME.
EH ?
ARE YOU SERIOUS?!
you'd talk to the cow--I mean, your mom?!
IT'D BE EASY. SHE SPOILS ME.
i'm an only child
SHE DOES WHAT I SAY. IN FACT, SO DOES MY DAD, THE COUNCILMAN.
ALL I'D HAVE TO DO IS TALK TO THEM.
I ....
YOU DO THAT, I'LL BE YOUR PET FOR LIFE. ♡
......

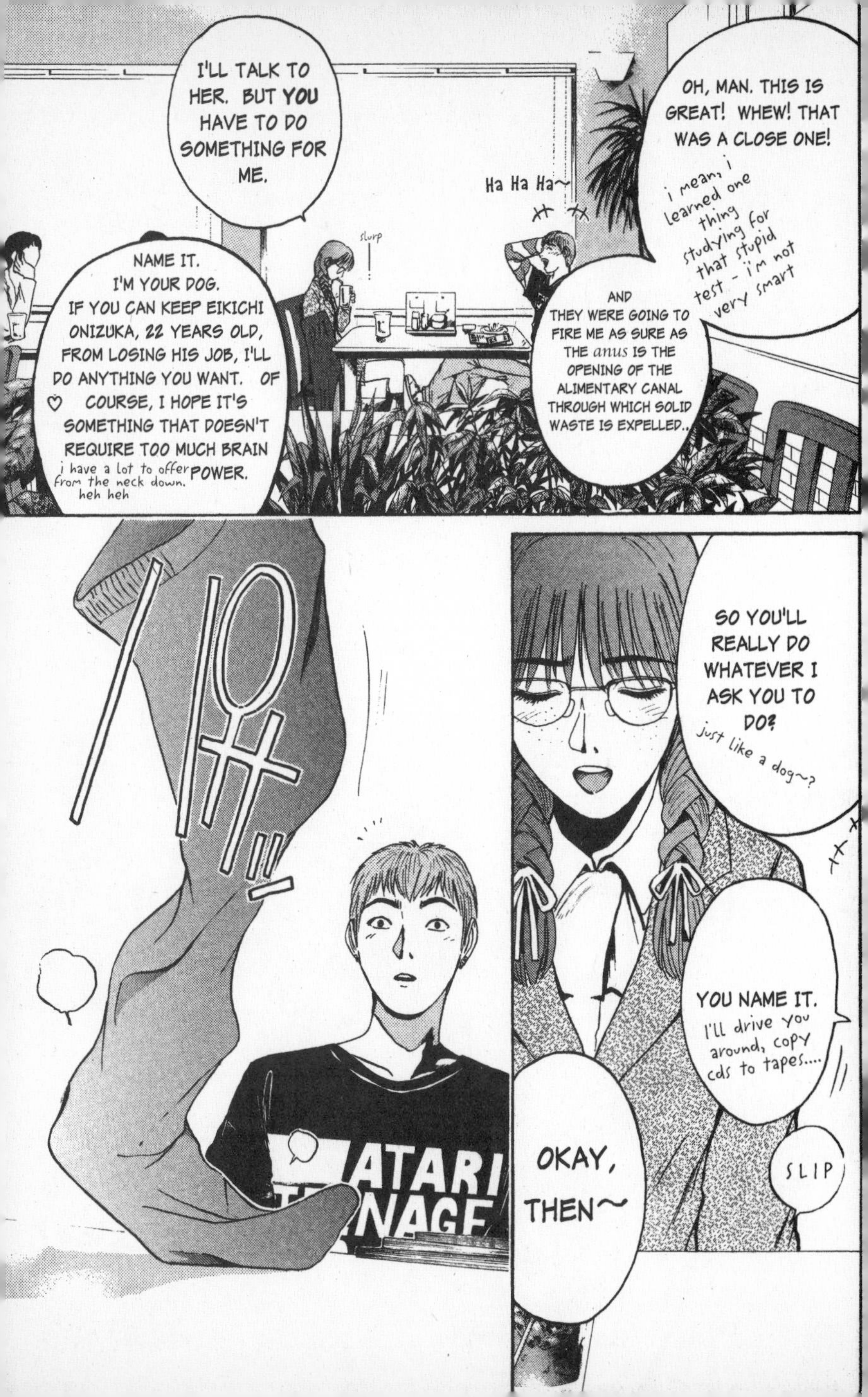

OH, MAN. THIS IS GREAT! WHEW! THAT WAS A CLOSE ONE!
i mean, i learned one thing studying for that stupid test - i'm not very smart
Ha Ha Ha~
AND THEY WERE GOING TO FIRE ME AS SURE AS THE *anus* IS THE OPENING OF THE ALIMENTARY CANAL THROUGH WHICH SOLID WASTE IS EXPELLED..
I'LL TALK TO HER. BUT **YOU** HAVE TO DO SOMETHING FOR ME.
slurp
NAME IT. I'M YOUR DOG. IF YOU CAN KEEP EIKICHI ONIZUKA, 22 YEARS OLD, FROM LOSING HIS JOB, I'LL DO ANYTHING YOU WANT. ♡ OF COURSE, I HOPE IT'S SOMETHING THAT DOESN'T REQUIRE TOO MUCH BRAIN POWER.
i have a lot to offer from the neck down. heh heh
SO YOU'LL REALLY DO WHATEVER I ASK YOU TO DO?
just like a dog~?
YOU NAME IT.
I'll drive you around, copy cds to tapes....
SLIP
OKAY, THEN~
ATARI TEENAGE

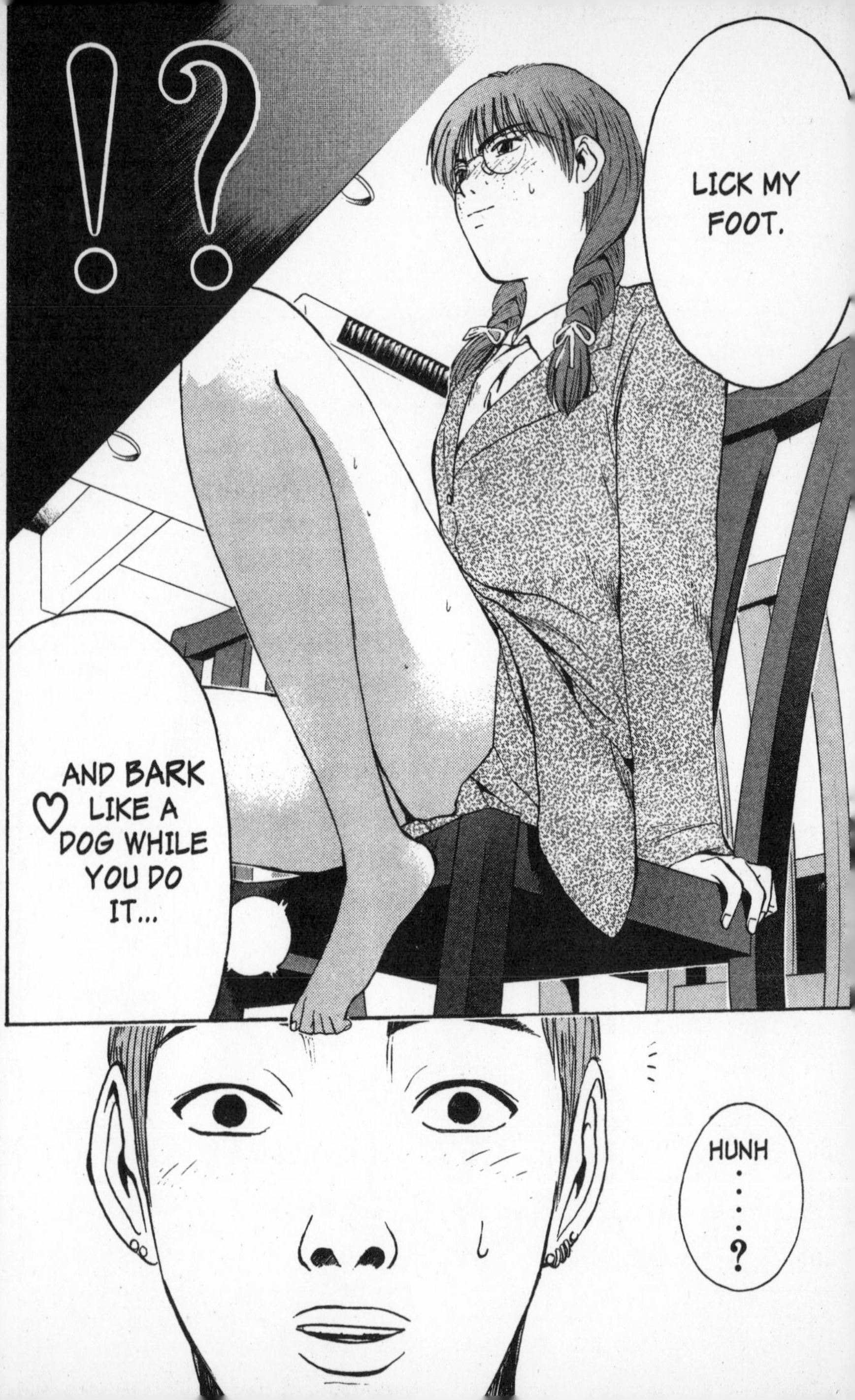
LICK MY FOOT.
!?
AND BARK LIKE A DOG WHILE YOU DO IT... ♡
HUNH.....?

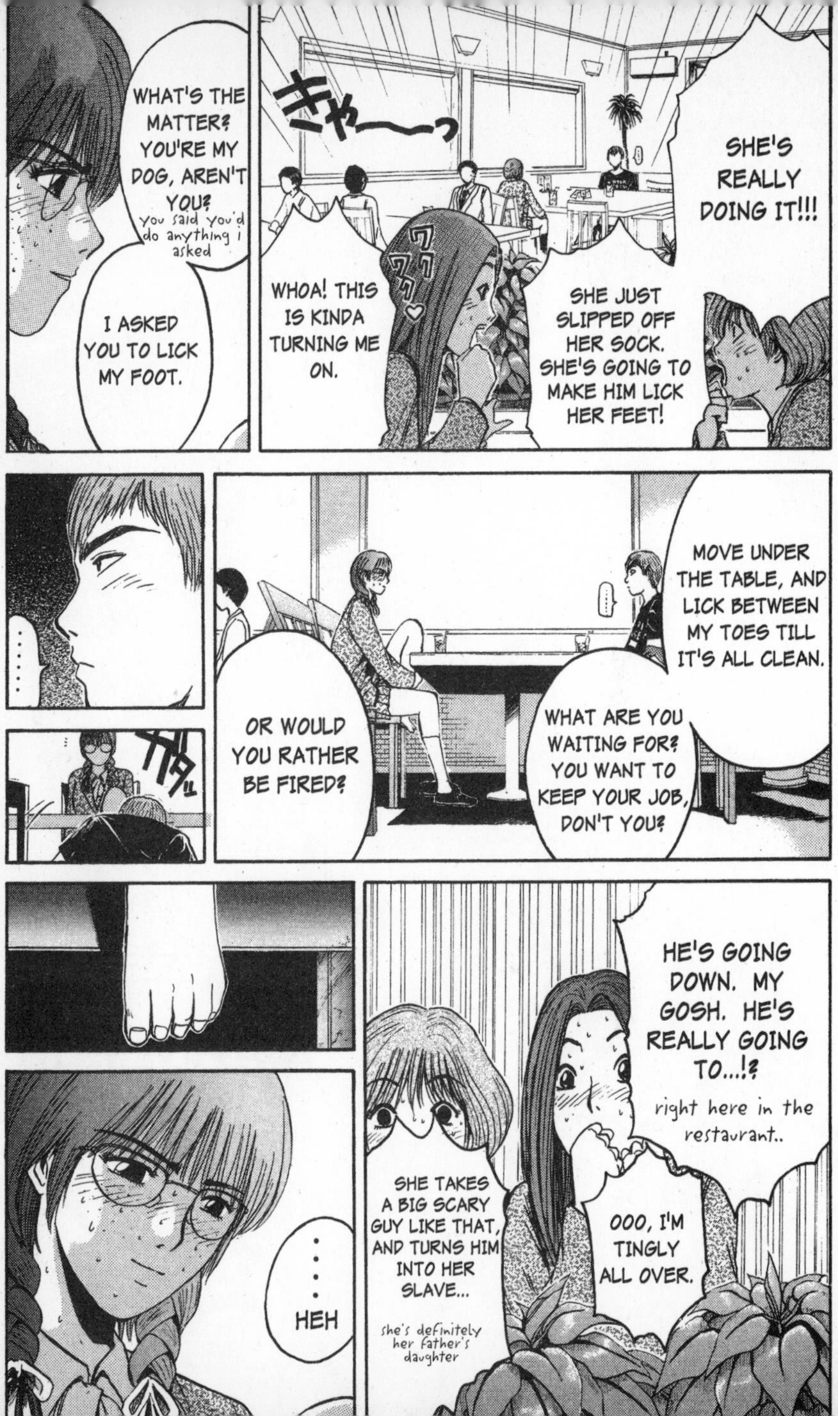

きゃ〜〜っ
SHE'S REALLY DOING IT!!!
SHE JUST SLIPPED OFF HER SOCK. SHE'S GOING TO MAKE HIM LICK HER FEET!
WHOA! THIS IS KINDA TURNING ME ON.
WHAT'S THE MATTER? YOU'RE MY DOG, AREN'T YOU?
You said you'd do anything i asked
I ASKED YOU TO LICK MY FOOT.
MOVE UNDER THE TABLE, AND LICK BETWEEN MY TOES TILL IT'S ALL CLEAN.
WHAT ARE YOU WAITING FOR? YOU WANT TO KEEP YOUR JOB, DON'T YOU?
OR WOULD YOU RATHER BE FIRED?
......
ガタッ
HE'S GOING DOWN. MY GOSH. HE'S REALLY GOING TO...!?
right here in the restaurant..
OOO, I'M TINGLY ALL OVER.
SHE TAKES A BIG SCARY GUY LIKE THAT, AND TURNS HIM INTO HER SLAVE...
she's definitely her father's daughter
..... HEH

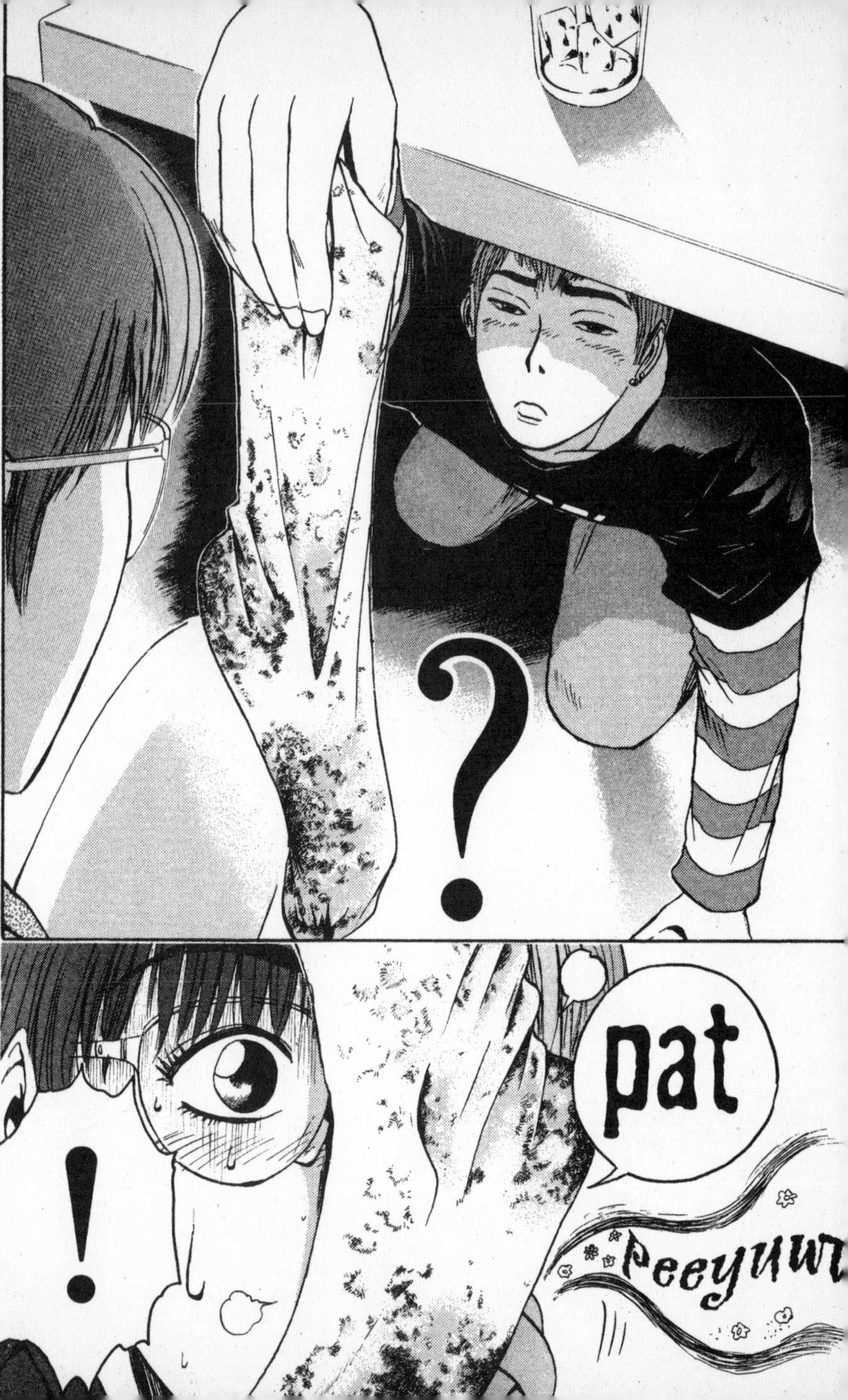
?
pat
Peeyuuu
!

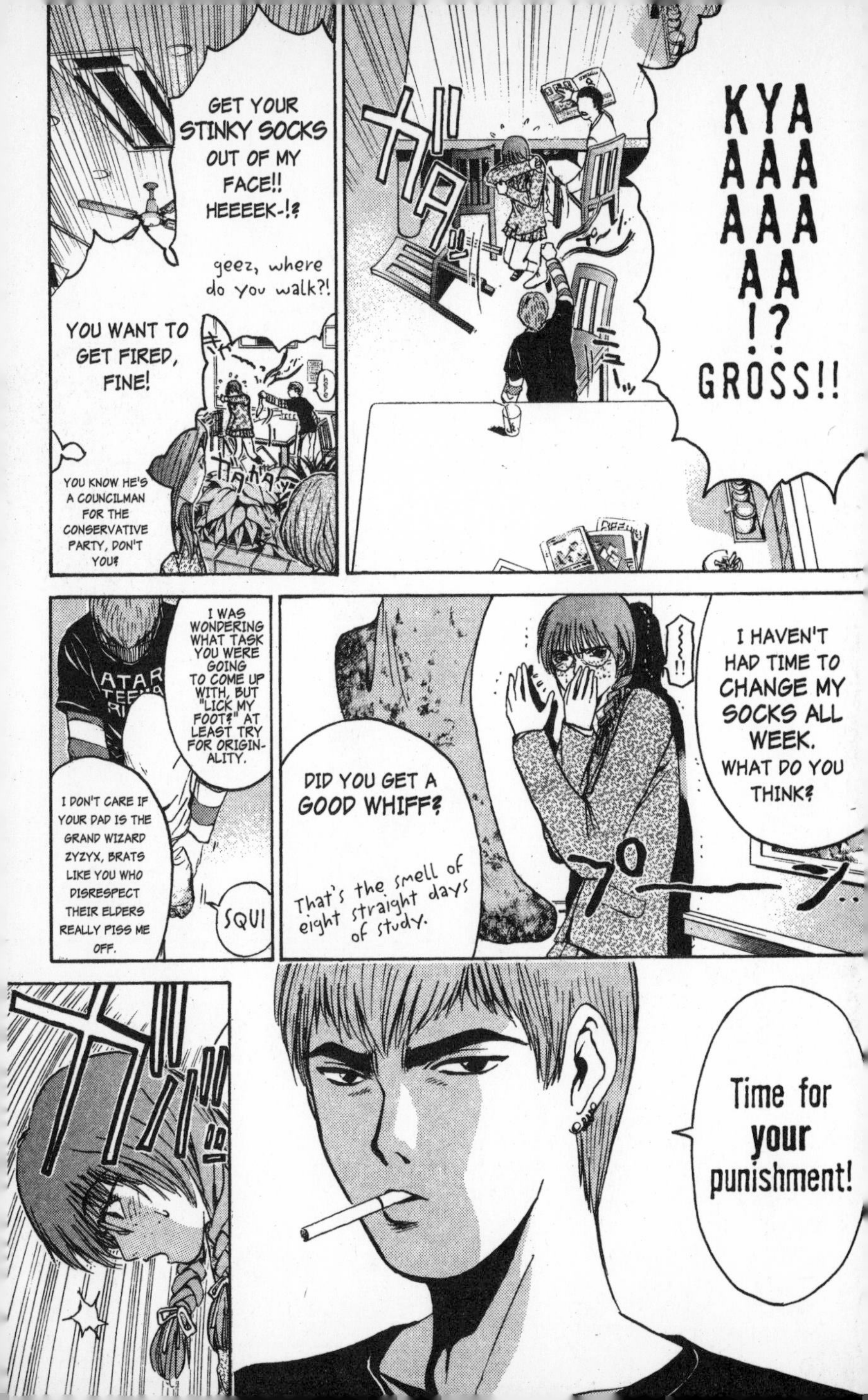
KYAAAAAAAAA!? GROSS!!
GET YOUR STINKY SOCKS OUT OF MY FACE!! HEEEEK-!?
geez, where do you walk?!
YOU WANT TO GET FIRED, FINE!
YOU KNOW HE'S A COUNCILMAN FOR THE CONSERVATIVE PARTY, DON'T YOU?
I HAVEN'T HAD TIME TO CHANGE MY SOCKS ALL WEEK. WHAT DO YOU THINK?
DID YOU GET A GOOD WHIFF?
That's the smell of eight straight days of study.
I WAS WONDERING WHAT TASK YOU WERE GOING TO COME UP WITH, BUT "LICK MY FOOT?" AT LEAST TRY FOR ORIGINALITY.
I DON'T CARE IF YOUR DAD IS THE GRAND WIZARD ZYZYX, BRATS LIKE YOU WHO DISRESPECT THEIR ELDERS REALLY PISS ME OFF.
SQUI
Time for your punishment!

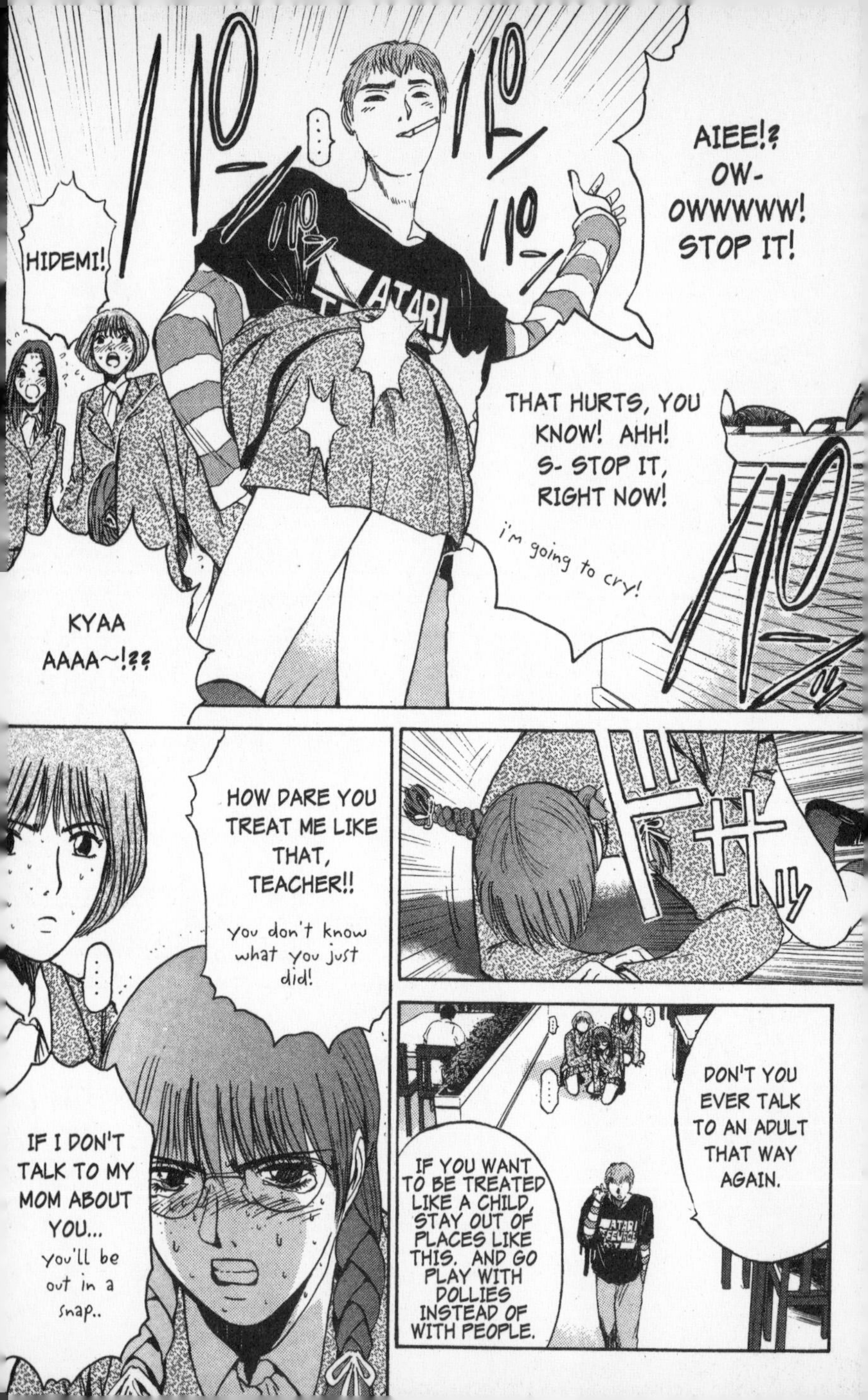
AIEE!? OW-OWWWWWW! STOP IT!
...
THAT HURTS, YOU KNOW! AHH! S- STOP IT, RIGHT NOW!
i'm going to cry!
HIDEMI!
KYAA AAAA~!??
DON'T YOU EVER TALK TO AN ADULT THAT WAY AGAIN.
IF YOU WANT TO BE TREATED LIKE A CHILD, STAY OUT OF PLACES LIKE THIS. AND GO PLAY WITH DOLLIES INSTEAD OF WITH PEOPLE.
...
...
HOW DARE YOU TREAT ME LIKE THAT, TEACHER!!
you don't know what you just did!
...
IF I DON'T TALK TO MY MOM ABOUT YOU... you'll be out in a snap..

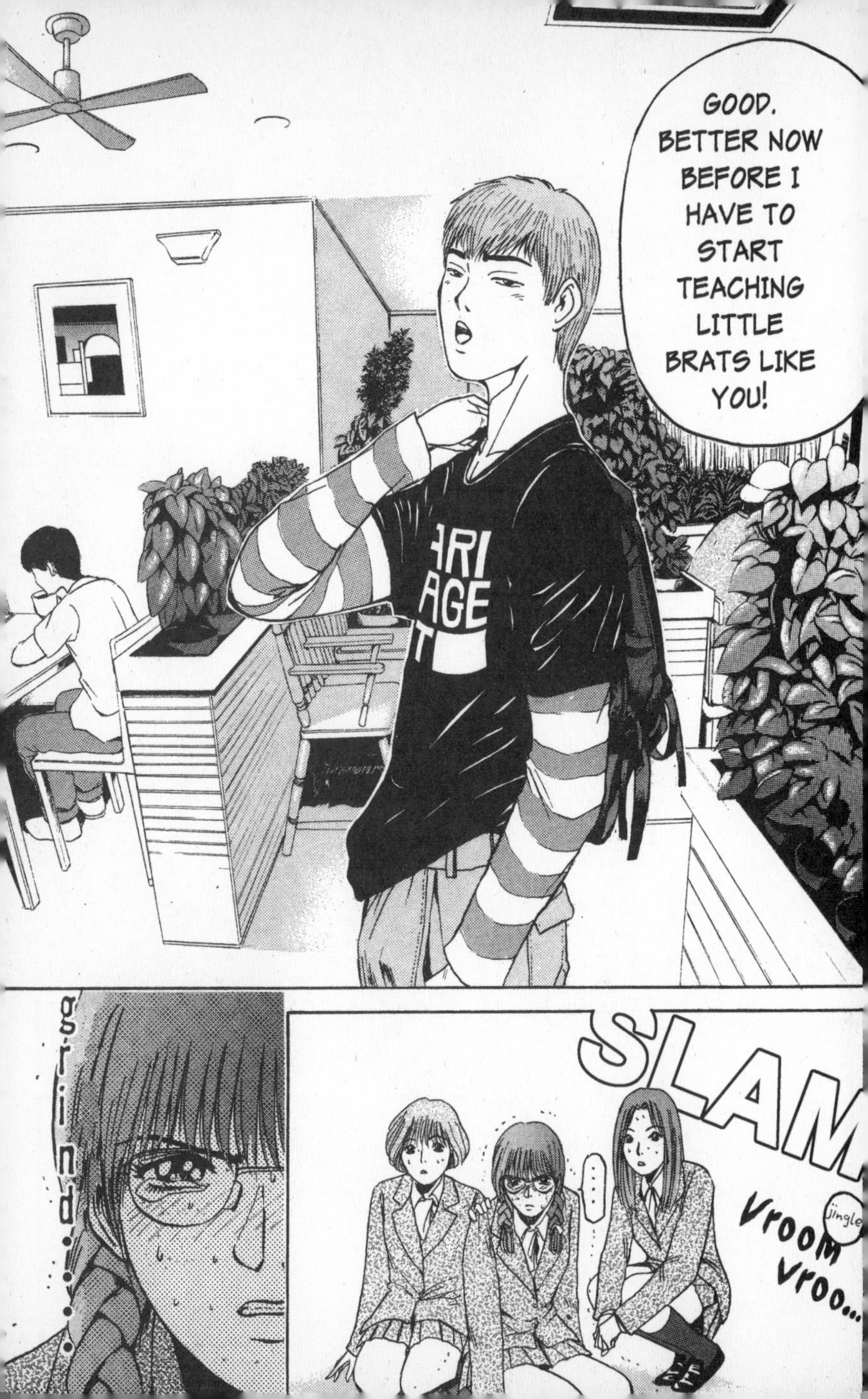
GOOD. BETTER NOW BEFORE I HAVE TO START TEACHING LITTLE BRATS LIKE YOU!
SLAM
jingle
Vroom Vroo...
...
grind......

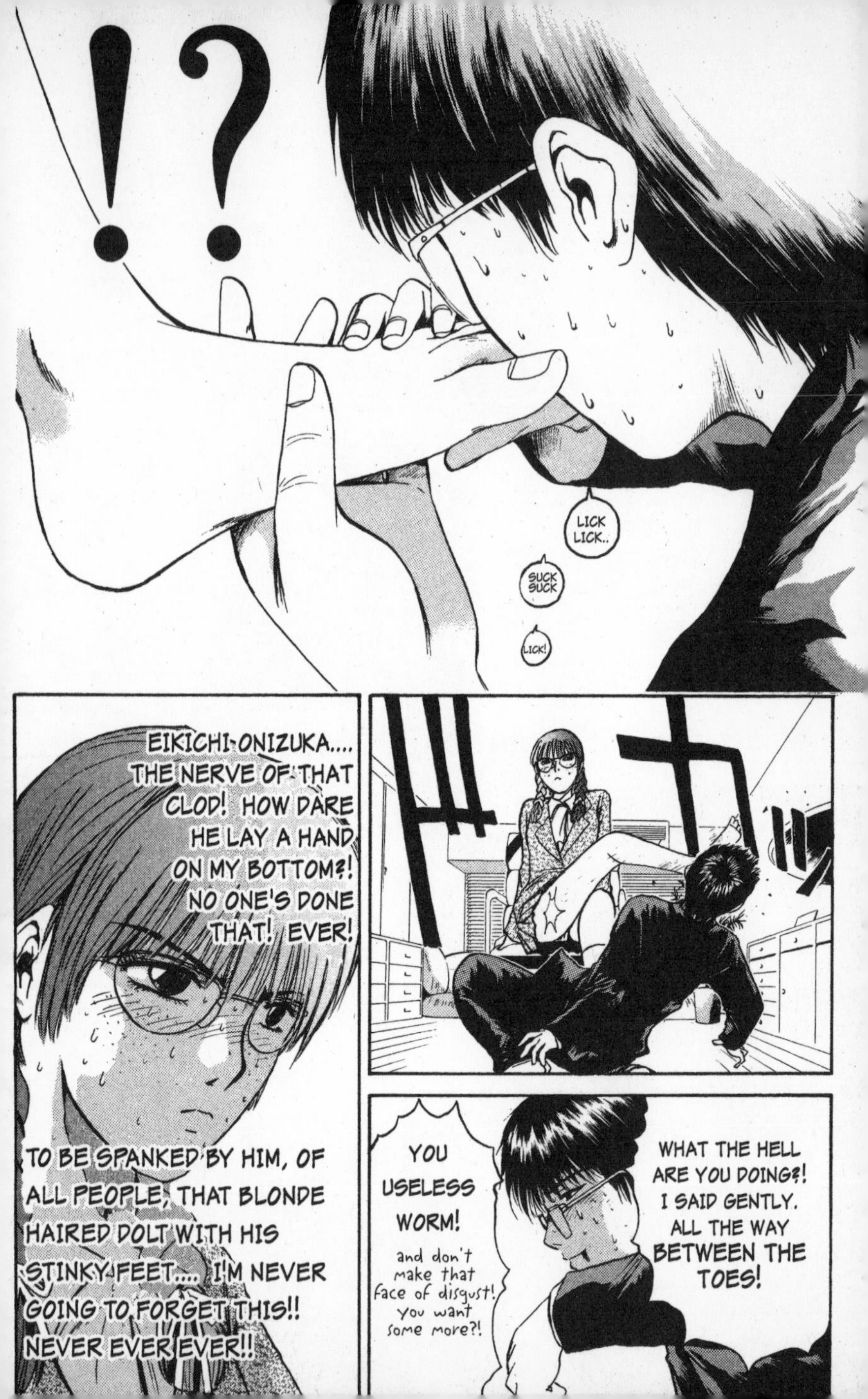
LICK LICK..
SUCK SUCK
LICK!
!?
WHAT THE HELL ARE YOU DOING?! I SAID GENTLY. ALL THE WAY BETWEEN THE TOES!
YOU USELESS WORM!
and don't make that face of disgust! You want some more?!
EIKICHI ONIZUKA.... THE NERVE OF THAT CLOD! HOW DARE HE LAY A HAND ON MY BOTTOM?! NO ONE'S DONE THAT! EVER!
TO BE SPANKED BY HIM, OF ALL PEOPLE, THAT BLONDE HAIRED DOLT WITH HIS STINKY FEET.... I'M NEVER GOING TO FORGET THIS!! NEVER EVER EVER!!

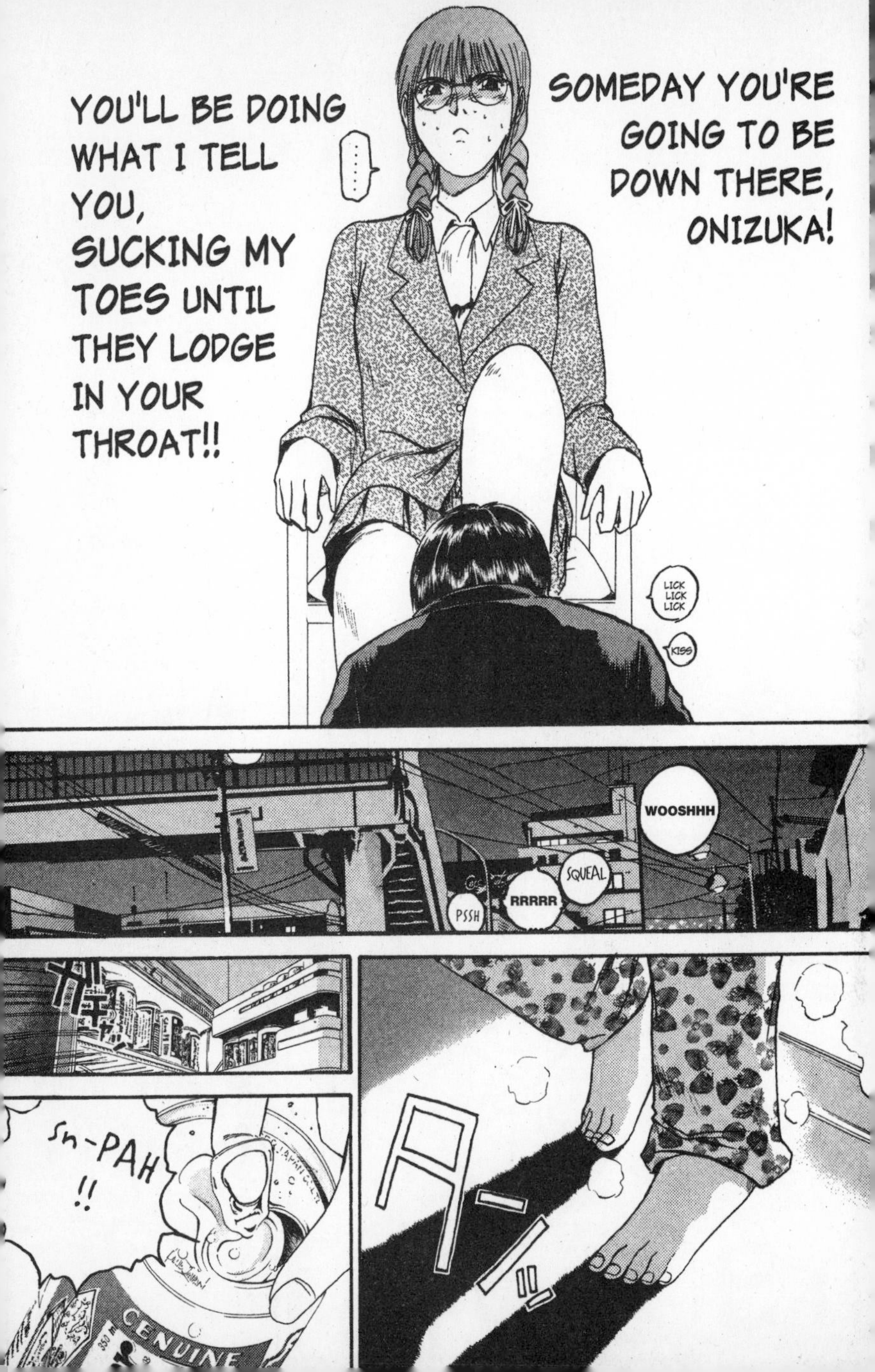
SOMEDAY YOU'RE GOING TO BE DOWN THERE, ONIZUKA!
......
YOU'LL BE DOING WHAT I TELL YOU, SUCKING MY TOES UNTIL THEY LODGE IN YOUR THROAT!!
LICK LICK LICK
KISS
WOOSHHH
SQUEAL
RRRRR
PSSH
Sn-PAH!!
GENUINE

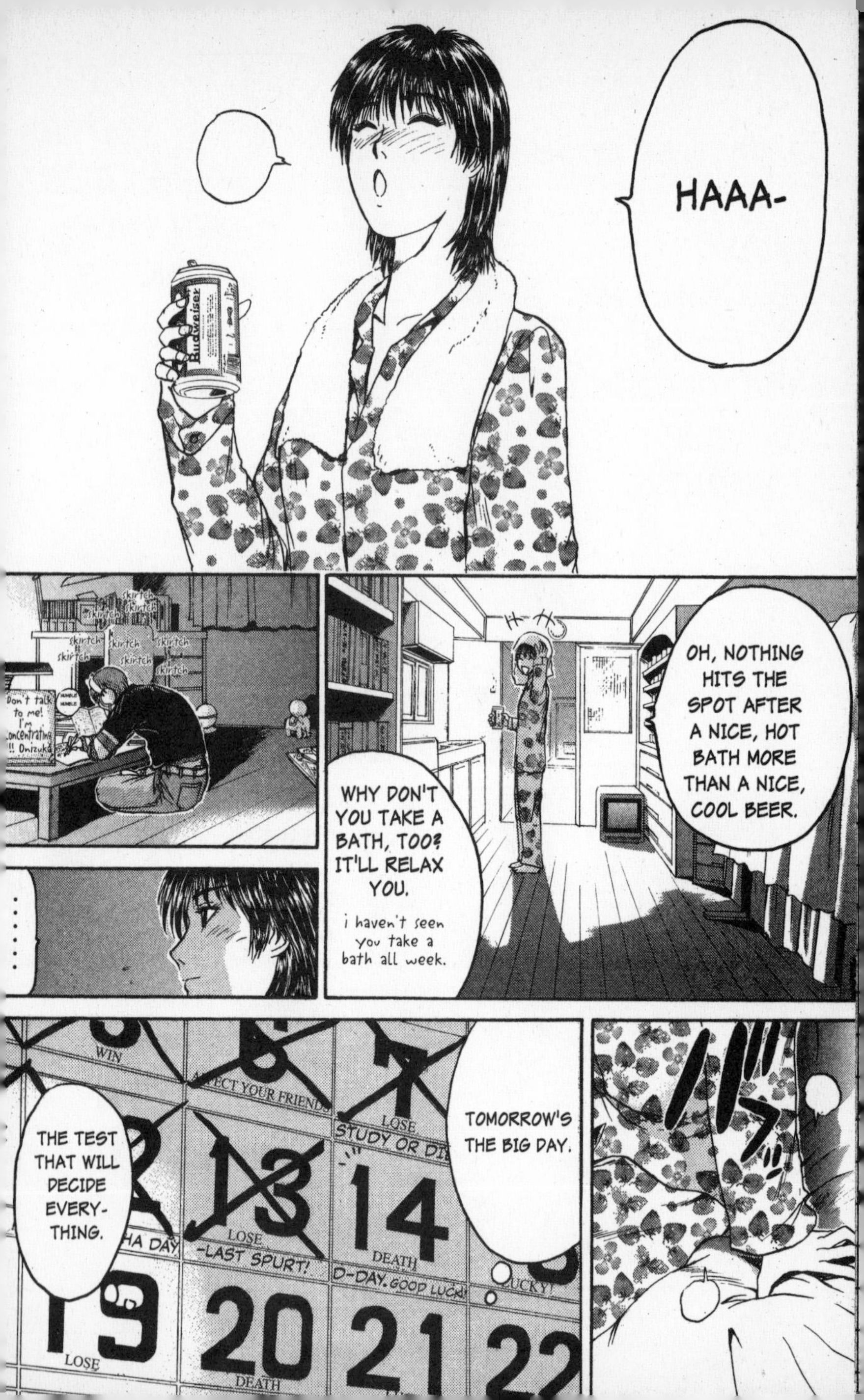
HAAA-
OH, NOTHING HITS THE SPOT AFTER A NICE, HOT BATH MORE THAN A NICE, COOL BEER.
WHY DON'T YOU TAKE A BATH, TOO? IT'LL RELAX YOU.
i haven't seen you take a bath all week.
skirtch skirtch skirtch skirtch skirtch skirtch skirtch skirtch skirtch
Don't talk to me! I'm concentrating!! Onizuka
......
TOMORROW'S THE BIG DAY.
THE TEST THAT WILL DECIDE EVERY-THING.
WIN
LOSE
13
14
LOSE
-LAST SPURT!
DEATH
D-DAY. GOOD LUCK!
19
20
21
22
LOSE
DEATH

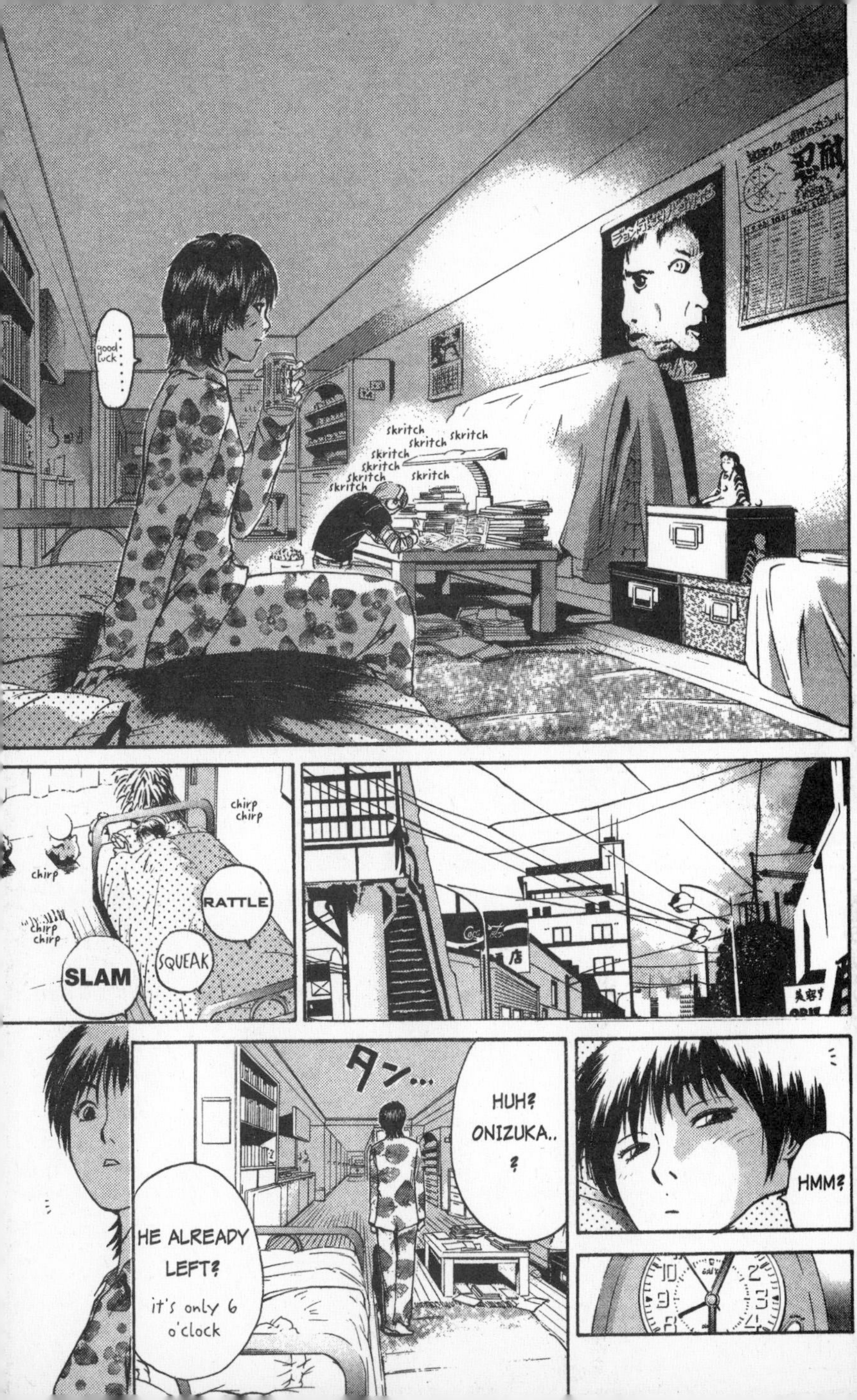
......good luck......
skritch skritch skritch
skritch skritch skritch skritch skritch
chirp chirp
RATTLE
chirp
chirp chirp
SQUEAK
SLAM
HMM?
タン...
HUH? ONIZUKA..?
HE ALREADY LEFT?
it's only 6 o'clock

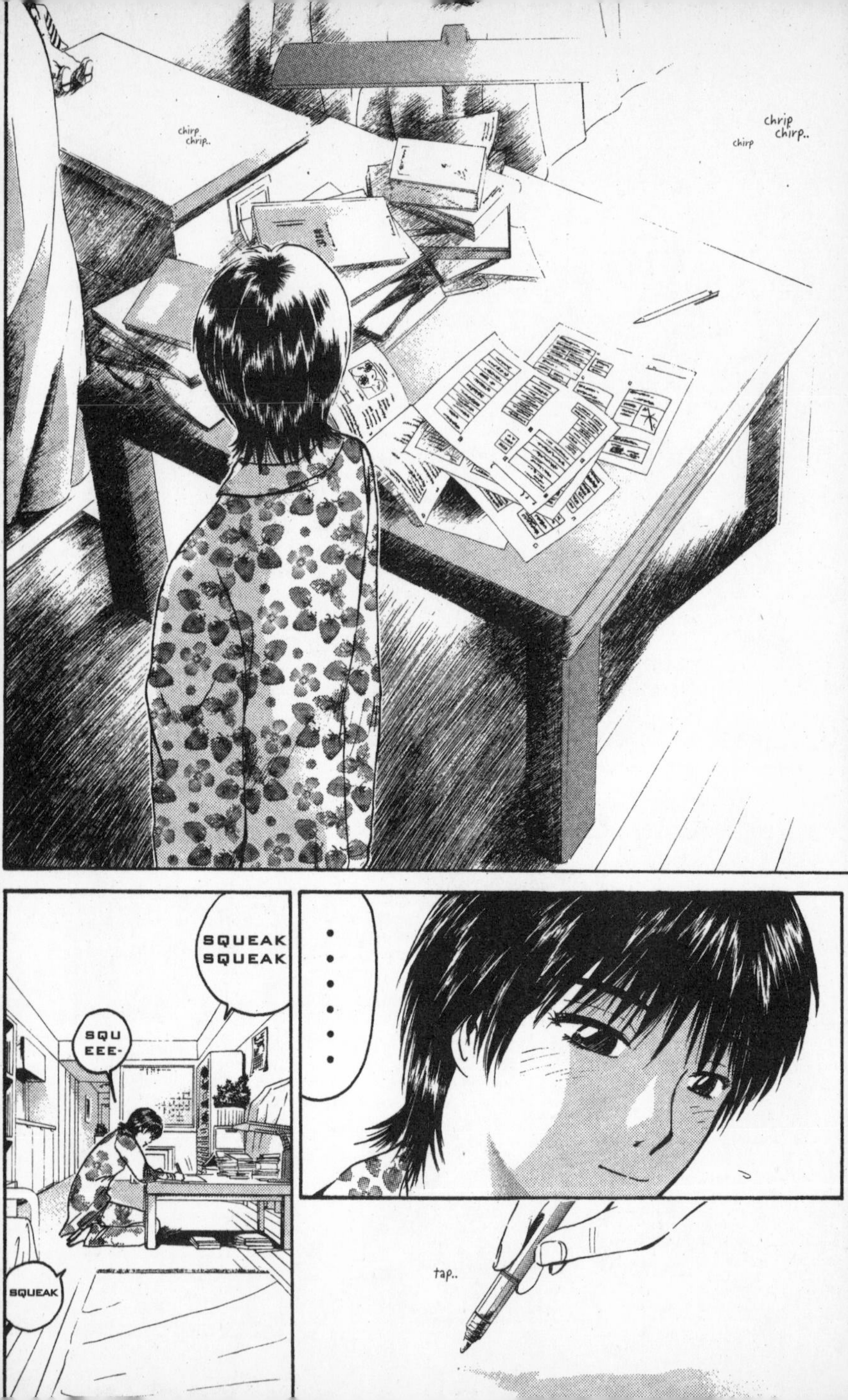

chrip chirp..
chirp
chirp chirp..
......
tap..
SQUEAK SQUEAK
SQU EEE-
SQUEAK

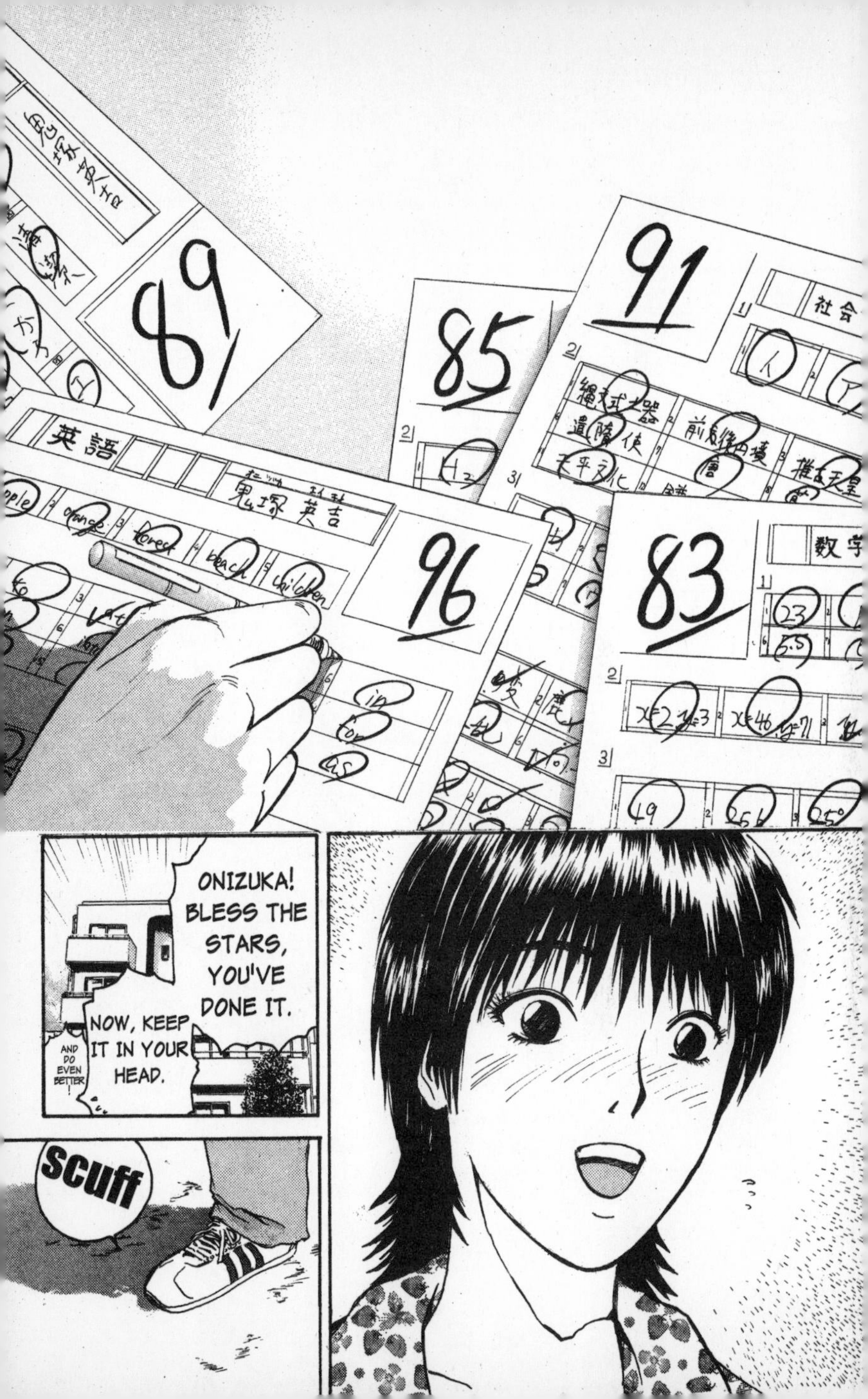

89
鬼塚英吉
91
社会
85
英語
鬼塚英吉
96
83
数学
ONIZUKA! BLESS THE STARS, YOU'VE DONE IT.
NOW, KEEP IT IN YOUR HEAD.
AND DO EVEN BETTER!
SCUFF

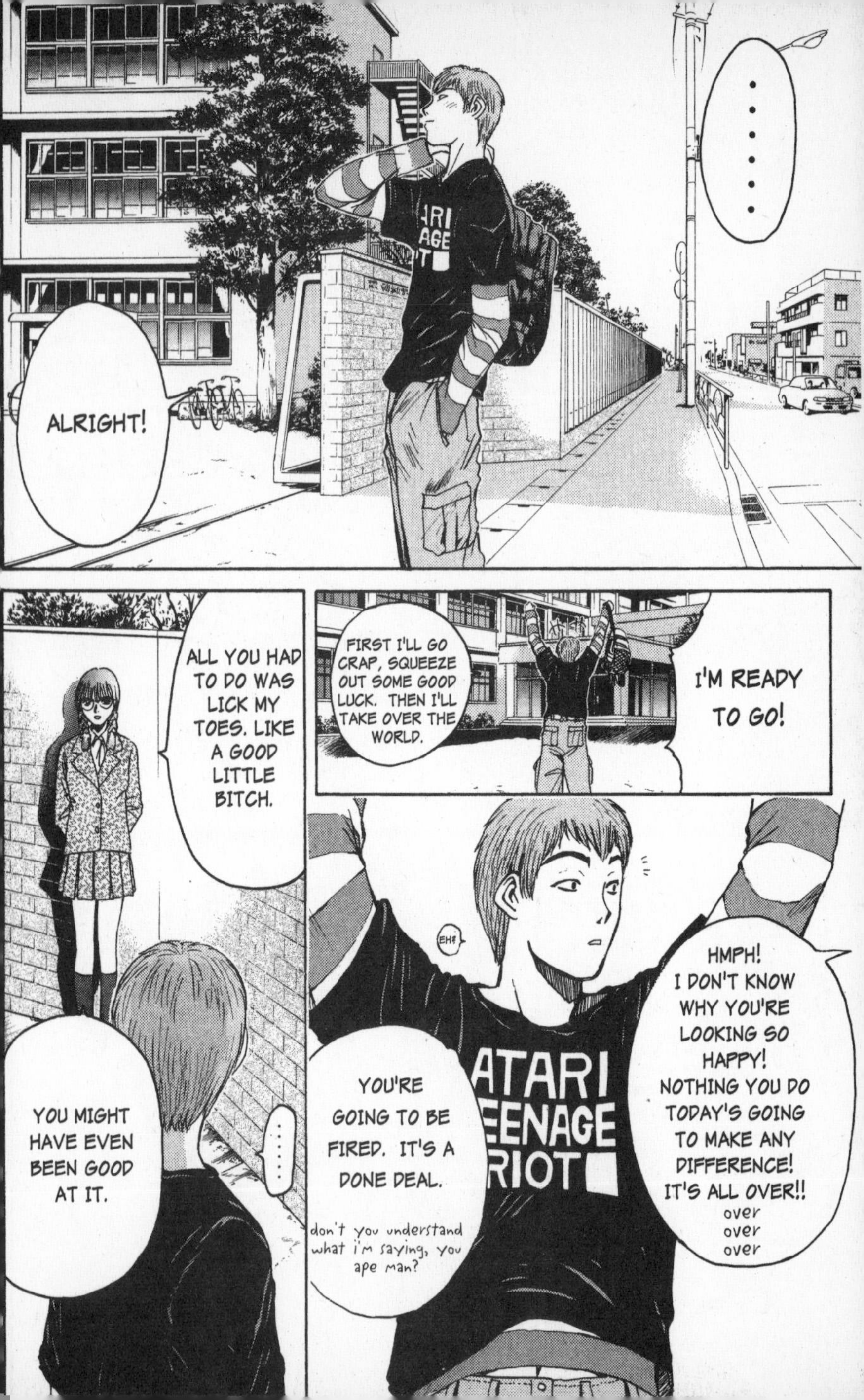

......
ALRIGHT!
I'M READY TO GO!
FIRST I'LL GO CRAP, SQUEEZE OUT SOME GOOD LUCK. THEN I'LL TAKE OVER THE WORLD.
EH?
HMPH! I DON'T KNOW WHY YOU'RE LOOKING SO HAPPY! NOTHING YOU DO TODAY'S GOING TO MAKE ANY DIFFERENCE! IT'S ALL OVER!! over over over
YOU'RE GOING TO BE FIRED. IT'S A DONE DEAL.
don't you understand what i'm saying, you ape man?
ALL YOU HAD TO DO WAS LICK MY TOES. LIKE A GOOD LITTLE BITCH.
......
YOU MIGHT HAVE EVEN BEEN GOOD AT IT.

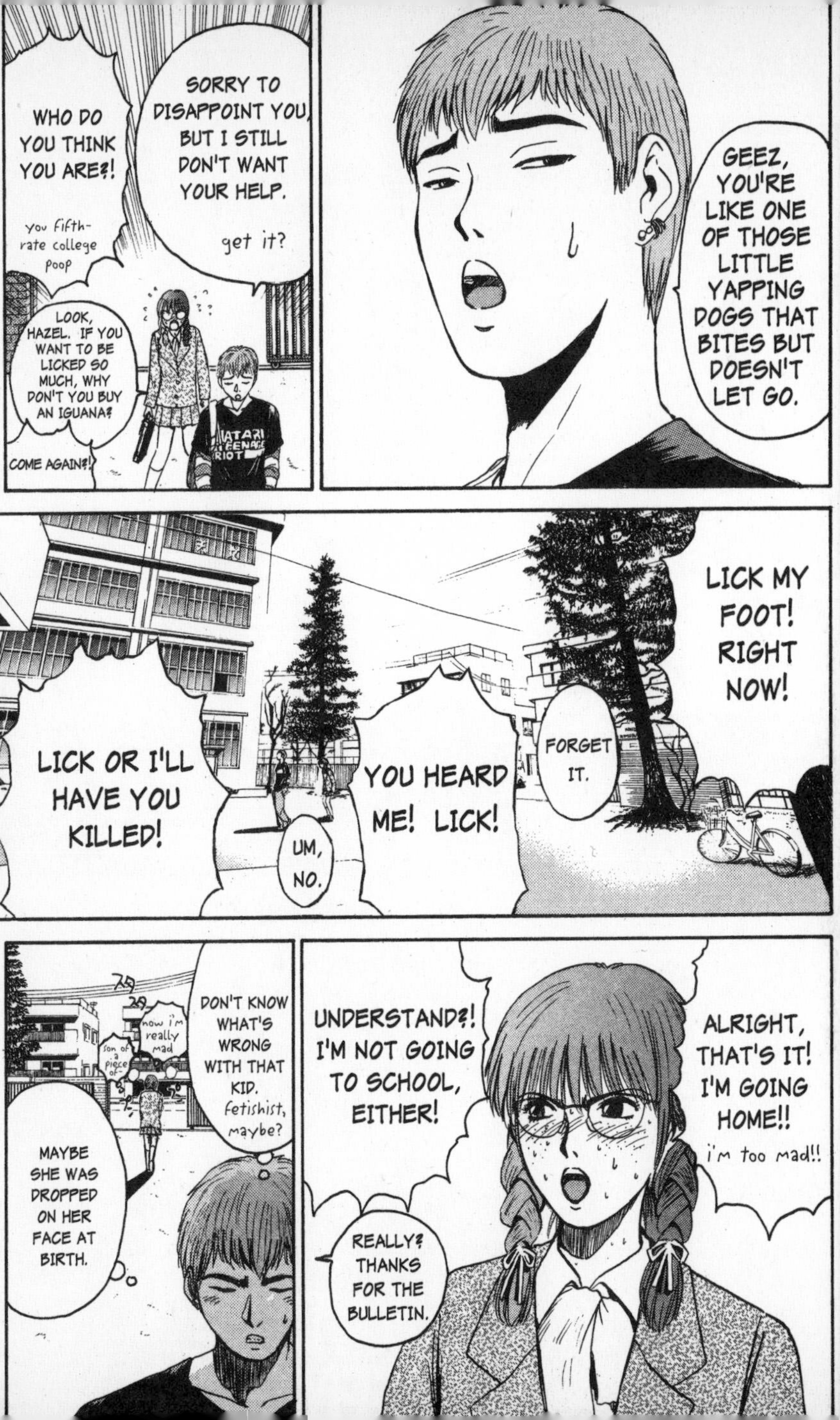

GEEZ, YOU'RE LIKE ONE OF THOSE LITTLE YAPPING DOGS THAT BITES BUT DOESN'T LET GO.
SORRY TO DISAPPOINT YOU, BUT I STILL DON'T WANT YOUR HELP.
get it?
WHO DO YOU THINK YOU ARE?!
You fifth-rate college poop
LOOK, HAZEL. IF YOU WANT TO BE LICKED SO MUCH, WHY DON'T YOU BUY AN IGUANA?
COME AGAIN?!
LICK MY FOOT! RIGHT NOW!
FORGET IT.
YOU HEARD ME! LICK!
UM, NO.
LICK OR I'LL HAVE YOU KILLED!
ALRIGHT, THAT'S IT! I'M GOING HOME!!
i'm too mad!!
UNDERSTAND?! I'M NOT GOING TO SCHOOL, EITHER!
REALLY? THANKS FOR THE BULLETIN.
DON'T KNOW WHAT'S WRONG WITH THAT KID.
fetishist, maybe?
now i'm really mad
son of a piece of-
MAYBE SHE WAS DROPPED ON HER FACE AT BIRTH.

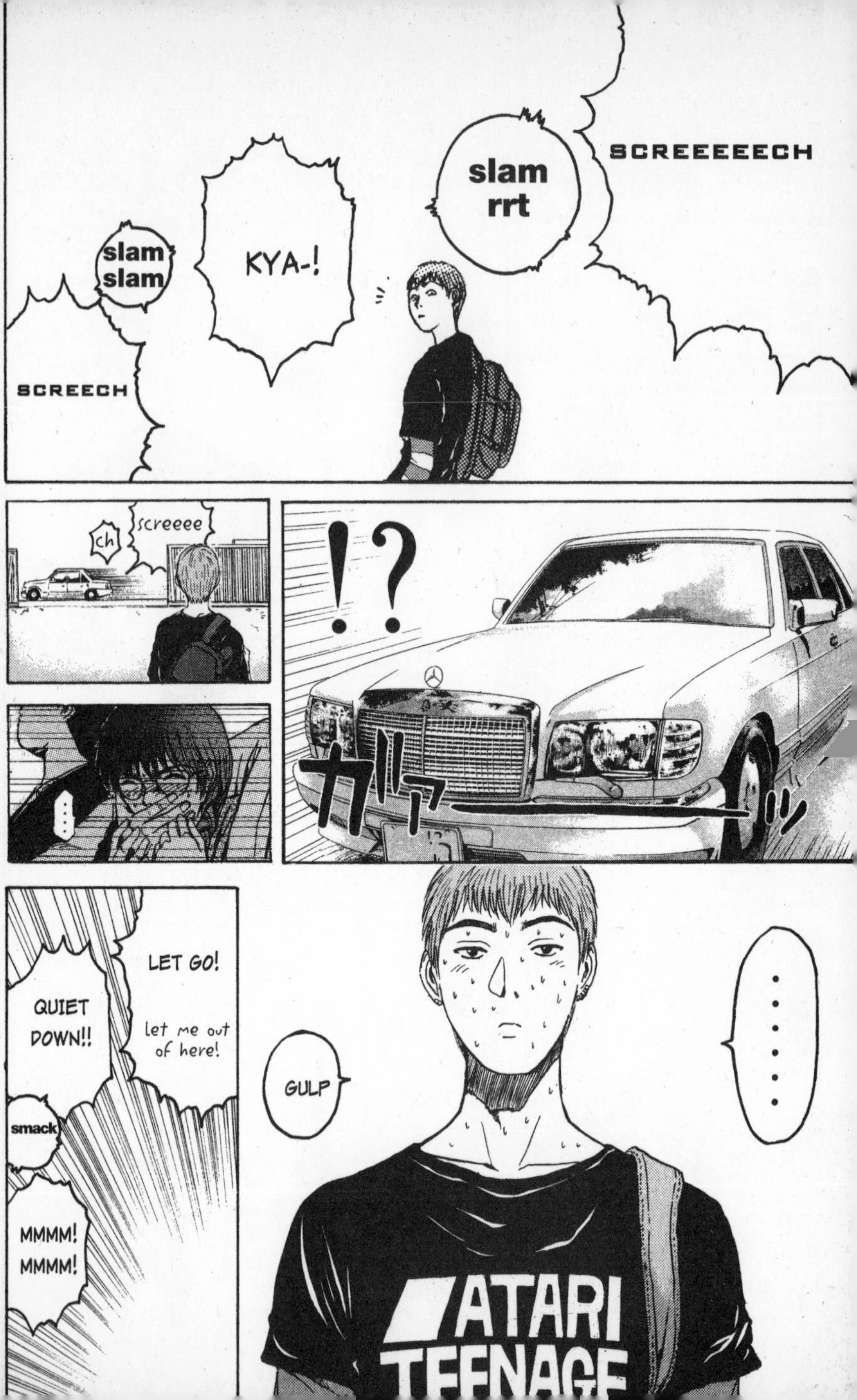
SCREEEEECH
slam rrt
KYA-!
slam slam
SCREECH
!?
screeee
ch
...
......
GULP
ATARI
LET GO!
let me out of here!
QUIET DOWN!!
smack
MMMM! MMMM!

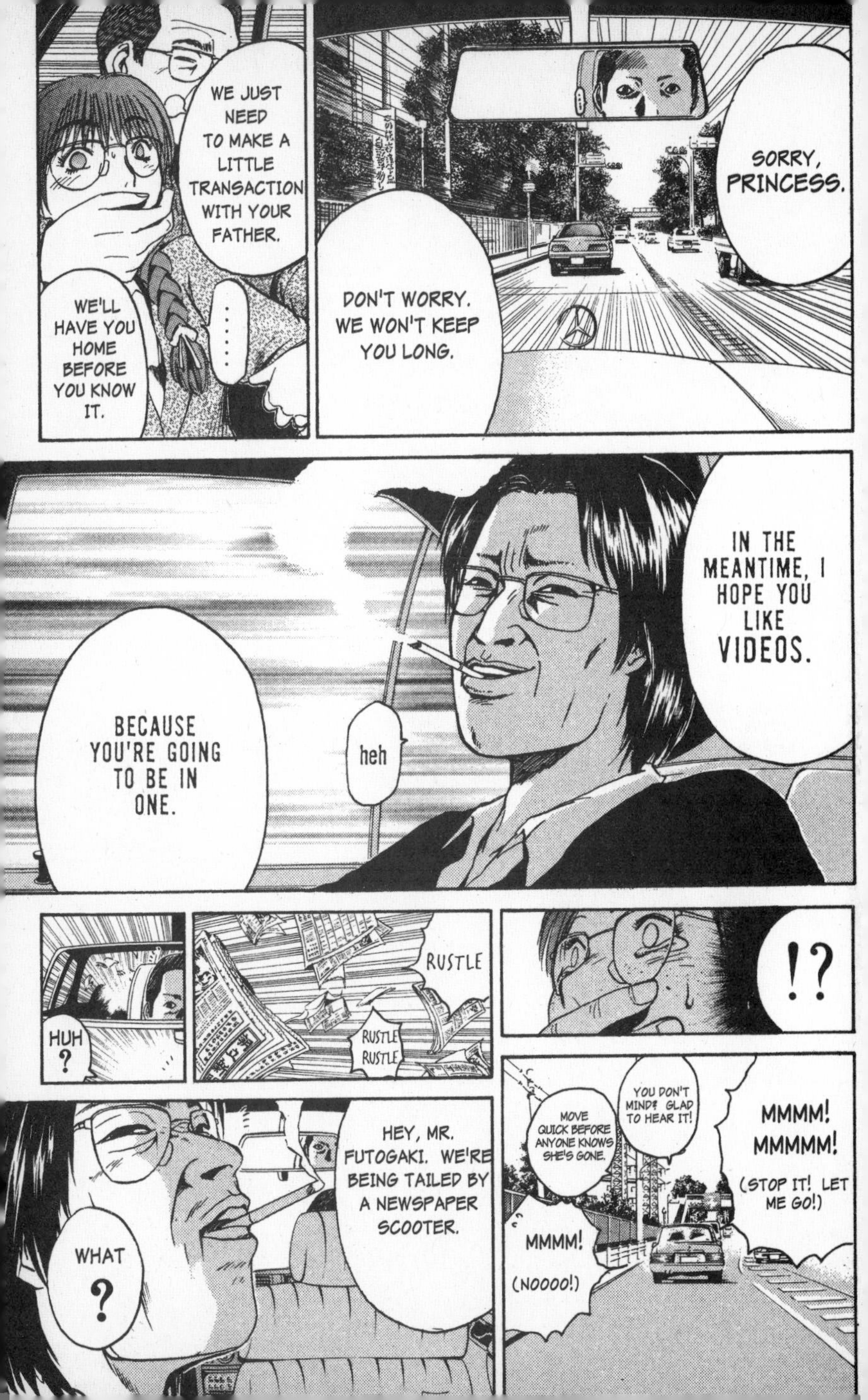
SORRY, PRINCESS.
DON'T WORRY. WE WON'T KEEP YOU LONG.
WE JUST NEED TO MAKE A LITTLE TRANSACTION WITH YOUR FATHER.
......
WE'LL HAVE YOU HOME BEFORE YOU KNOW IT.
IN THE MEANTIME, I HOPE YOU LIKE VIDEOS.
heh
BECAUSE YOU'RE GOING TO BE IN ONE.
!?
RUSTLE
RUSTLE RUSTLE
HUH ?
MMMM! MMMMM!
(STOP IT! LET ME GO!)
YOU DON'T MIND? GLAD TO HEAR IT!
MOVE QUICK BEFORE ANYONE KNOWS SHE'S GONE.
MMMM!
(NOOOO!)
HEY, MR. FUTOGAKI. WE'RE BEING TAILED BY A NEWSPAPER SCOOTER.
WHAT ?

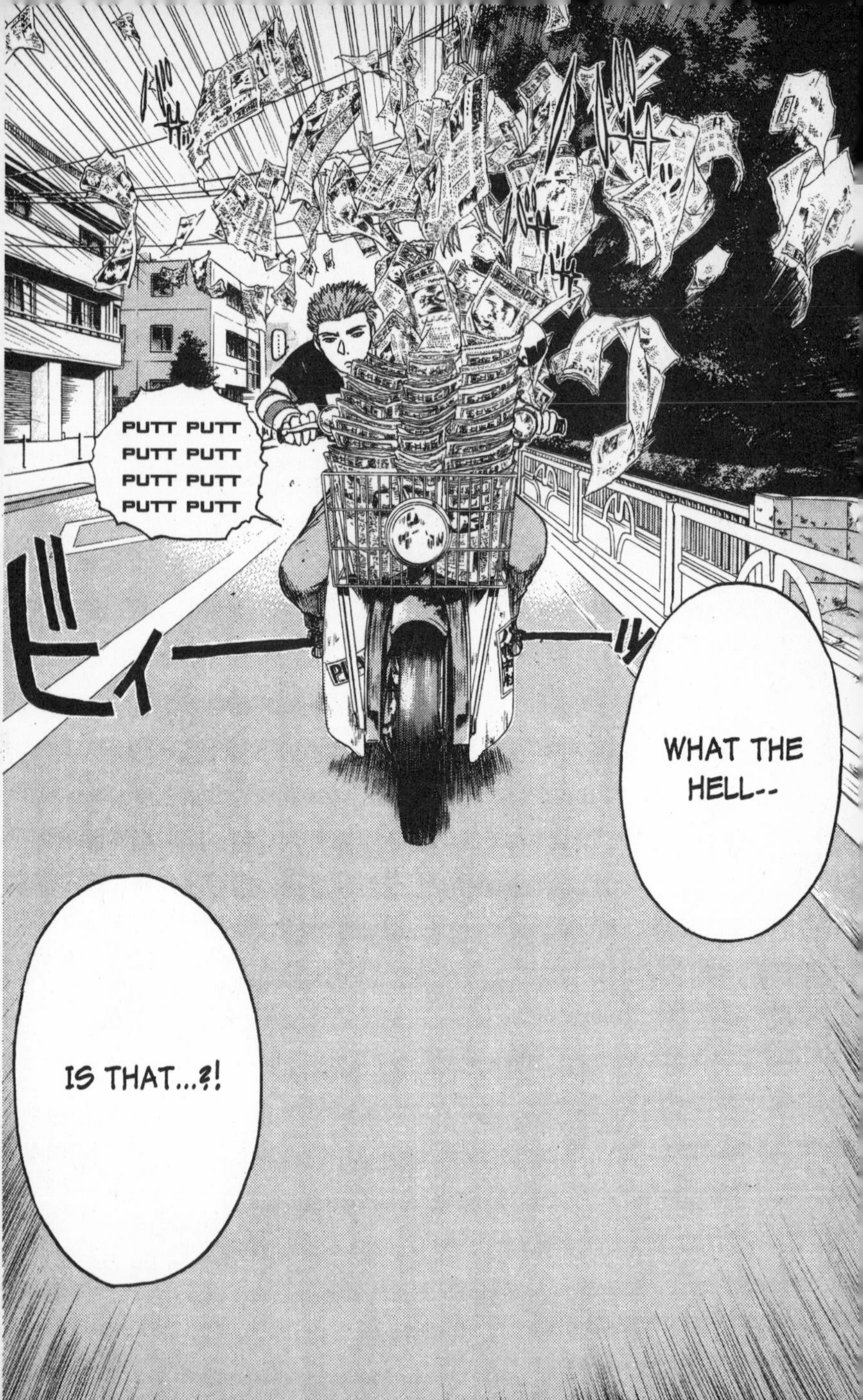
PUTT PUTT PUTT PUTT PUTT PUTT PUTT PUTT
WHAT THE HELL--
IS THAT...?!

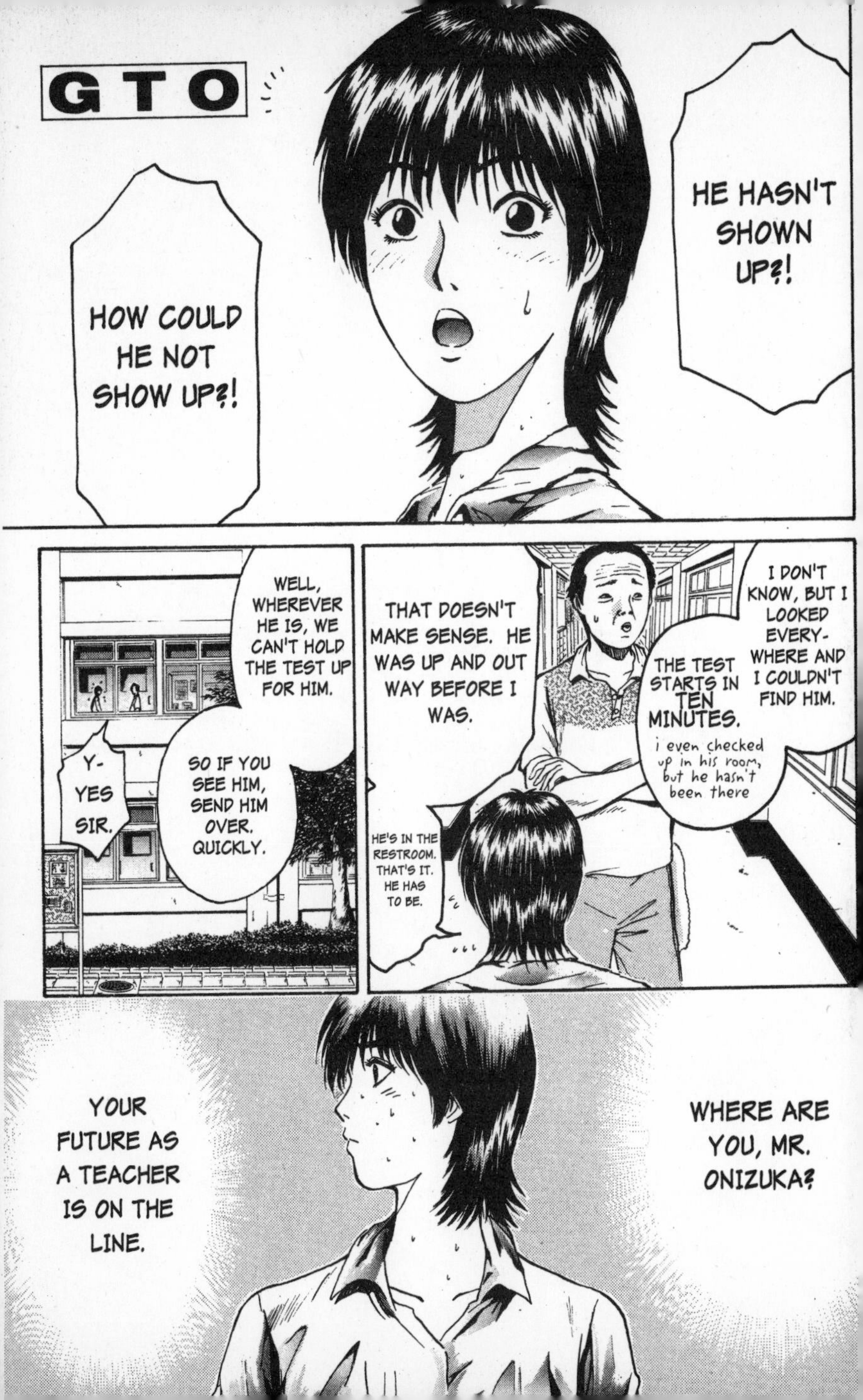
HE HASN'T SHOWN UP?!
HOW COULD HE NOT SHOW UP?!
I DON'T KNOW, BUT I LOOKED EVERY-WHERE AND I COULDN'T FIND HIM.
i even checked up in his room, but he hasn't been there
THE TEST STARTS IN TEN MINUTES.
THAT DOESN'T MAKE SENSE. HE WAS UP AND OUT WAY BEFORE I WAS.
HE'S IN THE RESTROOM. THAT'S IT. HE HAS TO BE.
WELL, WHEREVER HE IS, WE CAN'T HOLD THE TEST UP FOR HIM.
SO IF YOU SEE HIM, SEND HIM OVER. QUICKLY.
Y-YES SIR.
WHERE ARE YOU, MR. ONIZUKA?
YOUR FUTURE AS A TEACHER IS ON THE LINE.

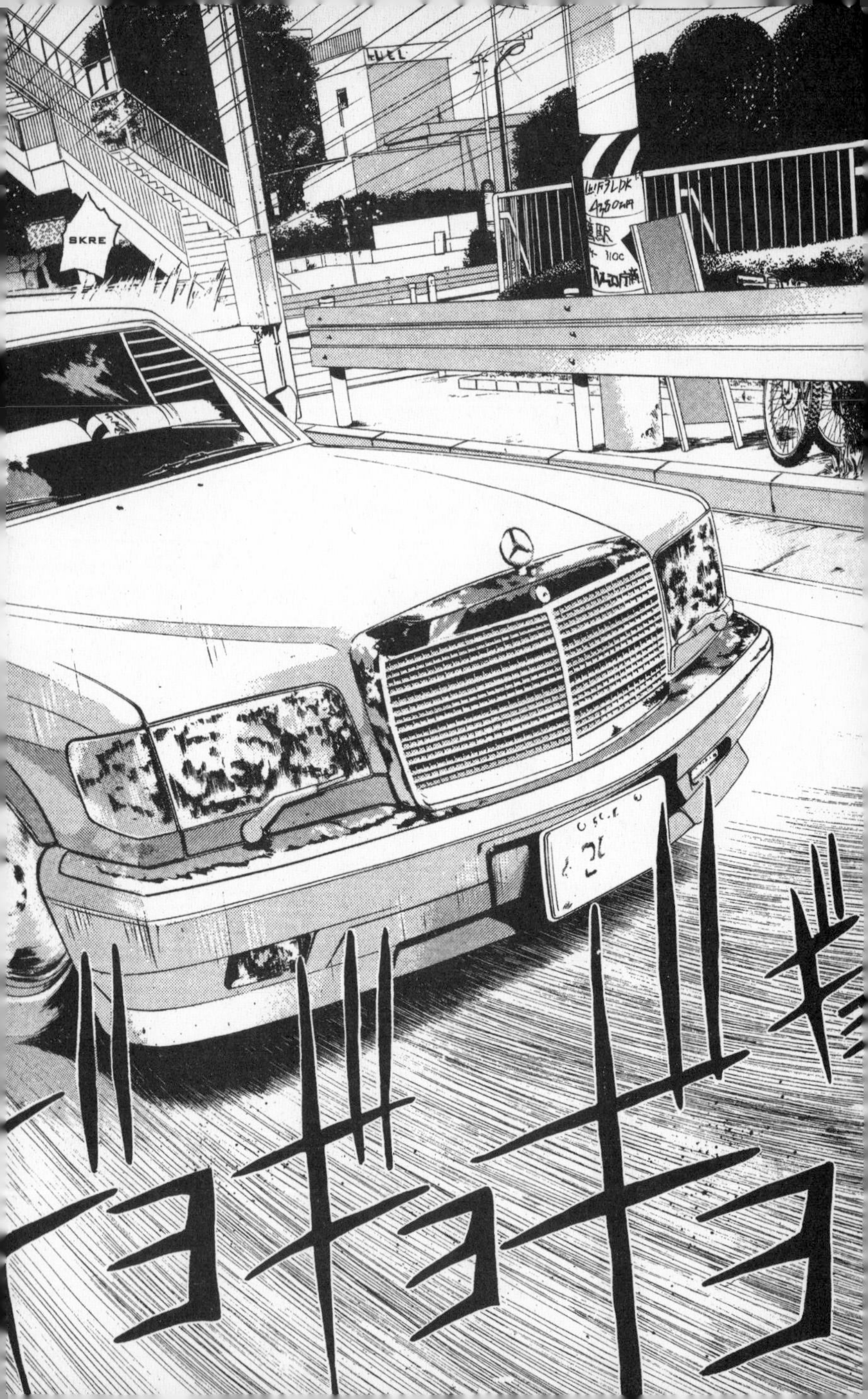
SKRE

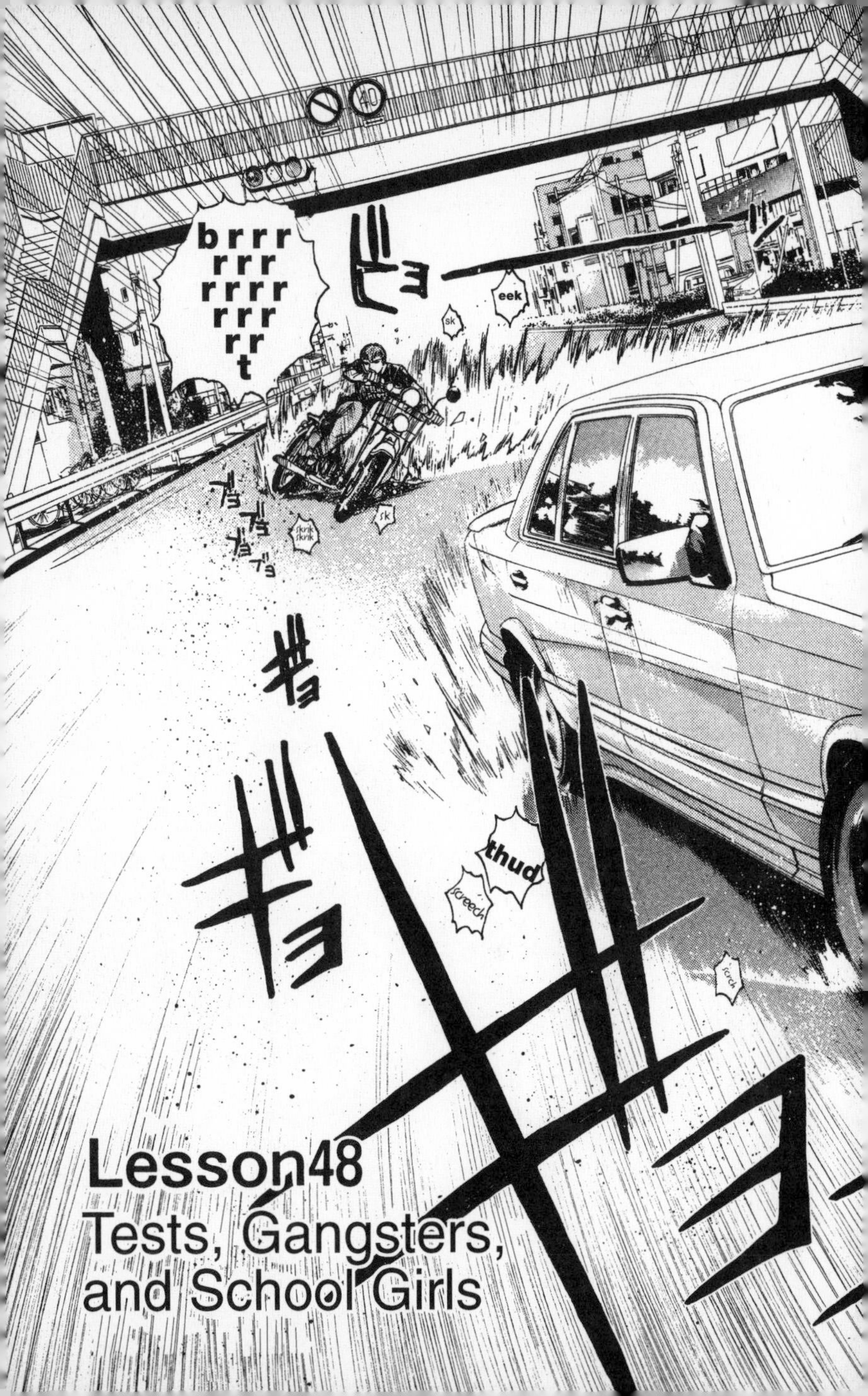
brrrrrrrrrrrrrrrt
eek
sk
sk
thud
screech
scrch

Lesson48
Tests, Gangsters, and School Girls

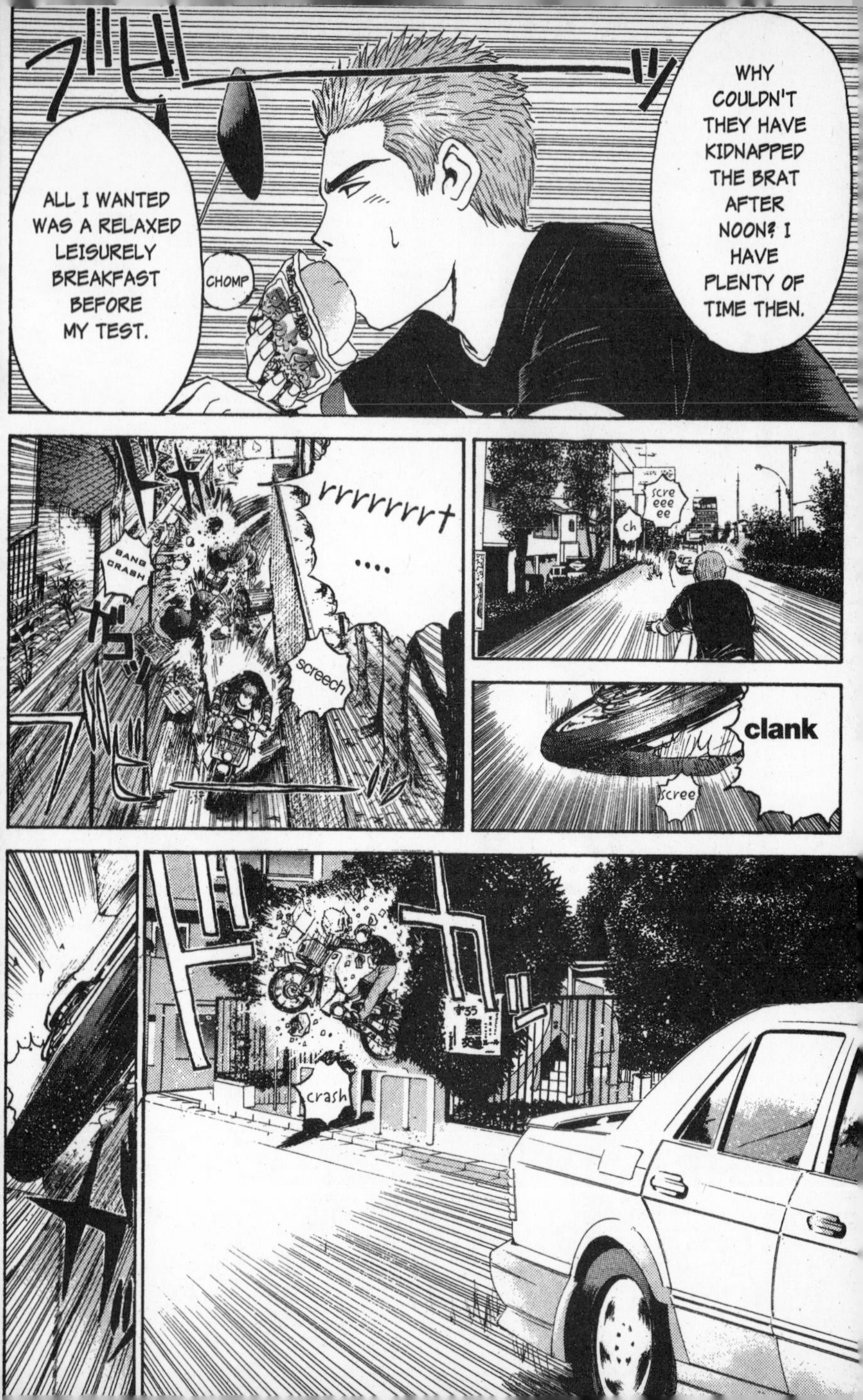
WHY COULDN'T THEY HAVE KIDNAPPED THE BRAT AFTER NOON? I HAVE PLENTY OF TIME THEN.
ALL I WANTED WAS A RELAXED LEISURELY BREAKFAST BEFORE MY TEST.
CHOMP
scre eee ee
ch
clank
scree
rrrrrrrrt
....
BANG CRASH
screech
crash

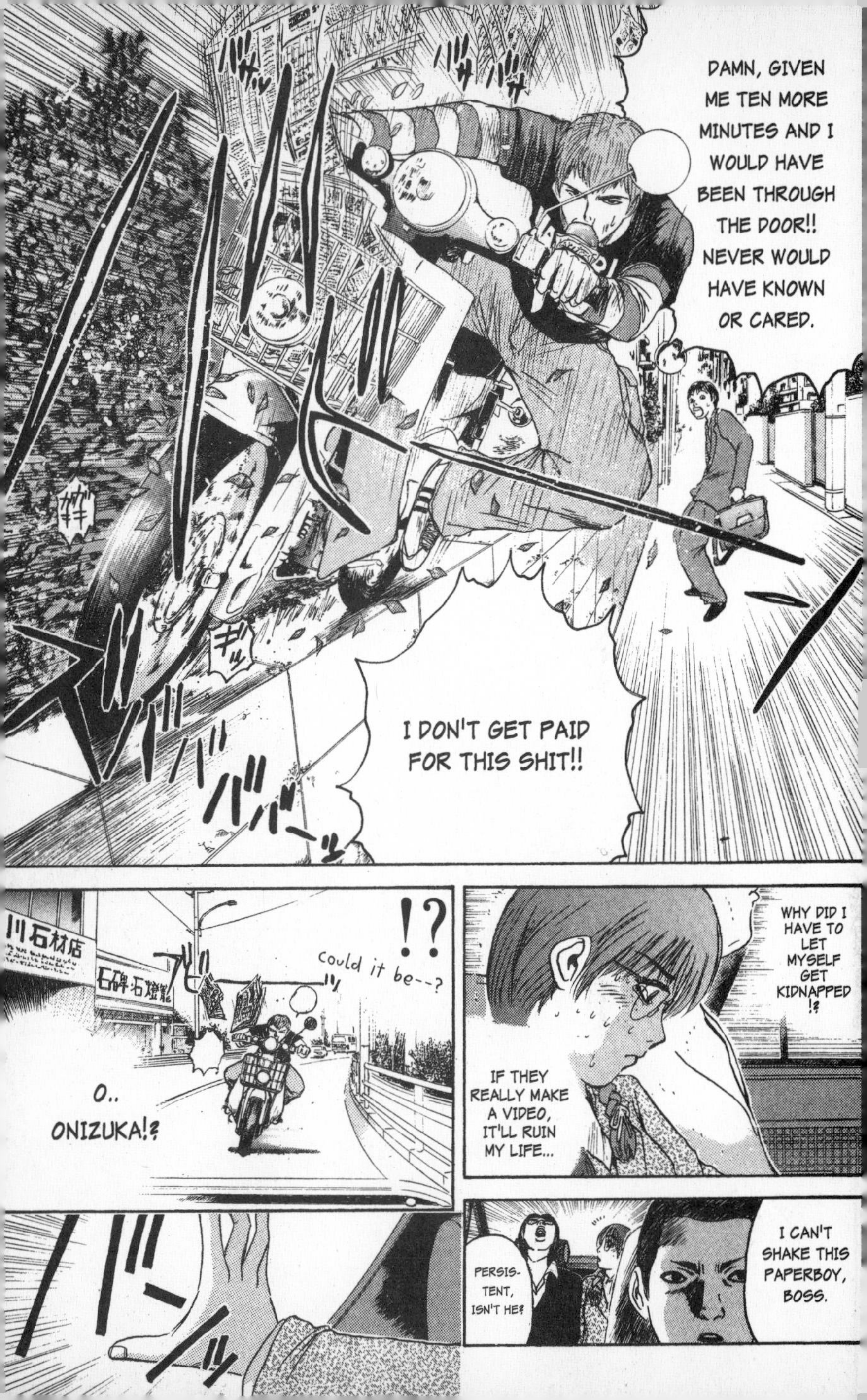
DAMN, GIVEN ME TEN MORE MINUTES AND I WOULD HAVE BEEN THROUGH THE DOOR!! NEVER WOULD HAVE KNOWN OR CARED.
I DON'T GET PAID FOR THIS SHIT!!
WHY DID I HAVE TO LET MYSELF GET KIDNAPPED!?
IF THEY REALLY MAKE A VIDEO, IT'LL RUIN MY LIFE...
!?
Could it be--?
川石材店
O.. ONIZUKA!?
I CAN'T SHAKE THIS PAPERBOY, BOSS.
PERSIS-TENT, ISN'T HE?

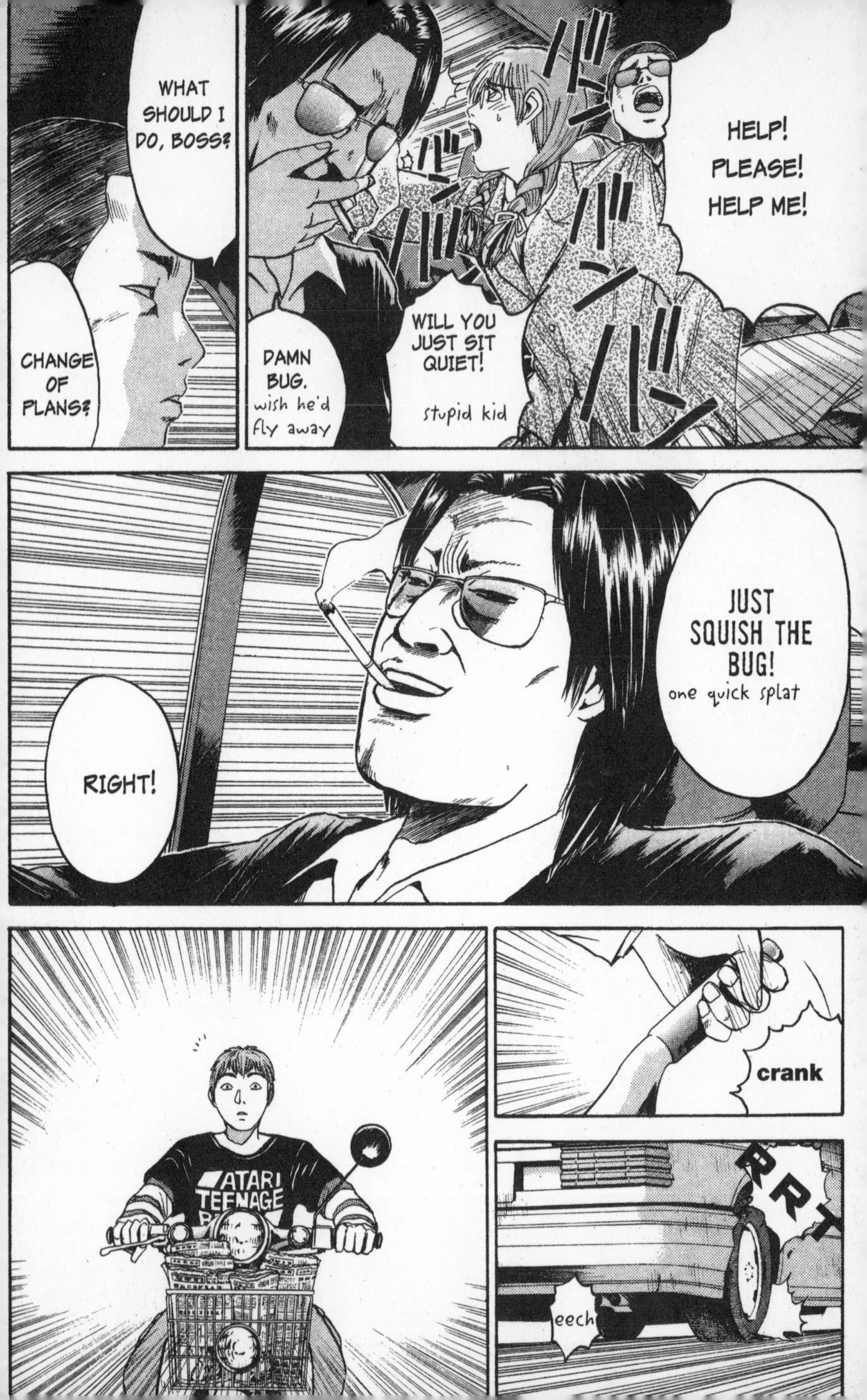
HELP! PLEASE! HELP ME!
WILL YOU JUST SIT QUIET!
stupid kid
DAMN BUG.
wish he'd fly away
WHAT SHOULD I DO, BOSS?
CHANGE OF PLANS?
JUST SQUISH THE BUG!
one quick splat
RIGHT!
crank
RRT
eech
ATARI TEENAGE

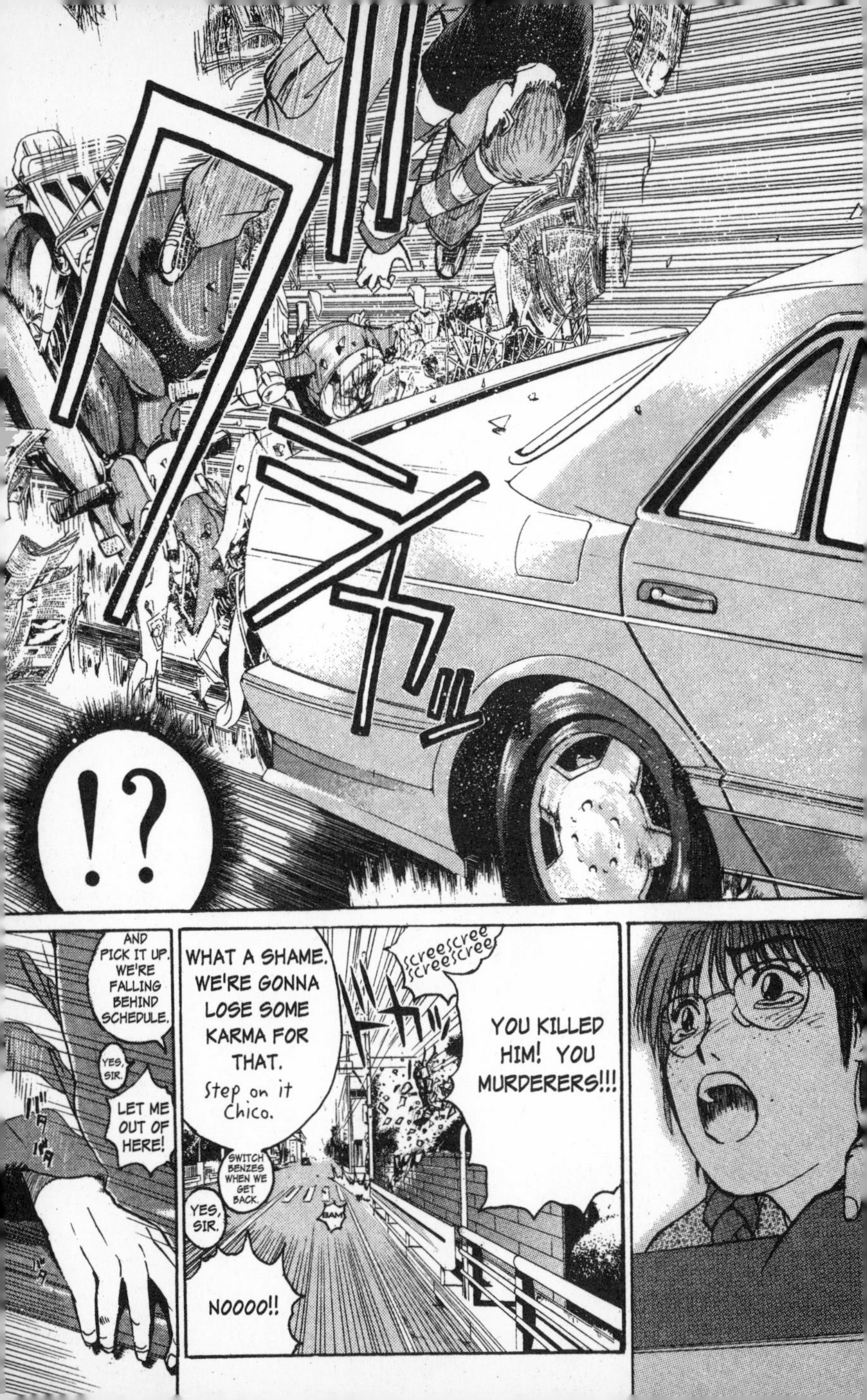
!?
YOU KILLED HIM! YOU MURDERERS!!!
screescree screescree
WHAT A SHAME. WE'RE GONNA LOSE SOME KARMA FOR THAT.
Step on it Chico.
SWITCH BENZES WHEN WE GET BACK.
YES, SIR.
BAM
NOOOO!!
AND PICK IT UP. WE'RE FALLING BEHIND SCHEDULE.
YES, SIR.
LET ME OUT OF HERE!

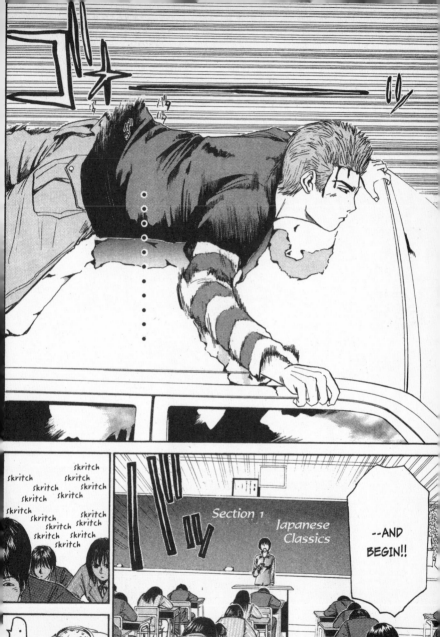

skritch skritch skritch skritch skritch skritch skritch skritch skritch skritch skritch skritch skritch skritch skritch skritch skritch

Section 1

Japanese Classics

--AND BEGIN!!

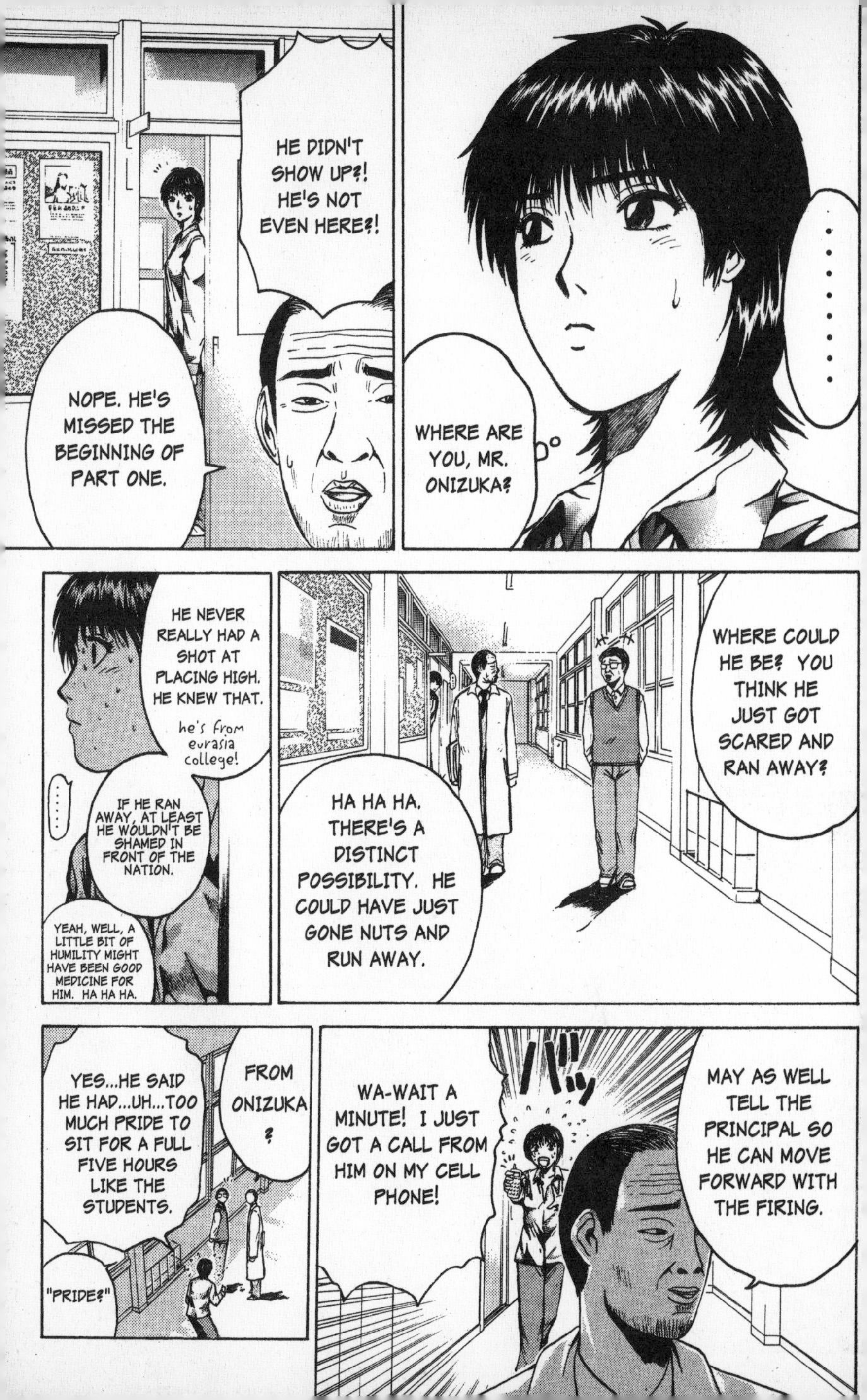
......
WHERE ARE YOU, MR. ONIZUKA?
HE DIDN'T SHOW UP?! HE'S NOT EVEN HERE?!
NOPE. HE'S MISSED THE BEGINNING OF PART ONE.
WHERE COULD HE BE? YOU THINK HE JUST GOT SCARED AND RAN AWAY?
HA HA HA. THERE'S A DISTINCT POSSIBILITY. HE COULD HAVE JUST GONE NUTS AND RUN AWAY.
HE NEVER REALLY HAD A SHOT AT PLACING HIGH. HE KNEW THAT.
he's from eurasia college!
......
IF HE RAN AWAY, AT LEAST HE WOULDN'T BE SHAMED IN FRONT OF THE NATION.
YEAH, WELL, A LITTLE BIT OF HUMILITY MIGHT HAVE BEEN GOOD MEDICINE FOR HIM. HA HA HA.
MAY AS WELL TELL THE PRINCIPAL SO HE CAN MOVE FORWARD WITH THE FIRING.
バッ
WA-WAIT A MINUTE! I JUST GOT A CALL FROM HIM ON MY CELL PHONE!
FROM ONIZUKA?
YES...HE SAID HE HAD...UH...TOO MUCH PRIDE TO SIT FOR A FULL FIVE HOURS LIKE THE STUDENTS.
"PRIDE?"

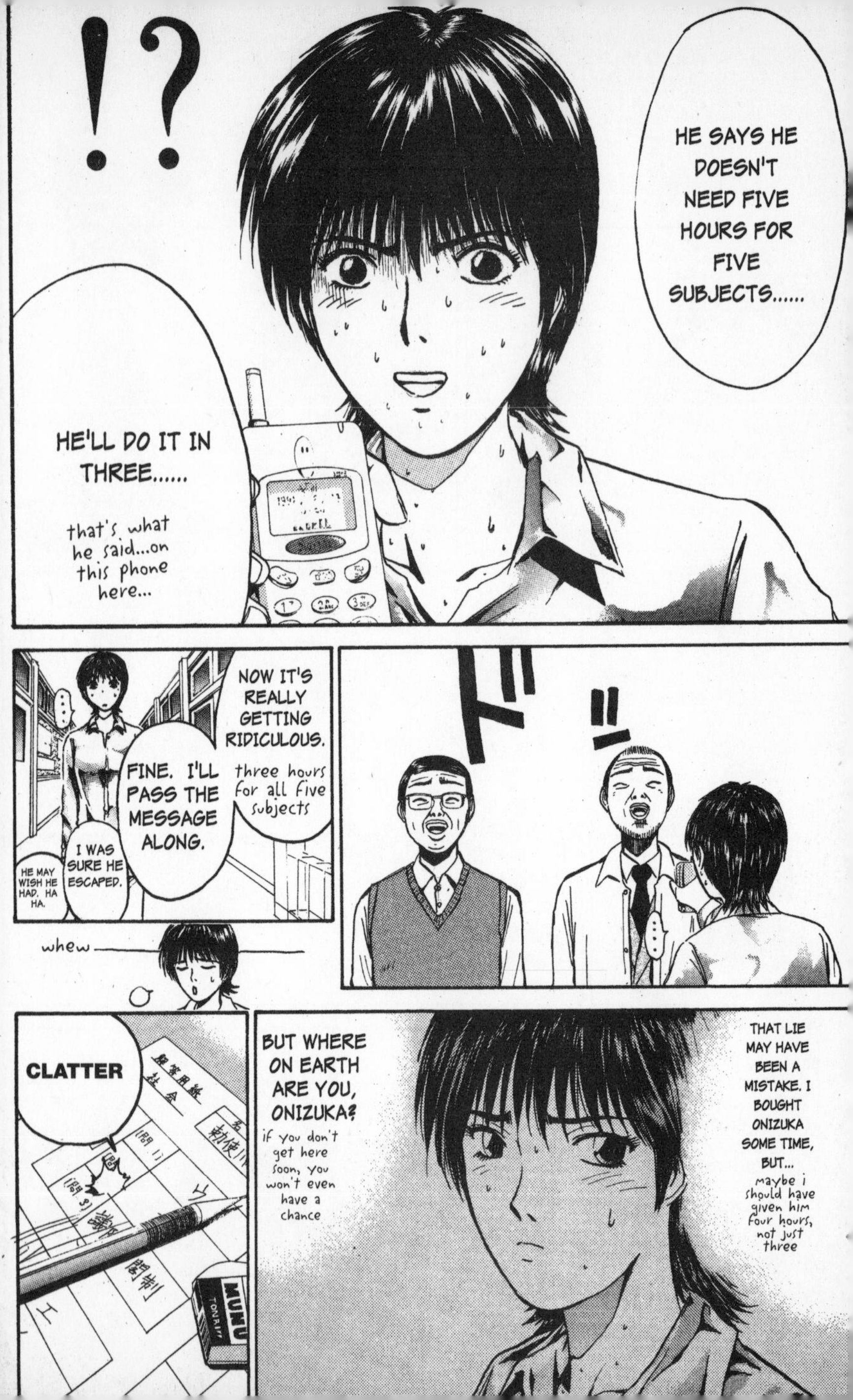
HE SAYS HE DOESN'T NEED FIVE HOURS FOR FIVE SUBJECTS......
!?
HE'LL DO IT IN THREE......
that's what he said...on this phone here...
NOW IT'S REALLY GETTING RIDICULOUS.
three hours for all five subjects
FINE. I'LL PASS THE MESSAGE ALONG.
I WAS SURE HE ESCAPED.
HE MAY WISH HE HAD. HA HA.
whew
THAT LIE MAY HAVE BEEN A MISTAKE. I BOUGHT ONIZUKA SOME TIME, BUT...
maybe i should have given him four hours, not just three
BUT WHERE ON EARTH ARE YOU, ONIZUKA?
if you don't get here soon, you won't even have a chance
CLATTER

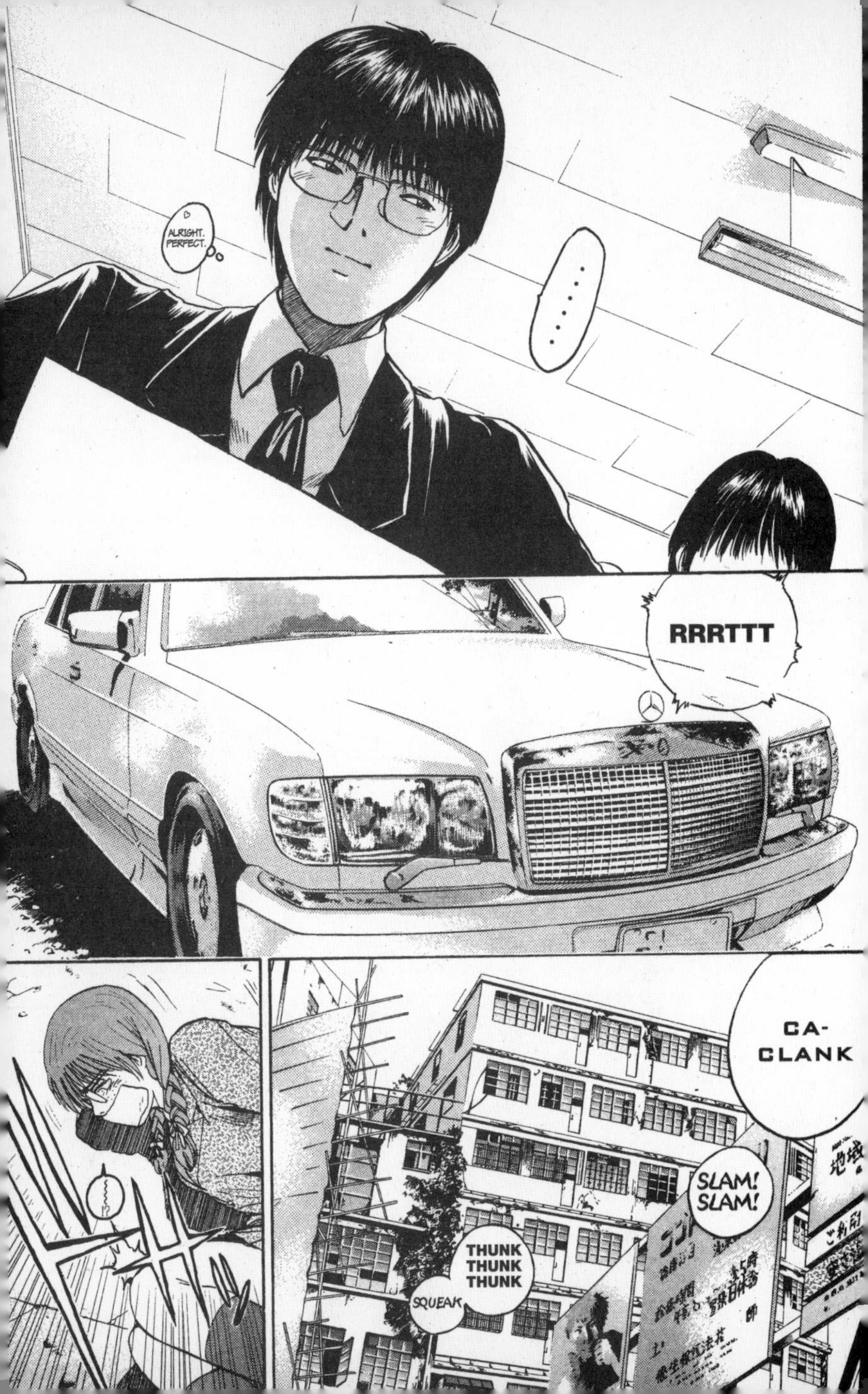
......
ALRIGHT. PERFECT.
RRRTTT
CA-CLANK
SLAM! SLAM!
THUNK THUNK THUNK
SQUEAK
...!?

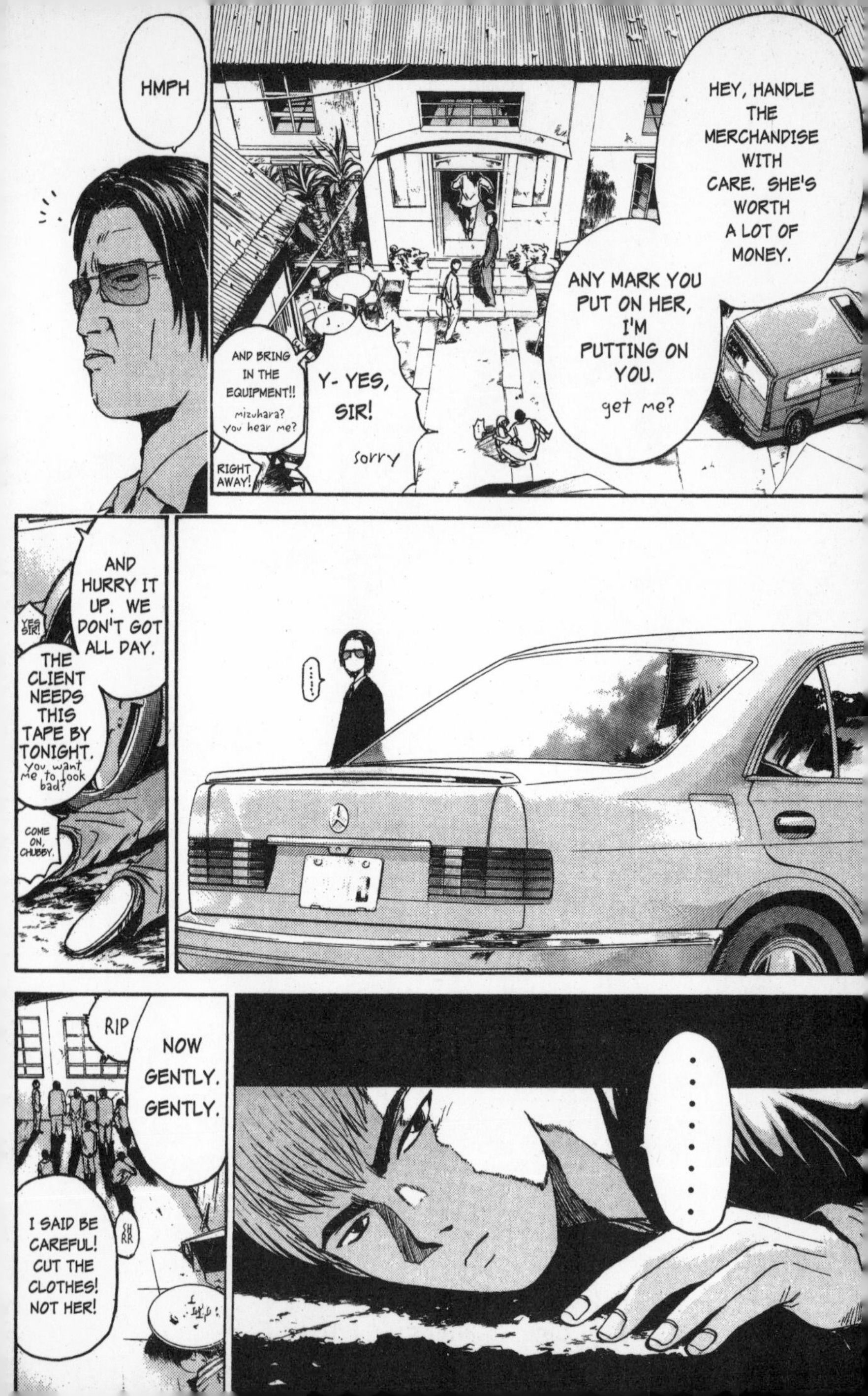
HEY, HANDLE THE MERCHANDISE WITH CARE. SHE'S WORTH A LOT OF MONEY.
ANY MARK YOU PUT ON HER, I'M PUTTING ON YOU.
get me?
Y- YES, SIR!
sorry
AND BRING IN THE EQUIPMENT!!
mizuhara? You hear me?
RIGHT AWAY!
HMPH
......
AND HURRY IT UP. WE DON'T GOT ALL DAY.
YES SIR!
THE CLIENT NEEDS THIS TAPE BY TONIGHT.
You want me to look bad?
COME ON, CHUBBY.
......
RIP
NOW GENTLY. GENTLY.
SHRR
I SAID BE CAREFUL! CUT THE CLOTHES! NOT HER!

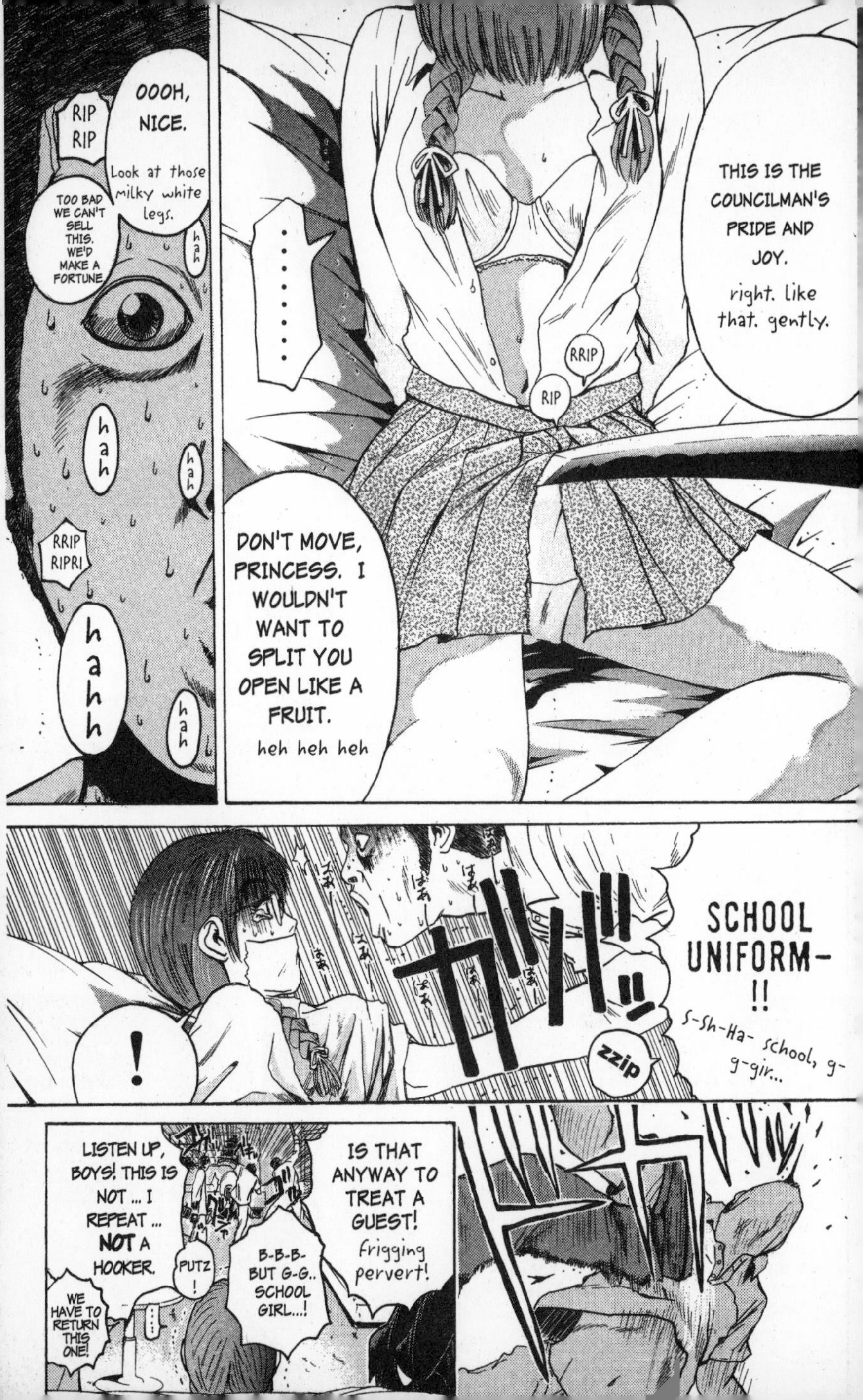
THIS IS THE COUNCILMAN'S PRIDE AND JOY.
right. like that. gently.
....
RRIP
RIP
DON'T MOVE, PRINCESS. I WOULDN'T WANT TO SPLIT YOU OPEN LIKE A FRUIT.
heh heh heh
OOOH, NICE.
Look at those milky white legs.
RIP RIP
TOO BAD WE CAN'T SELL THIS. WE'D MAKE A FORTUNE
hah
hah
hah
RRIP RIPRI
hahh
hah
SCHOOL UNIFORM-!!
S-Sh-Ha- school, g-g-gir...
zzip
!
IS THAT ANYWAY TO TREAT A GUEST!
frigging pervert!
LISTEN UP, BOYS! THIS IS NOT ... I REPEAT ... **NOT** A HOOKER.
B-B-B-BUT G-G.. SCHOOL GIRL...!
PUTZ !
WE HAVE TO RETURN THIS ONE!
...

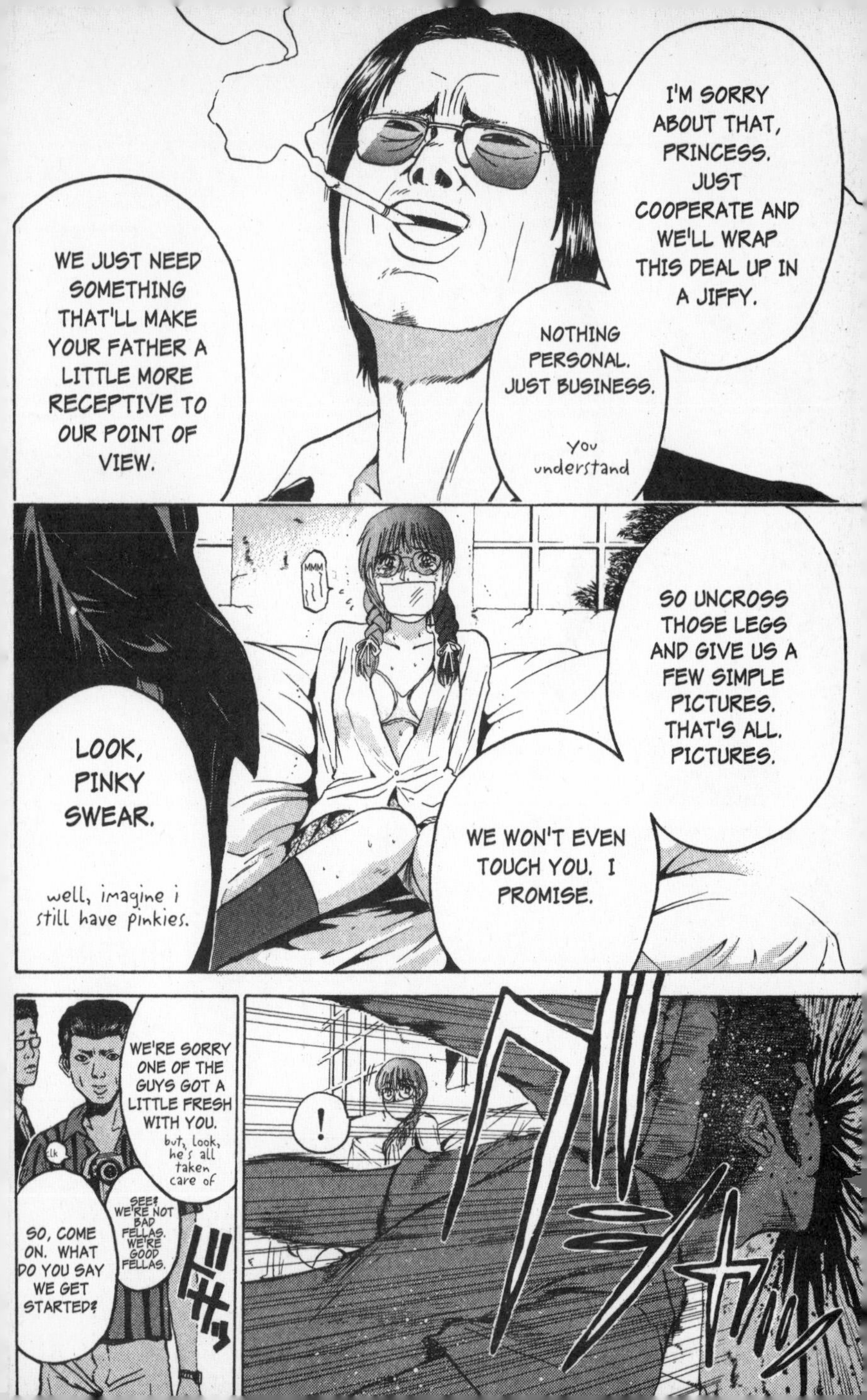
I'M SORRY ABOUT THAT, PRINCESS. JUST COOPERATE AND WE'LL WRAP THIS DEAL UP IN A JIFFY.
NOTHING PERSONAL. JUST BUSINESS.
you understand
WE JUST NEED SOMETHING THAT'LL MAKE YOUR FATHER A LITTLE MORE RECEPTIVE TO OUR POINT OF VIEW.
MMM
SO UNCROSS THOSE LEGS AND GIVE US A FEW SIMPLE PICTURES. THAT'S ALL. PICTURES.
WE WON'T EVEN TOUCH YOU. I PROMISE.
LOOK, PINKY SWEAR.
well, imagine i still have pinkies.
!
WE'RE SORRY ONE OF THE GUYS GOT A LITTLE FRESH WITH YOU.
but, look, he's all taken care of
clk
SEE? WE'RE NOT BAD FELLAS. WE'RE GOOD FELLAS.
SO, COME ON. WHAT DO YOU SAY WE GET STARTED?

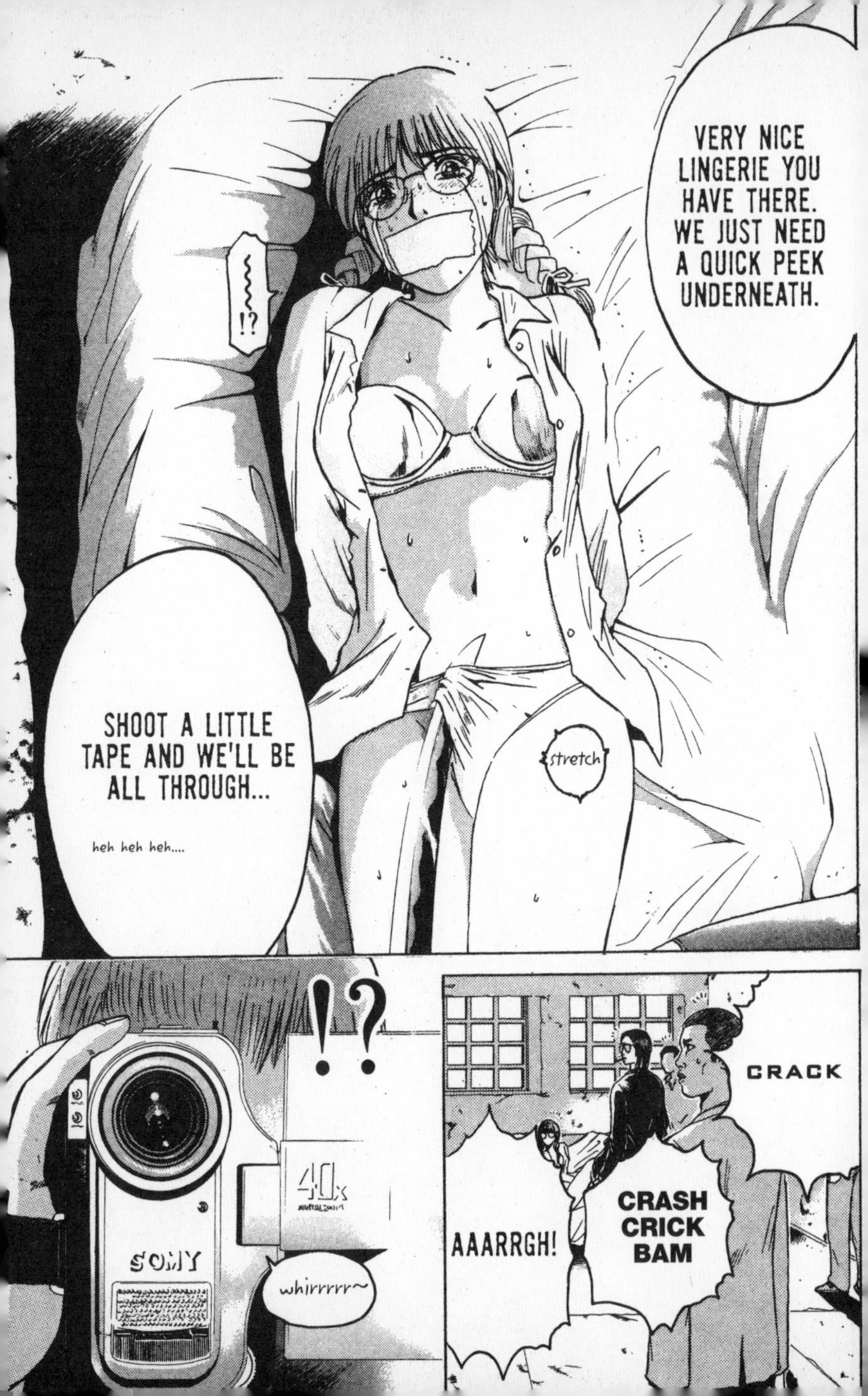
VERY NICE LINGERIE YOU HAVE THERE. WE JUST NEED A QUICK PEEK UNDERNEATH.
~~~~!?
stretch
SHOOT A LITTLE TAPE AND WE'LL BE ALL THROUGH...
heh heh heh....
CRACK
CRASH CRICK BAM
AAARRGH!
!?
40x
SOMY
whirrrrr~
~~~~

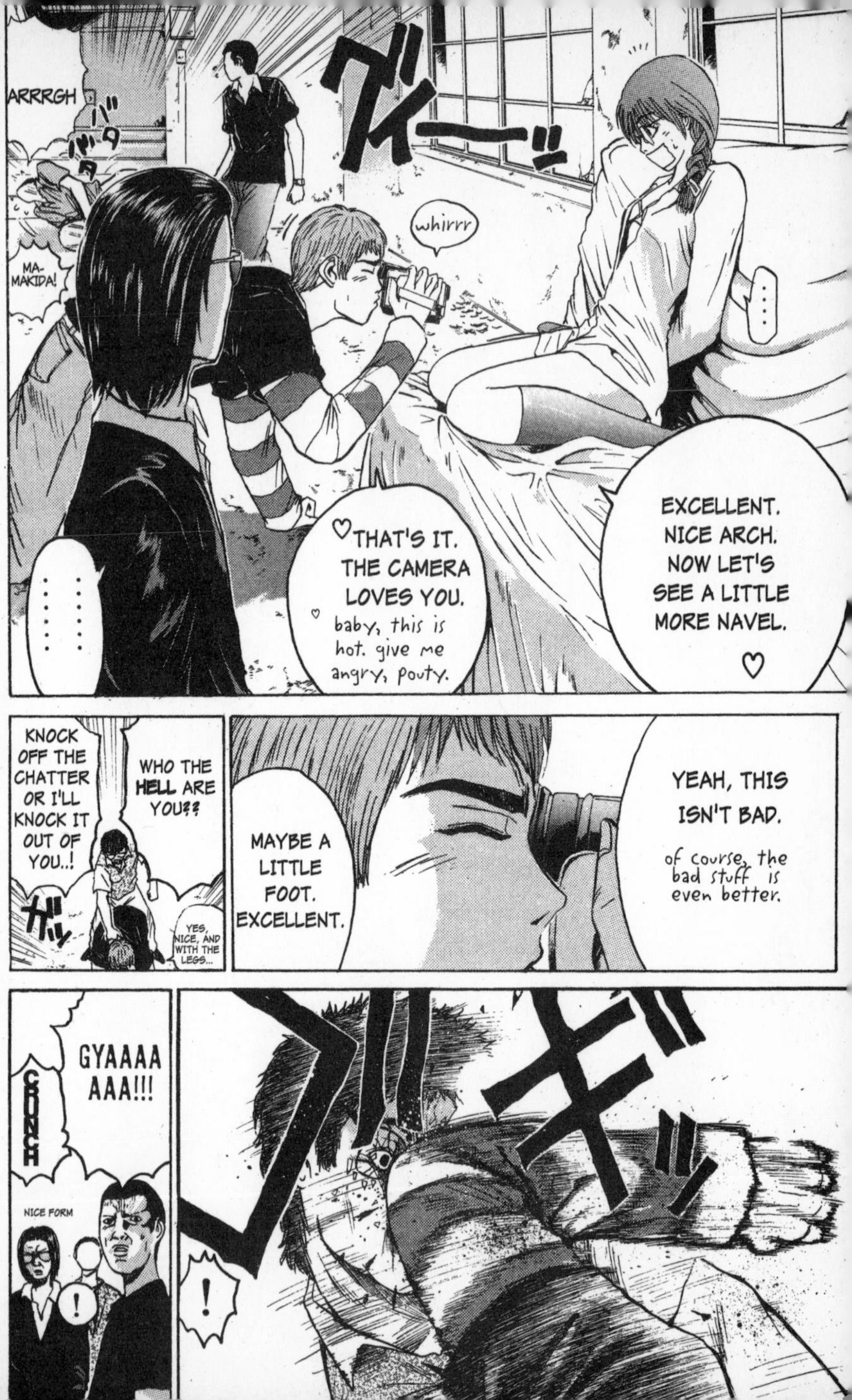
EXCELLENT. NICE ARCH. NOW LET'S SEE A LITTLE MORE NAVEL. ♡
....
ヴィーーヅ
whirrr
♡THAT'S IT. THE CAMERA LOVES YOU.
♡ baby, this is hot. give me angry, pouty.
ARRRGH
MA-MAKIDA!
......
YEAH, THIS ISN'T BAD.
of course, the bad stuff is even better.
MAYBE A LITTLE FOOT. EXCELLENT.
WHO THE HELL ARE YOU??
KNOCK OFF THE CHATTER OR I'LL KNOCK IT OUT OF YOU..!
YES, NICE, AND WITH THE LEGS...
!
GYAAAAAAA!!!
CRUNCH
NICE FORM
!

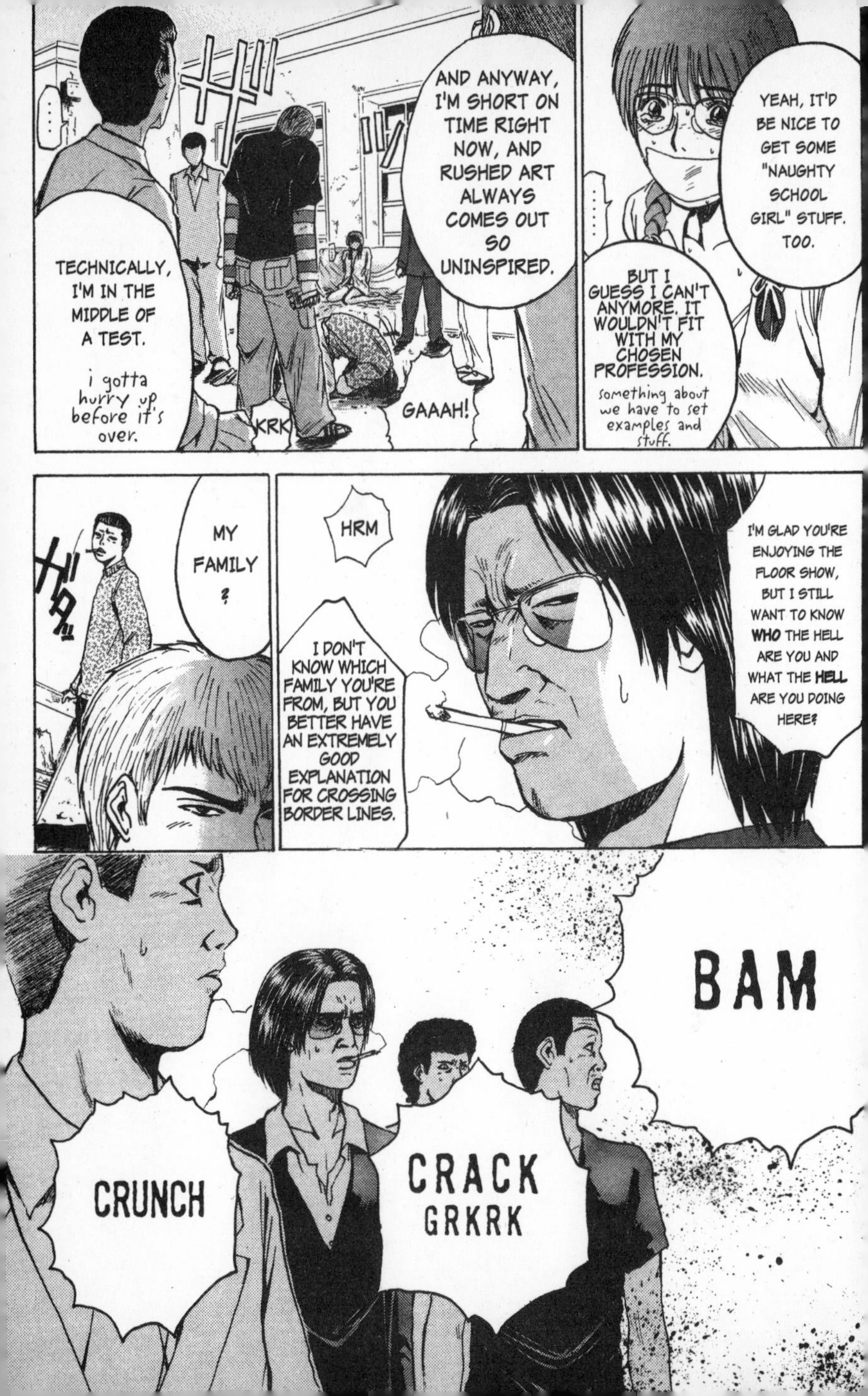
YEAH, IT'D BE NICE TO GET SOME "NAUGHTY SCHOOL GIRL" STUFF. TOO.
BUT I GUESS I CAN'T ANYMORE. IT WOULDN'T FIT WITH MY CHOSEN PROFESSION.
something about we have to set examples and stuff.
AND ANYWAY, I'M SHORT ON TIME RIGHT NOW, AND RUSHED ART ALWAYS COMES OUT SO UNINSPIRED.
GAAAH!
TECHNICALLY, I'M IN THE MIDDLE OF A TEST.
i gotta hurry up before it's over.
KRK
I'M GLAD YOU'RE ENJOYING THE FLOOR SHOW, BUT I STILL WANT TO KNOW **WHO** THE HELL ARE YOU AND WHAT THE **HELL** ARE YOU DOING HERE?
HRM
I DON'T KNOW WHICH FAMILY YOU'RE FROM, BUT YOU BETTER HAVE AN EXTREMELY GOOD EXPLANATION FOR CROSSING BORDER LINES.
MY FAMILY?
BAM
CRACK
GRKRK
CRUNCH

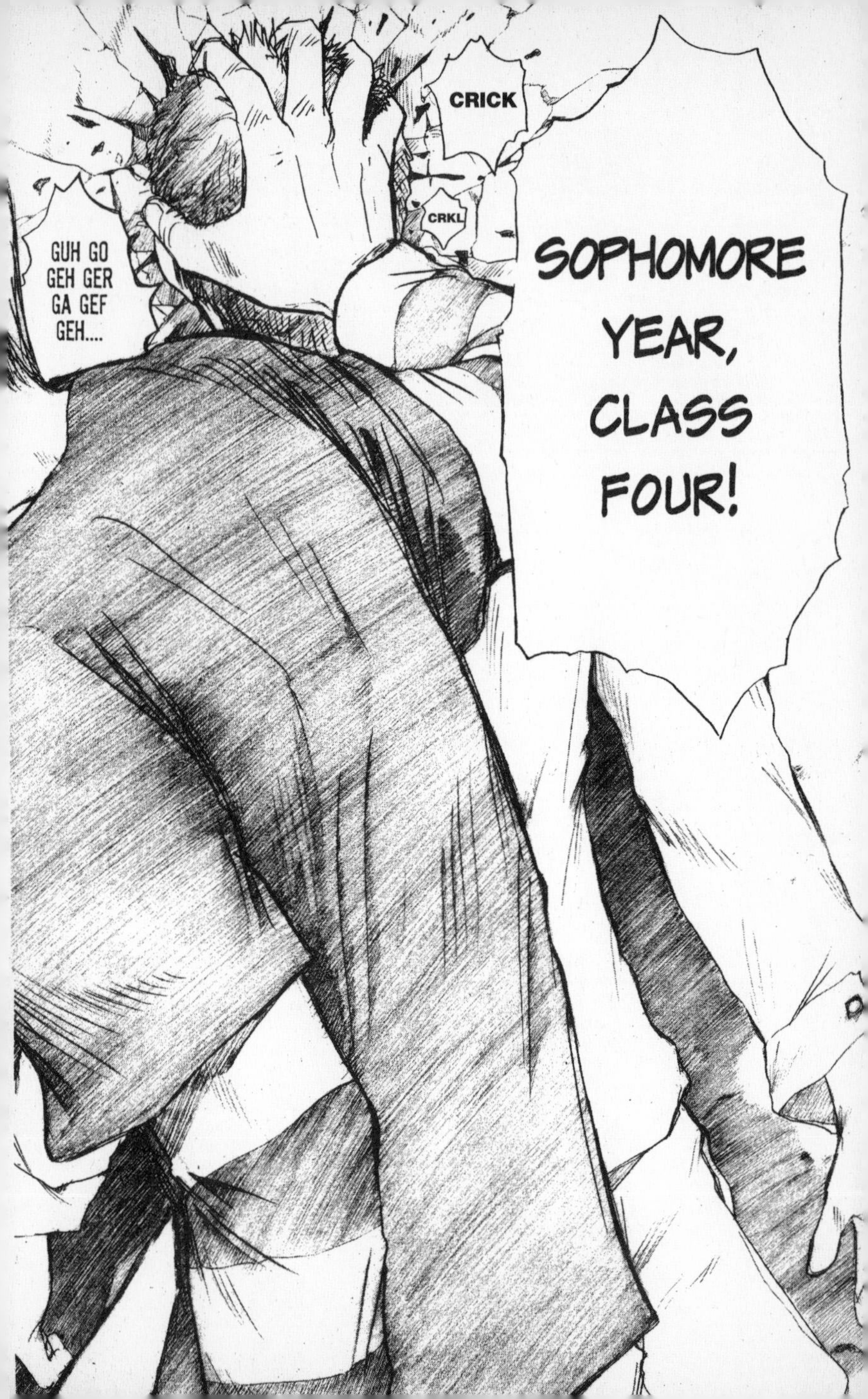
SOPHOMORE YEAR, CLASS FOUR!
CRICK
CRKL
GUH GO GEH GER GA GEF GEH....

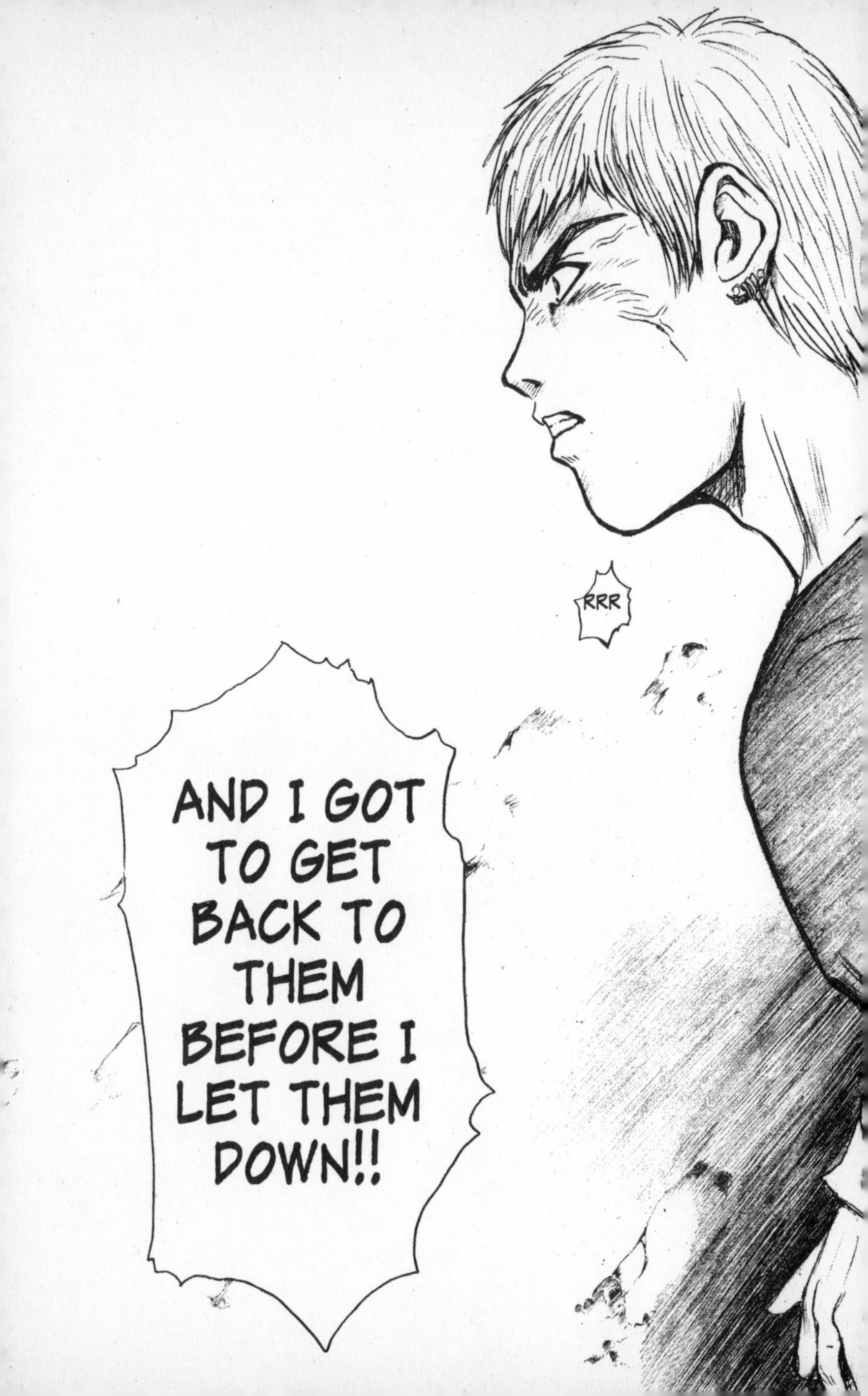
RRR
AND I GOT TO GET BACK TO THEM BEFORE I LET THEM DOWN!!

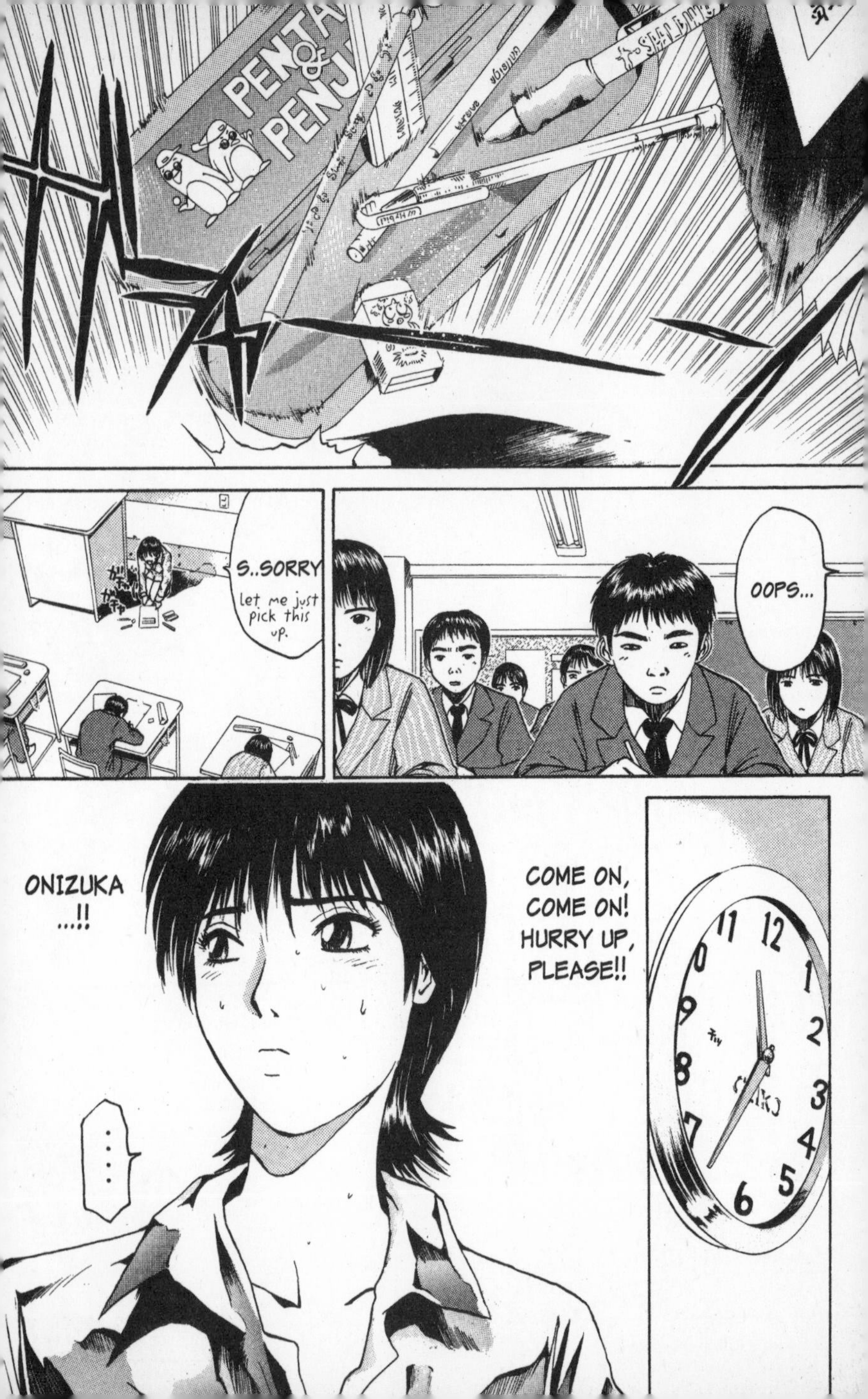
OOPS...
S..SORRY
let me just pick this up.
COME ON, COME ON! HURRY UP, PLEASE!!
ONIZUKA ...!!
....

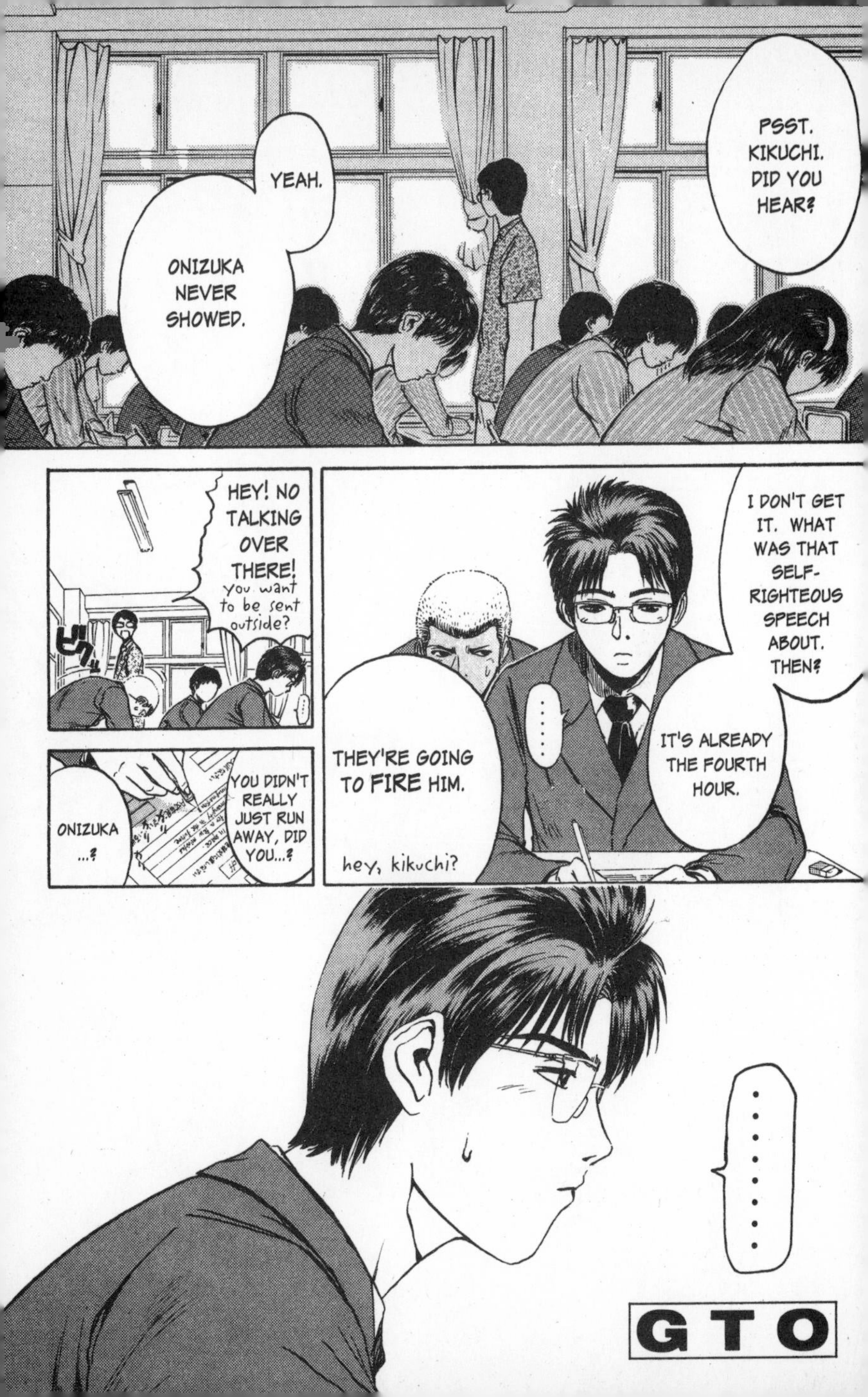
PSST. KIKUCHI. DID YOU HEAR?
YEAH.
ONIZUKA NEVER SHOWED.
I DON'T GET IT. WHAT WAS THAT SELF-RIGHTEOUS SPEECH ABOUT. THEN?
IT'S ALREADY THE FOURTH HOUR.
......
THEY'RE GOING TO FIRE HIM.
hey, kikuchi?
HEY! NO TALKING OVER THERE! you want to be sent outside?
ビクッ
...
YOU DIDN'T REALLY JUST RUN AWAY, DID YOU...?
ONIZUKA ...?
....
GTO

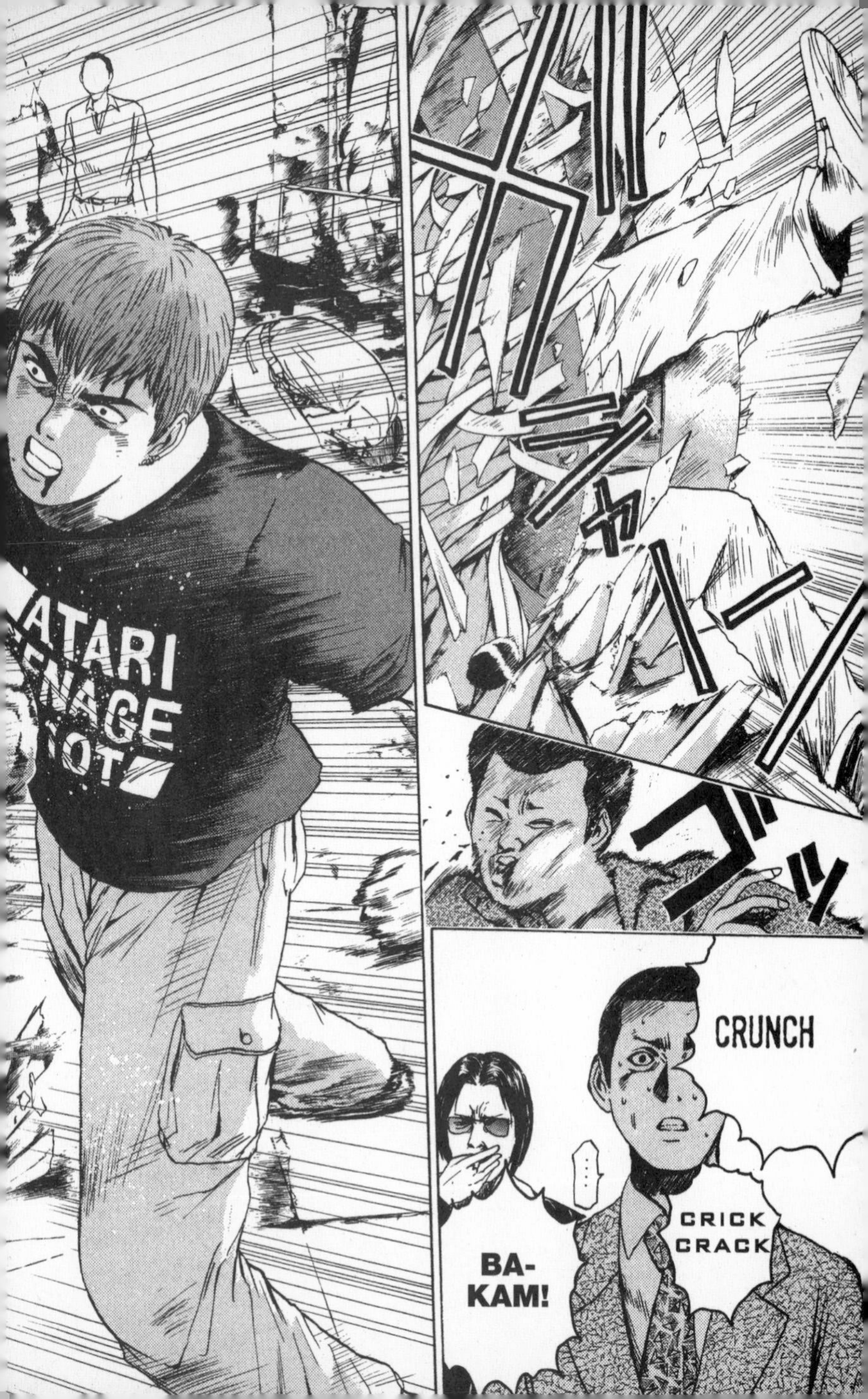
ゴッ
CRUNCH
CRICK CRACK
...
BA-KAM!
ATARI

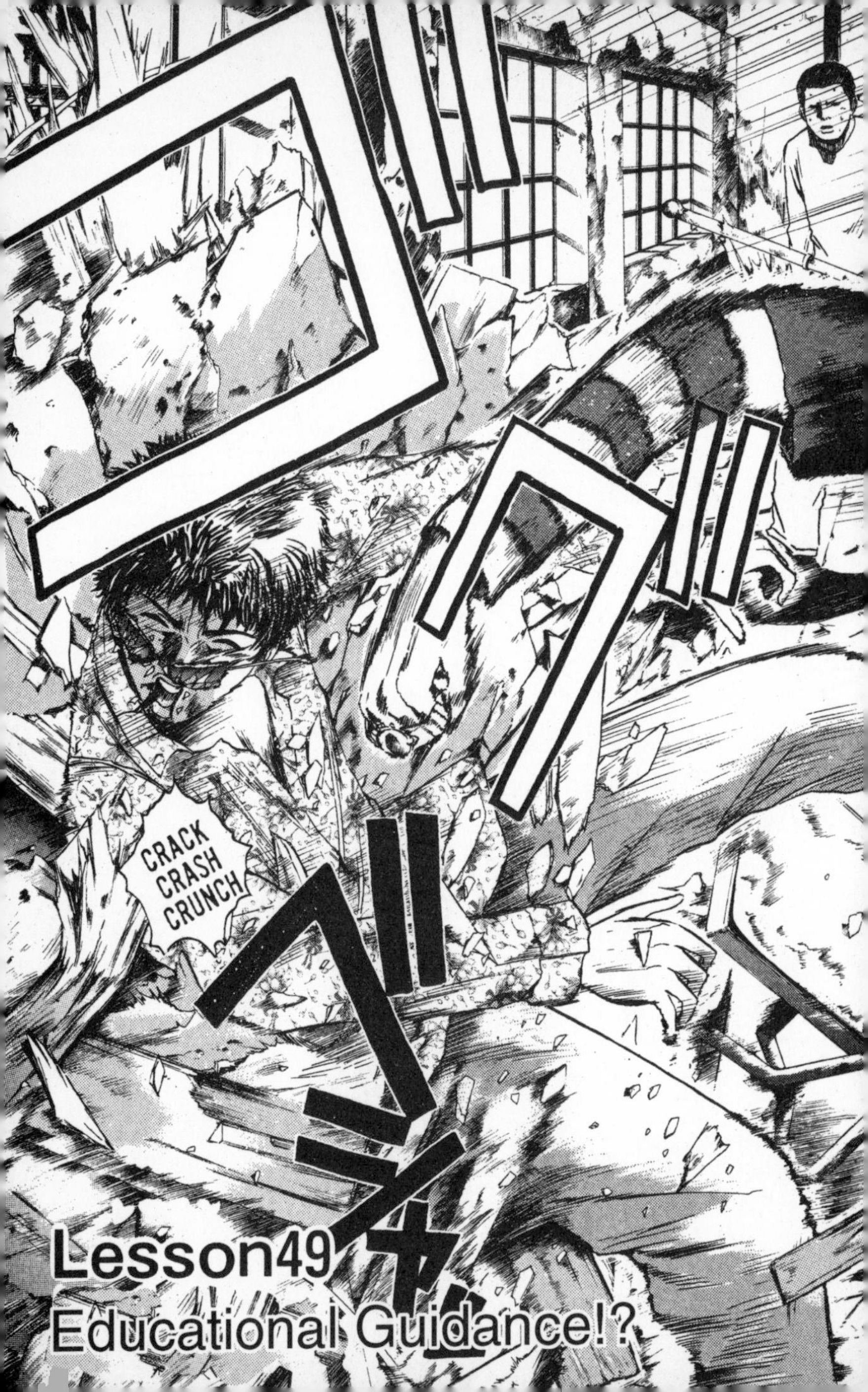
CRACK CRASH CRUNCH
Lesson49
Educational Guidance!?

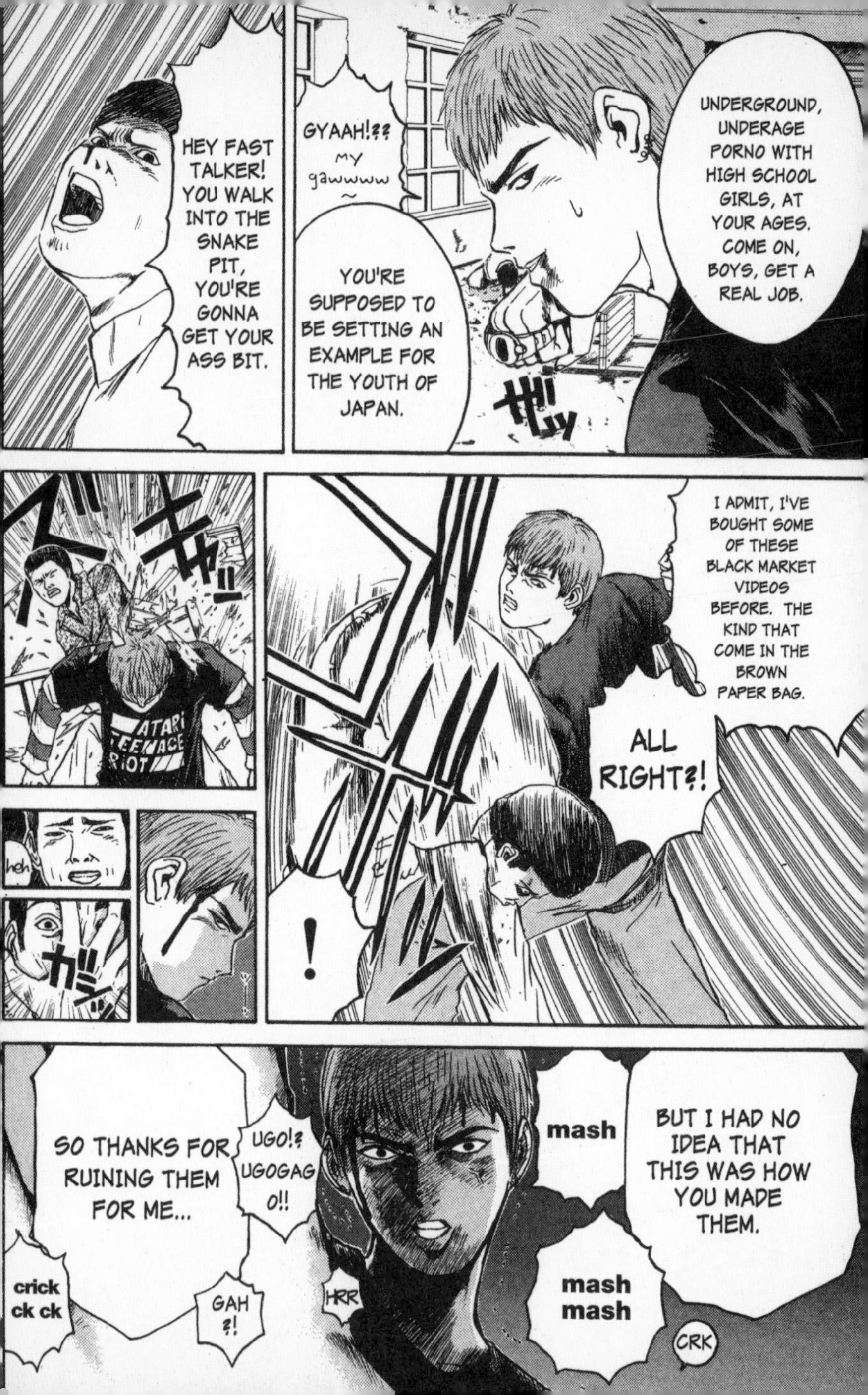
UNDERGROUND, UNDERAGE PORNO WITH HIGH SCHOOL GIRLS, AT YOUR AGES. COME ON, BOYS, GET A REAL JOB.
GYAAH!??
my gawwww~
YOU'RE SUPPOSED TO BE SETTING AN EXAMPLE FOR THE YOUTH OF JAPAN.
HEY FAST TALKER! YOU WALK INTO THE SNAKE PIT, YOU'RE GONNA GET YOUR ASS BIT.
I ADMIT, I'VE BOUGHT SOME OF THESE BLACK MARKET VIDEOS BEFORE. THE KIND THAT COME IN THE BROWN PAPER BAG.
ALL RIGHT?!
!
heh
BUT I HAD NO IDEA THAT THIS WAS HOW YOU MADE THEM.
mash
CRK
mash mash
HRR
UGO!? UGOGAG O!!
SO THANKS FOR RUINING THEM FOR ME...
GAH ?!
crick ck ck

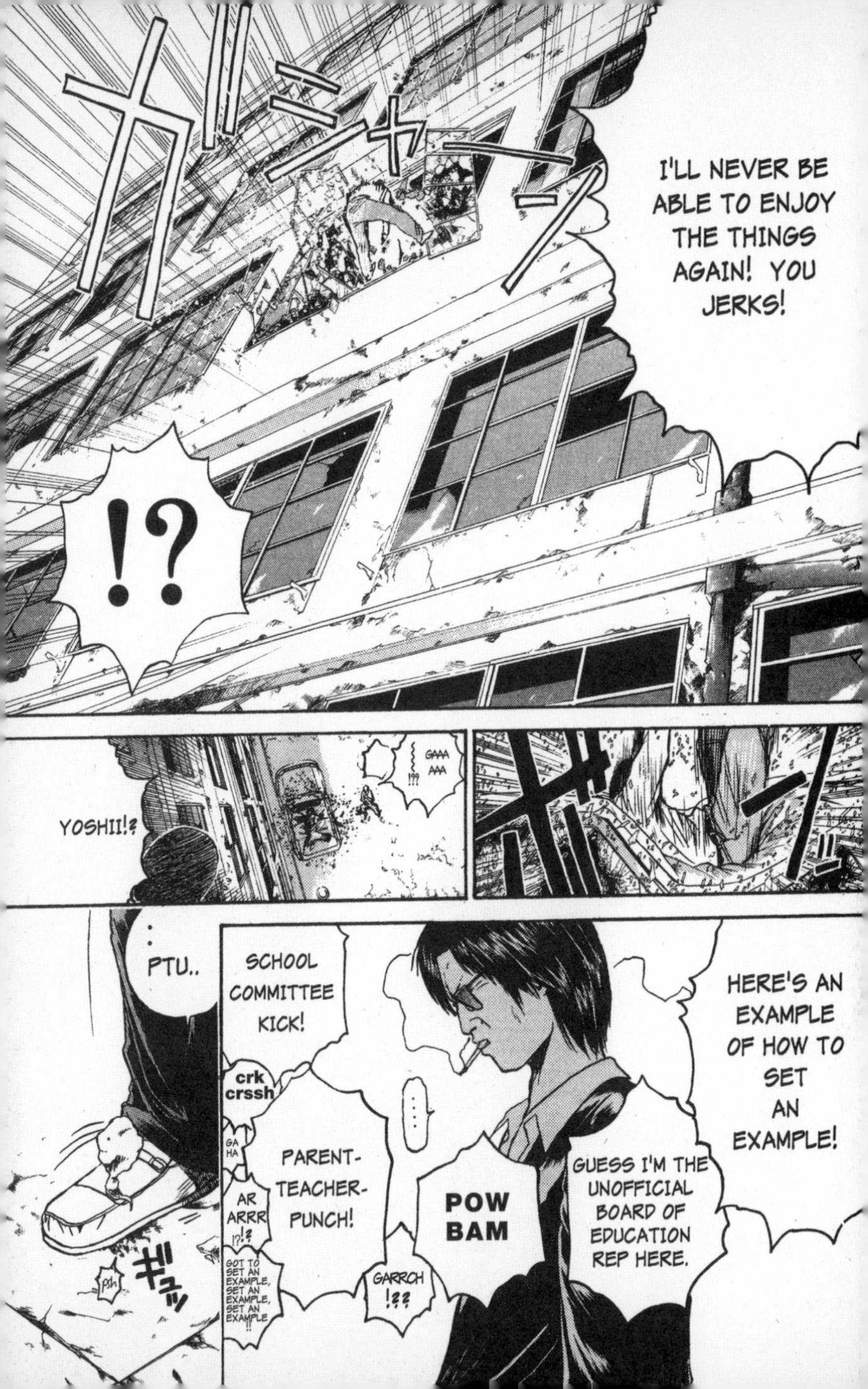
I'LL NEVER BE ABLE TO ENJOY THE THINGS AGAIN! YOU JERKS!
!?
GAAA AAA !??
YOSHII!?
HERE'S AN EXAMPLE OF HOW TO SET AN EXAMPLE!
GUESS I'M THE UNOFFICIAL BOARD OF EDUCATION REP HERE.
POW BAM
GARRCH !??
....
SCHOOL COMMITTEE KICK!
PARENT-TEACHER-PUNCH!
crk crssh
GA HA
AR ARRR !?!?
GOT TO SET AN EXAMPLE, SET AN EXAMPLE, SET AN EXAMPLE !!
... PTU..
pth

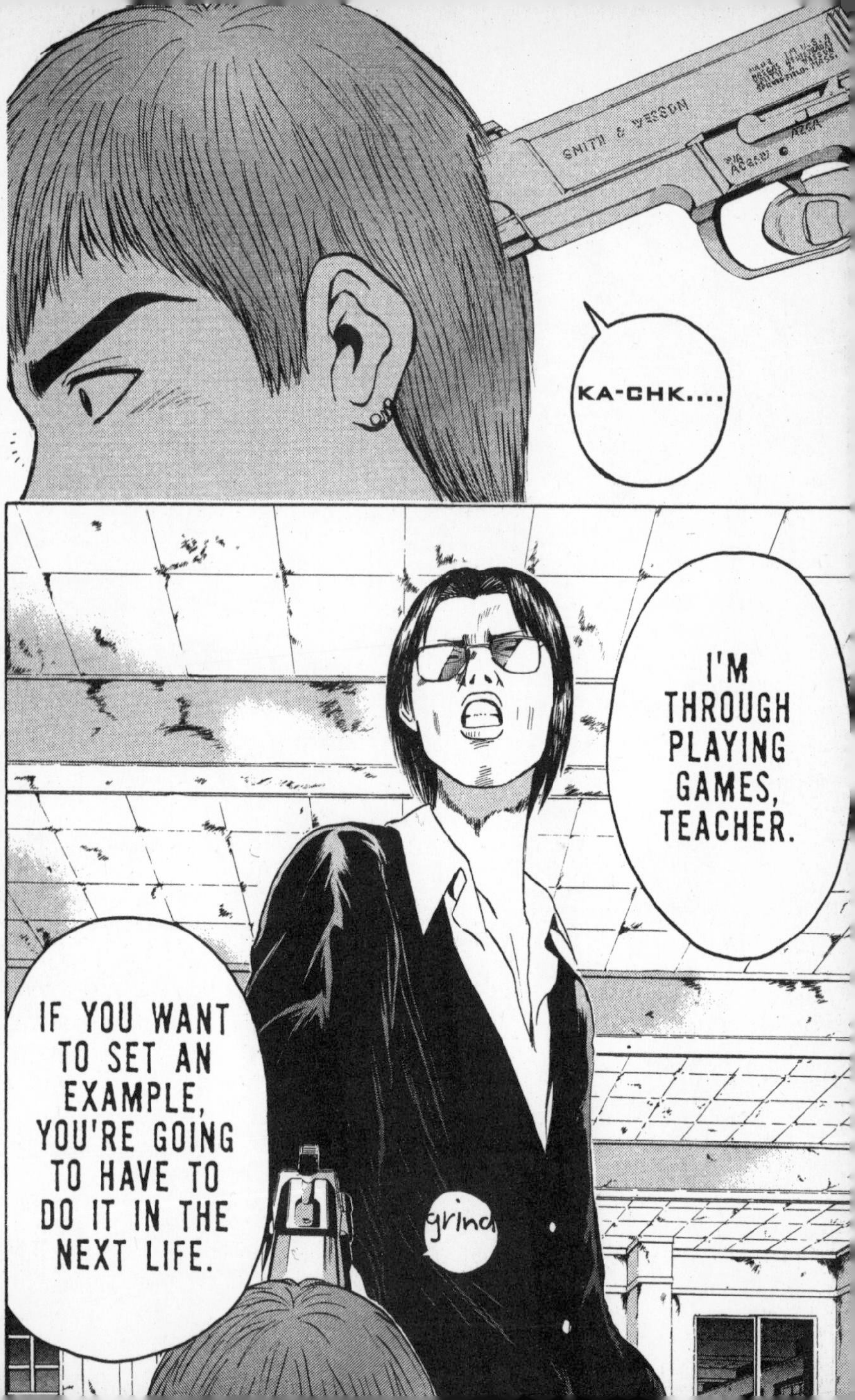
SMITH & WESSON
KA-CHK....
I'M THROUGH PLAYING GAMES, TEACHER.
IF YOU WANT TO SET AN EXAMPLE, YOU'RE GOING TO HAVE TO DO IT IN THE NEXT LIFE.
grind

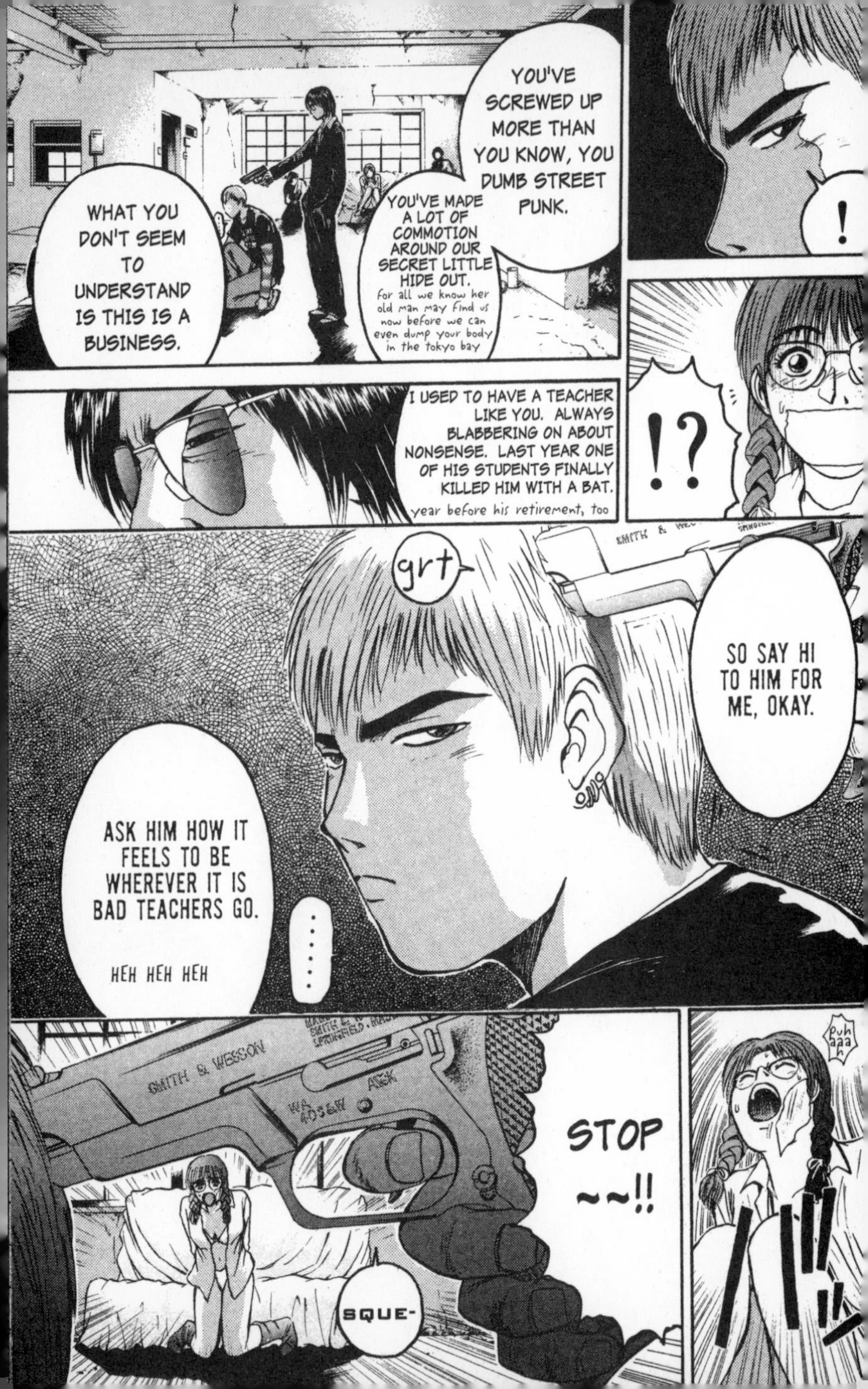
!
YOU'VE SCREWED UP MORE THAN YOU KNOW, YOU DUMB STREET PUNK.
YOU'VE MADE A LOT OF COMMOTION AROUND OUR SECRET LITTLE HIDE OUT.
for all we know her old man may find us now before we can even dump your body in the tokyo bay
WHAT YOU DON'T SEEM TO UNDERSTAND IS THIS IS A BUSINESS.
!?
I USED TO HAVE A TEACHER LIKE YOU. ALWAYS BLABBERING ON ABOUT NONSENSE. LAST YEAR ONE OF HIS STUDENTS FINALLY KILLED HIM WITH A BAT.
year before his retirement, too
SO SAY HI TO HIM FOR ME, OKAY.
grt
ASK HIM HOW IT FEELS TO BE WHEREVER IT IS BAD TEACHERS GO.
HEH HEH HEH
......
puh aaa h
STOP ~~!!
SMITH & WESSON
SQUE-

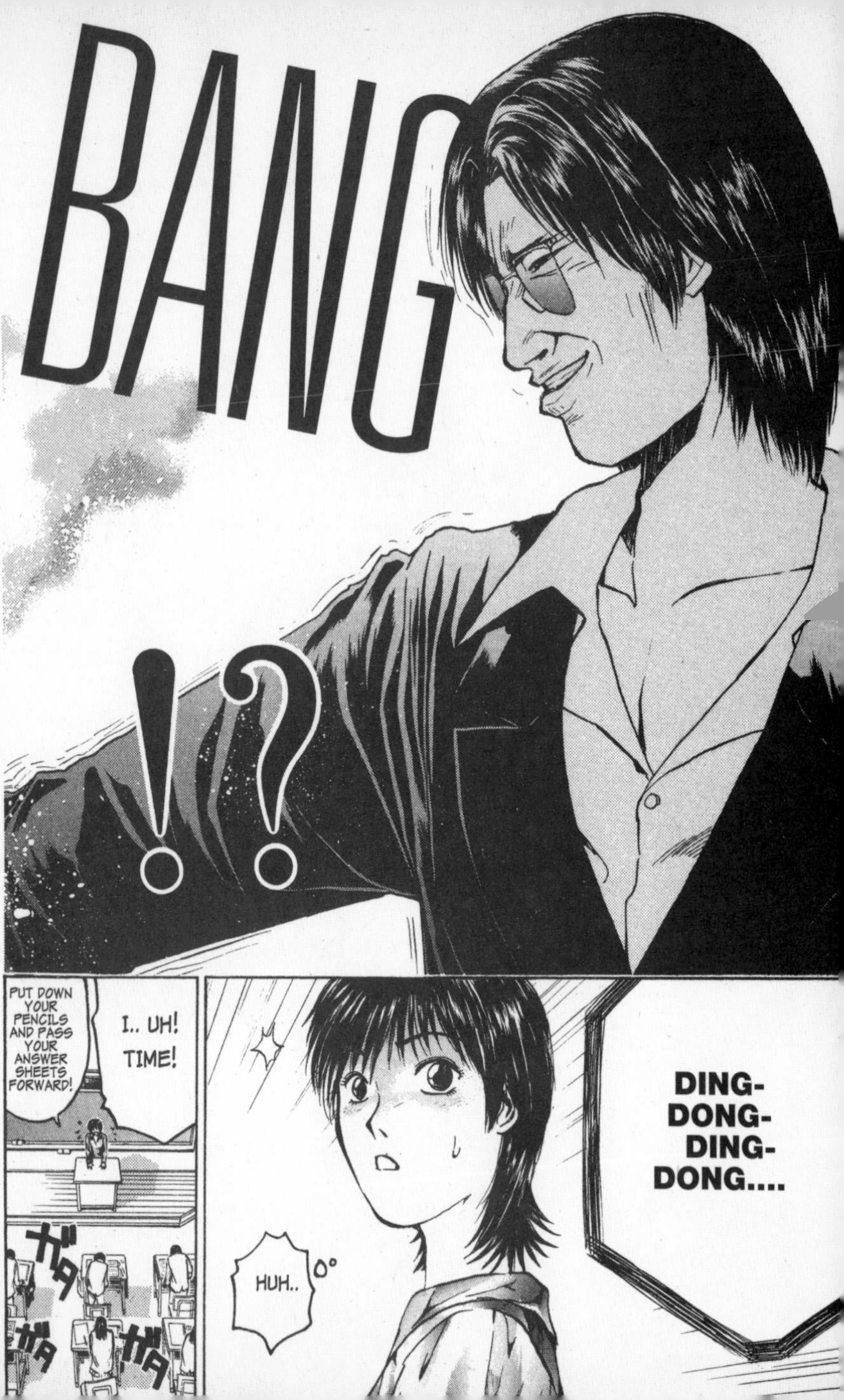
BANG
!?
DING-DONG-DING-DONG....
HUH..
I.. UH! TIME!
PUT DOWN YOUR PENCILS AND PASS YOUR ANSWER SHEETS FORWARD!
ガタ
ガタ
ガタ

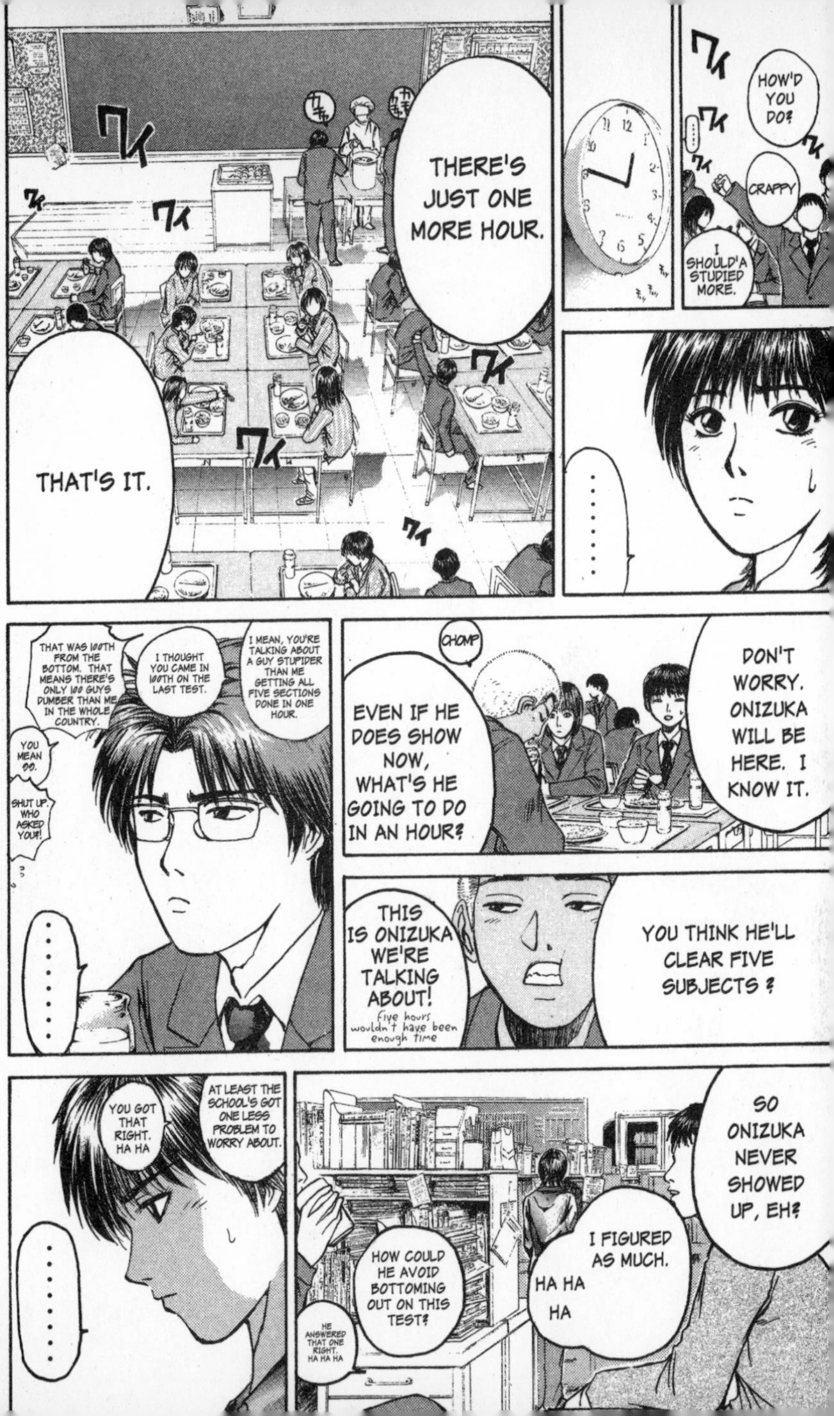
ワイ
HOW'D YOU DO?
ワイ
.....
CRAPPY
ワイ
I SHOULD'A STUDIED MORE.
......
THERE'S JUST ONE MORE HOUR.
ワイ
ワイ
ワイ
ワイ
ワイ
ワイ
THAT'S IT.
DON'T WORRY. ONIZUKA WILL BE HERE. I KNOW IT.
CHOMP
EVEN IF HE DOES SHOW NOW, WHAT'S HE GOING TO DO IN AN HOUR?
YOU THINK HE'LL CLEAR FIVE SUBJECTS?
THIS IS ONIZUKA WE'RE TALKING ABOUT!
five hours wouldn't have been enough time
I MEAN, YOU'RE TALKING ABOUT A GUY STUPIDER THAN ME GETTING ALL FIVE SECTIONS DONE IN ONE HOUR.
I THOUGHT YOU CAME IN 100TH ON THE LAST TEST.
THAT WAS 100TH FROM THE BOTTOM. THAT MEANS THERE'S ONLY 100 GUYS DUMBER THAN ME IN THE WHOLE COUNTRY.
YOU MEAN DO.
SHUT UP. WHO ASKED YOU?!
......
SO ONIZUKA NEVER SHOWED UP, EH?
I FIGURED AS MUCH.
HA HA HA
HOW COULD HE AVOID BOTTOMING OUT ON THIS TEST?
HE ANSWERED THAT ONE RIGHT. HA HA HA
AT LEAST THE SCHOOL'S GOT ONE LESS PROBLEM TO WORRY ABOUT.
YOU GOT THAT RIGHT. HA HA
......

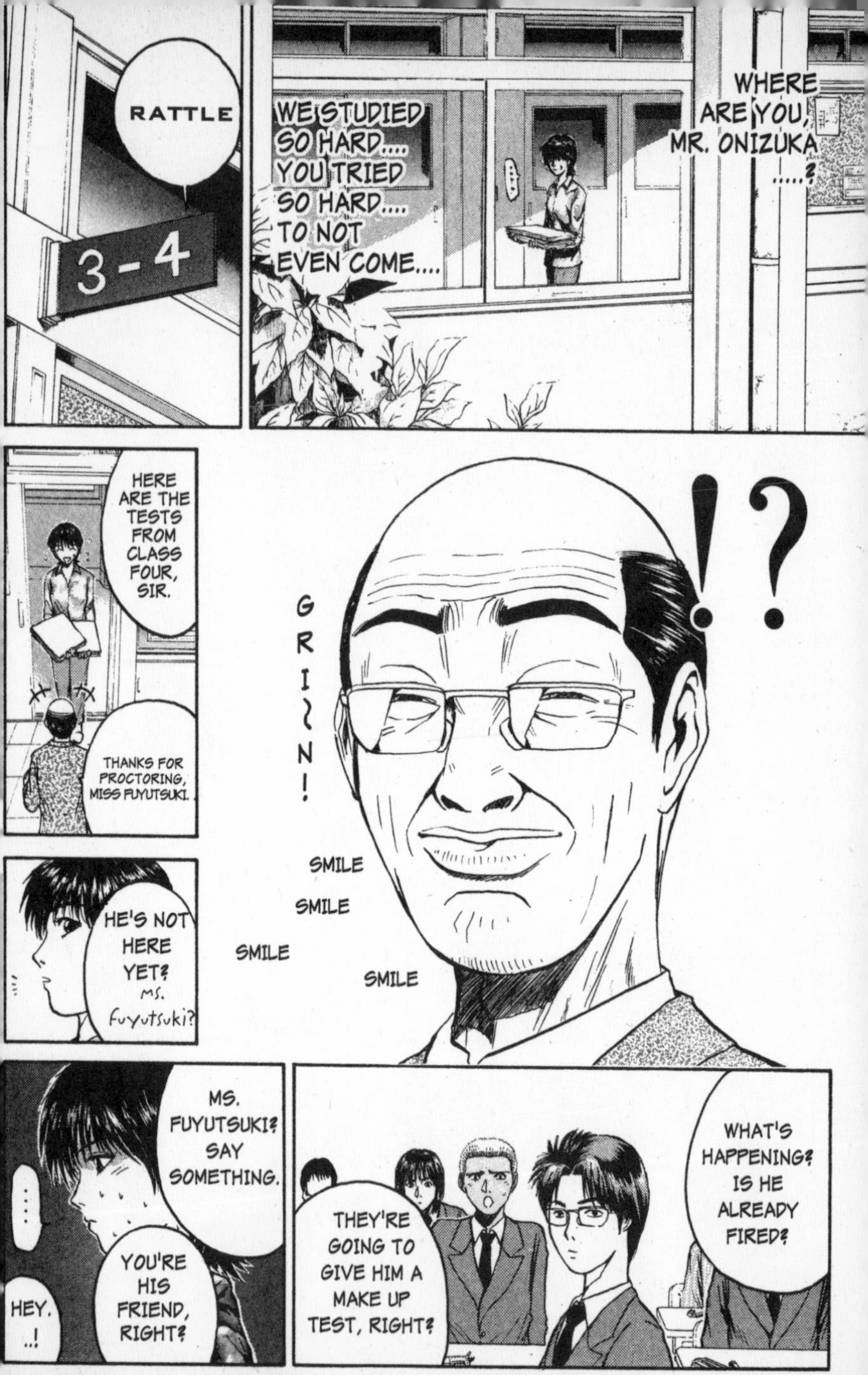

WHERE ARE YOU, MR. ONIZUKA .....?
WE STUDIED SO HARD.... YOU TRIED SO HARD.... TO NOT EVEN COME....
...
RATTLE
3-4
!?
GRI~N!
SMILE
SMILE
SMILE
SMILE
HERE ARE THE TESTS FROM CLASS FOUR, SIR.
THANKS FOR PROCTORING, MISS FUYUTSUKI.
HE'S NOT HERE YET? MS. FUYUTSUKI?
WHAT'S HAPPENING? IS HE ALREADY FIRED?
THEY'RE GOING TO GIVE HIM A MAKE UP TEST, RIGHT?
MS. FUYUTSUKI? SAY SOMETHING.
YOU'RE HIS FRIEND, RIGHT?
....
HEY. ..!

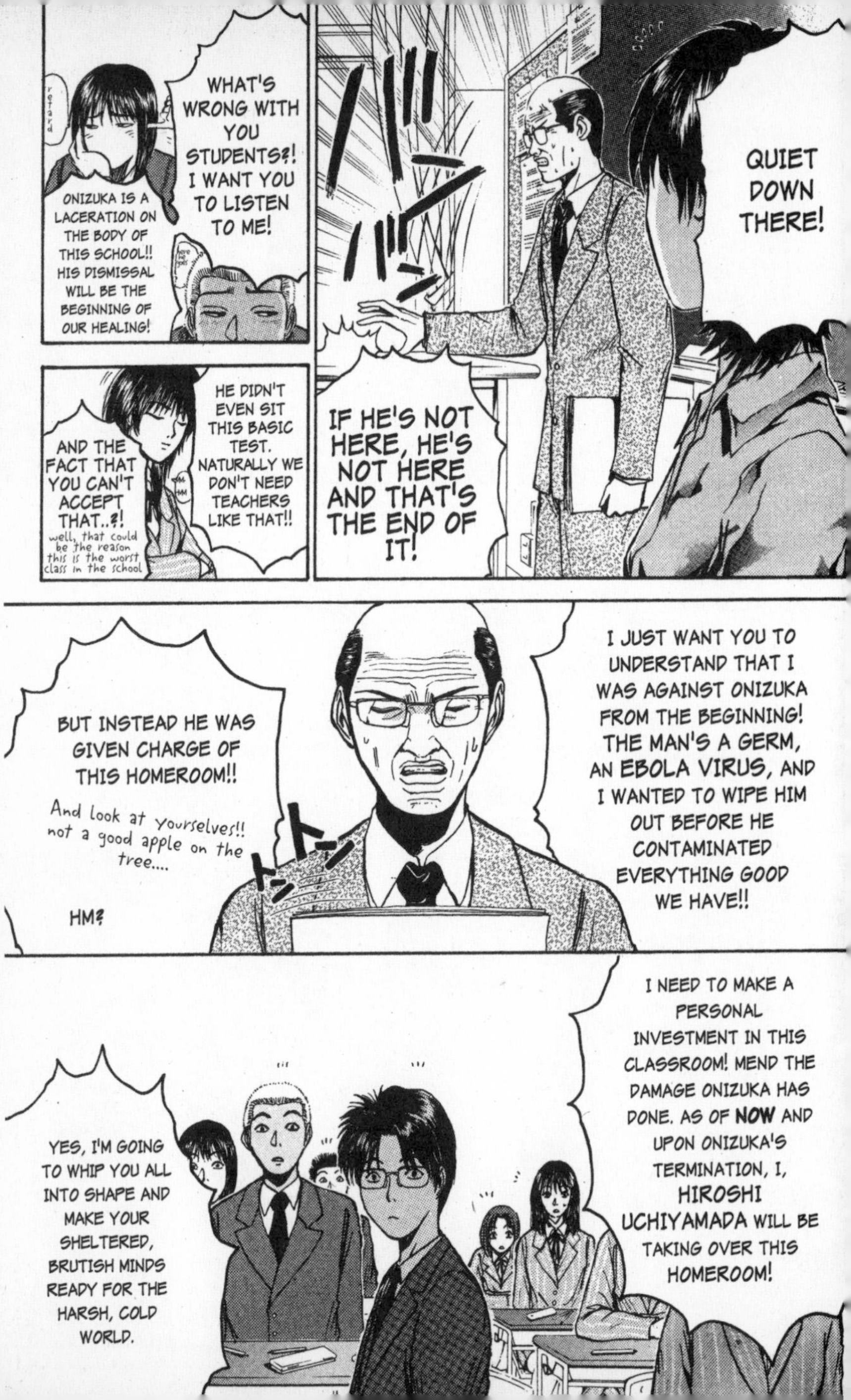
QUIET DOWN THERE!
IF HE'S NOT HERE, HE'S NOT HERE AND THAT'S THE END OF IT!
WHAT'S WRONG WITH YOU STUDENTS?! I WANT YOU TO LISTEN TO ME!
ONIZUKA IS A LACERATION ON THE BODY OF THIS SCHOOL!! HIS DISMISSAL WILL BE THE BEGINNING OF OUR HEALING!
HE DIDN'T EVEN SIT THIS BASIC TEST. NATURALLY WE DON'T NEED TEACHERS LIKE THAT!!
AND THE FACT THAT YOU CAN'T ACCEPT THAT..?!
well, that could be the reason this is the worst class in the school
I JUST WANT YOU TO UNDERSTAND THAT I WAS AGAINST ONIZUKA FROM THE BEGINNING! THE MAN'S A GERM, AN EBOLA VIRUS, AND I WANTED TO WIPE HIM OUT BEFORE HE CONTAMINATED EVERYTHING GOOD WE HAVE!!
BUT INSTEAD HE WAS GIVEN CHARGE OF THIS HOMEROOM!!
And look at yourselves!! not a good apple on the tree....
HM?
I NEED TO MAKE A PERSONAL INVESTMENT IN THIS CLASSROOM! MEND THE DAMAGE ONIZUKA HAS DONE. AS OF NOW AND UPON ONIZUKA'S TERMINATION, I, HIROSHI UCHIYAMADA WILL BE TAKING OVER THIS HOMEROOM!
YES, I'M GOING TO WHIP YOU ALL INTO SHAPE AND MAKE YOUR SHELTERED, BRUTISH MINDS READY FOR THE HARSH, COLD WORLD.

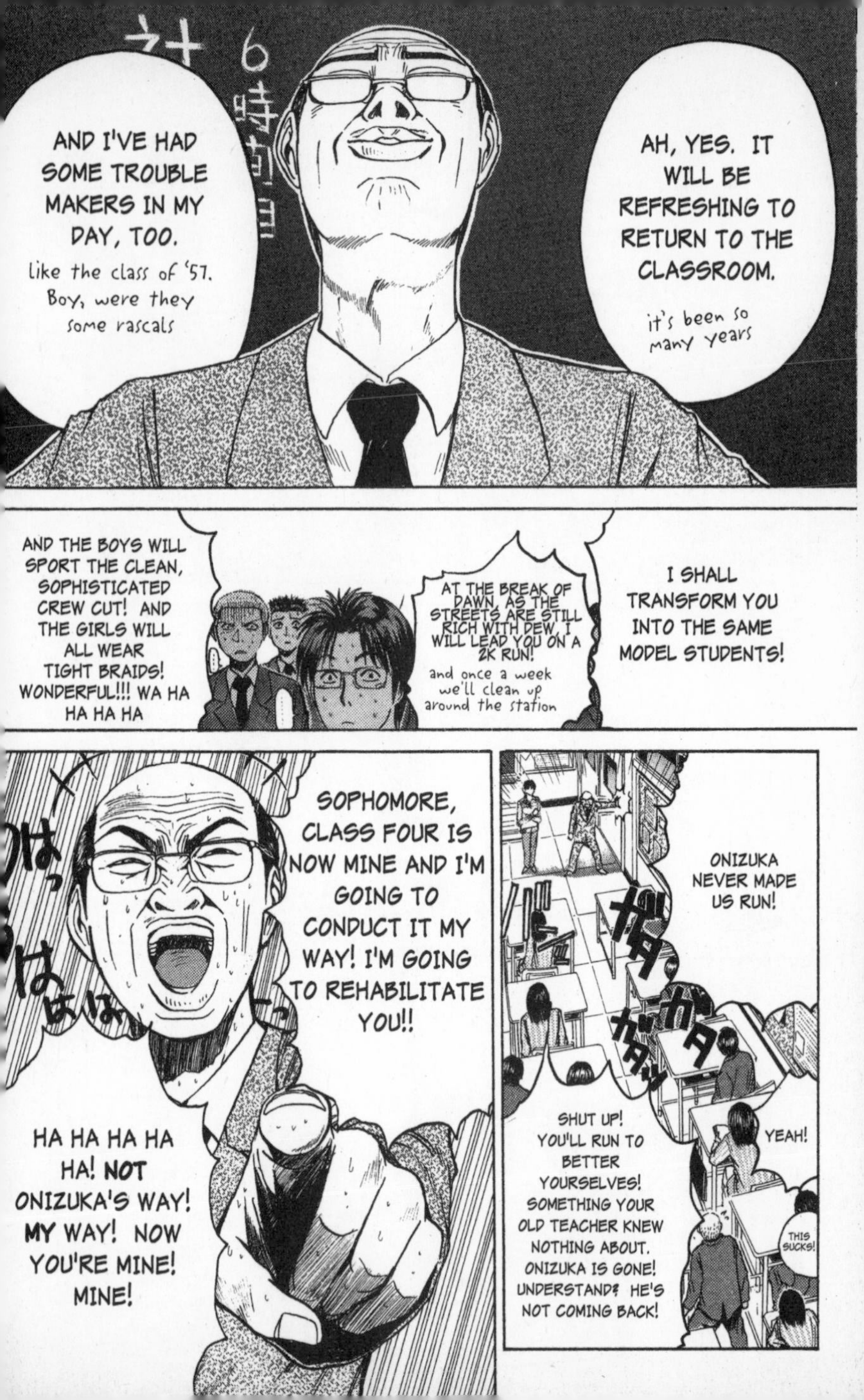

AH, YES. IT WILL BE REFRESHING TO RETURN TO THE CLASSROOM.
it's been so many years
AND I'VE HAD SOME TROUBLE MAKERS IN MY DAY, TOO.
like the class of '57. Boy, were they some rascals
I SHALL TRANSFORM YOU INTO THE SAME MODEL STUDENTS!
AT THE BREAK OF DAWN, AS THE STREETS ARE STILL RICH WITH DEW, I WILL LEAD YOU ON A 2K RUN!
and once a week we'll clean up around the station
AND THE BOYS WILL SPORT THE CLEAN, SOPHISTICATED CREW CUT! AND THE GIRLS WILL ALL WEAR TIGHT BRAIDS! WONDERFUL!!! WA HA HA HA HA
ONIZUKA NEVER MADE US RUN!
YEAH!
THIS SUCKS!
SHUT UP! YOU'LL RUN TO BETTER YOURSELVES! SOMETHING YOUR OLD TEACHER KNEW NOTHING ABOUT. ONIZUKA IS GONE! UNDERSTAND? HE'S NOT COMING BACK!
SOPHOMORE, CLASS FOUR IS NOW MINE AND I'M GOING TO CONDUCT IT MY WAY! I'M GOING TO REHABILITATE YOU!!
HA HA HA HA HA! **NOT** ONIZUKA'S WAY! **MY** WAY! NOW YOU'RE MINE! MINE!

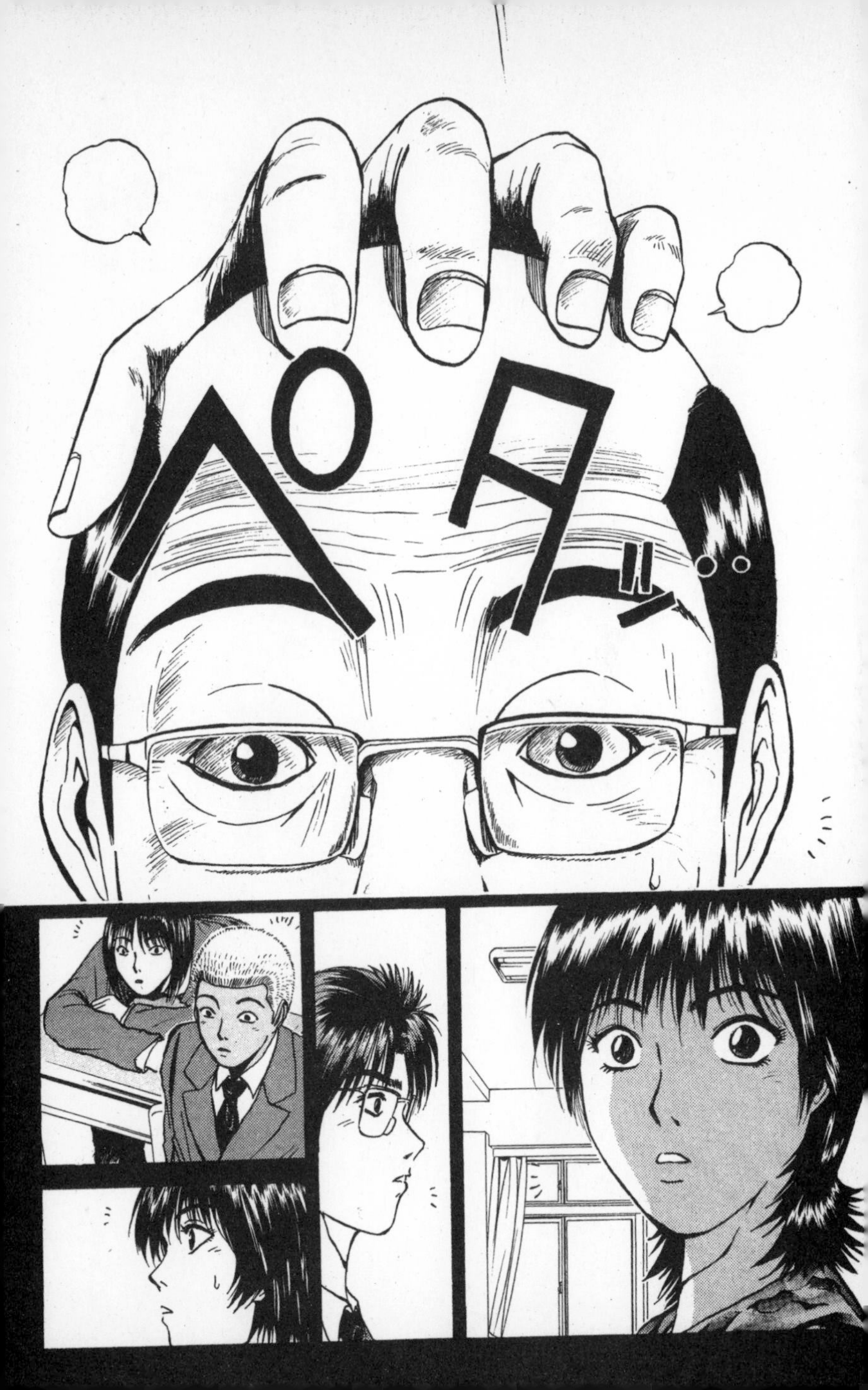

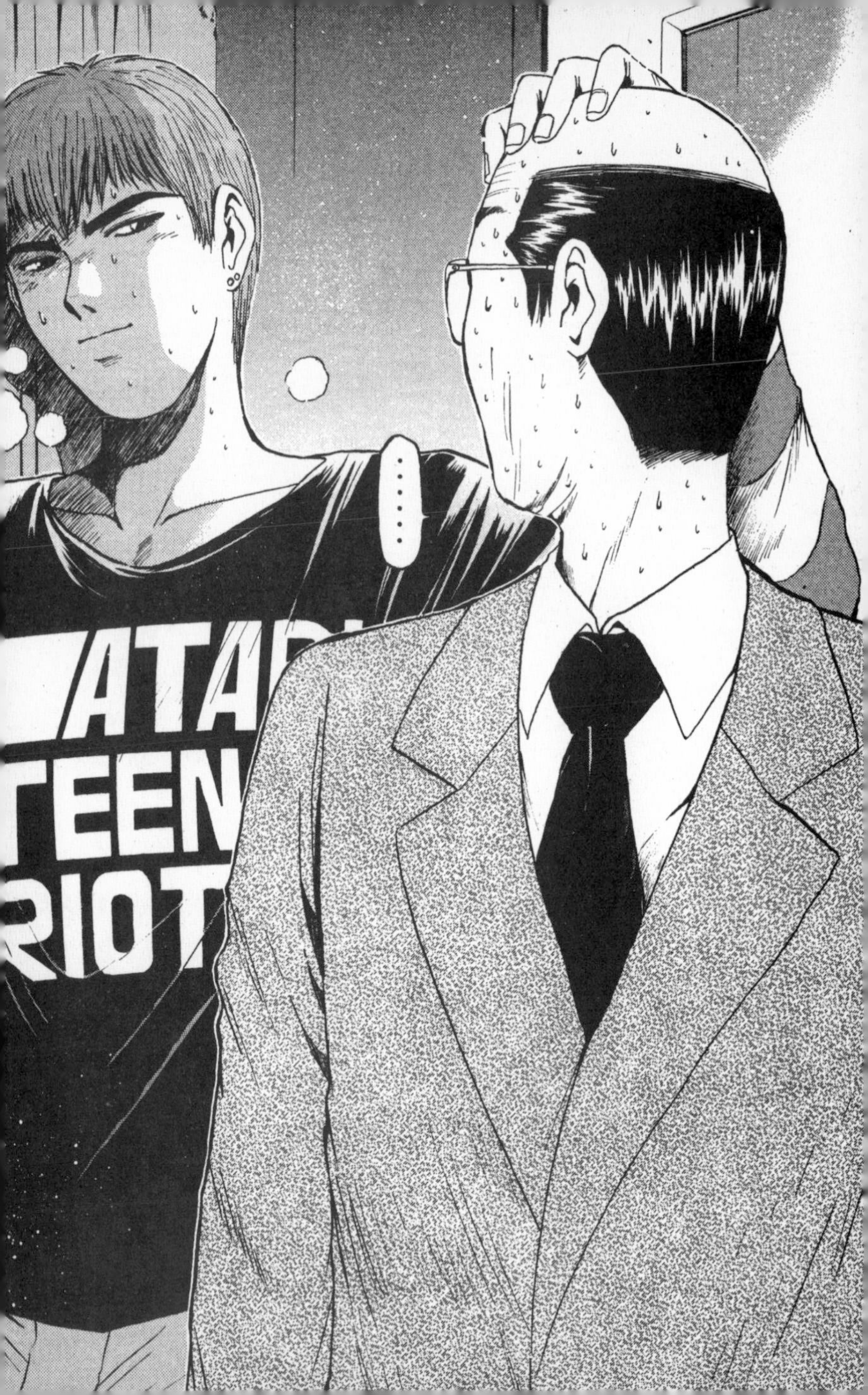
……
ATA
TEEN
RIOT

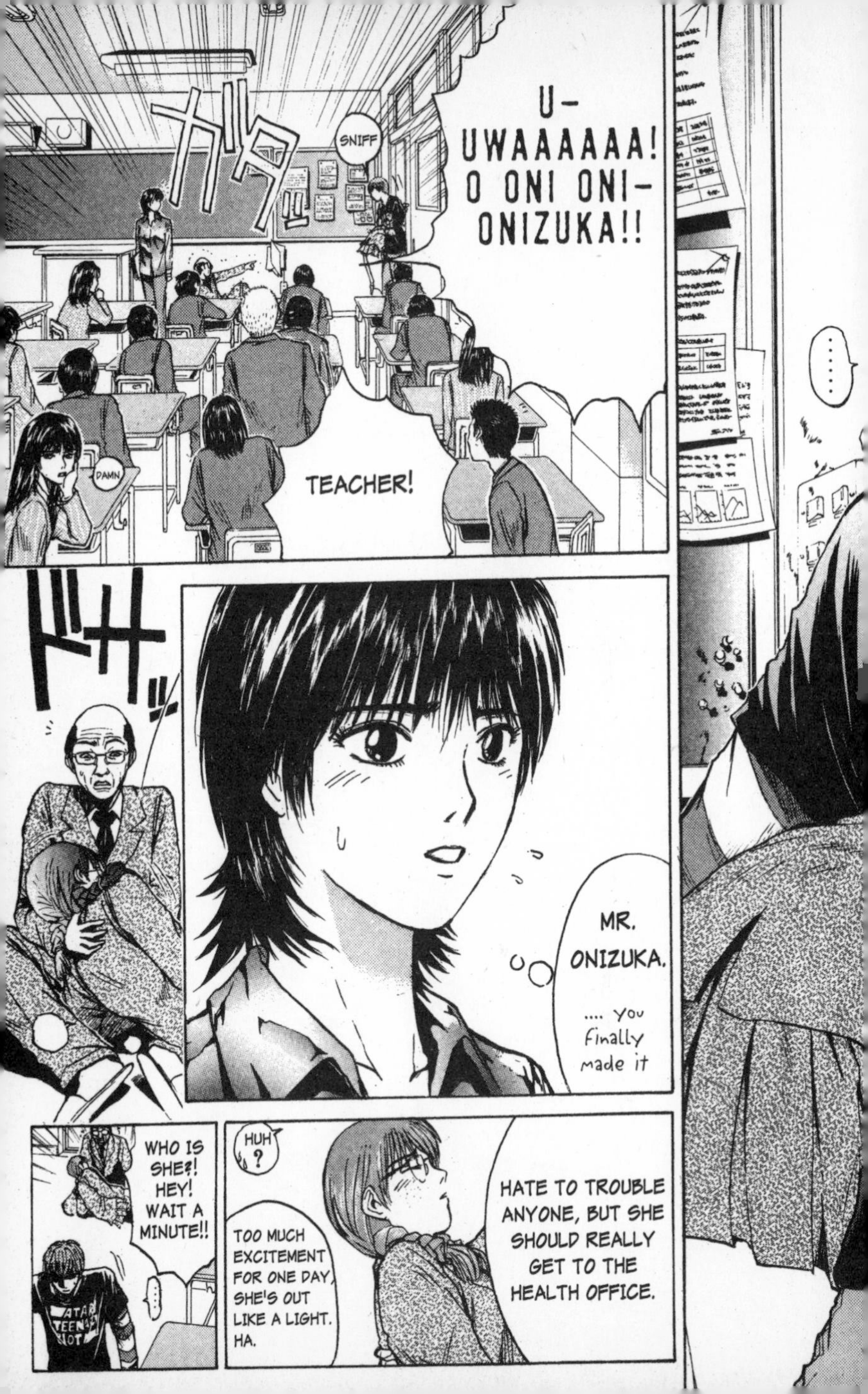
......
U-
UWAAAAAA!
O ONI ONI-
ONIZUKA!!
SNIFF
カタッ
TEACHER!
DAMN
MR. ONIZUKA.
.... you finally made it
ドサッ
HATE TO TROUBLE ANYONE, BUT SHE SHOULD REALLY GET TO THE HEALTH OFFICE.
TOO MUCH EXCITEMENT FOR ONE DAY, SHE'S OUT LIKE A LIGHT. HA.
HUH ?
WHO IS SHE?! HEY! WAIT A MINUTE!!
...

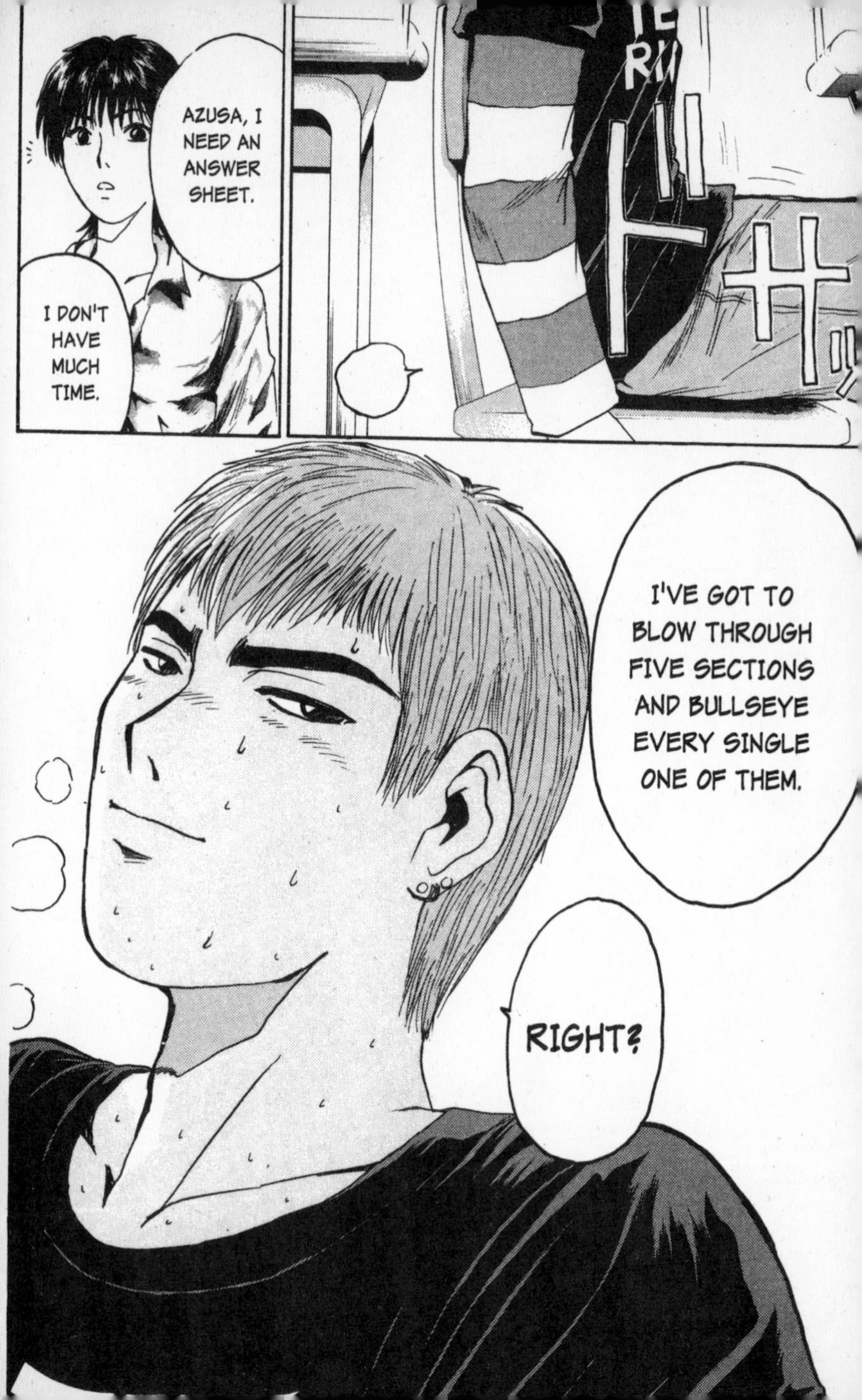
AZUSA, I NEED AN ANSWER SHEET.
I DON'T HAVE MUCH TIME.
I'VE GOT TO BLOW THROUGH FIVE SECTIONS AND BULLSEYE EVERY SINGLE ONE OF THEM.
RIGHT?

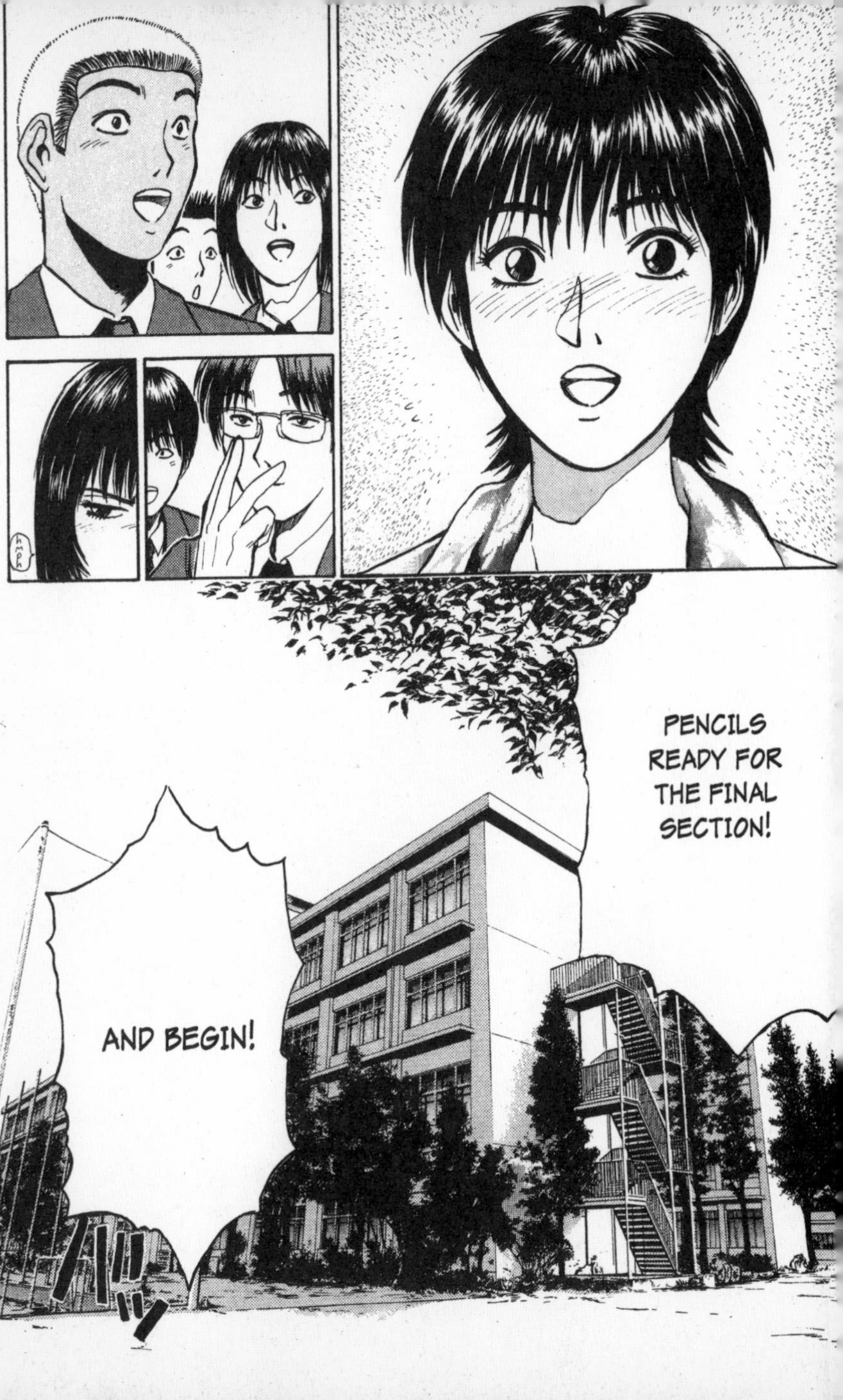
hmph
PENCILS READY FOR THE FINAL SECTION!
AND BEGIN!

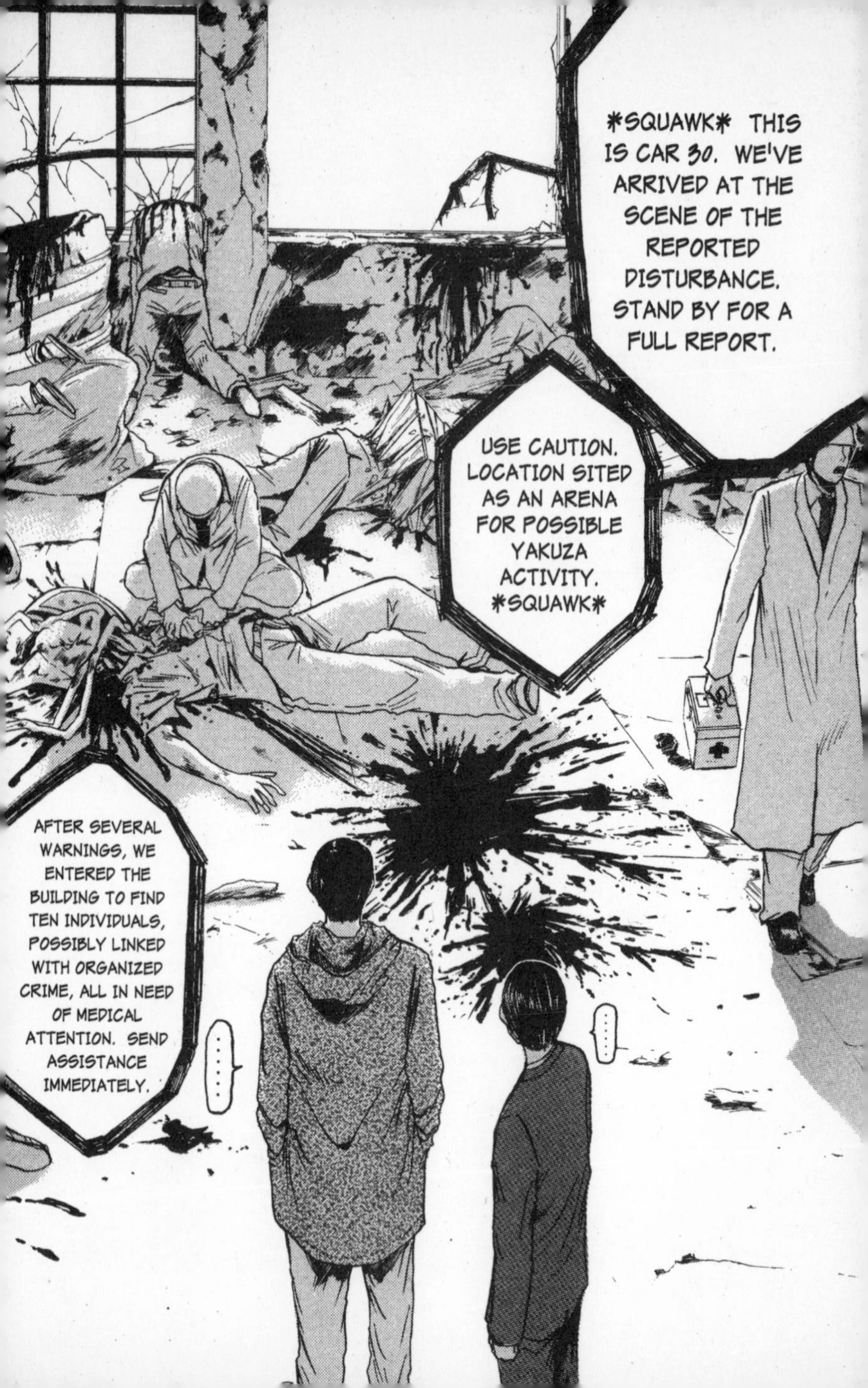
SQUAWK THIS IS CAR 30. WE'VE ARRIVED AT THE SCENE OF THE REPORTED DISTURBANCE. STAND BY FOR A FULL REPORT.
USE CAUTION. LOCATION SITED AS AN ARENA FOR POSSIBLE YAKUZA ACTIVITY. *SQUAWK*
AFTER SEVERAL WARNINGS, WE ENTERED THE BUILDING TO FIND TEN INDIVIDUALS, POSSIBLY LINKED WITH ORGANIZED CRIME, ALL IN NEED OF MEDICAL ATTENTION. SEND ASSISTANCE IMMEDIATELY.
......
......

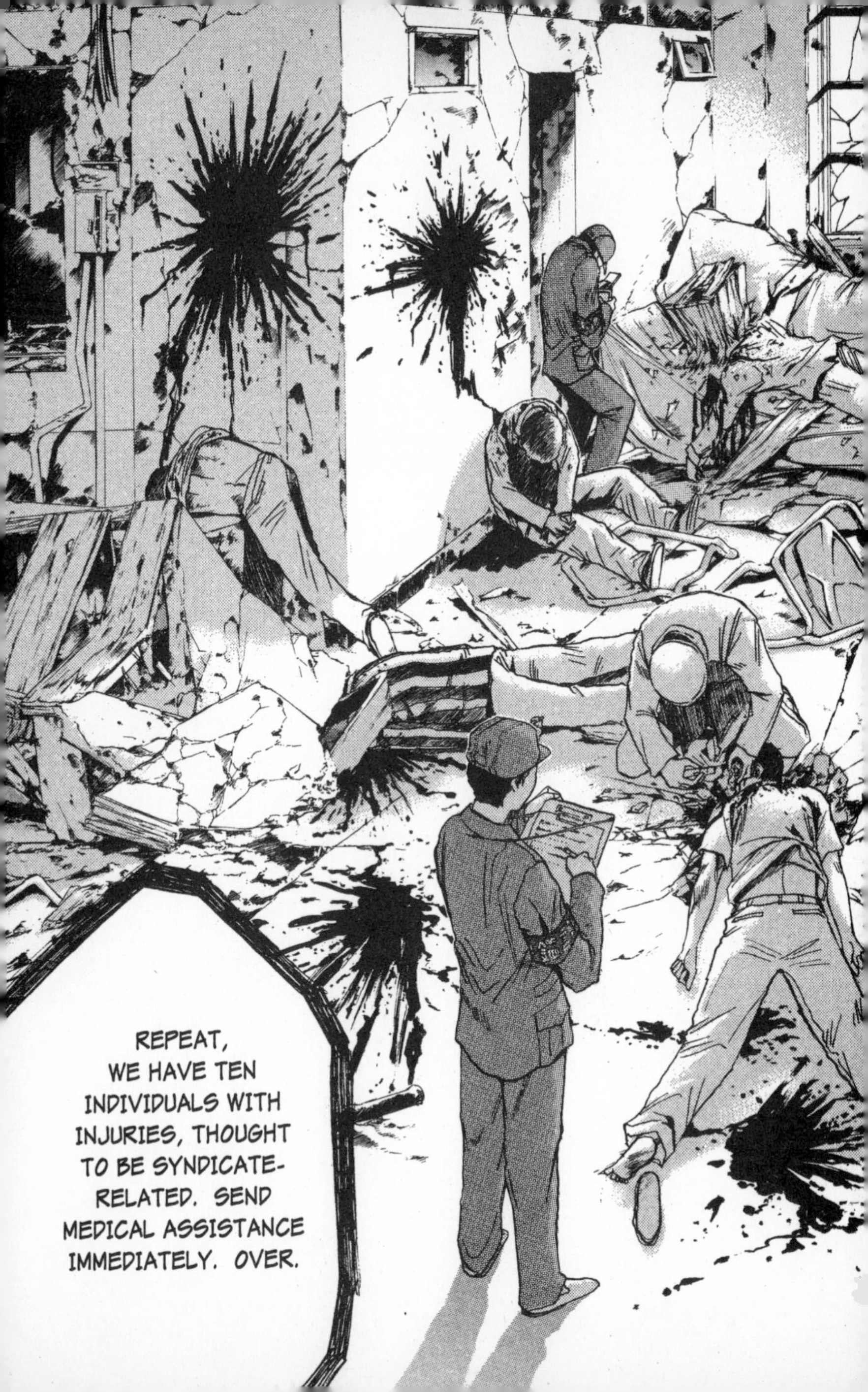
REPEAT, WE HAVE TEN INDIVIDUALS WITH INJURIES, THOUGHT TO BE SYNDICATE-RELATED. SEND MEDICAL ASSISTANCE IMMEDIATELY. OVER.

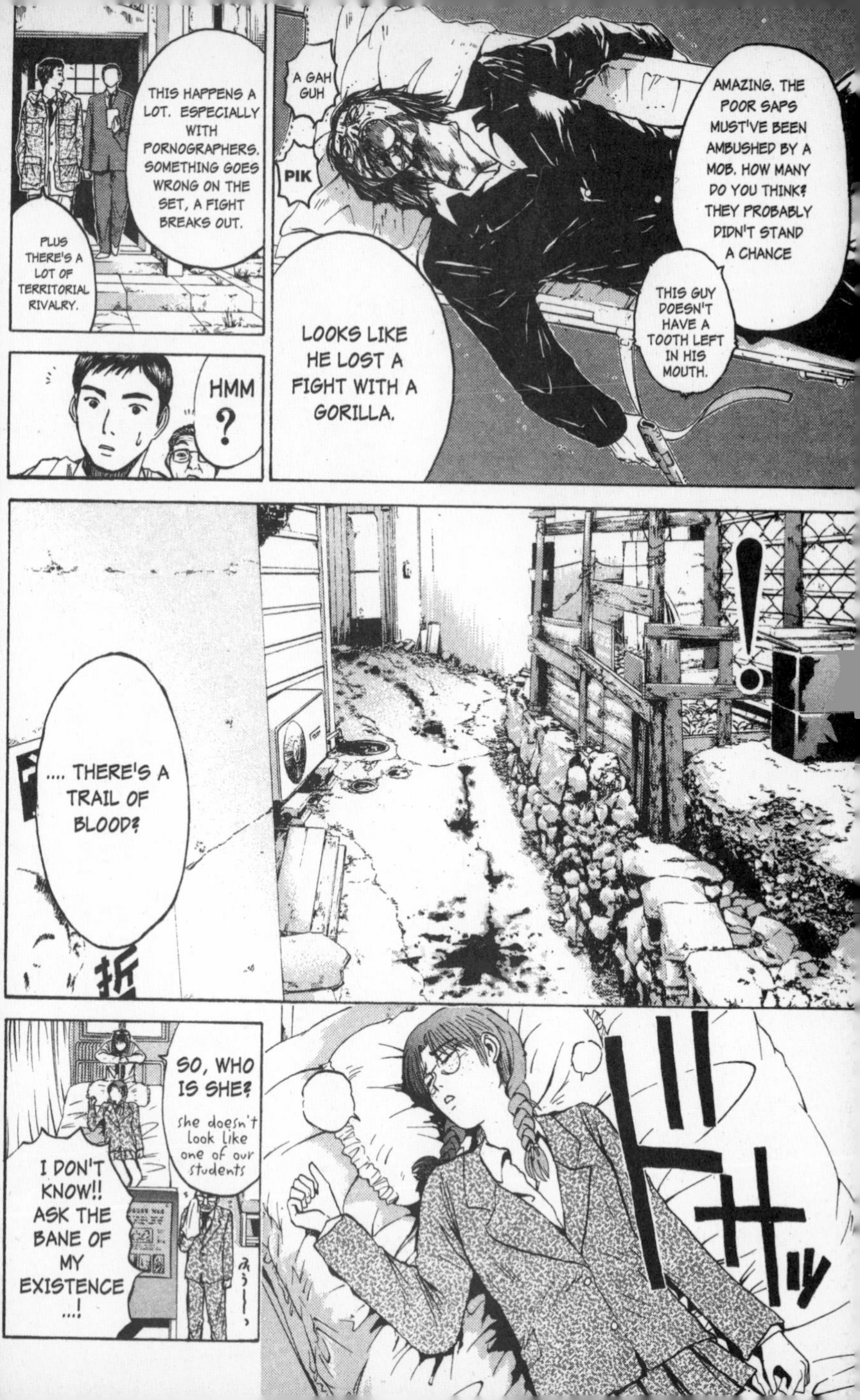
A GAH GUH
PIK
AMAZING. THE POOR SAPS MUST'VE BEEN AMBUSHED BY A MOB. HOW MANY DO YOU THINK? THEY PROBABLY DIDN'T STAND A CHANCE
THIS GUY DOESN'T HAVE A TOOTH LEFT IN HIS MOUTH.
LOOKS LIKE HE LOST A FIGHT WITH A GORILLA.
THIS HAPPENS A LOT. ESPECIALLY WITH PORNOGRAPHERS. SOMETHING GOES WRONG ON THE SET, A FIGHT BREAKS OUT.
PLUS THERE'S A LOT OF TERRITORIAL RIVALRY.
HMM ?
!
.... THERE'S A TRAIL OF BLOOD?
ドキッ
SO, WHO IS SHE?
she doesn't look like one of our students
I DON'T KNOW!! ASK THE BANE OF MY EXISTENCE ...!

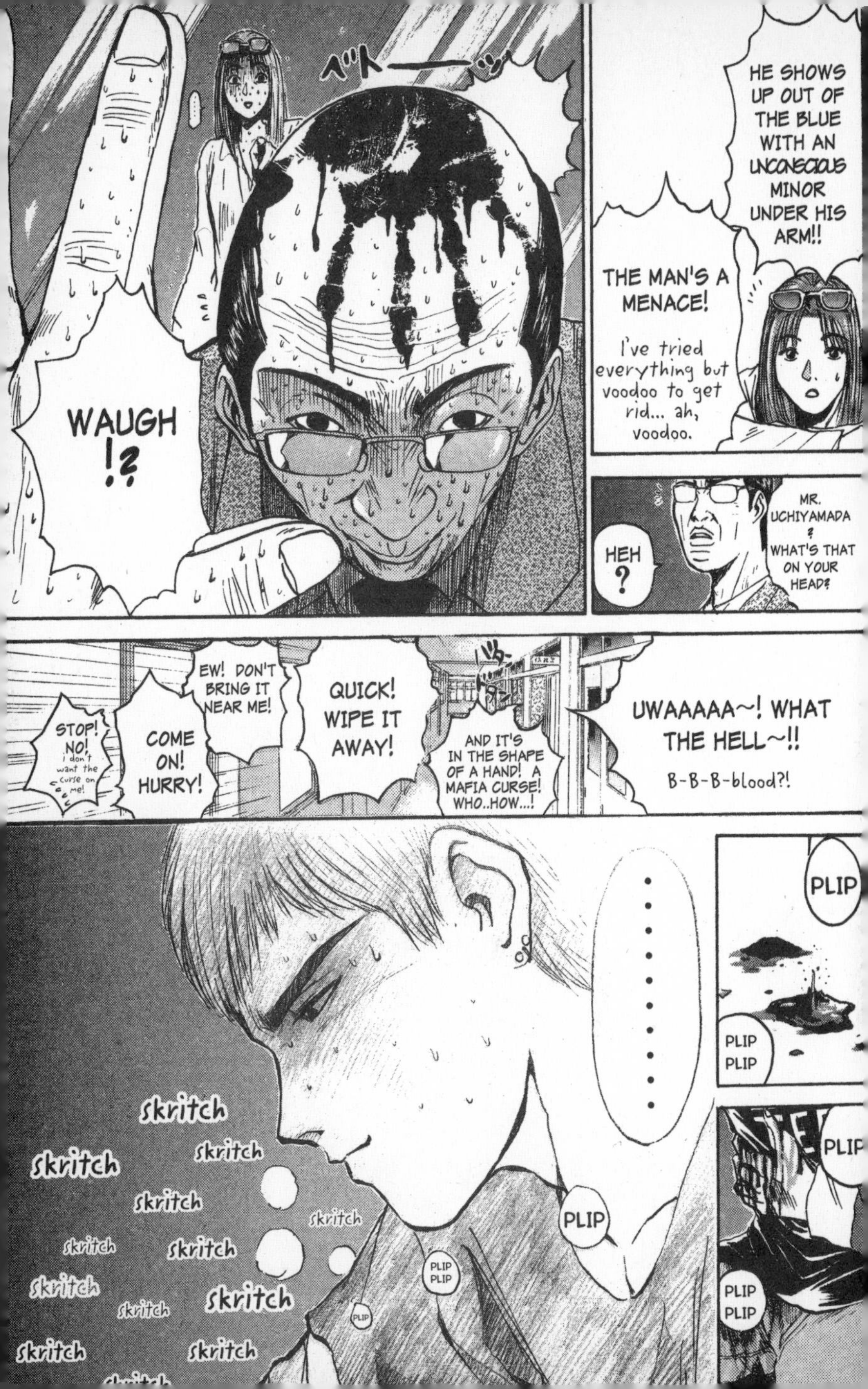
HE SHOWS UP OUT OF THE BLUE WITH AN UNCONSCIOUS MINOR UNDER HIS ARM!!
THE MAN'S A MENACE!
I've tried everything but voodoo to get rid... ah, voodoo.
MR. UCHIYAMADA? WHAT'S THAT ON YOUR HEAD?
HEH?
WAUGH!?
UWAAAAA~! WHAT THE HELL~!!
B-B-B-blood?!
AND IT'S IN THE SHAPE OF A HAND! A MAFIA CURSE! WHO..HOW...!
QUICK! WIPE IT AWAY!
EW! DON'T BRING IT NEAR ME!
COME ON! HURRY!
STOP! NO! I don't want the curse on me!
PLIP
PLIP PLIP
PLIP
PLIP PLIP
....
PLIP
PLIP PLIP
PLIP
skritch
skritch
skritch
skritch
skritch
skritch
skritch
skritch
skritch
skritch
skritch
skritch

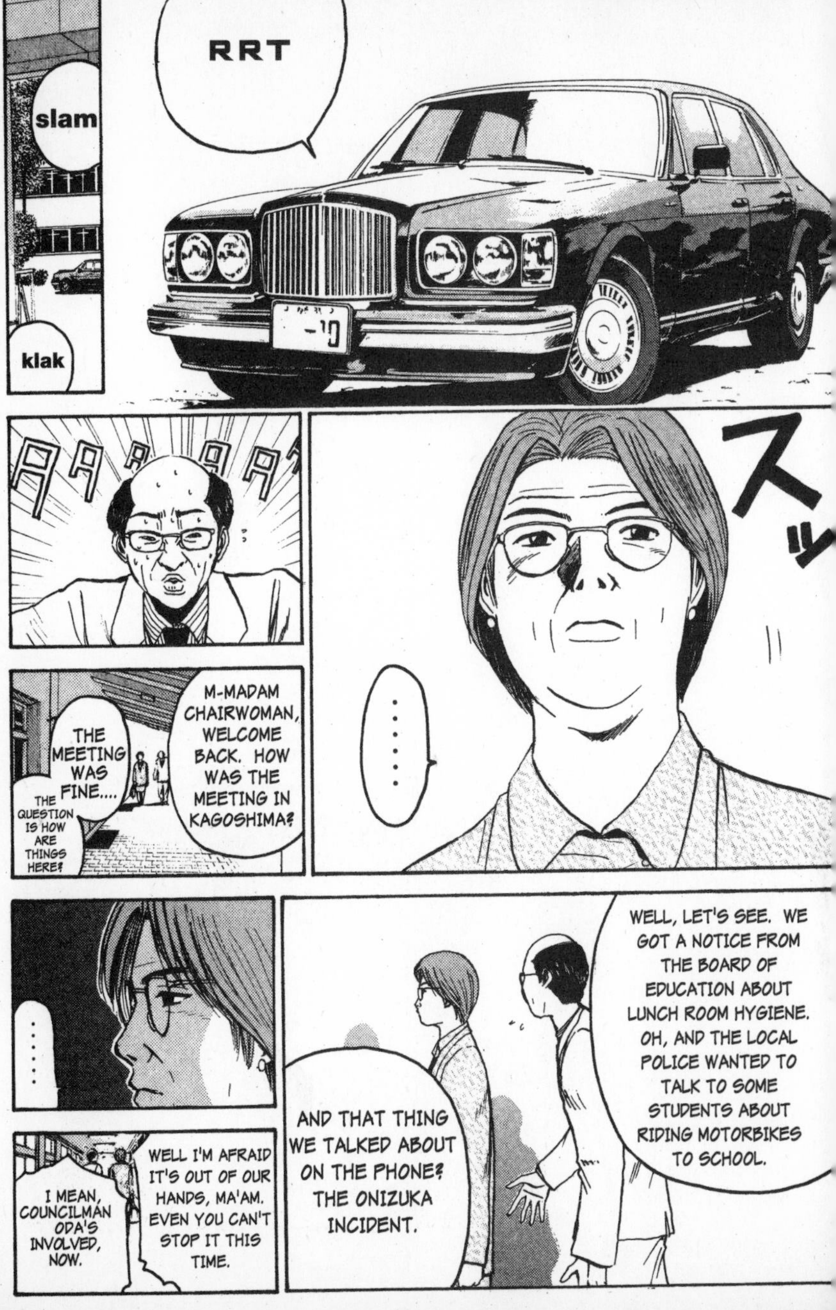
RRT
slam
klak
スッ
......
M-MADAM CHAIRWOMAN, WELCOME BACK. HOW WAS THE MEETING IN KAGOSHIMA?
THE MEETING WAS FINE....
THE QUESTION IS HOW ARE THINGS HERE?
WELL, LET'S SEE. WE GOT A NOTICE FROM THE BOARD OF EDUCATION ABOUT LUNCH ROOM HYGIENE. OH, AND THE LOCAL POLICE WANTED TO TALK TO SOME STUDENTS ABOUT RIDING MOTORBIKES TO SCHOOL.
AND THAT THING WE TALKED ABOUT ON THE PHONE? THE ONIZUKA INCIDENT.
......
WELL I'M AFRAID IT'S OUT OF OUR HANDS, MA'AM. EVEN YOU CAN'T STOP IT THIS TIME.
I MEAN, COUNCILMAN ODA'S INVOLVED, NOW.

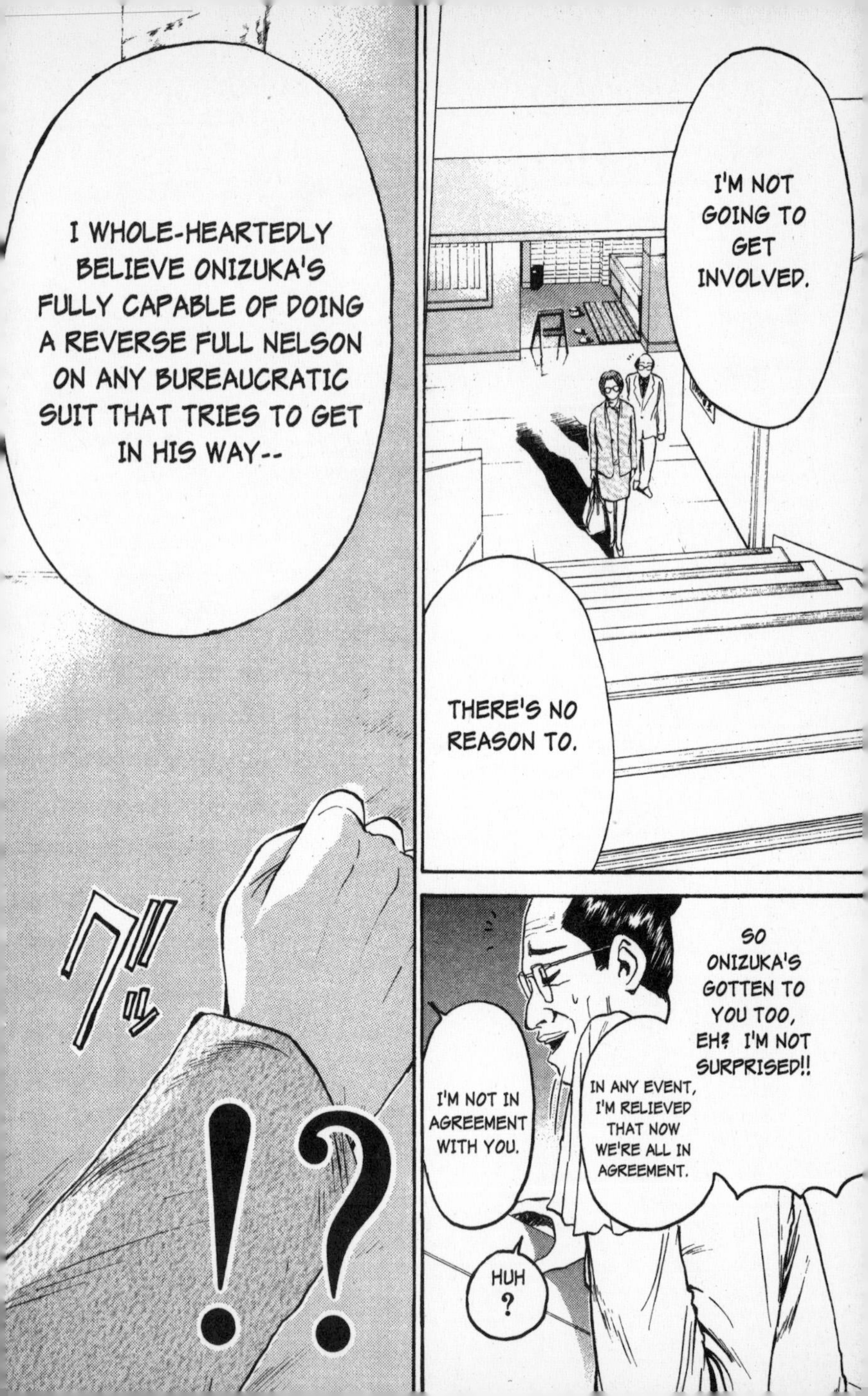
I'M NOT GOING TO GET INVOLVED.
THERE'S NO REASON TO.
SO ONIZUKA'S GOTTEN TO YOU TOO, EH? I'M NOT SURPRISED!!
IN ANY EVENT, I'M RELIEVED THAT NOW WE'RE ALL IN AGREEMENT.
I'M NOT IN AGREEMENT WITH YOU.
HUH ?
I WHOLE-HEARTEDLY BELIEVE ONIZUKA'S FULLY CAPABLE OF DOING A REVERSE FULL NELSON ON ANY BUREAUCRATIC SUIT THAT TRIES TO GET IN HIS WAY--
グッ
!?

Lesson50
The Academy's Greatest Crisis

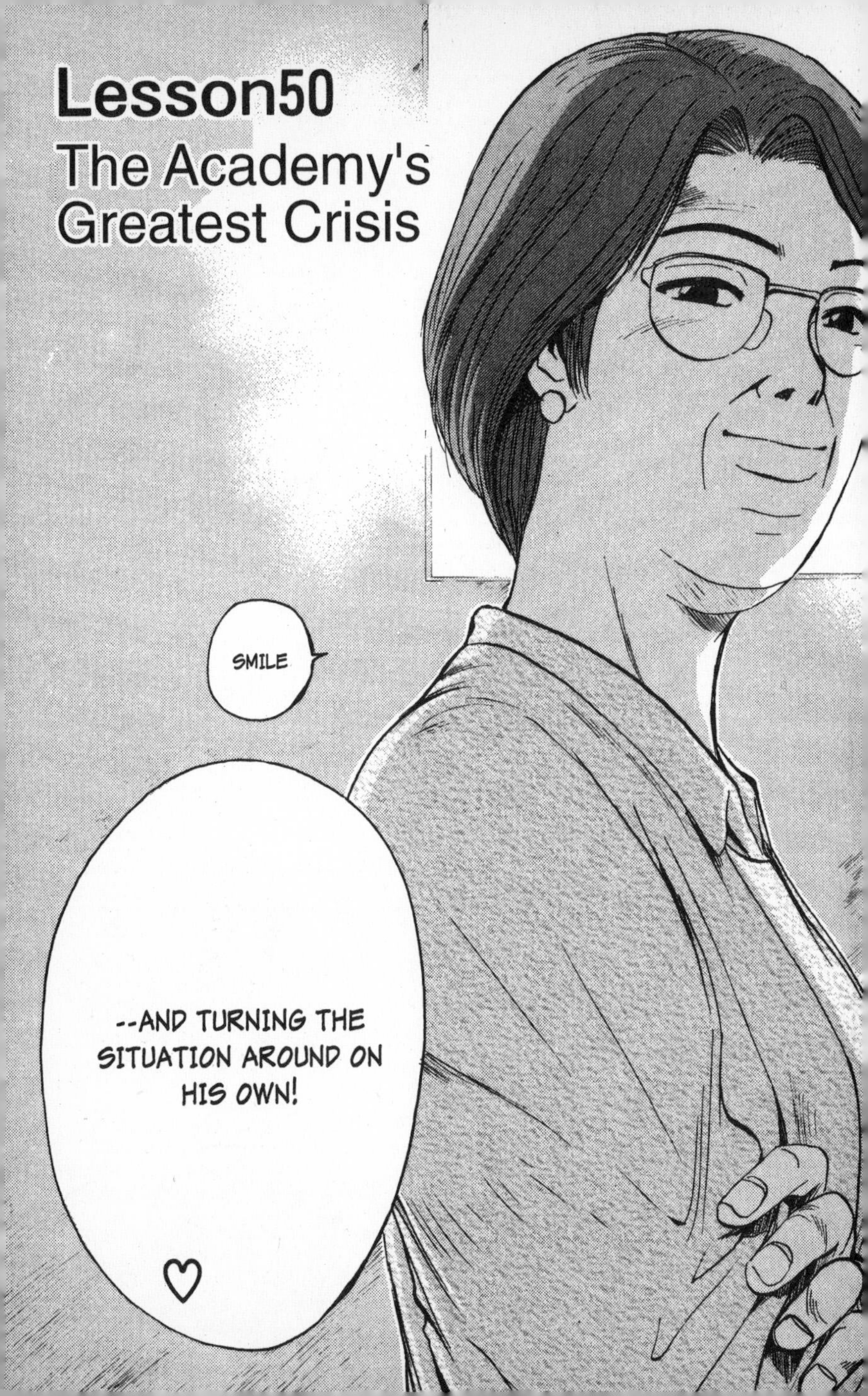
SMILE
--AND TURNING THE SITUATION AROUND ON HIS OWN!
♡

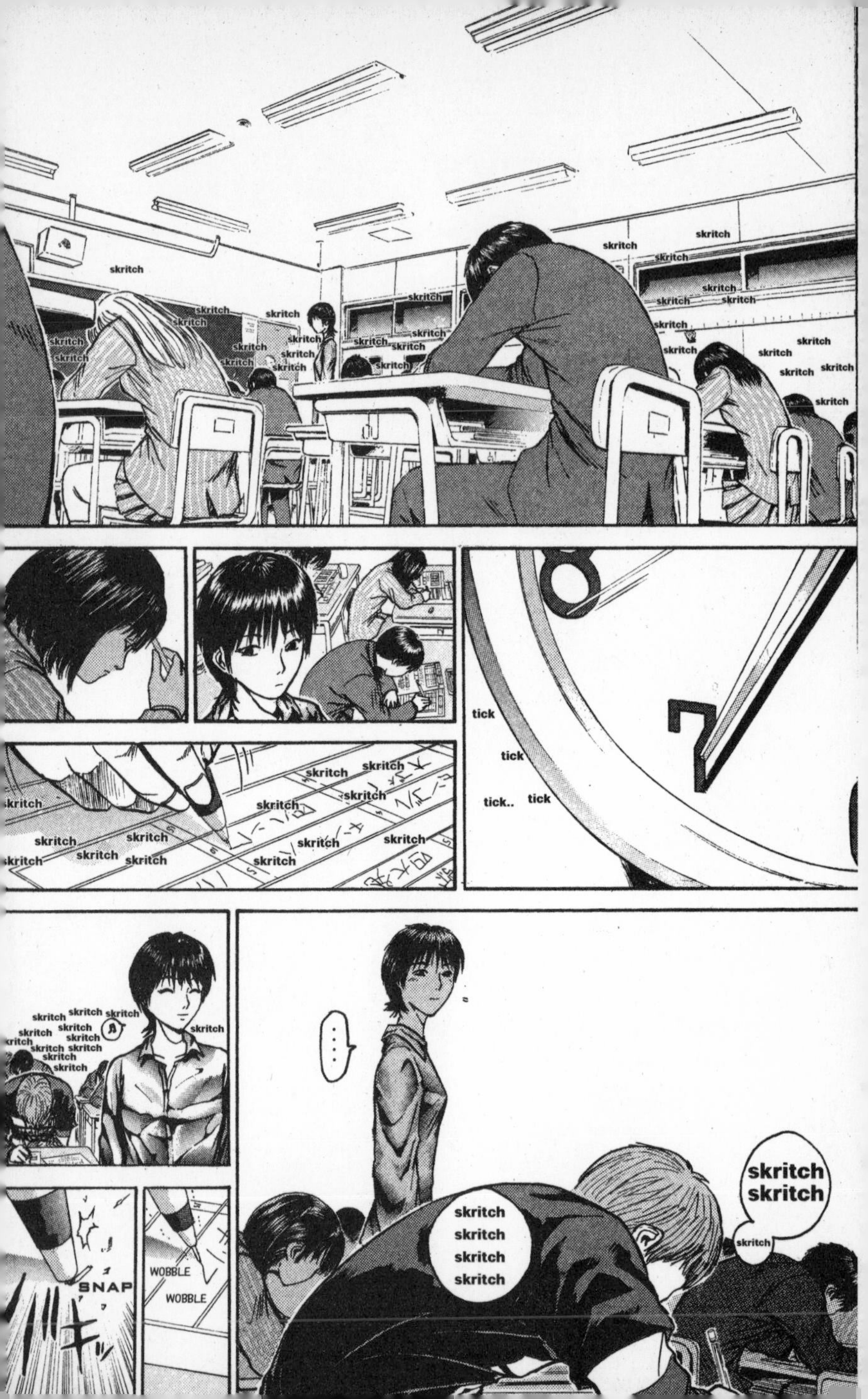
skritch
skritch
skritch skritch
skritch
skritch
skritch
skritch
skritch
skritch
skritch
skritch
skritch
skritch
skritch
skritch
skritch
skritch
skritch skritch
skritch
skritch
skritch
skritch
skritch
skritch
skritch
tick
tick
tick.. tick
skritch
skritch
skritch
skritch
skritch
skritch
skritch
skritch
skritch
skritch
skritch
skritch
skritch
skritch
. . . .
skritch skritch
skritch skritch skritch skritch
skritch
skritch skritch skritch
skritch skritch
skritch skritch
skritch skritch
skritch
skritch
skritch
WOBBLE
WOBBLE
SNAP

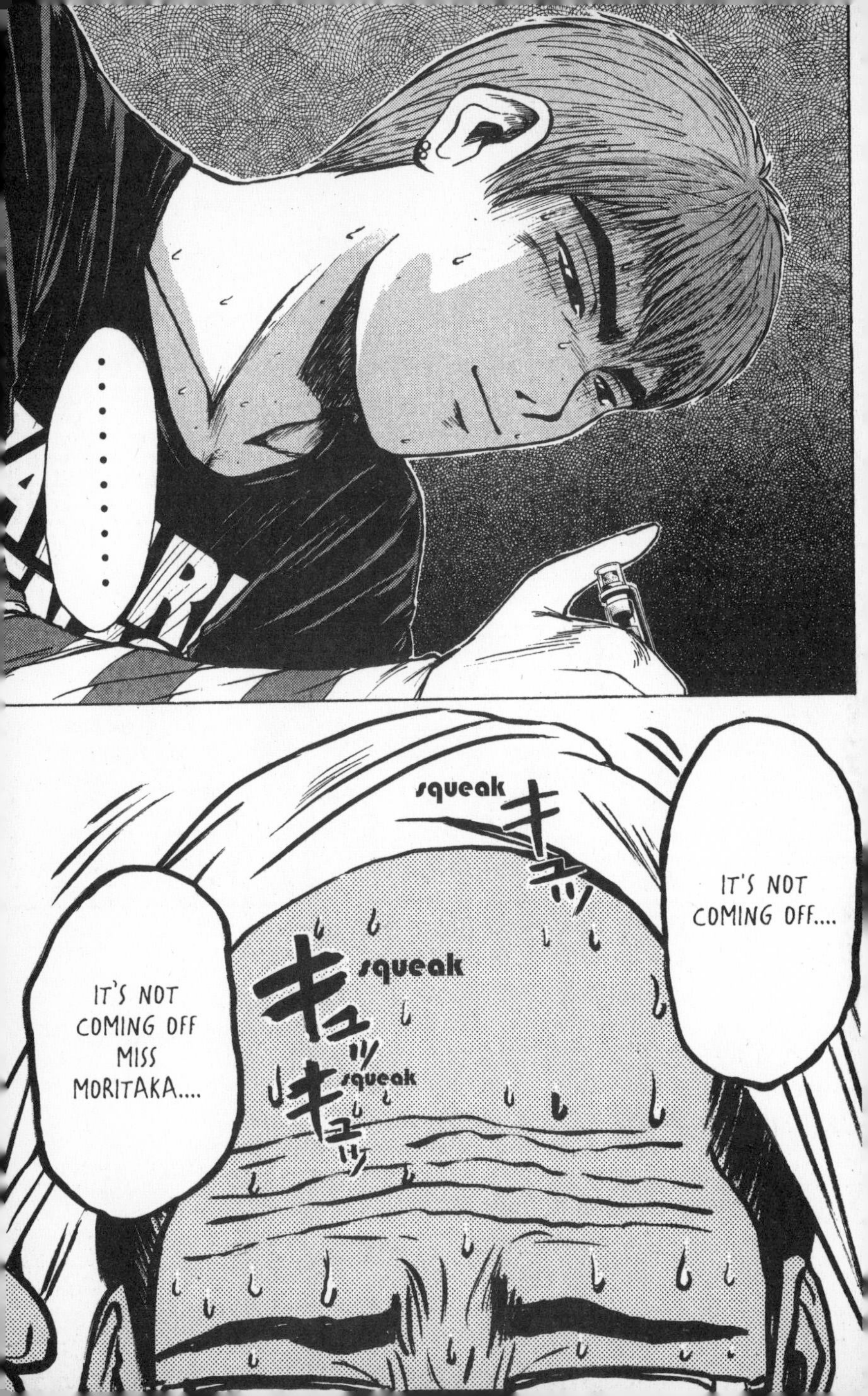

......
IT'S NOT COMING OFF....
squeak
squeak
squeak
IT'S NOT COMING OFF MISS MORITAKA....

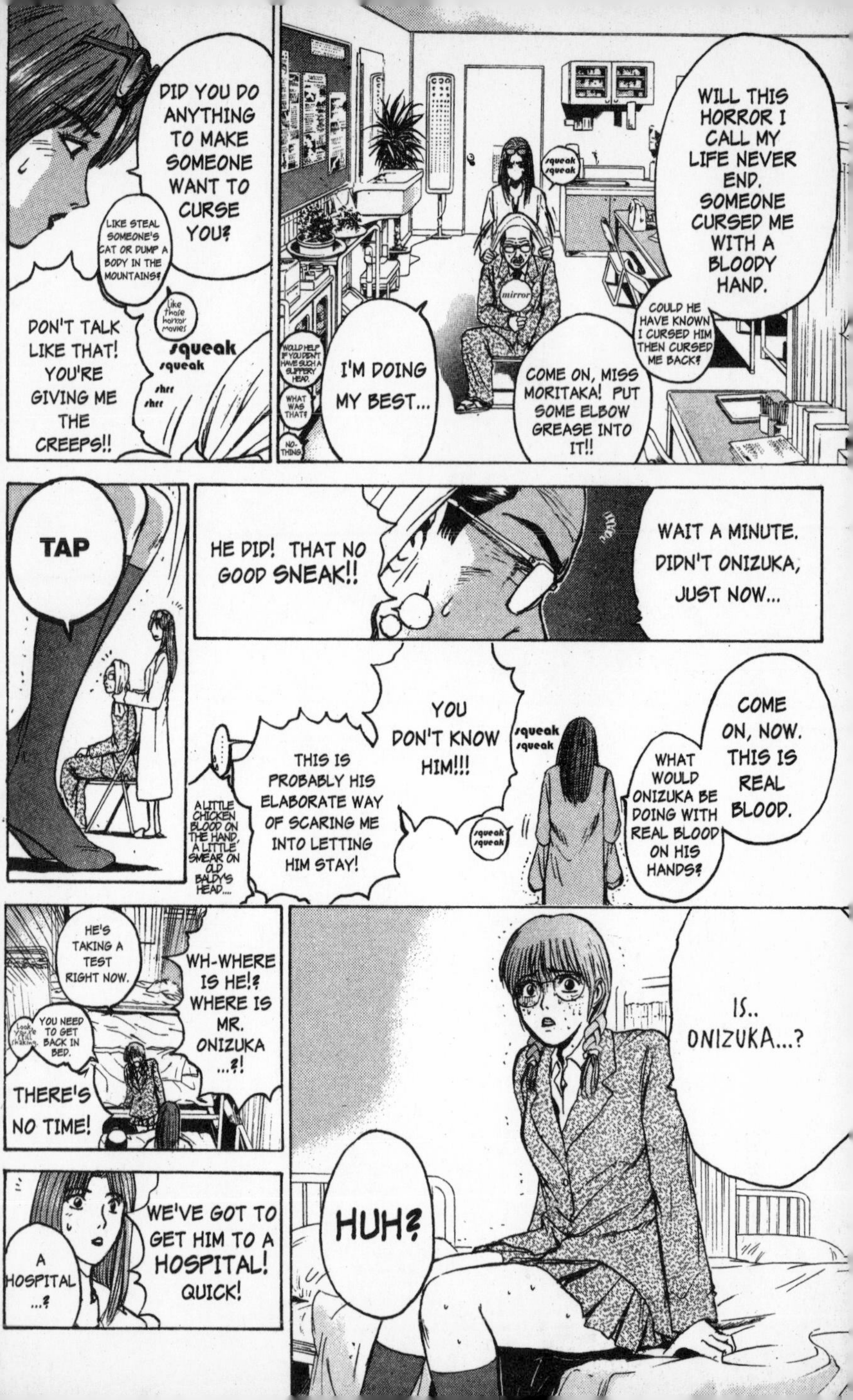
WILL THIS HORROR I CALL MY LIFE NEVER END. SOMEONE CURSED ME WITH A BLOODY HAND.
COULD HE HAVE KNOWN I CURSED HIM THEN CURSED ME BACK?
squeak squeak
mirror
COME ON, MISS MORITAKA! PUT SOME ELBOW GREASE INTO IT!!
I'M DOING MY BEST...
WOULD HELP IF YOU DIDN'T HAVE SUCH A SLIPPERY HEAD.
WHAT WAS THAT?
NOTHING.
DID YOU DO ANYTHING TO MAKE SOMEONE WANT TO CURSE YOU?
LIKE STEAL SOMEONE'S CAT OR DUMP A BODY IN THE MOUNTAINS?
like those horror movies
squeak squeak
shrr shrr
DON'T TALK LIKE THAT! YOU'RE GIVING ME THE CREEPS!!
WAIT A MINUTE. DIDN'T ONIZUKA, JUST NOW...
HE DID! THAT NO GOOD SNEAK!!
COME ON, NOW. THIS IS REAL BLOOD.
WHAT WOULD ONIZUKA BE DOING WITH REAL BLOOD ON HIS HANDS?
squeak squeak
YOU DON'T KNOW HIM!!!
squeak squeak
THIS IS PROBABLY HIS ELABORATE WAY OF SCARING ME INTO LETTING HIM STAY!
A LITTLE CHICKEN BLOOD ON THE HAND, A LITTLE SMEAR ON OLD BALDY'S HEAD....
TAP
IS.. ONIZUKA...?
HUH?
WH-WHERE IS HE!? WHERE IS MR. ONIZUKA ...?!
HE'S TAKING A TEST RIGHT NOW.
YOU NEED TO GET BACK IN BED.
Look, You're still shaking.
THERE'S NO TIME!
WE'VE GOT TO GET HIM TO A HOSPITAL! QUICK!
A HOSPITAL ...?

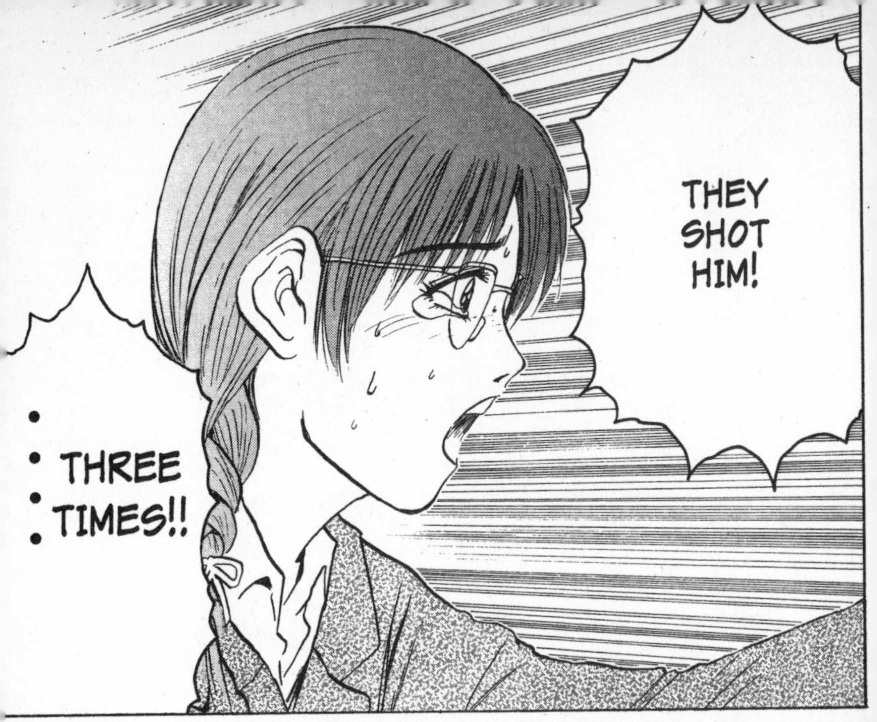
THEY SHOT HIM!
...THREE TIMES!!
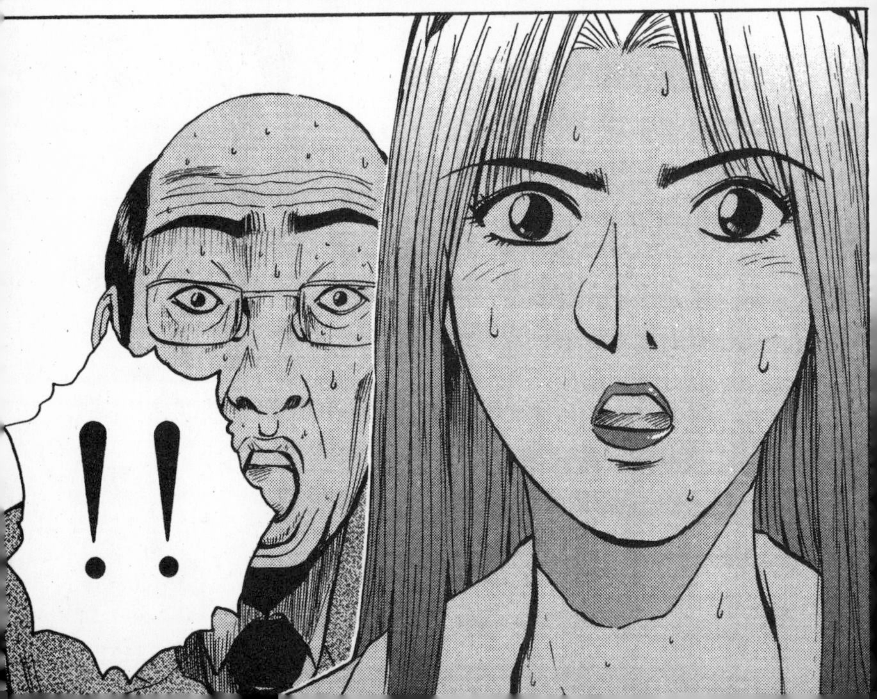
!!

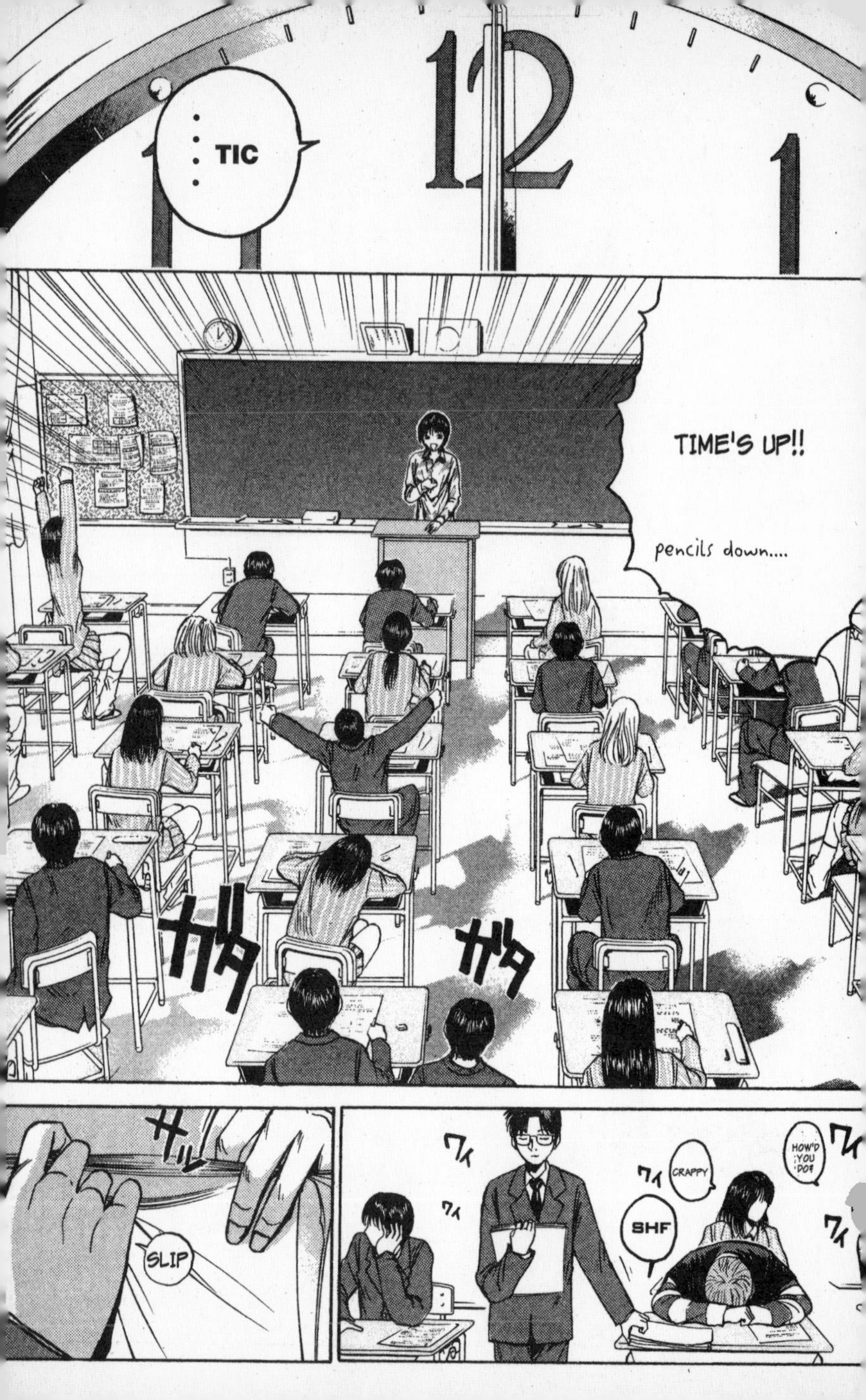
TIC
TIME'S UP!!
pencils down....
ガタ
ガタ
ワイ
HOW'D YOU DO?
CRAPPY
ワイ
SHF
ワイ
ワイ
ワイ
SLIP

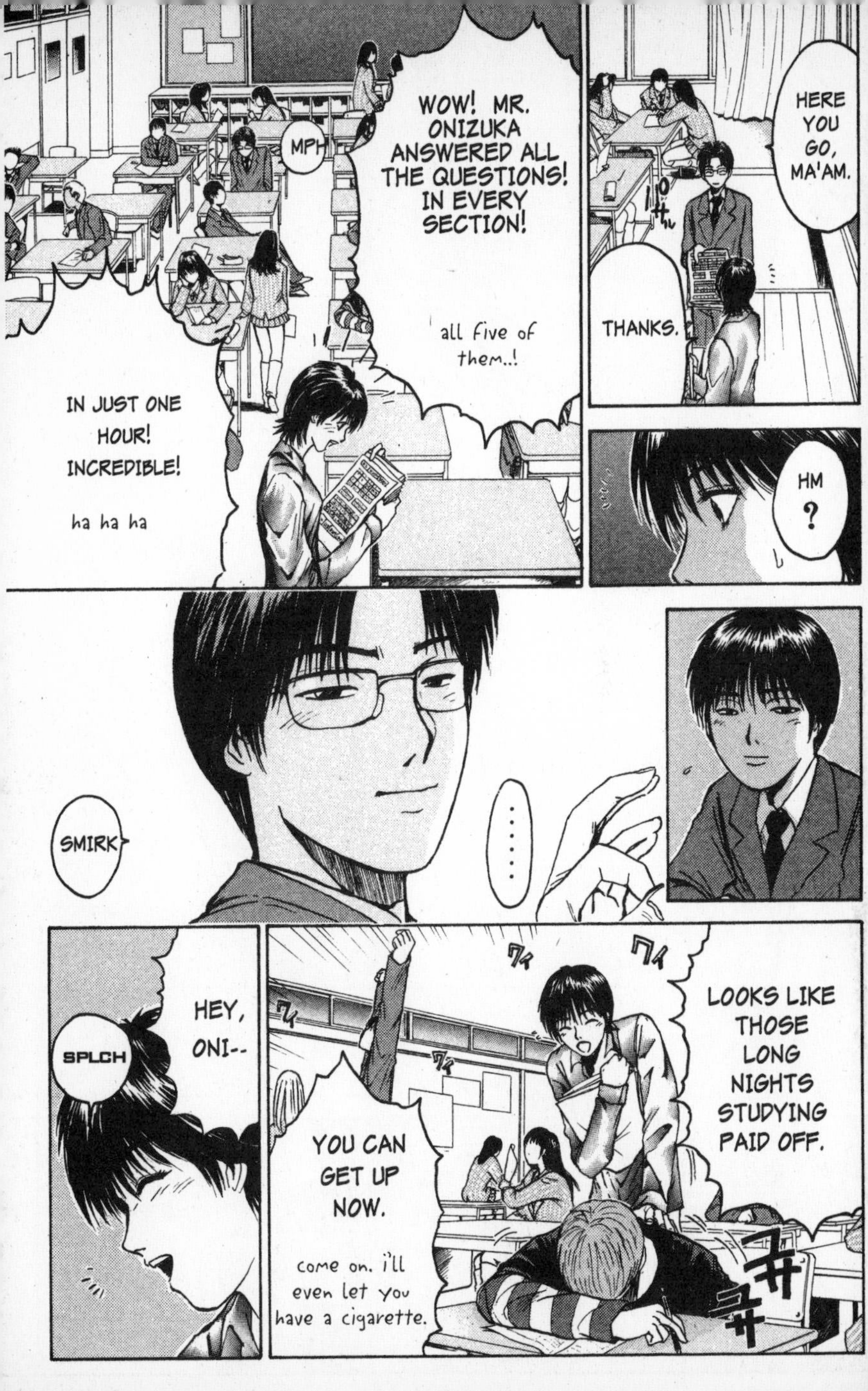
HERE YOU GO, MA'AM.
THANKS.
HM ?
WOW! MR. ONIZUKA ANSWERED ALL THE QUESTIONS! IN EVERY SECTION!
MPH
all five of them..!
IN JUST ONE HOUR! INCREDIBLE!
ha ha ha
......
SMIRK
LOOKS LIKE THOSE LONG NIGHTS STUDYING PAID OFF.
YOU CAN GET UP NOW.
come on. i'll even let you have a cigarette.
HEY, ONI--
SPLCH

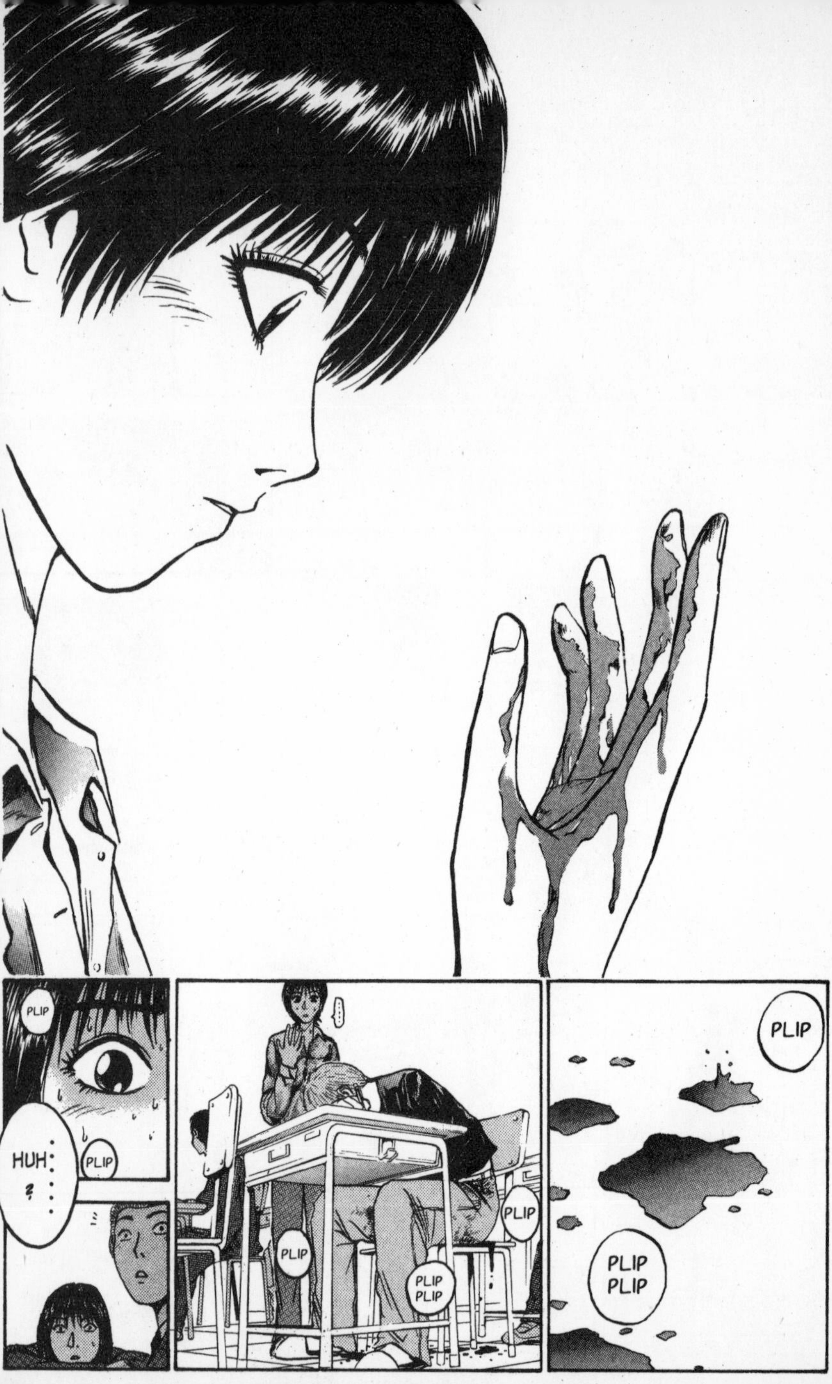
PLIP
PLIP
PLIP
......
PLIP
PLIP
PLIP
PLIP
PLIP
HUH......?
PLIP

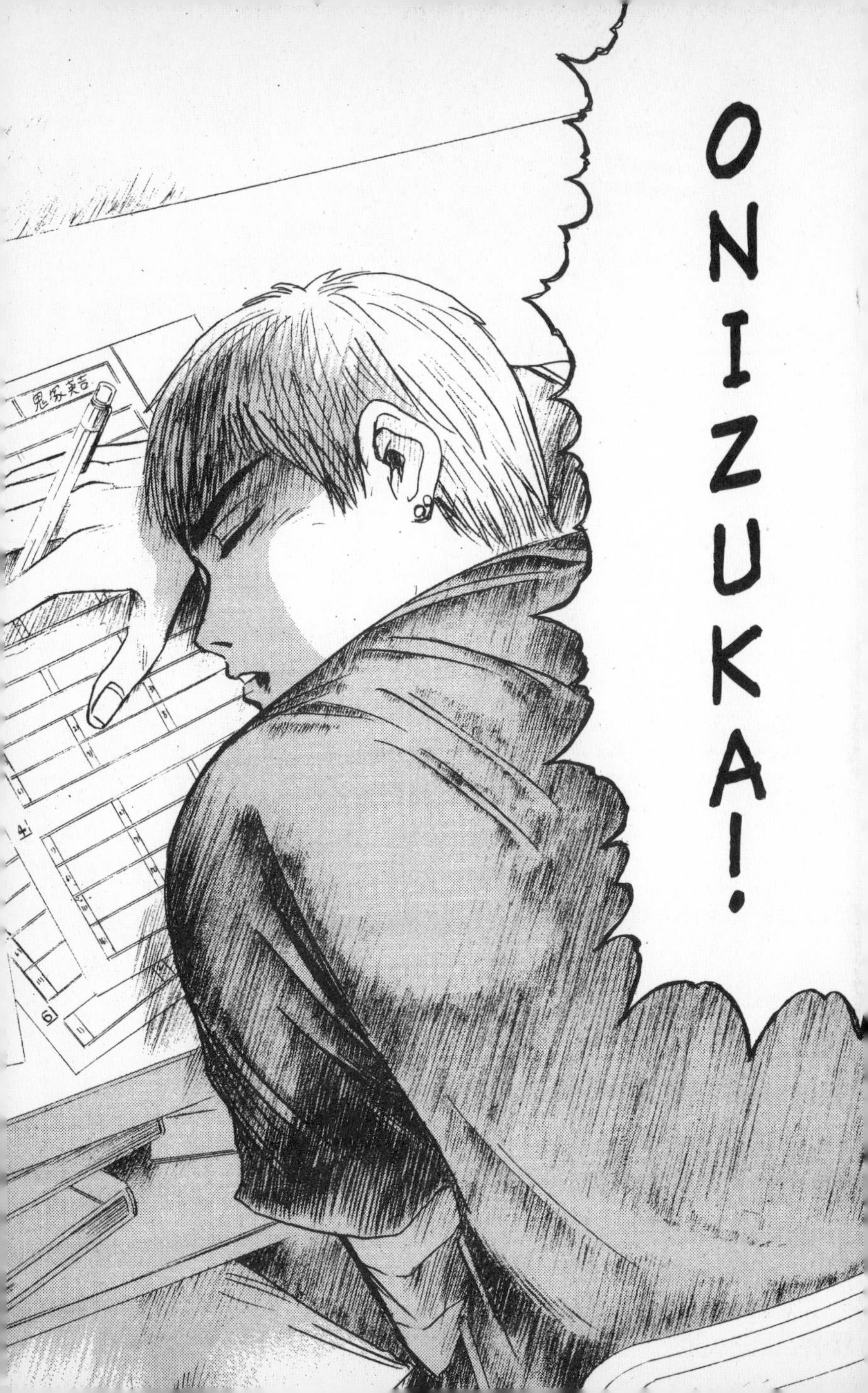
ONIZUKA!
鬼塚英吉

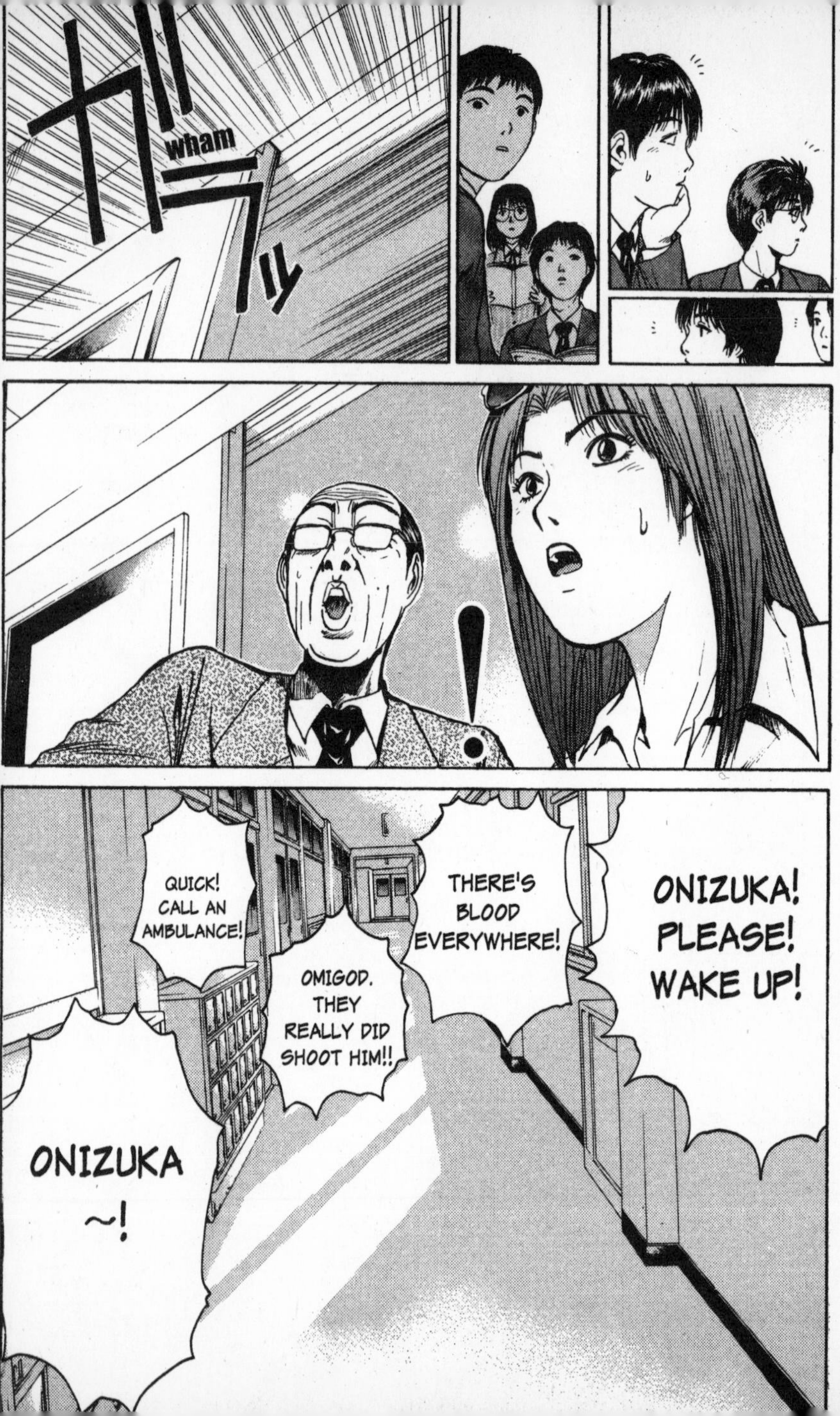
wham
!
ONIZUKA! PLEASE! WAKE UP!
THERE'S BLOOD EVERYWHERE!
OMIGOD. THEY REALLY DID SHOOT HIM!!
QUICK! CALL AN AMBULANCE!
ONIZUKA ~!

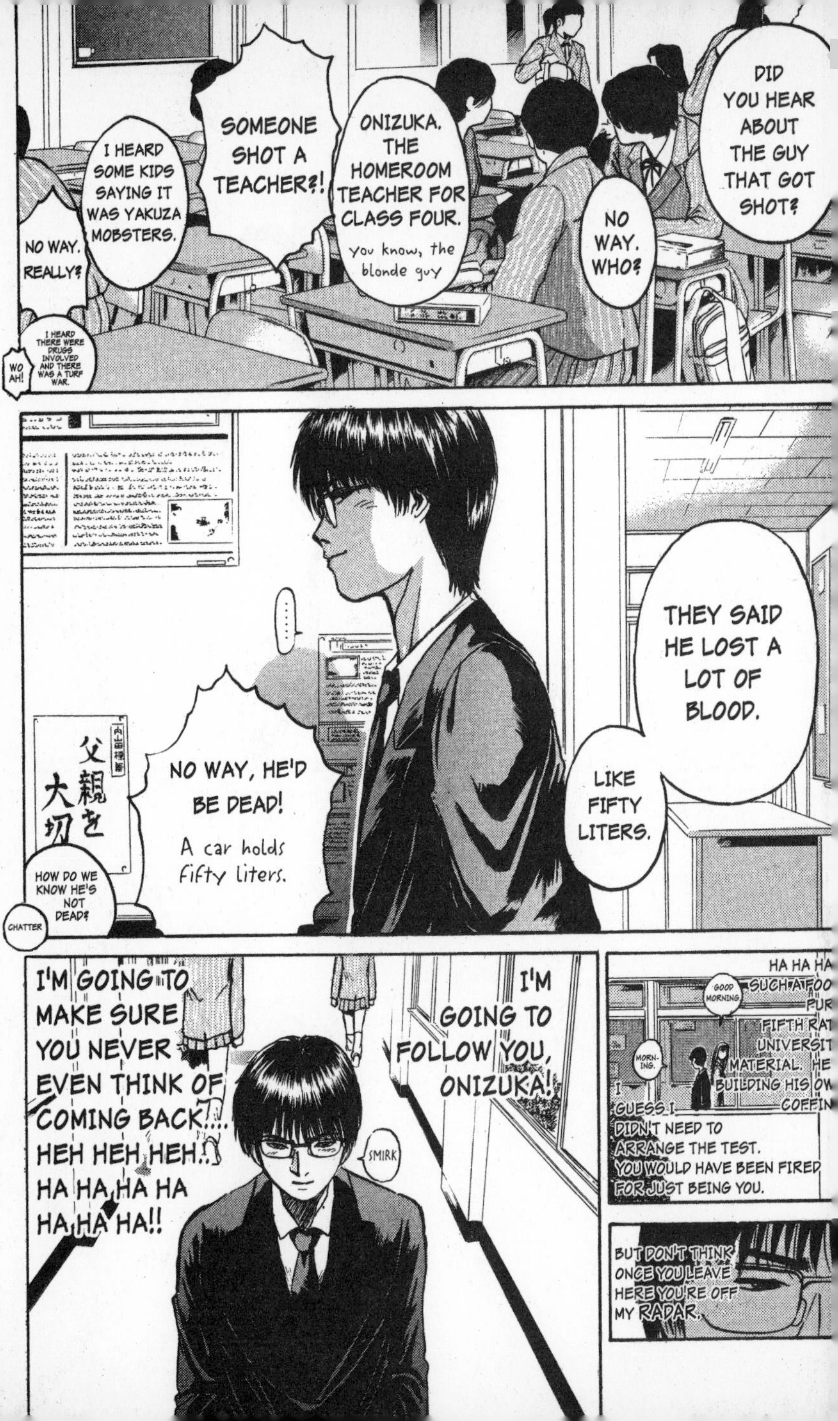
DID YOU HEAR ABOUT THE GUY THAT GOT SHOT?
NO WAY. WHO?
ONIZUKA. THE HOMEROOM TEACHER FOR CLASS FOUR.
you know, the blonde guy
SOMEONE SHOT A TEACHER?!
I HEARD SOME KIDS SAYING IT WAS YAKUZA MOBSTERS.
NO WAY. REALLY?
I HEARD THERE WERE DRUGS INVOLVED AND THERE WAS A TURF WAR.
WO AH!
THEY SAID HE LOST A LOT OF BLOOD.
LIKE FIFTY LITERS.
......
NO WAY, HE'D BE DEAD!
A car holds fifty liters.
父親を大切
HOW DO WE KNOW HE'S NOT DEAD?
CHATTER
HA HA HA SUCH A FOO FUR FIFTH RAT UNIVERSIT MATERIAL. HE BUILDING HIS OW COFFIN
GOOD MORNING.
MORN- ING.
I GUESS I DIDN'T NEED TO ARRANGE THE TEST. YOU WOULD HAVE BEEN FIRED FOR JUST BEING YOU.
BUT DON'T THINK ONCE YOU LEAVE HERE YOU'RE OFF MY RADAR.
I'M GOING TO FOLLOW YOU, ONIZUKA!
SMIRK
I'M GOING TO MAKE SURE YOU NEVER EVEN THINK OF COMING BACK.... HEH HEH HEH.. HA HA HA HA HA HA HA!!

SURGERY IN PROGRESS

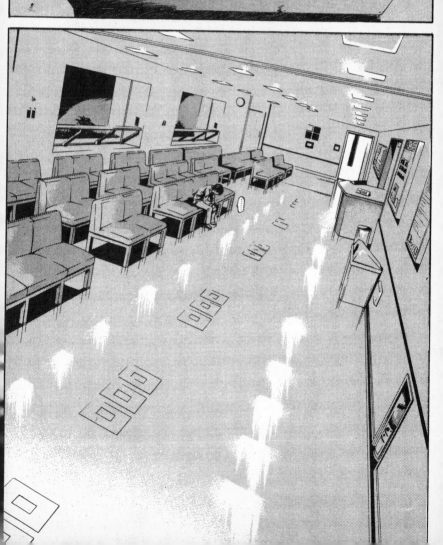

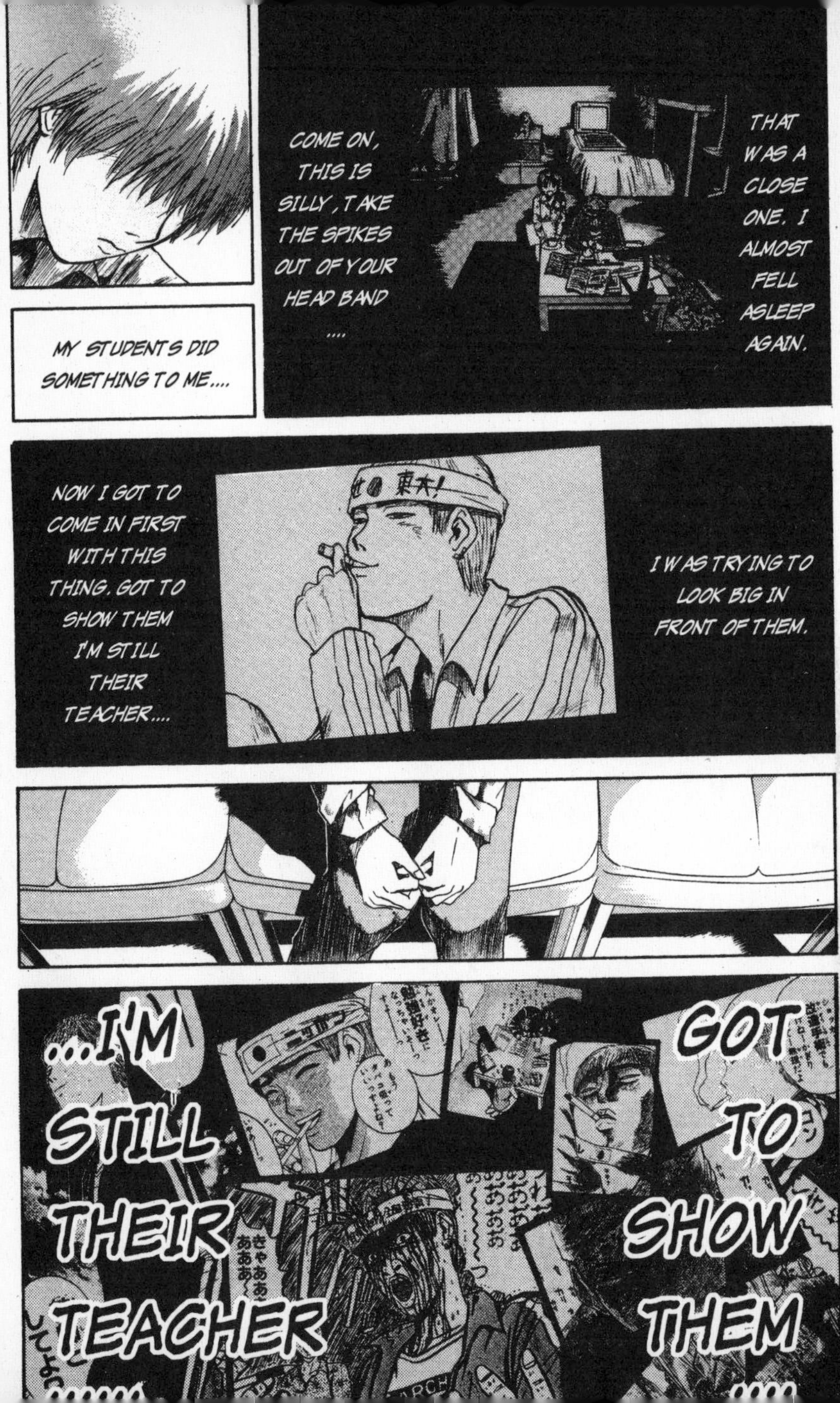
THAT WAS A CLOSE ONE. I ALMOST FELL ASLEEP AGAIN.
COME ON, THIS IS SILLY, TAKE THE SPIKES OUT OF YOUR HEAD BAND ....
MY STUDENTS DID SOMETHING TO ME....
I WAS TRYING TO LOOK BIG IN FRONT OF THEM.
NOW I GOT TO COME IN FIRST WITH THIS THING. GOT TO SHOW THEM I'M STILL THEIR TEACHER....
GOT TO SHOW THEM ....
...I'M STILL THEIR TEACHER ......

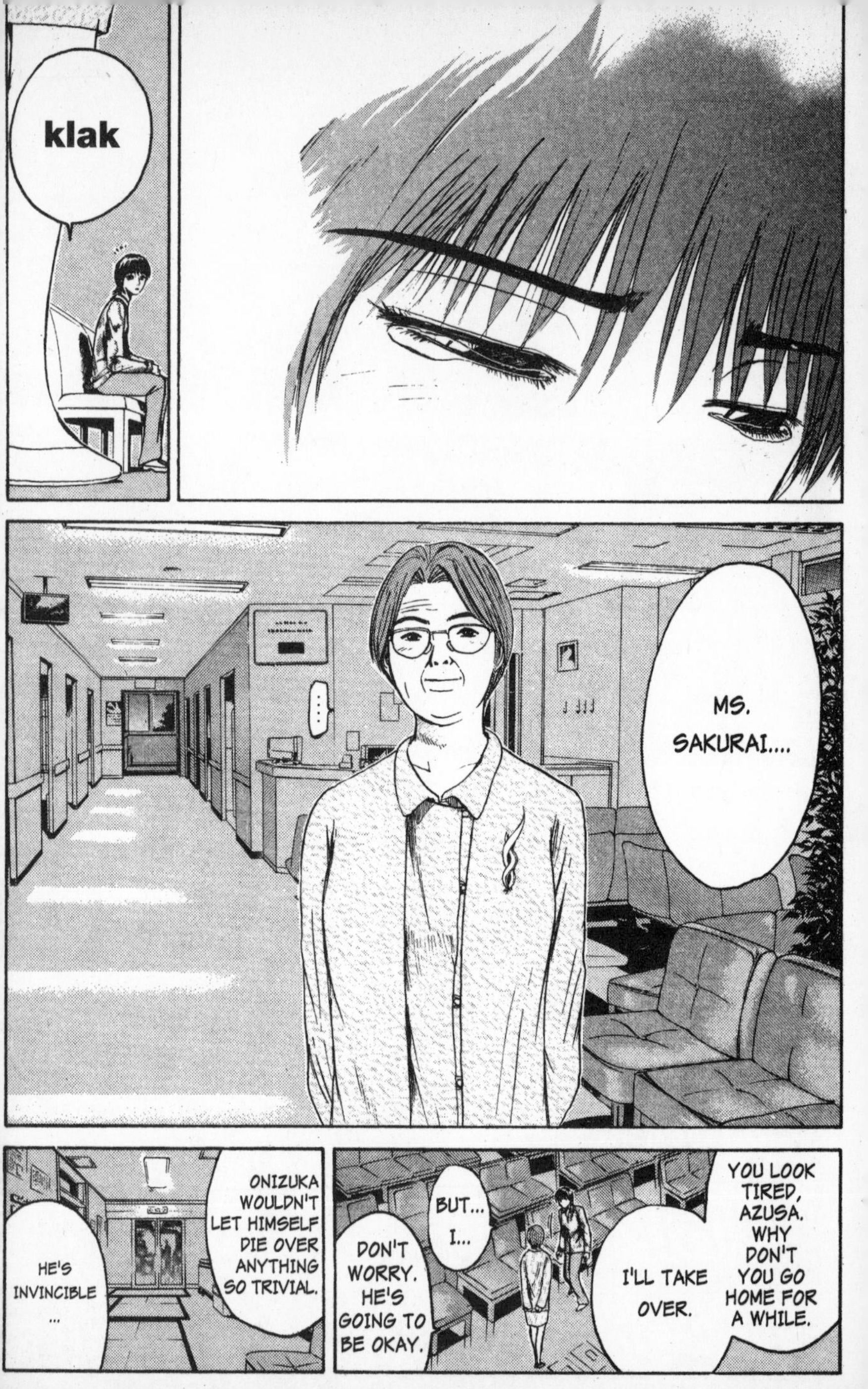
klak
MS. SAKURAI....
...
YOU LOOK TIRED, AZUSA. WHY DON'T YOU GO HOME FOR A WHILE.
I'LL TAKE OVER.
BUT... I...
DON'T WORRY. HE'S GOING TO BE OKAY.
ONIZUKA WOULDN'T LET HIMSELF DIE OVER ANYTHING SO TRIVIAL.
HE'S INVINCIBLE ...

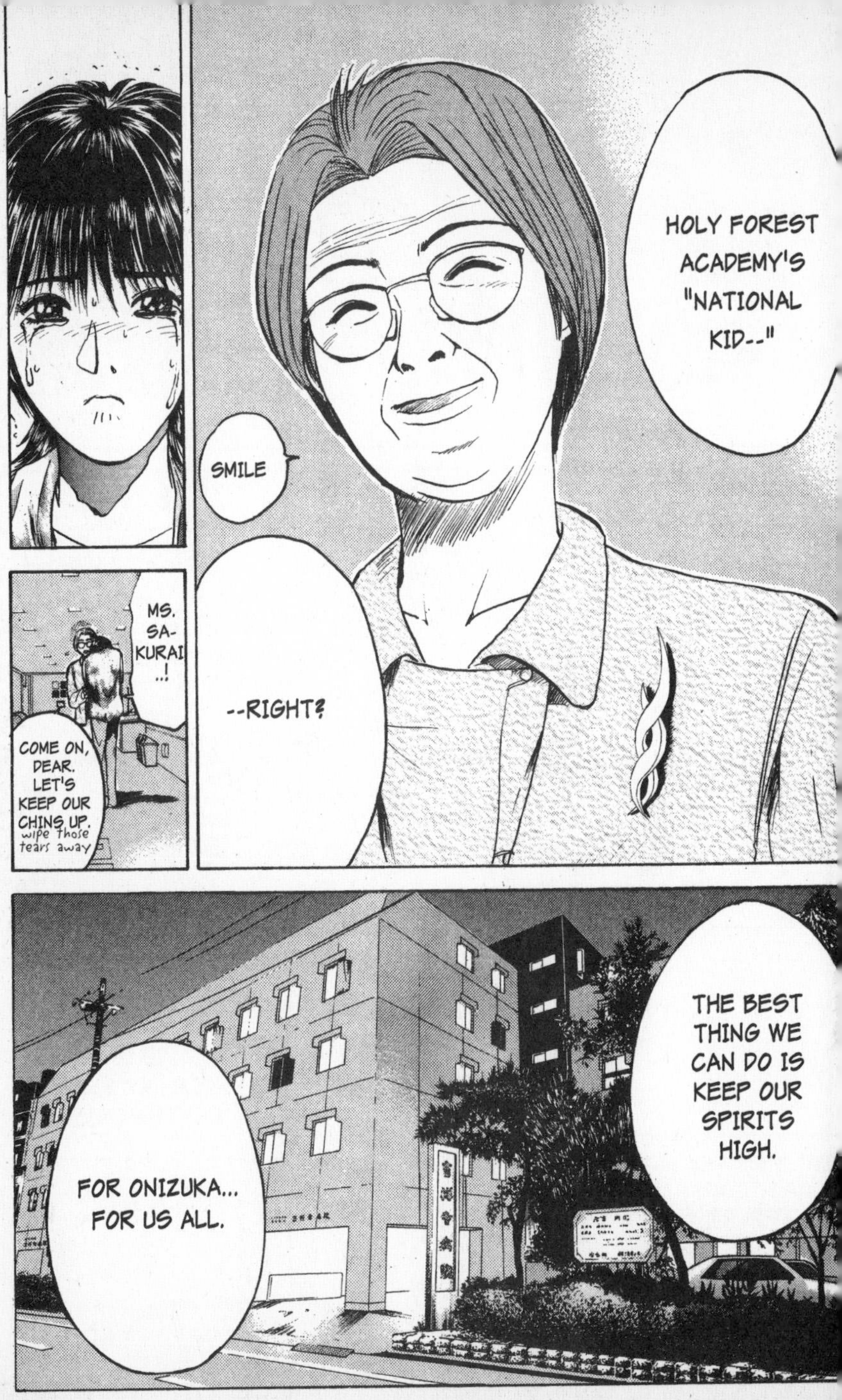
HOLY FOREST ACADEMY'S "NATIONAL KID--"
SMILE
--RIGHT?
MS. SA-KURAI ..!
COME ON, DEAR. LET'S KEEP OUR CHINS UP.
wipe those tears away
THE BEST THING WE CAN DO IS KEEP OUR SPIRITS HIGH.
FOR ONIZUKA... FOR US ALL.

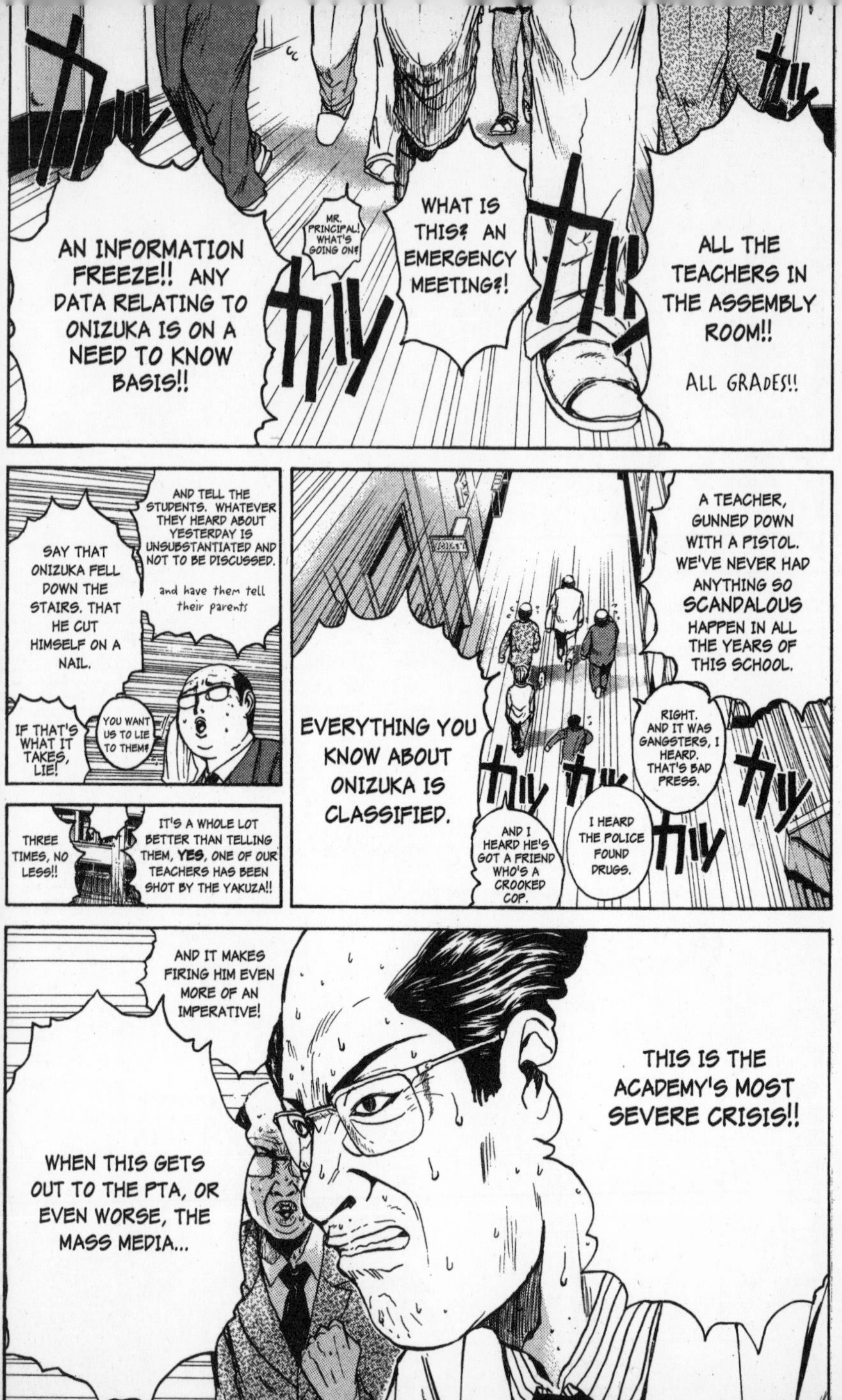
ALL THE TEACHERS IN THE ASSEMBLY ROOM!!
ALL GRADES!!
WHAT IS THIS? AN EMERGENCY MEETING?!
MR. PRINCIPAL! WHAT'S GOING ON?
AN INFORMATION FREEZE!! ANY DATA RELATING TO ONIZUKA IS ON A NEED TO KNOW BASIS!!
A TEACHER, GUNNED DOWN WITH A PISTOL. WE'VE NEVER HAD ANYTHING SO SCANDALOUS HAPPEN IN ALL THE YEARS OF THIS SCHOOL.
RIGHT. AND IT WAS GANGSTERS, I HEARD. THAT'S BAD PRESS.
I HEARD THE POLICE FOUND DRUGS.
AND I HEARD HE'S GOT A FRIEND WHO'S A CROOKED COP.
EVERYTHING YOU KNOW ABOUT ONIZUKA IS CLASSIFIED.
AND TELL THE STUDENTS. WHATEVER THEY HEARD ABOUT YESTERDAY IS UNSUBSTANTIATED AND NOT TO BE DISCUSSED.
and have them tell their parents
SAY THAT ONIZUKA FELL DOWN THE STAIRS. THAT HE CUT HIMSELF ON A NAIL.
YOU WANT US TO LIE TO THEM?
IF THAT'S WHAT IT TAKES, LIE!
IT'S A WHOLE LOT BETTER THAN TELLING THEM, YES, ONE OF OUR TEACHERS HAS BEEN SHOT BY THE YAKUZA!!
THREE TIMES, NO LESS!!
THIS IS THE ACADEMY'S MOST SEVERE CRISIS!!
WHEN THIS GETS OUT TO THE PTA, OR EVEN WORSE, THE MASS MEDIA...
AND IT MAKES FIRING HIM EVEN MORE OF AN IMPERATIVE!

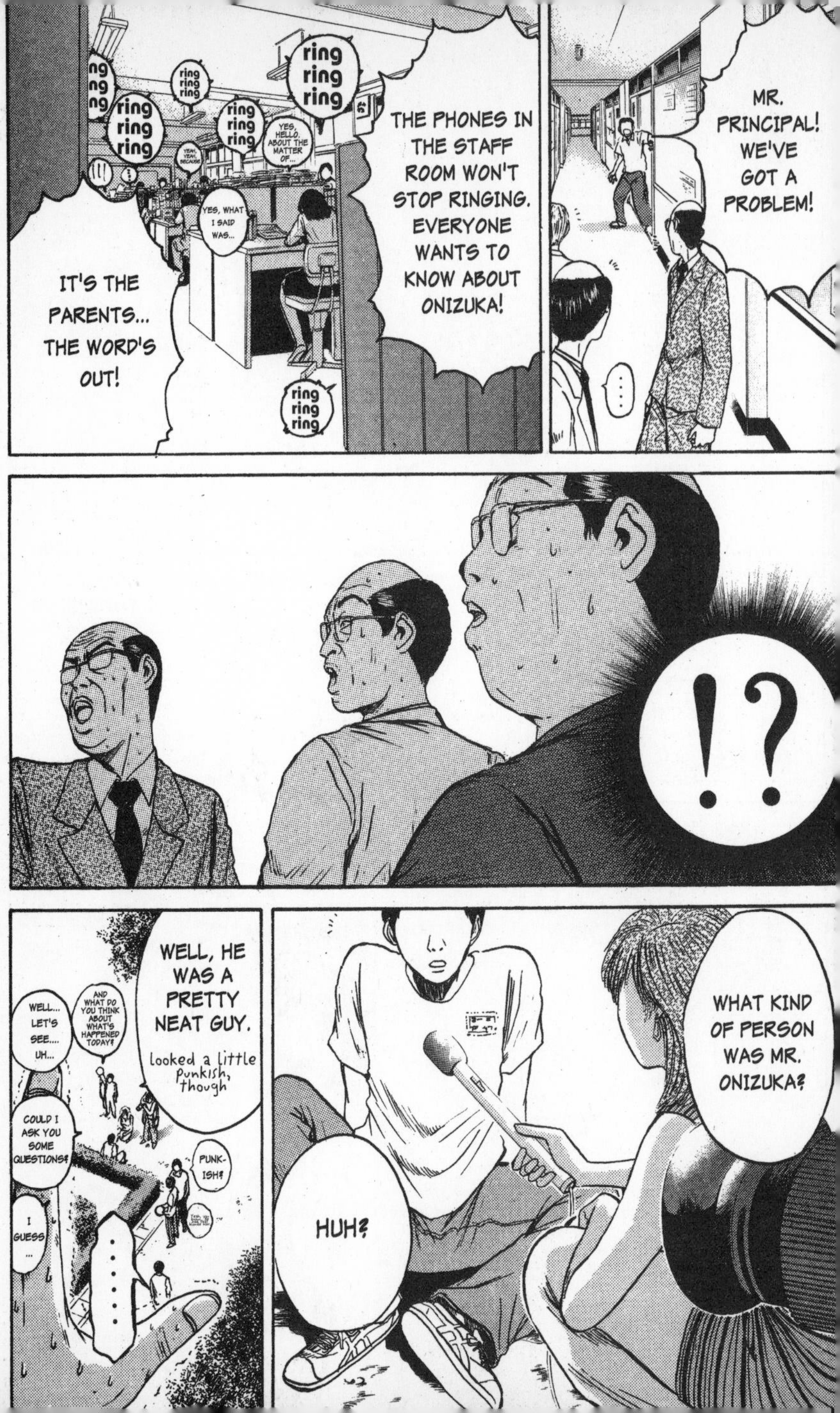
MR. PRINCIPAL! WE'VE GOT A PROBLEM!
. . . .
ring ring ring
THE PHONES IN THE STAFF ROOM WON'T STOP RINGING. EVERYONE WANTS TO KNOW ABOUT ONIZUKA!
YES, HELLO. ABOUT THE MATTER OF...
ring ring ring
ring ring ring
YEAH, YEAH, BECAUSE
ring ring ring
YES, WHAT I SAID WAS...
IT'S THE PARENTS... THE WORD'S OUT!
ring ring ring
!?
WHAT KIND OF PERSON WAS MR. ONIZUKA?
HUH?
WELL, HE WAS A PRETTY NEAT GUY.
looked a little punkish, though
PUNK-ISH?
AND WHAT DO YOU THINK ABOUT WHAT'S HAPPENED TODAY?
WELL... LET'S SEE.... UH...
COULD I ASK YOU SOME QUESTIONS?
I GUESS...
......

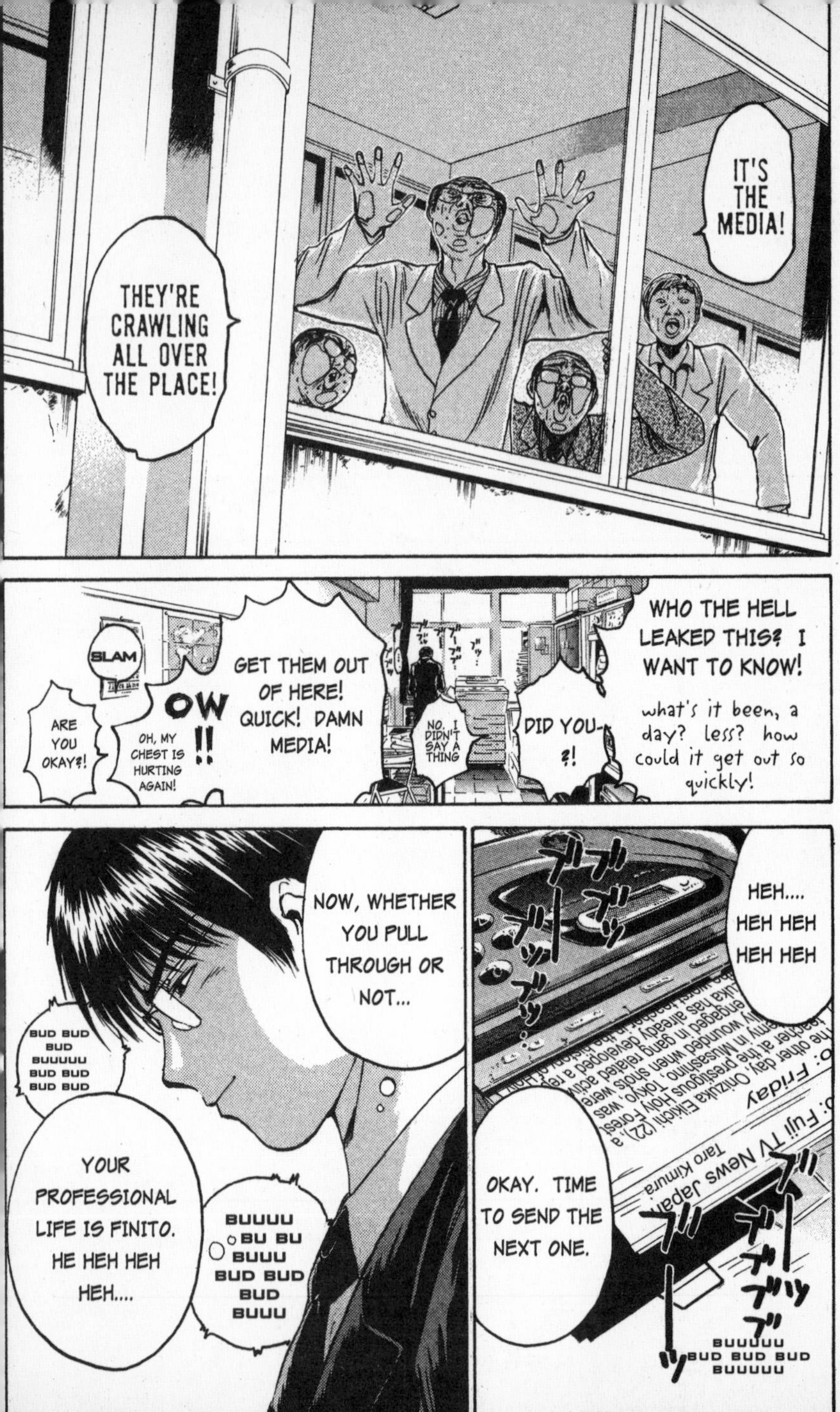
IT'S THE MEDIA!
THEY'RE CRAWLING ALL OVER THE PLACE!
WHO THE HELL LEAKED THIS? I WANT TO KNOW!
what's it been, a day? less? how could it get out so quickly!
DID YOU-?!
NO, I DIDN'T SAY A THING
GET THEM OUT OF HERE! QUICK! DAMN MEDIA!
SLAM
OW!!
OH, MY CHEST IS HURTING AGAIN!
ARE YOU OKAY?!
HEH.... HEH HEH HEH HEH
OKAY. TIME TO SEND THE NEXT ONE.
BUUUUU BUD BUD BUD BUUUUU
NOW, WHETHER YOU PULL THROUGH OR NOT...
BUD BUD BUD BUUUUU BUD BUD BUD BUD
YOUR PROFESSIONAL LIFE IS FINITO. HE HEH HEH HEH....
BUUUU BU BU BUUU BUD BUD BUD BUUU

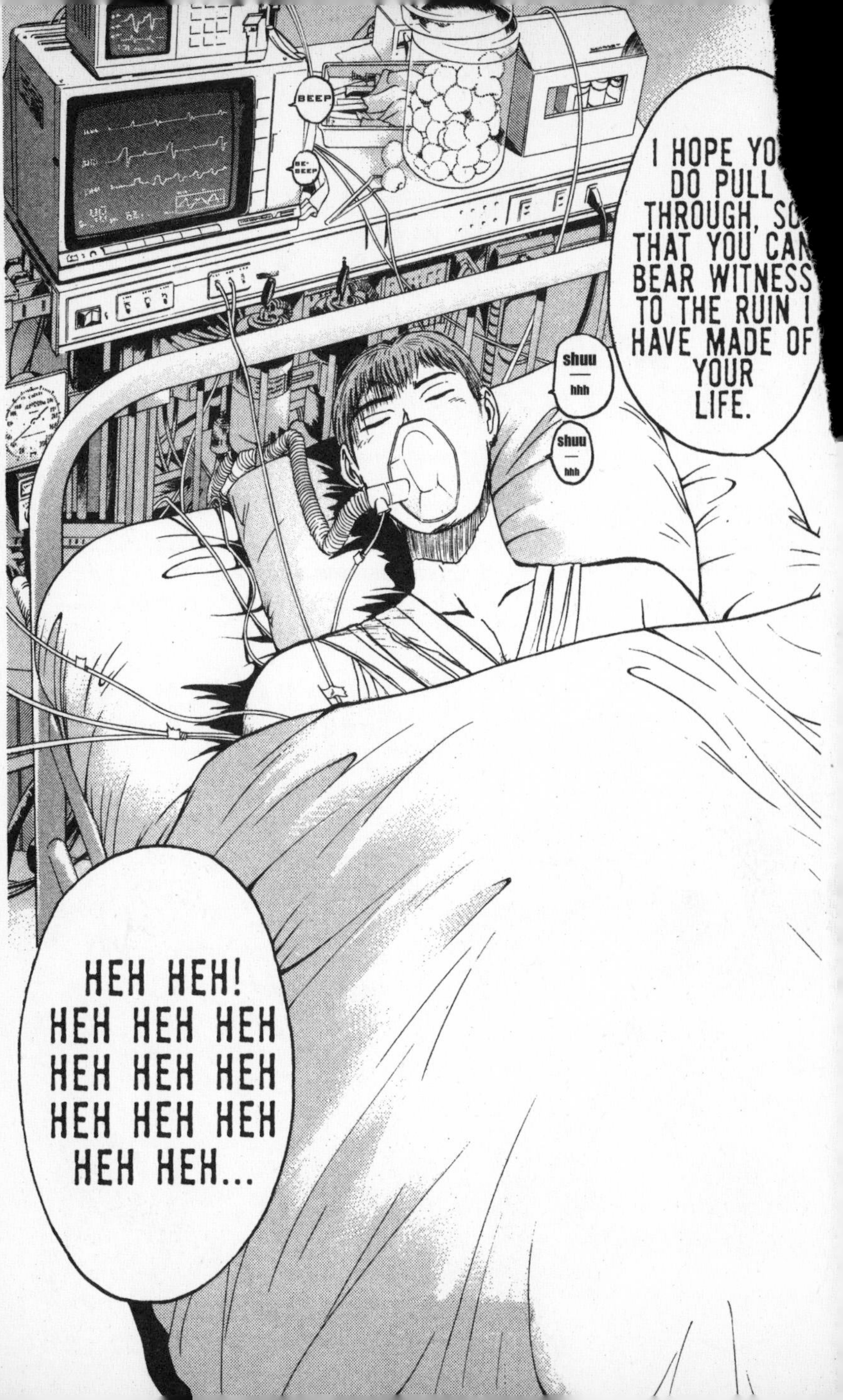
BEEP
BE-BEEP
I HOPE YOU DO PULL THROUGH, SO THAT YOU CAN BEAR WITNESS TO THE RUIN I HAVE MADE OF YOUR LIFE.
shuu—hhh
shuu—hhh
HEH HEH! HEH HEH HEH HEH HEH HEH HEH HEH HEH HEH HEH...

STOP!

This is the back of the book.
You wouldn't want to spoil a great ending!

This book is printed "manga-style," in the authentic Japanese right-to-left format. Since none of the artwork has been flipped or altered, readers get to experience the story just as the creator intended. You've been asking for it, so TOKYOPOP® delivered: authentic, hot-off-the-press, and far more fun!

DIRECTIONS

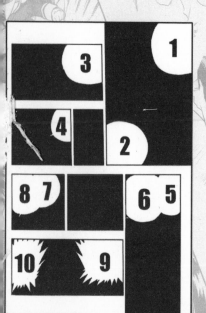

If this is your first time reading manga-style, here's a quick guide to help you understand how it works.

It's easy... just start in the top right panel and follow the numbers. Have fun, and look for more 100% authentic manga from TOKYOPOP®!